WHEN SEX THREATENED THE STATE

WHEN SEX THREATENED THE STATE

Illicit Sexuality, Nationalism,
and Politics in Colonial Nigeria,
1900–1958

SAHEED ADERINTO

UNIVERSITY OF ILLINOIS PRESS

Urbana, Chicago, and Springfield

Library of Congress Cataloging-in-Publication Data
Aderinto, Saheed, author.
When sex threatened the state: illicit sexuality, nationalism, and politics in colonial
Nigeria, 1900–1958 / Saheed Aderinto.
pages   cm
Includes bibliographical references and index.
ISBN 978-0-252-03888-4 (cloth : alk. paper)
ISBN 978-0-252-08042-5 (pbk. : alk. paper)
ISBN 978-0-252-09684-6 (ebook)
1. Sex—Political aspects—Nigeria—History—20th century. 2. Sex—Social aspects—
Nigeria—History—20th century. 3. Prostitution—Nigeria—History—20th century.
4. Child prostitution—Nigeria—History—20th century. 5. Prostitution—Law and
legislation—Nigeria. 6. Sexually transmitted diseases—Nigeria—History—20th century.
7. Sexually transmitted diseases—Great Britain—Colonies. 8. Great Britain—Colonies—
Africa—Social policy. 9. Nigeria—Social policy—20th century. 10. Nigeria—Politics and
government—To 1960.
I. Title.
HQ18.N55A33   2014
306.740966909'04—dc23   2014016324

For the memory of Madam Adunni Silifatu Aderinto
—*Kokoro ni o je un 'gbadun obi to 'gbo*
Iku ni o je un 'gbadun iya mi

CONTENTS

LIST OF ILLUSTRATIONS

LIST OF TABLES

ACKNOWLEDGMENTS

This book could not have been written without the generosity and assistance of many institutions, agencies, and individuals. My indebtedness goes to the staff of the three main Nigerian National Archives for helping to comb the repositories to pull out several rare documents that helped me write this book. I also thank Rasheed Hassan and Oyinkansola Ilori for their help in the archives. My numerous informants were not just a source of oral information about Lagos's past. They were true collaborators in my quest to understand the complex, yet fascinating history of twentieth-century Lagos. I thank them for enduring my often difficult questions about sexuality, and for allowing me to probe their memory for events that lay deep in the ocean of the past.

The feedback I received on various portions of this book at meetings, conferences, and symposia contributed immensely to shaping my thoughts. My heartfelt gratitude goes to Funso Afolayan and Gloria Chuku for their comments on versions of chapter 4 first presented at the African Studies Association (ASA) meeting in New Orleans in November 2009. Philippa Levine gave useful feedback on chapter 5 when I presented it at the Second British Scholar Conference at the University of Texas at Austin in February 2009. In June 2008 Eno Ikpe invited me to present an incarnation of chapter 6 at the Staff/Postgraduate Seminar of the University of Lagos's History and Strategic Studies Department. I first tested my arguments in the epilogue with participants at the Nigerian Studies Association's "Round Table on Nigeria at 50" at the 2010 ASA Meeting in San Francisco. Versions of chapters 3 and 7 were presented at the 14th Annual Emerging Scholarship in Women's and Gender Studies Conference and the Gender Symposium organized on the campus of University of Texas in 2007 and 2009, respectively. I thank all the participants at these gatherings for their comments and critique.

I owe several colleagues and friends—Babatunde Babalola, Kwame Essien, Bukola Gbadegesin, Abosede George, Laurent Fourchard, Chima Korieh, Raphael Njoku, Moses Ochonu, and Olatunji Ojo—a big thanks for offering useful advice on portions of this book at various stages of its existence. Judith Byfield, Gloria Chuku, Matthew Heaton, and Hakeem Ibikunle Tijani read the entire manuscript and gave highly useful critique that sharpened and refined my ideas. Bob Fullilove has been my copyeditor for five years. He not only read the manuscript for clarity and precision, he also offered deep editorial and conceptual questions as he plowed through every word I wrote. To the editors and anonymous reviewers of *Frontiers* and the *Journal of Colonialism and Colonial History*, where portions of chapters 4 and 7 previously appeared, I say thank you for your critical comments. I wrote the penultimate draft of the epilogue while serving as scholar-in-residence at the Ibadan office of the French Institute for Research in Africa in the summer of 2012. I am indebted to the director Gerard Chouin and his staff for providing the support that made writing pleasurable.

I received much financial and academic help from the History Department and the John L. Warfield Center for African and African American Studies of the University of Texas at Austin. The travel grants offered by the History Department and the Patrice Lumumba Research Fellowship of the Warfield Center allowed me to return to Nigeria in the summers of 2006 and 2008 to acquire more materials. I thank Aderonke Adesanya, Omoniyi Afolabi, Ruramisai Charumbira, Toyin Falola, Juliet E. Walker, and Emilio Zamora for their useful critique that pushed me to reprocess my ideas about the place of sex and sexuality in colonial Nigerian history. Joni L. Jones (Omi Osun Olomo), the former director of Warfield Center, personifies the true embodiment of Osun, the Yoruba goddess of fertility. I thank her for supporting my research in numerous ways.

I am grateful to my colleagues in Western Carolina University's History Department for providing the congenial and collegial environment for serious professional development. The useful advice I received from them at the department's Colloquia and Conversation in the spring of 2012 helped me to rethink and restructure portions of this book. The department's travel grants in the summers of 2012 and 2013 enabled me to return to Nigeria to collect more interviews and acquire materials from the new Lagos State Records and Archives Bureau. My colleagues David Dorondo, Gael Graham, and Richard Starnes gave a regular supply of encouragement, laugher, and caffeine that made the constant transitioning between teaching and writing enjoyable and rewarding. I tested some of my ideas with students in my graduate seminars and research assistants Mathew Baker and John Lance. I thank them for showing interest in my research and expressing deep curiosity that motivated me to consider new possibilities. The library staff enthusiastically aided my research, providing much needed items in a timely fashion. Bethany Ketting and JoAnn Marvel of the interlibrary loan section worked cheerfully with me to locate microfilms of colonial newspapers published in Nigeria but scattered in research libraries across the world. Thank you. That I was able to publish this book owes a lot to Larin McLaughlin, who acquired the manuscript for the University of Illinois Press. I cannot thank her enough for her efficiency and high level of professionalism. Her enthusiasm about this project right from when I first inquired about publishing my book with UIP encouraged me to complete the manuscript ahead of my planned schedule. I am thankful to Jennifer Clark, Kevin Cunningham, Maria E. denBoer, Dawn Durante, Dustin J. Hubbart, and Roberta J. Sparenberg for guiding me through the elaborate production process. My appreciation also goes to the anonymous readers for offering recommendations that improved the quality of this work.

The personal component of production of knowledge is as important as the academic. In June 2013, just a month after I submitted the first draft of the manuscript to the press, my mother, Madam Adunni Silifatu Aderinto (Iya alate), to whom I dedicate this book, passed on. Although Iya alate was not a member of the Ivory Tower, her irrepressible love for her son's progress drew her into the academic world, as she learned several vocabularies associated with the profession of history. Iya alate was my role model for intrepidity and perseverance. She taught me "not to die before death" and that I must confront, not run from, my fears. When my traveling plans to archives and my wife's college schedule affected our childcare arrangement in the summer of 2012, Iya alate sacrificed the comfort of her deep-rooted world in Mosfala/Odinjo and Oje Market in Ibadan for an unfamiliar domain in Waynesville, North Carolina, to stay with her grandchildren. Iya alate, although I could not physically present this book to you, I am sure you are smiling and appreciating, from wherever you are, what we have collectively worked for. My dad's, Alhaji Lateef Aderinto's, investment in my education is unquantifiable. Thank you, Baba onipako.

My deepest gratitude goes to my wife, Olamide, who journeyed the entire length of this project with me. She gives me the priceless gifts of love, perseverance, courage, and intellectual curiosity. There were so many moments we appeared unlovable as we both strove to meet our academic and professional goals. I hope this book compensates for several lost hugs and serves as a token of Olamide's priceless investment in me. Our children, Itandayo and Itandola, lived through the period of book writing. I thank them for giving me joy that manifests itself every day of my life, and pray this book compensates for all the time I disappeared into my home office, making myself invisible to their usual squabbles.

LIST OF ABBREVIATIONS

AVS	Anti-Vice Squad
BWAEGC	British West African Educated Girls' Club
CDAs	Contagious Diseases Acts
CWO	Colony Welfare Office
CYPO	Children and Young Persons Ordinance
DMSS	Director of Medical and Sanitary Service
LCN	Legislative Council of Nigeria
LLN	Ladies League of Nigeria
LPC	Ladies Progressive Club
LTC	Lagos Town Council
LWL	Lagos Women's League
NACA	National Agency for the Control of AIDS
NACBO	Native Authority Child Betrothal Ordinance
NAPTIP	National Agency for the Prohibition of Traffic in Persons
NAS	Nigerian Apothecary Society
NEACA	National Expert Advisory Committee on AIDS
NCNC	National Council of Nigeria and the Cameroons
NGO	Nongovernmental Organization
NNDP	Nigerian National Democratic Party
NPF	Nigeria Police Force
NPS	Nigerian Pharmaceutical Society
NWP	Nigerian Women's Party
NYM	Nigerian Youth Movement
PMO	Principal Medical Officer

RWAFF	Royal West African Frontier Force
SAP	Structural Adjustment Programme
SSO	Senior Sanitary Officer
TPPLEAA	Trafficking in Persons (Prohibition) Law Enforcement and Administration Act
UAO	Undesirable Advertisement Ordinance
UGPO	Unlicensed Guide (Prohibition) Ordinance
VDO	Venereal Diseases Ordinance
WACA	West African Court of Appeal
WAFF	West African Frontier Force
WOTCLEF	Women Trafficking and Child Labour Eradication Foundation
WWC	Women's Welfare Council

WHEN SEX THREATENED THE STATE

INTRODUCTION

Sex and Sexuality in African Colonial Encounter

When the Hunter Becomes the Hunted

On February 17, 1947, Justice Adetokunbo Ademola of Lagos Santa Anna magistrate court sentenced a female welfare officer, Ayodele Potts-Johnson, to six months in prison (without the option of a fine) for demanding and receiving bribes of £5. 30s. and 25s. 2d. from two prostitutes, Elizabeth Agadagwu and Alice George, respectively, in order not to repatriate them from their brothels located on Idoluwo Street, Lagos.[1] This judgment was witnessed by a "good number of privileged persons," most of whom were coworkers and relatives of Potts-Johnson, whose look "betrayed the severity of the ordeal through which she [had] been passing" in a court "taxed to its utmost capacity."[2] Christened by the press as a "sensational celebrated official corruption," this highly publicized scandal's documented facts are given below.

On the afternoon of Friday, December 13, 1946, Potts-Johnson, a supervisory officer with the Colony Welfare Office (CWO), a government institution that policed child prostitution, went to the homes of Agadagwu and George after receiving a tip from Joel Toviho, an ex-serviceman described as her "tout" and "unofficial" informant, that they were prostitutes engaged in girl trafficking.[3] In her testimony, Agadagwu said that Potts-Johnson did not trust her when she said her husband was a French sailor but referred to an unwritten informal convention that "it was against the law for an African to marry a whiteman."[4] When Potts-Johnson insisted that she must follow her to her office for full interrogation, Agadagwu enlisted the support of her landlord, a Yoruba man named Bakare, who spoke to Potts-Johnson in Yoruba and helped broker a £10 bribery arrangement. Bakare put £5. 30s. in Potts-Johnson's bag and asked her to return for the remainder the following day. George's testimony was similar to Agadagwu's.[5] She gave Potts-Johnson 5s. 2d. out of the £3 bribe imposed on her, with the promise to remit the balance at a later date.

The bribery arrangement went well for one main reason: Agadagwu and George admitted they were prostitutes and agreed with Potts-Johnson that it was better to pay a bribe than to be officially prosecuted. The agony of the criminal justice system and punishment for prostitution and girl trafficking were truly severe: two years in prison, a £50 fine, and repatriation from Lagos. What started as an internal arrangement between consenting lawbreakers became a criminal issue when Agadagwu and George reported Potts-Johnson to the police the following day. A crude method of crime detection was enough to establish Potts-Johnson's criminality—the police made the inscription *"wayo"* (meaning fraud) on the currency to be given to Toviho, whom Potts-Johnson had sent to retrieve the balance of the bribe, and planted an undercover cop to witness the illegal transaction. Toviho was promptly arrested as he put the marked currency in his pocket.[6] Neither Agadagwu nor George, who broke the law by keeping a brothel, nor Bakare, who as the landlord of prostitutes violated the criminal code by "living on proceeds of prostitution," was arrested or prosecuted.

Potts-Johnson's scandal was not a conventional one. By all indications it represented a turning point in the history of sexual politics and was indeed a first-class legal tussle involving some of Nigeria's finest legal experts engaged in an unusual manner for an uncommon purpose. First, Potts-Johnson's defense team comprised four African and British lawyers (E. A. Akerele, J. A. Kester, N. O. A. Morgan, and V. O. Munis) led by F. R. A. Williams, noted in a 1946 directory of prominent Lagosians as "an influential politician and Barrister-at-law of good standing."[7] Widely recognized as the father of modern legal practice in Nigeria, Williams was also the general secretary of the Nigerian Youth Movement (NYM), which James S. Coleman described as "Nigeria's first genuine nationalist organization."[8] The presiding judge, Ademola, whom a contemporary thought was "a kind, courteous, human judge" whose "displeasure could be quickly stirred against those who had deliberately flouted the law or who willfully caused unnecessary suffering to others," was one of very few African magistrates and the prince of the reigning *alake* (king) of Abeokuta.[9] He would later become Nigeria's first chief justice, the head of the entire judiciary at the country's independence; Williams became the first senior advocate, the most prestigious honor for a legal practitioner. The fact that Potts-Johnson hired five lawyers to defend a bribery scandal involving less than £6 reveals the length to which she was willing to go to decriminalize herself, escape a prison sentence, and protect her reputation.

Second, the trial lasted for an unusual length of time and was heard in multiple courts. While most corruption cases were determined at the magistrate court, Potts-Johnson's was heard at every level of the judiciary: from the lowest court (the magistrate); to the Nigerian Supreme Court; to the West African Court of Appeal (WACA), the final arbiter for judicial matters in the whole of British West Africa.[10] Dressed in a "cream, thick, Indian-tailored ensemble with a navy blazer" during one of the trials, Potts-Johnson made more than five court appearances over eight months (from December 1946 to July 1947).[11] Even serious criminal cases like murder seldom lasted beyond two magistrate court sessions, let alone a bribery charge, which was usually determined in a single trial.[12] In addition to the caliber of personalities involved, this case reached the apex court in British West Africa because Potts-Johnson's counsel invoked a technical component of the Nigerian Criminal Code (section 404) that punished "corruption under the colour of employment" but overlooked "extortion" by government employees. The legalistic assumption was that "extortion" by a government employee was not an "offense" provided it did not undermine official duties or influence the employee's judgment in a manner that would bring disrepute on the colonial state. Williams and his legal team did not contest the established fact that their client "extorted" money from the prostitutes, but they argued that her action could not have prevented her from initiating criminal charges against Agadagwu and George. Like the lower courts, the WACA was unconvinced that Potts-Johnson had not used her position to "enrich" herself or bring the government into disrepute, and insisted that she must serve a prison sentence like the prostitutes, the so-called undesirables she was entrusted to police.

Third, and most important, the case was about sexual politics, which carried a significant burden of moral responsibility because of the class of people involved (prostitutes) and the projected implications of Potts-Johnson's action on the colonial state's ideal of progress. To be sure, the 1940s represented a milestone in the history of prostitution and corruption. Having tolerated sex work for decades, the British launched a prohibitory regime by introducing a number of anti-prostitution laws and establishing the CWO to protect underage girls who were trafficked and sexually exploited. While corruption was not unknown in the interwar years, it was during this period that it became fully entrenched in virtually every sphere of Nigerian life. Indeed, the popular notion that bribery is a postcolonial problem of development that suddenly erupted in the wake of military dictatorship is ahistorical given the spate of corruption during the 1940s. Since the government had already convicted some officers of the Nigeria Police Force (NPF) for a similar offense of collecting a bribe, the Potts-Johnson scandal showed its determination to rid Lagos of the "undesirables" by punishing all corrupt law enforcement officials who abetted their activities. In a similar way, the case embarrassed those Lagos moralists who had clamored since the 1920s for effective policing of prostitutes and dented the image of the CWO, whose top official was convicted for committing a moral crime, contributing to the sexual exploitation of girls through the very establishment meant to address it. What is more, the Potts-Johnson scandal clearly shows that the problems of sexual morality and law and order could not be levied solely on prostitutes and criminals, but also on educated elites and moralists whose failure to ensure that "undesirables" were brought to account actually facilitated their illegal activities. Above all, it offers a critical point of entry into the intricate politics of sex in colonial Nigeria.

This book is concerned with sexual politics but also with nationalism. At the heart of the story I am about to tell is the idea of dangerous sexuality and how it intersects with broader issues of colonial progress and civilization from the first decade of the twentieth century when VD began to constitute a sexo-moral panic to 1958 when the age of consent was raised from 13 to 16. In writing sexuality into Nigeria's past, I attempt to construct deep analyses around an ideological sinew about sex and perversion exhibited by a variety of individuals and groups that were drawn along multiple social, racial, and power boundaries and were operating at local, regional, and international levels. I examine how sex, an aspect of human behavior considered to be private and much repressed, generated massive public and institutional concern, thus affirming its significance to people's existence and the construction of normalcy. Indeed, if historians of Nigeria think sexuality research is about obscenity, to be scholarly repressed, it is worth noting that the makers of the country's past (men and women; Africans and colonialists alike) did not think so. They voiced their opinion about sex through various information outlets, producing a wealth of accessible and useful data.

As complex as the history of Nigerian sexual politics is, I want to make three overarching arguments that form the centerpiece of the spectrum of ideas engaged in this book. First, sexuality as a component of human behavior cannot be understood in isolation from wider historical processes.[13] The language of sex is not just about such vague categories as "immorality" but also about contestation normally couched in the vocabulary of civilization. Indeed, a cluster of conflicted representations around sexual danger provides a metaphor for negotiating wider problems arising from the inability to reconcile such opposing binaries as "legitimate and illegitimate," "traditional and modern," "progress and failure," and "normal and abnormal," among other dialectic values. Sexuality, as I demonstrate throughout this book, was one of the intricate sites through which several core ideas of colonial practices and thinking about modernity were configured and reconfigured.

Second, the age of females who practiced prostitution played a significant role in molding the perception and institutional attention toward sex work, exemplifying the constructed difference between child and adult sexualities. The emergence of the idea of an erotic child became a sociopathological problem because both colonialists and Nigerians framed the girl-child as asexual, as an individual incapable of utilizing her emotions and intellect in making informed decisions about sexuality. The intersectionality of race, gender, and class remains of importance in dissecting sexual politics, but what we know about this aspect of Africa's past would be incomplete without a consideration of age. Conventional approaches have failed to recognize that prostitution, in addition to being conditioned by race, gender, and class, also must be viewed through an age-specific lens.[14]

Third, the intersection between sexuality and nationalism in Africa is far more complex than the present literature reveals. I argue that in Nigeria sexualized nationalism, or what I call the sexualization of nationalism, was an aspect of the moral, cultural, economic, and political nationalisms championed by both men and women who felt that certain expressions of sexuality threatened nation-building. But this nationalistic drive took a gendered form and was wrought with conflict. Throughout the era covered in this book, the nationalists (both men and women) did not speak with one voice partly because they could not reconcile the incongruous "danger" that sex posed to the state. Indeed, while prostitution was the subject of the popular debate, the underlying issues being contested often revolved around the protection of individual and group interests. The issue of prostitution became a camouflage for negotiating threats to the social, political, and sexual ideologies of a wide range of people.

The following definitions of terms, despite their limitations, are important for understanding the numerous connotations attributed to socio-sexual behavior and the politics of naming. Prostitution is conceptualized as the commoditization of sex, or a form of casual labor that involves payment for sexual services.[15] Women who sold sex and men who paid for it were involved in relationships that were mostly transient and geared toward erotic and material satisfaction. Regardless of the period and location, women traditionally practiced prostitution outside their native communities—hence prostitution, like most forms of labor that emerged under colonialism, was associated with migration.[16] I recognize that prostitution was not the only form of socio-sexual behavior or identity in colonial Lagos and that Nigerian sexuality was far more diverse than the sources (especially written) usually tell. But I concentrate mainly on heterosexual relations in Nigeria's past. Meanwhile, it is a truism that the morality of prostitution has been a subject of debate among scholars of various ideological standpoints—from liberal to Marxist feminist.[17] However, this is not the appropriate venue to review the theoretical and ideological controversies that cut across contours of power, patriarchy, agency, and exploitation.[18] My primary objective in this book is first to emphasize the significant place of sex in the Nigerian colonial encounter and, more imperatively, to encourage historians specializing in other colonial sites to rethink existing approaches to the story of prostitution. Occasionally, I differentiate between "adult" and "child" prostitution to reflect Nigerians' and colonialists' perceptions of class and sex work and the constructed negative implications. Although underage prostitution also appears as "juvenile" prostitution in some Africanist literature, I have decided to stick with the term "child" to emphasize its synchronic usage.

In order to obtain a critical focus on the interplay between sexuality and respectability on one hand, and the notion of colonial progress on the other, I have chosen Lagos as the main scene of the events that this book reconstructs. As a port city and colonial Nigeria's capital, it is the best place to unearth the sexual past partly because it was the first part of modern Nigeria to be brought under colonial rule and the locale of a scale of ideals of respectability traversing race, social class, ethnicity, and power. As one of Africa's most urbanized cities, Lagos affords the opportunity to chart the multilayered nuances of colonial progress espoused by both colonialists and Nigerians who vied to control political resources in the name of modernity and civilization. Although the bulk of my data come from Lagos, my findings have broader implications for discourses of sexuality in other parts of Africa and the former British Empire. In terms of identity framing, I alternate between the designations "Nigerians" to mean the citizens of Nigeria, a country that came into existence officially in 1914, and "Lagosians" to mean the Nigerian residents of Lagos. It is important to differentiate between "Lagosians" and "Nigerians" because prostitution debates occasionally took a nativist dimension, exemplified in the agitation by Lagos residents to protect their "beloved" city from the moral scourge perpetuated by "foreigners" from other parts of the country and abroad. Numerous city ordinances sought to reinforce nativism and anti-immigration by establishing a rigid differential between the "indigenes" and the "foreigners." The extent to which narratives of sexual impropriety were "nativist" or "national," "Lagosian" or "Nigerian," depended on the time, the issues at stake, and the ideologies of nationalists or commentators. Taken as a whole, a combination of local and national manifestations of modernity intersected with global ideas about the place of colonial subjects in world politics to put illicit sexuality at the center of rhetoric of colonial progress.

A "Total" History of Sexuality?

When I started this project, my intention was to write the history of gender and prostitution in Nigeria by examining the correlation between sex work and social class under colonial rule. Deeply inspired by Luise White's seminal work, *The Comforts of Home*, I wanted to expand on the existing literature by comparing and contrasting sex work with "respectable" careers of those few Nigerian educated elite women. I wanted to understand how family backgrounds, ethnicity, and location shaped women's professional careers. Archival materials and oral interviews solidified some, but not all, of my initial assumptions; they also led me into a new array of attractive possibilities. Based on the depth and diversity of these sources and the historical reality of Nigeria they brought to light, I opted to expand my focus beyond prostitution and intra-gender class differences.

Because of my conviction that as an interpreter of the past, I could not just write what I like, I had to grapple with the past as revealed through the sources closer to what "actually" transpired. I faced the daunting challenge of writing what appeared like a "total" history of sexuality that captures the historical "actuality." Since academic knowledge production is normally situated within geographical and disciplinary confines, writing such a history would mean learning the language or vocabulary of a gamut of subfields and becoming conversant with all the published literature in the various regions in Africa. It also would involve combing the entire Nigerian archival collections for comprehensive data on sexuality in the legal, medical, military, and social welfare records, as well as fragmentary yet useful information from minutes of meetings of the Lagos Town Council (LTC). The fact that none of the secondary sources dealing both with West Africa and with other regions of the continent satisfactorily engage sexuality history in its "completest" form was quite frustrating. When I started the project, there was no published work on prostitution in colonial Lagos; there was no book-length study of prostitution in any part of Anglophone West Africa covering the colonial era.[19] There is no gainsaying the fact that the silencing of sexuality in West African historical production has significantly undermined the prime position that sex occupied in the history of colonial encounter.

My project reached a turning point when I decided to engage the literature on sexuality in other regions of the British Empire, especially Asia and the Middle East. Philippa Levine's *Prostitution, Race and Politics*, which provides a detailed account of the contestation over venereal disease and sexuality regulation in the British colonies of Hong Kong, India, Queensland, and the Straits Settlements, was instrumental to my task. Right on page 1, I found the statement that, more than any other, effectively represents the ideas I hope to encompass herein. According to Levine, her book engages the "medical and military history, political and social history, and cultural and feminist history in an effort not only to understand the central importance of laws and practices around prostitution and disease control but also in an effort to integrate these widely different strands of history."[20] One could add ethnic and even urban history to the possible dimensions to which a society's sexual past is relevant. Levine demonstrates that sex is reflected in virtually all sites of the encounter between the colonizer and the colonized. In this book, I go beyond mentioning the political, legal, socioeconomic, medical, military, and urban perspectives on sexuality to effectively demonstrate how they all coalesced in the making of Nigeria's sexual past. This work is influenced by *Prostitution, Race and Politics*, and there are many historical parallels across cultures, locations, and polities. However, it departs from it in many ways.

Colonialism not only produced new regimes of class differences among both Africans and Europeans, it also introduced new elements of tension about how to tackle the alleged medico-moral implications of prostitution as an "underclass" profession. Yet race played a significant role in molding imperial perceptions toward prostitution since it was framed as an expression of sexual primitivity that was "distinctively African" and that imperialism sought to address through its so-called civilizing mission.[21] The idea of racial backwardness provided the justification for colonialism, and racialized sexuality as a component of racial prejudice not only satisfied colonialists' assumptions of the African's sexual perversion but paved the way for regimes that policed private debauchery in the interest of public virtue. Aside from sexual objectification, racialized sexuality justified the sexual exploitation of African women by white colonial officers and other foreign invaders. Imperial sexual exploitation, like other forms of expropriation, was anchored on the identity of the colonies as a tabula rasa—a blank slate of sexual desire where colonialists could experiment with new forms of sexual behavior rarely permissible in the metropole. Applying Michel Foucault's discourse of sexuality as "an especially dense transfer point for relations of power" to the study of imperialism, scholars have argued that sex and colonial exploitation are inseparable.[22] Ronald Hyam affirms that European imperialism "was not only a matter of 'Christianity and commerce,' it was also a matter of copulation and concubinage." Levine, however, presents the paradox: "Prostitution was a critical artifact of colonial authority, a trade deemed vital to governance but urgently in need of control."[23] Yet, without Western biomedicine, an integral arm of the European civilization project that *medicalized* sex, administrators might not have been equipped with the "scientific" language to justify sexoracist laws that punished Africans for their alleged sexual waywardness, while limiting their choices and initiating significant forces of social change. Sexual travesty was not genderless. In colonialists' ordering, its identity was female. According to Sander Gilman, the "primitive" in the European's gaze "is the black, and the qualities of blackness, or at least of the black female, are those of the prostitute."[24]

It is evident from the foregoing that the present literature does not lack an engagement with the intersections of sex, class, race, and gender.[25] What is lacking is proportionate engagement of these categories in close relation with the character of the colonial state as a site of ruthless capitalist expropriation, especially regarding some regions of Africa, and effective representation of diverse African voices that affirm the uniqueness of the colonial city as a container for cultures. Indeed, I would argue that at the present, Africanist literature on sexuality has been "overcompartmentalized," yielding a dearth of opportunities to approach the subject from wider angles. For instance, the intersection of class and sexuality is far more complex and fluid than the present literature suggests. In fact, the class factor tends to be collapsed into the so-called undesirables and the reformers (predominantly colonial administrators and traditional African agencies) who attempted to regulate sex. However, the politics of sex occasionally transcends interclass intrigues between the "outcast" and the "saints"; witness the intra-class manipulations among the so-called moralists. As we have seen in the case of Potts-Johnson, although she took a bribe from the prostitutes Agadagwu and George, the political row over incarceration that ensued was not between her and the prostitutes but between her and the colonial state, represented by the criminal justice system. In addition, the dimensions her case took on were dictated by her status and the civic expectations placed on her as an African, educated elite woman and high-ranking government officer.

Moreover, the interconnectivity between social class and prostitution has tended to be deployed esoterically without full engagement of the shades and contours it took over time and across locations. In order to decenter the class factor in sexual politics, I attempt to establish a distinction between multiple categories of class systems that emerged under colonial rule and those that had a precolonial foundation but which underwent transition under alien rule: civilian and military; elite and lower class; traditional and modern; children and adults; Africans and Europeans; men and women; rural and urban; educated and uneducated. These stratifications were informed by race, place, gender, and power in differing contexts. Although scholars, including Megan Vaughan, contend that the generalization of black female sexuality as the source of disease and moral corruption must be qualified and that the "extent to which it appeared 'male' or 'female' varied according to particular circumstance [and imperial setting]," they have committed less energy to explicating how it played out.[26] In the case of Nigeria, the colonialists, aside from the civilians (especially women), also identified African male soldiers as the demographic group whose sexual excessiveness needed to be policed, for an exigent purpose of enhancing the security of the colony and prolonging the life of the empire (see chapter 4). In addition, it is a truism that class tension and sexism were responsible for the traditional elites' quest to contain women's migration, under the guise of protecting cultural integrity. It is also a fact that the British established a rigid and often complementary distinction between civilian and military sexualities and sought to attend to each in accordance with perceived implications for the security of the colonial state. The present Africanist literature on sexuality regulation and VD has focused almost entirely on the civilian population to the detriment of the highly important colonial military force.[27] The very few sources that reference military prostitution do not address the VD campaign in terms of the struggle to balance attention to sexual vice within the civilian and military demographics.[28]

Consequently, this book argues that new research into African prostitution history must effectively disaggregate the identity of various classes of people involved in sexual politics and holistically demonstrate how their stance changed over time, as did the conditions responsible for the transition. It must also critically address prostitution as a significant aspect of social welfare and humanitarian politics. Not all British officers moralized against sex work, and not all Nigerian commentators and politicians believed prostitution should be policed. Moreover, the British approach to prostitution, more than any factor, was shaped by the position each colonial officer occupied in the colonial hierarchy. Although medical and civil authorities both agreed that sexual pathology was the enemy of civilization, they differed on the best approach to take. If VD received serious attention among the soldiers, as we will see, it was because the colonial military officials viewed the wellness of the so-called guardian of the empire as more important than the health of civilians.

Historical studies on the relationship between sex and race in Africanist literature (especially those focusing on the settler colonies of East Africa and southern Africa) is vast.[29] The justification for the colonialists' anti-prostitution movement in these regions is not far-fetched: prostitution allegedly increased the rate of VD, which posed a threat to the notion of white "purity," or "whiteness." In other words, the distribution of palliative resources for VD was tied to race, as the white communities tended to be better served than the black ones partly because of the notion that VD was synonymous with blackness or that the color of VD was black.[30] In addition, anxiety over rape and the sexual safety of white women in settler colonies "tended to spill over borders, incorporating other controversies, borrowing rhetoric, undermining reform, and creating political opportunities."[31] Nigeria, like other parts of West Africa, was not a settler colony, no doubt. But race was one of the central planks on which British thinking about sex and all its ascribed medico-moral implications rested. The dearth of scholarship has downplayed the connection between race and sexuality in West African history.[32] Unlike in South Africa, racial prejudice was not an official policy of the British in Nigeria. However, it did shape, explicitly and implicitly, how Africans were governed, in terms of the culture of socialization, urban planning, remuneration for work, health and sanitation, bodily habits, and vertical and horizontal human relations. In moving beyond the mere mentioning of race and sex in West Africanist literature, to showing how these matters really manifested in everyday interactions between the colonized and the colonizer, I intend to demonstrate that the history of sexuality in Nigeria would have taken a completely different turn without the colonialists' rigid construction of prostitution as a "moral crime" for Nigerians and as a "treat" for the whites. Racism therefore influenced the introduction and implementation of anti-prostitution laws that punished or spared individuals based on the color of their skin (see chapter 5). Aside from influencing the moral implications of commercial sex, and the identity constructed for the people involved, race also determined the nomenclature imposed on where it took place. Sexual nomenclature and racial ordering were not just a contrast between "white" and "black"—the gradation of "whiteness," tied to social class within the colonial establishment and nationality, guided the reading of sexual laxity among dissimilar groups of European populations.

Men (both colonialists and African chiefs) were at the apex of sexuality regulation in Africa for one principal reason: colonialism was a male-centered edifice that was erected by men and controlled almost entirely by men. Western and African brands of male authority were contradictorily deployed to stigmatize all women, regardless of social class and location, as elements whose dangerous sexuality needed to be tamed. However, one of the major lacunae in the present literature on sexuality and gender is the paucity of analysis on the involvement of African educated women. The impression one gets is that men monopolized the debate or mobilized to subdue the productive and reproductive power of women who practiced prostitution. The story of Lagos seems unique because of the presence of a small but highly influential group of Western-educated African women who campaigned against illicit sexuality as part of their larger project of improving the social and economic condition of women and girls (see chapters 2 and 7). I am not aware of any part of Africa where educated African women were so intimately involved in the politics of sexual regulation as in Lagos.

The Idea of the Erotic Child

There is no doubting the fact that the factors of race, gender, and class informed sexual regulation. But I would argue that age is another prism that sheds a powerful light on social surveillance, one that historical studies have overlooked. Existing works have tended to emphasize prostitution mainly as a profession of adult women who acted on their own to achieve social and economic independence from mainstream norms of sexual respectability.[33] Even when mention is made of girls who practiced prostitution, an engaging analysis of the complexity of differentiating between a "girl" or "underage" female and an "adult" prostitute is missing. Moreover, the dichotomy between a "girl" and "adult" female affected such issues as domesticity, missionary education, and the cliterodectomy controversy, among others, as seen in recent literature; but it also concerned psychosexual and physio-sexual development in relation to medico-moral anxiety over the future of African womanhood.[34] In Nigeria, the idea of an erotic child, or a child as an object of sexual pleasure, emerged alongside the struggle against sexual perversion. Indeed, both British colonialists and Lagosians differentiated between the sexuality of adult women and that of young girls, not mainly in terms of their physiological appearance, but also in relation to the implications of their "social deviance" for the wellness of the colonial state. While adult prostitutes were viewed as women who acted voluntarily in defiance of the colonial states' values of dignity, underage prostitutes were treated as passive girls without any agency. If child prostitutes were in moral decadence, it was because of the criminal activities of adult procurers and the breakdown of state paternalism, the last resort for remedying social problems.

This book brings into conversation two areas of substantive historical inquiry—prostitution and childhood. Legal and social fixations on the girl-child's docility and her place within the colonial society meshed to create often ambiguous outcomes about sexual degeneration. But the legal construction had stronger administrative power because the criminal justice system used chronological age as the marker of childhood and adulthood. However, when social and legal constructions of childhood innocence collided, the former prevailed because the practices and interpretation of statutes could not operate outside the core structures of the society. The contradictions between legal and social constructions of childhood went beyond the administration of justice, extending to the state's intervention in the family's private affairs as it attempted to fulfill a paternalistic responsibility to protect girls from sexual exploitation in order to forestall immediate and future social instability that could jeopardize the security and smooth running of the colonial state. Hence girls were subjected to paternalistic influences of both the family and state. In uncovering the phenomenon of illicit underage sex, I explore the complicated definitions of childhood from multiple perspectives and demonstrate that new colonial ideas of childhood did not overrun the preexisting African-centered attitudes, but coexisted with them, creating often irreconcilable perspectives (see chapter 3).

A host of theoretical expositions by British welfare officers anchored on the relationship between chronological age and psychosexual development surfaced. On the one hand, adolescence arrived earlier among African girls, compared to their Western counterparts; but these girls were, welfare officers concluded, incapable of making wise decisions about their sexuality until around age 18. Closely read, the British welfare officers, like Donald Faulkner, whose career is synonymous with the emergence of the crude colonial science of childhood, extended racial prejudice to the politics of children's welfare by insisting that the traits of sexual pathology, responsible for such deviant behavior as prostitution, did not mature until females reached adulthood since the prepubescent child was deemed to be asexual. In short, sexual pathology was age specific. Attention on child and juvenile welfare went beyond presumptions or theoretical expression of endangerments—the British government, through the efforts of Faulkner, even established the CWO, primarily to police delinquency among boys and girls because the office took a development approach to vice. The CWO believed that child prostitutes would grow up to become adult prostitutes who would abhor the institution of marriage and healthy heterosexuality. Thus, a child prostitute of today would become the adult and "criminal" of tomorrow.

As it turned out, while the government believed that child prostitutes and other sexually exploited girls deserved rehabilitation after being removed from brothels, the adults were treated as criminals and were subjected to fines, imprisonment, and repatriation. The British committed more resources to rehabilitating delinquent children and went the extra mile in punishing procurers and culprits like Potts-Johnson, whose action undermined the state's determination to rid Lagos of child prostitutes. In fact, Potts-Johnson's court case might have ended differently or not even been initiated at all if she had not been in charge of reclaiming underage girls from brothels. A strong element of failed moral responsibility on the part of adults in protecting sexually exploited children played out in the proceedings and the eventual outcome of the case. The scandal was about not only bribery but, more important, the implications of her action, which the criminal justice system believed would lead to the proliferation of child prostitution. As chapters 6 and 7 further explicate, the response to anti-prostitution laws was based on the categories of prostitutes it affected and was emblematic of the panic over broader social instability.

Sexualized Nationalism and Selective Modernity

Thanks to the historian George Mosse's pioneering study *Nationalism and Sexuality*, scholars now firmly acknowledge that sexuality and the nation are not autonomous and discrete constructs.[35] Whether in Africa or other parts of the world, sexuality has played a significant role in molding the idea of statehood and progress. Nationalism, perhaps the most powerful ideology of the modern era, is significant not only because it gives individuals and groups across societies something to live and die for, but also because its expression is largely coded in the historical moments peculiar to each society. Hence nationalism is not transhistorical. To be sure, references to the interplay between sexuality and nationalism in African historical research are legion. When African patriarchs attempted to forbid women's migration into the city, they were expressing a sort of cultural nationalism—an attempt to protect the so-called pristine African womanhood.[36] Women who contested cliterodectomy and missionaries' and the colonial government's concocted reproduction policies were expressing socioeconomic sentiments about their sexuality and bodies.[37]

But the correlation between nationalism and sexuality goes far beyond the colonialists' and African elites' anti-migration polices or the politics of the womb.[38] My goal in this book is to put nationalism and sexuality in a conversation in a manner that unmasks the numerous contours of nationalistic ferment and how they connect to the ideas of respectability and progress among those who espoused them. Colonial Nigeria was a country not only of many ethnicities, but also of disparate ideological positions on sexuality. And one does not need to look far to come to grips with this. On the pages of the major nationalists' newspapers—the *West African Pilot*, the *Comet*, the *Lagos Daily News*, and the *Daily Service*, among others—during the 1930s and 1940s one finds a barrage of commentaries, detailed articles, thought-provoking editorials, and columnists' debates that vividly unveil a Nigerian-centered interpretation of the relationship between sex and nationalism. Lagos elites who tripled as politicians, professionals, and public intellectuals did not allow the British to monopolize the rhetoric of illicit sexuality; rather, they used the newspapers and the sprouting culture of public lectures to give a Nigerian meaning to the politics of sex.

In fact, it is not an overstatement to assert that sexualized nationalism took a more vociferous dimension in Nigeria than in any other British African colony. The early lead the country took in education, literacy, and print culture, coupled with its vast population and position as one of Britain's most prosperous colonies, all conspired to give it a history of sexualized nationalism rarely found in Africa. Between the 1920s and 1950s, the British colonialists found themselves contending with groups of well-educated and politically relevant African women and men who defined sexual respectability to suit their vision of a modern colonial state, which they intended to inherit after the anticipated demise of imperialism. For the nationalists, decolonization was not just about political self-determination but also about the notion that social problems like prostitution, constructed as a backlash to imperialism, would all be eradicated once the Union Jack was lowered. Hence, there was a bearing between decolonization and sexuality that obviously featured in the rhetoric of nationalism. Prostitution was not just about secret "sinful" affairs between consenting adults or sexual exploitation of underage girls. It was about nation-building.

Nigerian nationalists' sexual politics was couched in terms of what I call selective modernity, the notion that Nigeria could follow the path of modern European nation-states by selectively appropriating "positive" practices of social advancement and doing away with those constructed as "negative." It was a practice and way of thinking riddled with contradictions and inconsistencies. The elites wanted a progressive modern city like London but disliked some of the consequences of urbanization like prostitution. Moreover, sexual politics took on a paternalistic dimension as the semantics of sexual degeneration found expression in the failure of the colonial masters to fulfill the "fatherly" responsibility of "civilizing" the natives. Indeed, when nationalist politicians condemned the colonialists' toleration of prostitutes, they invoked what one could call a covenant of moral responsibility between the colonizer and the colonized. This "broken" moral covenant was confronted by moral nationalism as Lagosians blamed the British for promoting immorality by not policing prostitutes. One sees the fusion of moral and political nationalism when the educated elites believed that the British deliberately tolerated sexual decadence in order to undermine the emergence of a strong Nigerian society capable of standing on its own after the projected withdrawal of the colonialists. But sexualized nationalism was not a common front parading uniformly and coherently against degeneration. Rather, individuals and groups based on location, power, and gender presented their ideas in a conflicting manner. Indeed, Frederick Cooper's complicated view of the role of the African "collaborators" under colonial regimes is appropriate to an understanding of the terrain of contestation over prostitution regulation.[39] As I show, the rigid binary of "resisters" and "collaborators" is not useful for understanding the response of Nigerians. Some Nigerian supporters of anti-prostitution legislation did become critics and vice versa, responding both to the evolving debate and to their own shifting socioeconomic locations.

The core structure of nationalism, like empire-building, was male centered. But in the case of Nigeria, the activities of a few educated elite women broadened the terrain of anticolonial sentiments. It is important to recognize this gendered nationalism in retracing the different ways in which nationalist men and women constructed sexual danger and the articulated solutions to it. The following historiographical issues make the study of educated African women's sexual politics important for understanding the gendered character of African nationalism.

First, the inclusion of elite women in the history of prostitution clarifies that it was not only men (as previously noted) who launched repressive attacks on African women's sexuality and existence; elite women, in the case of Lagos, were actually at the forefront of this project.

Second, elite women's involvement in sexual politics opens another window on the relationship between intra-gender relations and sexual politics. The women through such associations as the Lagos Women's League (LWL), the Women's Welfare Council (WWC), and the Nigerian Women's Party (NWP) felt that prostitutes, due to their deviation from the dominant virtue of respectability, did not qualify for political protection. This notion is currently missing in the historiographies of elite African women, which fail to recognize that women nationalists were selective in their mobilization against the colonial state's poor attitude toward female empowerment. The elite women stood for or were the mouthpiece of only "good" and "law-abiding" women who earned "legitimate" income, not the "criminally minded" ones who polluted the moral serenity of the society.

Third, the elite women's construction of "badness" for prostitutes fit into the colonialists' practice of organizing individuals and groups in accordance with their importance and their perceived peril to mainstream conventions.

Fourth, in terms of comparative gender politics, one could identify and contextualize the difference between elite women's sexual politics in Nigeria and their sexual politics in Western Europe and North America. While elite European and North American women were divided over the prejudiced implementation of anti-prostitution and VD laws, as seen in the movement against the Contagious Diseases Acts (CDAs) in Britain and its empire, elite Lagos women throughout the first half of the twentieth century spoke with one voice.[40]

A Note on Sources and Methodologies

The sources and methodologies I deploy for this book reflect both the interdisciplinary character of scholarly production on sexuality and the significant position that sex occupied in African colonial experience. My primary archival documents include those generated by military and medical establishments of the colonial force, the West African Frontier Force (WAFF), and the Department of Medical and Sanitary Service, respectively. This earliest body of thick documents dating to the first decade of the twentieth century largely contains colonialists' perspectives on the medical impact of VD among the military and civilian populations. They include "fact-finding" reports and annual returns of the incidence of VD produced by colonial medics. The colonial office dispatches (or circulars) on VD and on the progress of the British civilizing mission not only generated information pertaining to Nigeria but also allowed me to evaluate broader imperial practice and draw comparative insights from other colonies across the globe. Largely treated with utmost confidentiality by the colonialists, these documents firmly establish the centrality of dissident sexuality to colonial security and the sustenance of the hegemonic status quo. I used this genre of documents (especially for chapter 4) to map out the shifting concern over VD within the military and civilian populations.

The establishment of the CWO in 1941 led to the institutionalization of child and juvenile delinquency programs and the production of extensive reports mainly by welfare officers on child prostitution and its impact on the colonial state. This spectrum of data brings researchers closer to the identity of adult and child prostitutes and the entire prostitution underworld. They are peppered with statistics on the occurrence of child prostitution and on the ages and physical appearance of child prostitutes. Other information includes the life histories of some child prostitutes, how they were recruited into sex work, and the methods adopted for rehabilitating them. Without the massive documents of the CWO, it would have been impossible to establish any clear difference between adult and child sexualities. In addition, the CWO records in conjunction with those of the prison service provide vivid insight into the

science of colonial childhood that emerged as the colonialists sought to p(
juvenile delinquency.

Between 1916 and 1944, the British passed more than one hundred anti-
prostitution statutes, codified into five broad pieces of legislation. A review
of these anti-prostitution laws revealed quite clearly that a holistic approach
would be the best method of coming to terms with the place of sexuality in
Nigeria's past. This body of documents is unusual in that they are all published
primary sources and, unlike other categories of documents, are available in
several research libraries in Europe and North America. In order to strengthen
one of my core arguments—that age was a major factor in the politics of
sex—I divide anti-prostitution laws into "child" and "adult" and create an
intersection between them and the prevailing practices of power and agency.
Another typology, namely "VD laws," strengthens my contention about the
need to address sexuality from both the civilian and the military angles. Anti-
prostitution laws had metropolitan and local origins; whereas a couple of them
were customized for Lagos in that they dealt specifically with the situation in
the city, others such as the Venereal Diseases Ordinance, or VDO (1943), an
adaptation of the notorious Contagious Diseases Acts passed in Britain and
later introduced to some of its colonies during the second part of the nineteenth
century, and the Children and Young Persons Ordinance, or CYPO (1943),
were adapted from the metropole (see chapter 5). Regardless of their source,
anti-prostitution laws satisfied the British conviction that the criminal justice
system was the best means of policing illicit sexuality.

All the aforementioned data, despite their depth and vastness, are one-sided
since they largely present the colonialists' perspective on vice and criminality.
Nigerian sources are highly important for cross-examining and/or corroborat-
ing the colonialists' sources. Petitions from Lagos elites and "ordinary law-
abiding" citizens from the 1920s help me to pinpoint the difference between
"regulation" and "prohibition" and identify the main advocates of each agenda.
These petitions are found in the official files of the various elite women's associations and the minutes of meetings of chiefs. One must read beyond the
conventional moralizing tone of the genuine attempt to extol core values of
"decent" society because they were composed mainly by men who decried
the financial and social independence of women practitioners of prostitution.
Petitioners also supply a researcher with useful information on the political
economy of sex work—from their letters, we know that prostitutes made
"tons" of money from sex work and that it was a wise choice for women who
sought financial and social independence. Other Nigerian-centered information has been gathered from the records of the ethnic associations that were
deeply involved in prostitution policing since colonial authorities blamed them
(as "foreigners") for being the purveyors of immorality. Various sections of

the ethnic association documents also contain laws to punish members for prostitution and to lay down the procedures for aiding their repatriation.

Another body of documents comprises court records, which offer insight into courtroom experiences of individuals and groups accused of breaking anti-prostitution laws. Without the court records, it would be impossible to unearth the contradictions between legal and social conceptions of criminality and the social changes and continuities they produced. In addition, colonial laws did not have a full human implication until people were arraigned for violating them and until they were subjected to opposing interpretations as accused persons attempted to circumvent the law. As useful as court records are, they pose a number of challenges, one of which is that they could represent the perspective of a court clerk who took proceedings of cases, transcribing and translating them, sometimes from local languages. In the process of judging what testimony to record based on its perceived relevance, a clerk could knowingly or unknowingly omit or silence information that might have enhanced a historian's balanced interpretation. More worrisome is the fact that court documents are handwritten and sometimes illegible. However, this challenge can be surmounted by placing cases within specific historical contexts. In addition, because some proceedings were also reported in the newspapers, these accounts can help to cross-examine original court documents and fill some interpretative gaps. Unlike court records, the newspapers paint the picture of courtroom drama, the atmosphere under which proceedings took place, and the emotions of the actors.

Newspapers make up the most comprehensive source of information on Nigerians' attitudes toward prostitution; they are arguably the largest repository of written data on colonial Nigeria produced by Nigerians. The history of the newspaper press is synonymous with the story of the British presence in Lagos. In 1863, just two years after Britain added Lagos to its worldwide empire, the *Anglo-African* appeared as the city's first newspaper.[41] Lagos remained the hub of the print media, which featured close to two hundred newspapers and magazines during Britain's one hundred years of colonial presence in Nigeria. The print culture was popular not only because it gave expression to anticolonial voices, but also because it came (at least from the 1930s on) to define the gradual, but slow progression toward a Nigerian-defined modernity project. The newspapers traditionally sensationalized prostitution stories and appeared to have exploited sexual politics to promote sales. They published news, the minutes of meetings of elite women, public lectures given by prominent Lagosians on prostitution, and announcements of new anti-prostitution laws. Beyond these, powerful editorials shaped the tenor of public discourse, while columns edited by popular women and men not only reflected developments in the society, but also allowed "ordinary" Lagosians to air their opinions, mostly in unedited form. Hence more than any other sources, it was the newspapers that accommodated divergent views on prostitution. In all, sexual politics constituted one component of the newspapers' contribution to the anticolonial movement and added flavor to the print media, which assumed a "popular" culture dimension from the 1930s through the 1950s.

I approached my oral interviews in the same manner as I engaged this study. It would have been difficult to mine the wealth of information about sexuality in oral accounts if I went around asking questions specifically about sex work. Rather, I wanted to understand the social life of Lagos in holistic terms. How people socialized or congregated to share music, time, and love made up just a fraction of my inquiry. Other investigations included public perceptions about VD and reactions to anti-prostitution laws. So well entrenched was prostitution in the social life of colonial Lagos that virtually all my male and female informants (both "indigenes" and "foreigners") remembered the main red-light streets and popular brothels, interesting stories or jokes about prostitution, and famous prostitutes of the final four decades of the colonial era. They even remembered a famous novel about a Lagos prostitute (see chapter 2) and how it influenced popular culture. Songs about prostitution during the interwar years survived decades of sociopolitical and economic transformations and were reference points to "sweet" and "dark" old days, as my informants ambivalently described life under British colonialism.

The language in which my interviews were conducted also reflected the linguistic realities of Lagos. Most of my interviews were conducted in Pidgin English, the most widely spoken "dialect" in multiethnic Lagos. Aside from facilitating easy communication across cultures, Pidgin English has expanded its urban dictionary through its flexibility and creativity. On rare occasions, interviewees preferred to communicate in Yoruba or English, both of which I speak fluently. It is normal for some interviewees to want to speak in Yoruba since Lagos was originally a Yoruba town. In addition, I discovered that some respondents, regardless of ethnicity, felt comfortable speaking in Yoruba since my ethnicity is obvious—I bear conspicuous Yoruba facial marks. The dichotomy between an insider/emic and an outsider/etic in relation to the identity or ethnicity of a researcher also exists in Lagos—for instance, my Yoruba respondents tended to treat me as an insider, while the non-Yoruba viewed me as an outsider.[42] These attitudes were not so much impediments to unlocking the repository of oral history. This is probably because over the course of colonial and postcolonial eras, Lagosians, both the "indigenes" and the "foreigners," have learned to accommodate ethnic differences. I am not suggesting that inter- and intra-ethnic relations in Lagos are wholly harmonious. Actually, inter- and intra-ethnic tension permeated virtually all spheres of life in the city; as we will see in various sections of this book, the politics of sex also took on a nativist dimension. A Nigerian researcher, regardless of ethnicity, would encounter limited problems conducting interviews in Lagos, compared to most parts of Nigeria. However, the reverse would be the case for a foreign researcher, who would be treated as an outsider but would still be able to navigate the cultural landscape with the aid of research guides and assistants.

The Chapters in Brief

This book's seven chapters are fused thematically and chronologically to reflect the changing and episodic character of sexual politics in relation to the activities of the main actors and the issues at stake. The first chapter, "'This Is a City of Bubbles': Lagos and the Phenomenon of Colonial Urbanism," sets the historical stage by introducing the socioeconomic, gendered, and racial structure of colonial Lagos and unveiling the identities of individuals and groups that shaped sexual politics. It draws on a fairly conventional history of colonial Lagos but sheds new light in contextualizing the chapters that follow. Since prostitution was an urban phenomenon that did not take place in isolation from broader social processes, this chapter depicts urban social life, locating it within the context of Lagos's rapid transformation from a backwater coastal community in the nineteenth century to one of Africa's most culturally diverse cities and the capital of the colonial state of Nigeria. It explores inter-ethnic and intra-ethnic relations and concludes that the politics of sex fit into the existing tension over urban citizenship, class stratification, and social privileges accruing from the pigmentation of the skin. It argues that the agitation against prostitution reflected a social ambivalence that I term "selective modernity."

Chapter 2 is the first of three chapters that explicate how prostitution was constructed as a cog in the wheel of the modern colonial society that the colonialists and Nigerian elites wanted to create. Titled "'The Vulgar and Obscene Language': Prostitution, Criminality, and Immorality," it focuses specifically on adult prostitution and the physical, ethnic, and racial geography of sex work. It details the ethnic identities of Lagos prostitutes and asserts that sex work mirrored the diversity of the colonial urban economy and consumption patterns of Lagosians. A glimpse into the political economy of prostitution is necessary in apprehending some of the reasons women chose it as a career path or a temporary solution to financial hardship. As this chapter demonstrates, prostitution was not only a profitable profession, it also directly and indirectly contributed to the colonial state's agenda of maintaining the city as a hotspot of migrants. How did moralists define and construct sexual immorality and the relationship between prostitution and urban crime? Did gender, race, and power influence the attention given to urban crime? I trace the changing attitudes of the government toward prostitution, the activities of Lagos elite men and women, and how their ideas converged and diverged over time. When the colonial government during World War II decided to abandon its regulatory stance toward prostitution and embrace prohibition, it was doing what the Lagos elites had demanded for two decades. However, in whose interest was this new policy change? In answering these questions and others, I concentrate on the activities of delinquent youth known in the urban dictionary as *boma* and *jaguda* boys and how their identity and behavior gave new connotations to prostitution as a profession that must be proscribed.

Building on chapter 2's concern with adult sex work and urban crime, in chapter 3, "Childhood Innocence, Adult Criminality: Child Prostitution and Moral Anxiety," I turn my attention to underage sex work and the emergence of the idea of the erotic child. This chapter allows me to rearticulate one of my main contentions that prostitutes' age played a major role in determining the disposition of the colonialists and Lagosians to sexual politics. I argue that the idea of child prostitution as a sex crime against children and the framing of the sexual child strengthened state paternalism. This chapter complicates the definition of a child from legal and social angles and explores how the attempt to identify children as belonging to a "delinquent" demographic produced inconsistent outcomes. All categories and forms of prostitution were a sexo-moral aberration, but child prostitution went beyond sexual degeneration to encompass an ethical guilt and the failure of "responsible" adults to protect endangered girls—the future of African womanhood. As this chapter shows, from the early 1940s, the idea of "sexually endangered" children became the target of the state, which attempted to "save" children from the clutches of violence in order to uphold its values of colonial progress, tranquility, and continuity. Numerous and complicated ideas of the psychosexual development of the girl-child emerged, not only in response to the trafficking for sexual exploitation but also in the CWO's quest to institutionalize a "development approach" to social vice.

But the concern over prostitution transcended alarms over urban insecurity and sex crimes against underage girls—VD also constituted a medical panic because of the assumption that it led to a decline in population and endangered the health of the military, the defender of the empire. In chapter 4, "The Sexual Scourge of Imperial Order: Race, the Medicalization of Sex, and Colonial Security," I posit that sex had broader implications for the future of the British Empire, while also showing that the generalization that women were the moral scourge of the empire whose sexuality needed to be curtailed must be qualified. Indeed, the African rank-and-file of the colonial army, like women, became another demographic whose sexuality was treated as dangerous. What is more, by using a civil-military approach, I reveal that the colonialists' perception of the effect of moral danger was not monolithic but was based on the identities they constructed for civilian and military populations and their contributions to colonial capitalism. A discussion of the tension among military and civilian authorities establishes that the colonialists' ideas of sexual savagery and their methods of dealing with it were class specific and were constantly in a state of flux. This disequilibrium to a large extent was based on the weighting of the medical consequences of gonorrhea and syphilis against other communicable diseases like influenza. I argue that the medicalization of sex reflected the quest by colonial medics to appropriate the panic over prostitution as a means of repositioning themselves as a vital tool of civilization.

In chapter 5, "Sexualized Laws, Criminalized Bodies: Anti-prostitution Law and the Making of a New Socio-Sexual Order," we begin to move away from the narratives of the medical and moral danger of sex work to a discussion of how the criminal justice system assumed a prime position in the policing of prostitution. Law mirrors how a society is structured, and vice versa. Laws not only lead to massive social change but also reflect attempts to order citizens' conduct to concur with powerful persons' understanding of "respectable" living and "wise" management of time, resources, and their bodies. By differentiating between adult and child prostitution laws, I show that the legal system played a significant role in molding public and official perceptions toward the identity of adult and underage practitioners of prostitution and the perceived menace each type of prostitution allegedly posed. This is not to say that the society did not socially construct the identities of adult and child prostitutes differently. Indeed, before the 1940s, the dominant rhetoric of sexual danger hinged on the social construction of sex work as morally degrading. But the new legal regime from the early 1940s, unlike the social interpretation of sex work, institutionalized the criminalization of transactional sex as a component of social and public order. Prostitution became a component of the colonial state's maintenance of law and order, which was cardinal to the effective exploitation of the colonies. This chapter further untangles one of my major claims that prostitutes' age influenced both how prostitution was viewed and the level of institutionalized attention it received.

Chapters 6 and 7, "Men, Masculinities, and the Politics of Sexual Control" and "Lagos Elite Women and the Struggle for Legitimacy," detail the contradiction and consequences—intended and unintended—of anti-prostitution law from the perspectives of men and women, respectively. Lagosians inevitably reacted to the content and implementation of anti-prostitution laws for the following reasons, among others: the laws were ineffective and poorly implemented; their enforcement involved racial and gender discrimination; and, more important, they affected the lives of several individuals and groups outside the prostitution subculture. Collectively, the two chapters argue that if support for the prostitution regulatory regime was gendered in nature, one should also expect the reaction to it to be gendered. More than 90 percent of anti-prostitution laws were introduced during World War II, one of the most unstable periods in modern British imperial history. Aside from the breakdown of law and order as a result of wartime emergency measures, massive immigration created a degree of social backlash that increased the difficulty of policing the city. As it was, the British could only make laws; they needed Nigerians like Potts-Johnson (as law enforcement officers) to implement them during a period when corruption reached an all-time high. In explaining why legal prohibition could not solve the "problem" of prostitution, I argue that the challenges of policing sex work could not be dissociated from the broader crisis of the maintenance of law and order and colonial legitimacy.

I disaggregate the response of men and women, by looking at how social class, power, and location influenced their stance. It is a fact that men, leaning on European- and African-style patriarchy, tended to be puritanical in their approach to illicit sexuality. But on rare occasions, some were actually prostitution advocates, by appropriating the rhetoric of moral licentiousness to lambast the colonialists for initiating the social changes that led to urban vice. The reaction of elite women to anti-prostitution laws dovetailed with their longstanding agenda to augment women's agency in a man's world. More important, they revised their attitudes toward the enforcement of anti-prostitution laws to reflect the emerging concern over the rehabilitation of child prostitutes and attempted to feminize the policing of prostitution. This emerging crisis of gender and legitimacy would see the elite women launching new attacks on the colonial government, while attempting to maternalize sexual danger.

The epilogue, "Prostitution and Trafficking in the Age of HIV/AIDS," links the colonial history of sexuality with the contemporary politics of HIV/AIDS and girl-child trafficking in Nigeria. If the nationalists and politicians felt that independence would usher in social transformation that would eradicate socially constructed problems of prostitution, the postcolonial crises of nation-building exemplified in political instability, coups d'état and military intervention in politics, and civil war have proved them totally wrong. The continuity and change in the institutional response to illicit sexuality mirrored the transformative process in the core structures of Nigeria's political and economic ordering. Unlike in the 1940s, when the NPF and the CWO were chiefly responsible for policing prostitution, postcolonial Nigeria witnessed the emergence of new organizations like the National Agency for the Prohibition of Traffic in Persons (NAPTIP), which monitors sexual exploitation of underage girls. The rehabilitation of prostitutes in Nigeria's Fourth Republic (since 1999) has become the focus of a newly created women's agency, supported by the wives of politicians and senior government officials who appropriate the anti-trafficking cause as a means of demonstrating their political relevance. The character, intensity, and composition of regulatory agencies have changed to meet the new challenges of urbanization, HIV/AIDS, underdevelopment, and the globalization of sex in post-independence Nigeria. Regardless of how one chooses to approach sexual politics, the colonial background remains vital.

CHAPTER I

"This Is a City of Bubbles"
Lagos and the Phenomenon
of Colonial Urbanism

The title of this chapter is a phrase from Cyprian Ekwensi's *People of the City* (1954), which was "acclaimed as the first major novel in English by a West African to be widely read throughout the English-speaking world."[1] Aside from being of immense importance in the development of contemporary African writing, *People of the City* in so many ways affirmed the significant position that Lagos occupied in the 1950s—a bridge between the demise of colonialism and the birth of an independent Nigerian state. What made Lagos a city of bubbles, as Ekwensi rightly emphasizes, was not only the multiple road lanes, electricity, and tall buildings that adorned the main business districts but the superfluous social life of its residents. Amusa Sango, the main character of the novel, leads a socially complementary existence as a 26-year-old bachelor from eastern Nigeria, a "ladies' man," dance bandleader of calypso and *konkoma*, and crime reporter for a local newspaper. In attempting to capture Lagos of the 1940s and 1950s, Ekwensi situates Sango within the ambiance of nocturnal socialization, gender relations, popular culture, and even the politics of nationalism. "Every Sunday in this city," Ekwensi attempts to capture Sango's "play boy" feeling toward Aina, one of his lovers, "men met girls they had never seen and might never see again. They took them out and amused them. Sometimes it led to a romance and that was unexpected, but more often it led to nowhere. Every little affair was a gay adventure, part of the pattern of life in the city. No sensible person who worked six days a week expected anything else but relaxation from these strange encounters."[2] But urban living had its darker side and offered inconveniences, not just the pleasures of transient socio-sexual networking. Poverty, bribery and corruption, violent crime, the high cost of living, and noise pollution emanating from the "sounds of buses, hawkers, locomotives, the grinding of brakes, the hooting of sirens and clanging of church and school bells" were only a short list of the ills of city life.[3]

For students of African history familiar with the history of colonial urbanism, Ekwensi's narrative, though fictional, aptly and vividly captures the social changes accentuated by the transformation of Lagos from a little island "of pristine simplicity of a cantonment of African huts and compounds" on the eve of British colonization in 1861 "to the dignity of the Queen city of the West Coast" by the first half of the twentieth century.[4] In this chapter, I lay out the socioeconomic, racial, political, and ethnic contexts of the story of prostitution in Lagos. I introduce Lagosians, placing their experience within the rapidly modernizing colonial society, struggling to reconcile the contradictions between colonial progress and colonial failure. If the story of African involvement in sexual politics in Lagos is different from what obtained in most parts of Africa, it is because the city's social and economic structures are unique. Moreover, prostitution, like other aspects of human socio-sexual relations, did not take place in isolation from other components of society's larger experience but within the broader urban space that served as a melting pot of cultures and ideas. The city more than any other location was flexible in accommodating myriads of social behaviors rarely permissible in the countryside and was a significant site for measuring the "success" or "failure" of the imperialist project.

A "No-Man's Land"

Research has shown that the popular sentiment "Lagos is a no-man's land," which gained currency from the first half of the twentieth century, not only is ahistorical, but also overrides the civilization of the people that inhabited the coastal city before it became a British colony in 1861.[5] The exact date of the founding of Lagos is unknown because of a lack of written records and conflicting oral traditions. What we do know is that it was settled before the sixteenth century by the Awori subgroup of the Yoruba, who were compelled to leave Ile-Ife, the ancestral home of the Yoruba, by *ifa* (divination) because of a chieftaincy dispute.[6] The migratory group was commanded to follow the path of a basin along the Ogun River and to settle at the point it sank. The name Awori derives from the response to the question: "Where is the basin?" Answer: "Awori—'the basin has sunk.'" The settlement's popular Yoruba name Eko probably derived from the Yoruba word for farm, *oko*.[7] It could also be from the Bini word *eko*, meaning "war camp," used by Benin conquerors in the mid-seventeenth century. Lagos, as the settlement would later be called, is derived from the Portuguese designation *lago* (lake).[8] The earliest immigrants first established a settlement at Ebute Metta (the three landing places), on the mainland, until the need for greater security pushed them to Iddo on the island.[9]

Unlike other polities like Oyo, Ijebu, and Benin in what is now Nigeria, which registered their formidable presence in the Atlantic economic order from the fifteenth century, Lagos remained a backwater settlement for much of the sixteenth and seventeenth centuries.[10] Its earliest inhabitants definitely engaged in farming—despite the fact that the sandy soil was unsuitable for agriculture—canoe building, iron working, salt making, and fishing. A gendered division of labor must have taken a form akin to that in other Yoruba towns: while men engaged in clearing the farm and planting, women harvested, processed, and sold the produce. Children's involvement in economic activities was important, not only as additional help, but also as one means of passing skills to future generations. Political organization was patterned along the lines of conventional Yoruba power distribution.[11] The earliest ruler, named *Olofin*, defended the community from invaders, made laws of succession, and distributed political power among his immediate family and some members of the larger community. However, he would later be overthrown by the powerful Benin Empire by the mid-seventeenth century. The relationship between Lagos and the Benin Empire went beyond having been conquered militarily, and extended to the creation of a new political institution that has survived to the present: in gratitude for helping to return the corpse of his warrior son killed during the battle with Lagos, the *oba* of Benin proclaimed the *ashipa* of Lagos as the new ruler of the town; the latter thus became the progenitor of the dynasty from which Lagos *oba* (kings) were subsequently chosen since around the 1630s.[12]

Lagos would remain economically and politically insignificant in the Atlantic world until around the 1760s, when it joined powerful states like Dahomey and Asante in the transatlantic slave trade. Popular history recounts that Oba Akinsemoyin (ruled 1760–75), the fourth king of Lagos, and his Portuguese friend, Joao de Oliveira, began to export slaves from the lagoon, first to the Gold Coast and later to the Americas. Akinsemoyin and Oliveira had met in Badagry, where the former was exiled before being enthroned. An estimate of about 575 slaves was exported yearly during the second half of the 1760s. It expanded from almost 4,000 to 14,000 between the first and second halves of the 1780s, respectively. Most of the slaves were captives and prisoners of wars taking place in nearby Badagry and Dahomey. But it was in the first half of nineteenth century that Lagos would become a major slave port, rivaling and surpassing its contemporaries in the Bight of Benin.[13] It became the largest slave exporter north of the equator by the 1820s—as other outposts were succumbing to the firepower of the British Anti-Slave Trade Squadron that policed the waters off the West African coast. The reasons for Lagos's eminent position during this era can be located in developments both within and outside Africa.

One external factor was the increasing demand for slaves in Brazil, where prices remained high. Although the prosperity of the Bahian sugar trade declined around 1820, the flourishing of the intra-Brazilian slave trade continued to create demand for human cargo. The decline in slave trading in the Bight of

Biafra and the Gold Coast allowed Lagos to take their place. Perhaps the most significant factor was the Yoruba civil wars, which started with the defeat of Owu in 1817, its sacking in 1823, and the collapse of Old Oyo Empire between 1817 and 1826.[14] The end of the Old Oyo Empire, the most powerful Yoruba state before the nineteenth century, created a vicious circle of violence in the whole of Yorubaland, as polities were destroyed to give way for others. The ensuing refugee crisis created enabling conditions for slave raiding, while the endless wars put a premium on slaves as the most important booty. More than 37,000 enslaved Africans who departed from Lagos between 1846 and 1850 came from the war-ravaged Yoruba hinterland.[15] In addition, the sheltered location of Lagos offered protection against the British naval squadron.

Lagos and the Phenomenon of Colonial Urbanism

Although the slave trade brought Lagos into global prominence, it also was responsible for sounding a death knell to its autonomy. The flourishing of the port's trade embarrassed the British and proved the antislavery campaign ineffective. A crack in the internal politics of Lagos exemplified in a chieftaincy dispute between two princes (Kosoko and Akintoye) was all the British needed to invade the town in 1851 under the pretext of stamping out the slave trade. Ten years after its bombardment, Lagos officially became the first part of modern Nigeria to be formally colonized.[16] The immediate impact of the imposition of colonial rule was a decline in slave trading and massive immigration to the city, which permanently changed the structural landscape of Lagos as immigrants established their economic, artistic, and cultural presence there. Among the first set of immigrants were the liberated African ex-slaves who had been converted to Christianity and received Western education through missionary activities in Sierra Leone.[17] They were soon followed by another set of immigrants from the Atlantic world—ex-slave returnees from Brazil, who numbered around four thousand to six thousand in 1873.[18] During the first half of the 1870s, an acting administrator in Lagos remarked that the Brazilian *emancipados* were the most populous residents after the natives.[19] They and their Sierra Leonean counterparts (the Saro) settled the Olowogbowo and Popo Aguda Districts of the town, respectively.

These two groups of immigrants from the Americas and West Africa laid the foundation of an African-centered entrepreneurial and professional class.[20] They would compete (albeit unfavorably) with large European firms for the importation of European goods, form trade unions, and contribute directly to the effective integration of Lagos into the world capitalist system. All the professionals in Lagos in 1920—numbering some twenty lawyers, twelve doctors, several engineers, as well as architects and surveyors—were of Aguda and

Saro origins.[21] But the contributions of the Saro and Aguda transcended the economic and professional spheres; they were also instrumental in the rise of the cultural nationalism that was a significant element of sociopolitical engineering from the 1880s on. Without them, the history of Nigeria's political nationalism and decolonization might have taken a completely different turn or been delayed because they laid the foundations of anticolonial sentiment through Western education. Trailblazers like Dr. James Africanus B. Horton and Dr. William Davies (the first "Nigerian" medical doctors), Christopher Sapara Williams, David Vincent (later known as Mojola Agbebi), and Herbert Macaulay (the so-called father of Nigerian nationalism), among others, received education in some of the most prestigious disciplines of the era such as medicine and law. They also pioneered an African-centered lifestyle that blended African and European cultures to create a distinctive hybrid that appealed to future generations of frontline politicians like Dr. Kofoworola Abayomi, Dr. C. C. Adeniyi Jones, F. R. A. Williams, and Adeyemo Alakija, among others.[22] It was therefore no coincidence that this class of pioneer literates, their descendants, and others they influenced would dominate Lagos elite culture during the first half of the twentieth century.[23] As leading public intellectuals, their stance on sexual morality, among other key social issues, would influence public opinion.

No doubt, the foundation of Lagos's primacy as the economic and infrastructural epicenter of Nigeria was laid in the mid-nineteenth century; however, it was not until the first two decades of the twentieth century that it would fully maximize its strategic location and head start as the bastion of colonial modernity. First, the massive investment in anti-malaria campaigns and improvements in sanitation—after Sir Ronald Ross, a winner of the Nobel Prize for Physiology or Medicine, discovered in 1897 that the female *Anopheles* mosquito was the vector of the disease—significantly reduced the mortality rate from about 100 per 1,000 in the 1890s to 30 per 1,000 in the 1920s.[24] Slum clearance and swamp reclamation did not totally end Lagos's unsanitary conditions, but it decongested the island and opened up several districts on the mainland.[25] Second, and most important, the choice of Lagos as the capital of southern Nigeria in 1906 and of the amalgamated Nigerian state in 1914 was both cause and effect of massive migration to the area and the attendant economic boom. The population rose from 39,387 in 1901 to 230,256 and then to 650,000 in 1950 and 1963, respectively.[26]

The largest number of the new immigrants, who came mainly from the hinterlands of Nigeria, arrived in search of jobs made possible by the government's investment in major capital projects like the construction of ports, rail and road networks, water and electricity plants, and wharves.[27] Railroad construction—perhaps the most expensive capital project embarked on by the colonialists, following the "pacification" of much of southern Nigeria—started from Lagos in 1895 and reached Kano in 1912. Indeed, throughout the colonial period the Railway Department was the largest employer of wage labor.[28] Aside from opening up Lagos and the interior of Nigeria to international commerce, railways facilitated the massive influx of provincial Nigerians into Lagos. The city also offered several amenities—electricity, public water supply, and educational and medical institutions—that were far beyond the reach of most Nigerians. Electricity was first introduced to Lagos in 1898, and by 1923 the Ijora Power Station was generating 29 megawatts from steam turbines and coal fires.[29] In the 1940s the second phase of the Ijora Power project increased supply to 80 megawatts.[30] In 1915 a public water scheme that was the biggest of its kind in West Africa, with the capacity to supply 2.5 million gallons of water daily to more than 100,000 inhabitants, was completed. Construction of two major wharves in the 1920s (the Apapa and Coal Wharves) further enhanced Lagos's intermediary position between domestic and international commerce.[31]

Not all immigrants sought jobs in the expanding government service and private enterprises. A large number from the 1860s came purposely to join the army. Apart from the pay, which was better than what was offered in lowest-paying government jobs, enlistment in the army afforded men the opportunity to exhibit masculinity, honor, and valor. Indeed, during the nineteenth century and much of the twentieth century, Lagos was essentially a military base where soldiers were deployed for both domestic and international expeditions. To be sure, the history of the colonial army is as old as the history of the British incursion into Nigeria. The establishment of the Lagos Constabulary in 1863, two years after the annexation of Lagos, signaled the emergence of a well-financed and organized military outfit for Britain's imperial project in what is now Nigeria. The strength of this predominantly African army (known from the 1890s as the Nigeria Regiment of the West African Frontier Force, or WAFF, and later as the Royal West African Frontier Force, or RWAFF, increased from some 200 Hausa men in 1863 to about 14,000 and 130,000 during World War I and World War II, respectively. The army was one of the most important institutions of colonial hegemony in Nigeria, and in Africa at large. Not only was it used against states and empires during the British subjugation of the Nigerian geographical area, but it also played a role in maintaining peace and order in the conquered territories. It was normally the security option of last resort, called in when the local police proved incapable of suppressing the numerous "riots," "revolts," and "insurgencies" that threatened colonial administration. Although by the 1950s the WAFF was composed of virtually all the major Nigerian ethnic groups, up to the 1920s it was largely dominated by the Hausa-Fulani of the North, who were tagged the "martial race" or "combatant tribes" of West Africa.[32] In the nineteenth and early twentieth centuries, southerners, especially the Igbo, were officially excluded from enrolling in the army during peacetime because authorities thought they were "mentally and physically far inferior" and "useless as combatant troops."[33]

Employment opportunities and the availability of modern infrastructure were not the only reasons people moved into Lagos in large numbers—education was another immigrant pull factor. Several parts of the Nigerian interior were exposed to Western education through Christian missionary outreach from the nineteenth century, but Lagos offered expanded access and diverse choices in the areas of curriculum, specialization, and job opportunities after graduation.[34] With 29 formal schools and about 2,200 students in 1881, Lagos had more educational institutions and higher enrollment than any other part of Nigeria.[35] At independence in 1960 more than 80,000 students were attending more than 140 schools—arguably the largest enrollment in the whole of British Africa.[36] The concentration of professionals in Lagos was one visible, positive manifestation of the lead the coastal city maintained in education. During the 1940s there were far more African doctors in Lagos than elsewhere in Nigeria, which prompted a call for doctors to extend their practice to the provinces in order to help improve the health of non-Lagosians.[37] But the majority of Lagos's literate class was to be found in lower-level white-collar jobs as bookkeepers, clerks, stationmasters, and printing assistants, among other occupational designations, in the expanding civil service, commercial, and public works sectors.[38]

Perhaps the most significant consequence of education was the consolidation of a modern social class system with its corresponding features such as differentials in income, ideology, standard of living, and political capital. What people consumed, where they lived, and how they socialized mirrored their educational attainment and social status in ways peculiar to the new colonial cities. While the Saro and Aguda—whom J. F. A. Ajayi referred to as the "New Elites" because of their acquisition of Western education—monopolized the elite culture in the second half of the nineteenth century, the twentieth-century class structure was far more diverse, comprising several Nigerian ethnic groups whose ascribed social status was determined by the level of education they attained.[39] Although scholars have highlighted the complexity of defining an "elite" in colonial urban Africa or attempting to impose a social hierarchy akin to that obtainable in Europe, the lawyers, medical doctors, newspaper editors, and publishers, among others, surely qualified as "elite or upper class" because they earned far above the minimum wage, which was about £36 per annum in 1941.[40] Office or account clerks and bookkeepers working with a high-school certificate/diploma qualified as "middle, working, or lower class," not only because they made less than the upper class but because they were not the "movers and shakers" of the colonial state. During the 1940s, an African magistrate's maximum annual income was around £720, a stark contrast to the £48 earned by most middle-class Nigerians working with a high-school diploma.[41] I agree with Ajayi that ethnicity, not social class conflict, was the most important factor in intergroup relations in Nigeria.[42] But I also contend

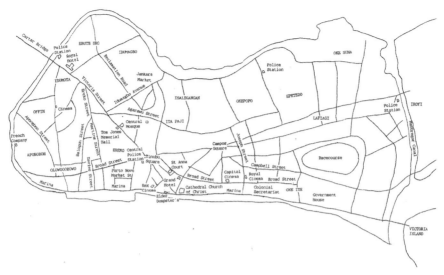

Figure 1.1. Map of Lagos Island, c. 1950s. Reproduced by courtesy of the National Archives Ibadan.

that when it comes to issues like prostitution, class differences significantly influenced how individuals and groups framed and sustained their positions. As we will see, upper-class ideologies about socialization, public conduct, and grassroots identity varied remarkably from those of the lower class. The elites' attempt to mold the city in their own image by making prescriptive recommendations for the pathway to a "modern," "respectable," and "safe" social existence was influenced by their education, status, and political capital within both the African and the European ranks.

Aside from effecting the consolidation of a new social class system, education was also pivotal to the efflorescence of the print media. Lagos did not pioneer the print culture; the first Nigerian newspaper, *Iwe Irohin fun awon ara Egba ati Yoruba* (Newspaper for the Egba and Yoruba), was established in Abeokuta, "the bastion of Christianity in Yorubaland," in 1859, mainly to improve literacy and facilitate evangelism among its early Yoruba converts.[43] However, from the 1860s to the end of Britain's colonial presence in Nigeria, Lagos would dominate the newspaper industry, which was arguably the only modern enterprise monopolized by Nigerians.[44] From this same period, newspapers' messages and ideologies changed radically from their evangelical origin to become largely a tool and symbol of anticolonial sentiments. By the 1930s, print media would establish themselves as shapers of "popular" culture as opposed to their predominantly elitist outlook in the nineteenth century. The trend the print culture assumed from the 1920s on is attributable, in part, to the colonialists' direct involvement in education, which increased literacy and thus readership and market size. Through advertisements, columnist features, debates, and other forms of writing, the newspaper played a major role in the consolidation of an urban culture that borrowed from both European and African ideals of socialization and identity formation. No other written sources portray consumer culture, fashion, love, and romance, quite like the newspapers.

Although Western education was a significant factor in social change, it was also discriminatorily gendered in that girls' enrollment in school remained very low throughout the colonial era. The view on women's education as taught by the missionaries and enhanced by the colonialists held that women's ideal place was in the courtyard. When girls received education under the missionaries' instruction, emphasis was placed on domestic science, needlework, home hygiene, and in general skills needed to train girls as future Christian wives and mothers.[45] By paying lip-service to girls' education, the missionaries and the colonialists laid the foundation of the disempowerment of women in virtually all the modern spheres of the society and made gender inequality an official policy of the state. Women's political, economic, and social activities, though important, were not firmly established or acknowledged unless in periods of crisis like the World Wars when they were persuaded to contribute to the Win-the-War efforts of the imperial government.[46] By 1944, Alexander Paterson, a British welfare officer invited to survey social problems in Nigeria, would blame the skewed inattention to women's education and the feminization of poverty for prostitution. "In many countries," Paterson asserted comparatively, "two main occupations absorb the labour of the unmarried girl. One is factory work and the other is domestic. Both of these are denied to the Nigerian girl, and if she wants to escape from the close grip of the family, prostitution is almost the only alternative open to her."[47] Paterson definitely exaggerated the options available to Nigerian girls and held a sexist position, for studies of migration have revealed that women moved into the city to acquire education, engage in trade, or learn skills deployed for economic activities.[48] Be that as it may, what remained indisputable is that colonial society introduced policies that placed women at the bottom rung of the sociopolitical ladder.

The colonialists' prejudice toward female education did not go unchallenged. A group of highly educated women, some of whom were second-generation Saro, were at the forefront of campaigns for women's empowerment. Influential personalities like Charlotte Olajumoke Obasa, Oyinkan Abayomi, and Kofoworola Ademola, among others, received a Western education in disciplines ranging from music, law, and social science to education, nursing, and journalism, in both Nigeria and the United Kingdom.[49] They broke notable barriers and taboos characteristic of the Victorian and post-Victorian eras. For instance, Ademola was the first African woman to attend and receive a degree from the

University of Oxford in 1933.[50] The same year Stella Jane Thomas was called to the bar at the Middle Temple (London), becoming the "first lady barrister in West Africa." She would later be appointed as West Africa's first female magistrate in 1942 after establishing "an extensive and lucrative [legal] practice."[51] Similarly, in 1938 Lagos newspapers gave wide publicity to the achievement of Dr. Elizabeth Akerele, "the first full-blooded Nigerian lady" to qualify as a medical doctor and surgeon, while E. Ronke Ajayi's emergence as the first female newspaper editor in 1931 opened the floodgate of representation of diverse aspects of gender relations in mainstream print media.[52] Not all elite women who shaped social life and sexual politics in Lagos were born or raised there. For instance, Henrietta Millicent Douglas, a journalist and Pan-Africanist from Grenada who relocated to Nigeria in 1939, played a significant role in Lagos sexual politics in the 1940s as the secretary of the Women's Welfare Council (WWC), the umbrella body of elite women's associations.[53]

Although some elite women, like the newspaper editor Ajayi, appeared to have worked independently, writing critical editorials about gender bias, they mostly organized themselves into voluntary associations including the Lagos Ladies League (later the Lagos Women's League, or LWL), the British West African Educated Girls' Club (BWAEGC; later the Ladies Progressive Club, or LPC), the WWC, and the Nigerian Women's Party (NWP), formed in 1901, 1920, 1942, and 1944, respectively. It appeared that working through associations allowed the women to pursue a coherent and long-term agenda. They campaigned vigorously against the colonialists' lack of interest in girls' education and were in fact well-recognized public intellectuals on issues concerning women's welfare.[54] For them, education was the pathway to the socioeconomic progress of African women and the solution to social problems like prostitution that formed a component of their politics from the early 1920s (see chapters 2 and 7).[55] Their agitation paved the way for the establishment of Queen's College, the first government girls' secondary (high) school in Lagos in 1927. Starting from 1923, the LWL clamored for the enrollment of women in the colonial service, criticized the practice of giving European women (mostly wives of colonial administrators) jobs that African women could successfully undertake, and demanded equal pay for men and women.[56] The manifestos of the NWP clearly established the relationship between education and social mobility: "Education of women and politics, to become useful and loyal citizens, to know their rights and the right way to demand them, to love and admire the highest standard of morals, to keep women of less average ability busy on industrial or domestic science pursuits, to start mass education of women so that in a year to two there will be more literacy among women for whom suitable employment should be given as teachers, mid-wives and nurses, supervisors, lecturers and in various other departments and capacities."[57]

At its inception in 1944, the NWP received a cold reception from male nationalists (particularly the Nigerian Youth Movement, or NYM), who were skeptical of the ability of a predominantly female party to advance the cause of women. Even the *Daily Service*, the official organ of the NYM that served as a major channel through which the women propagated their programs, expressed the belief that nothing could be achieved by an exclusively female organization.[58] However, this criticism had a background in the politics of gender within the ranks of the NYM. Abayomi, also the founder of the LPC, established the NWP out of the women's wing of the NYM when she discovered that the male nationalists were not advancing women's interests. Meanwhile, a few months after condemning the NWP, the *Daily Service* recanted. "Judging from its programme of work, its activity and the way it has handled one or two questions of public interest," commented an editorial of August 25, 1944, "we feel it cannot but inspire the confidence of the women of this country. The way the business of the Party is handled and the active and intelligent leadership it enjoys are happy augury for the fast approaching day when the Nigerian women shall fully come into their own and exert influence befitting them in the public life of their country."[59]

This shifting recognition mirrored one of the challenges elite women faced as they attempted to negotiate politics among both colonialists and male nationalists who subscribed to Afrocentric male authority. Indeed, the elite women were usually criticized by the press controlled by male nationalists for either not doing enough to promote women's welfare or for attempting to impose Western gender practices that were "un-African" or not in tune with the challenges of most economically marginalized women.[60] "No fair minded person should regard this Editorial as an attack either on the Ladies Progressive Club or any other women's organization in Nigeria," disclaimed the *West African Pilot* of May 3, 1941. "Our point is that our womenfolk, in the majority think more of fineries, jewelleries, millineries, haberdasheries etc than performing distinct community service. Nigeria cannot afford to produce womenfolk who are more interested in straightening their hair, wearing petite dresses, Parisian hats."[61] To be sure, the ideological conflict between Nigerian male and female nationalists has not been satisfactorily explored.[62] Existing studies tend to focus mainly on the elite women's conflict with the colonialists over issues of social mobility and the grassroots mobilization of uneducated women over taxation and unfair economic policies.[63] Although more-educated women participated in the politics of decolonization in the 1950s than in previous decades, the literature tends to paint wholly harmonious relations—that did not exist—between female and male nationalists. How the struggle for political relevance configured and reconfigured relations between male and female nationalists, and its effect on the drive toward political self-determination, requires critical attention.

Figure 1.2. *Left to right:* Justice Adetokunbo Ademola, Lady Oyinkan Abayomi, and Sir Kofoworola Abayomi, and Adebisi Vincent, a Nigerian student studying in the United Kingdom paying her respect after Abayomi's investiture as a knight. Buckingham Palace, July 31, 1951. Reproduced by courtesy of the National Archives Ibadan.

Urban Life, Selective Modernity, and Class Conflict

If there is anything that made city life attractive and charming, it was the expanded opportunities for individuals and groups, regardless of ethnicity and class, to experiment with new and diverse forms of social behavior, such as were rarely tolerated or available in the countryside. Lagos was the most unsafe of Nigerian urban centers, judging by the annual police reports. But urban insecurity—manifested in robbery, theft, and public disorder—did not prevent a vibrant nightlife.[64] Indeed, juju, a genre of popular music that emerged in the interwar years, got its name from the mysterious character of nightlife—"tailor-cut for the enjoyment of nocturnal spirit."[65] New forms of social expression supplanted the old, and in a number of cases they complemented or were syncretized into preexisting forms. By the 1930s, a cinema culture had matured fully. Many Lagosians had disposable income to visit popular cinemas, such as the Rex, Royal, Regal, Capitol, Le Coliseum, and Odeon—despite the epileptic character of the colonial economy, which was reflected in poverty and the high cost of living.[66] Two shillings would earn an entry into most Lagos cinemas that screened European movies of different genres in the 1940s. Going by the advertisement for films in the leading newspapers, it is obvious that movies about crime, love, and romance were the most popular. A September 1945 advertisement for a film at the Capitol Cinema, titled *Spider Women*, had the following description: "Mistress of murder! Love in her eyes . . . murder in her mind."[67] Lagosians also socialized in pubs, restaurants, and hotels, run mostly by locals. Most pubs and hotels, like the famous Ritz Hotel, had dance floors and featured popular musical styles like *asiko*, juju, highlife, and brass band, as well as ballroom dance music.[68] Admission to weekend dances ranged from 2s. to 3s. for men—women and soldiers usually received free passes. Unlike other genres of popular music such as *apala* and *sakara* that were distinctively "local," brass band, ballroom, highlife, and juju were all cosmopolitan, in that they borrowed from African, European, and American styles and idioms and were enjoyed across the continent.[69] They suited the urban dwellers who craved musical expressions that were both innovative and modern yet reflected their daily struggles.

Without places of socialization like hotels, pubs, and cinemas, the business of sexual favors would not have become an urban staple. These venues provided the settings that brought people together for love, sexual desire, relationship, business networking, and other purposes. Indeed, the lines between socialization for sexual pleasure and nonsexual desires were easily blurred as men and women congregated mostly under the cover of darkness and anonymity to ease the pressure and stresses of work and the busyness of city life. So profitable were drinking places by the early 1940s that a lead editorial in the *West African Pilot* lamented that most residential homes had been converted into pubs. It claimed that every street had at least one pub.[70] The editorial was written against the backdrop of escalating rents in Lagos and their impact on the standard of living.[71] Another editorial of March 5, 1943, worried about the unavailability of bookings for Glover Memorial Hall, the most popular event center in Lagos, accusing youths of depriving "charitable and profitable" organizations the opportunity to use the hall by booking up to a year ahead of planned events to satisfy the "new craze" for dancing and immorality.[72] Criticism of excessive partying also extended to the constructed difference between "civilized" and "uncivilized" nightclubs. Some critics argued that in "civilized" societies, nightclubs provided the venues for showcasing history and culture through music, food, and dance. To ensure that Lagos nightclubs performed a function akin to those of the "civilized" societies, they should operate under the close supervision of the police and "well-meaning" Nigerians. A proposed nightclub law should, according to these critics, "compel every nightclub to close at midnight, prohibit nightclubs on Sundays, bar unescorted women from nightclubs and critically assess the social reputation of a would-be nightclub proprietor."[73]

When the *West African Pilot* referenced the use of Glover Memorial Hall for "charitable and profitable" functions, as earlier noted, it was referring to the high-level social and political functions that defined the elite habit of exclusionary socialization and professional networking. Opened in 1887 and named after Sir John Glover (nicknamed Oba Goloba), the governor of Lagos between 1863 and 1872, Glover Hall was not a conventional civic center.[74] Rather, it was in all respects one of the hallmarks of modernity in Lagos; it hosted some of the monumental events that shaped modern Nigerian history, such as the 1922 inaugural meeting of the Nigerian National Democratic Party, the "first well-organized political party in Commonwealth West Africa."[75] If the elites appeared to have monopolized the use of the hall up to the 1920s, from the 1930s on they were compelled to share it with individuals and groups whose interests transcended elite politics and nationalism. The elites could only nag about the hall's unavailability for "charitable" events; they could not stop those who put it to "noncharitable" use because the ordinance that established it did not differentiate between "charitable" and "noncharitable" events.

Criticism of the ubiquity of pubs, contraction of residential dwelling, or *aso ebi*, which supposedly encouraged wasteful spending and excessive partying, reflected the widening ideological gap in values between upper-class Lagosians and the overwhelming lower-class and economically marginalized ones.[76] As the population of Lagos expanded, so also did the demand for recreation sites, which put pressure on social space. It would appear that the elites' recreation options were shrinking, while those of the lower class kept expanding. In addition, attempts were made to impose the language of criminality and indecency on the recreation habits of the lower class, as opposed to those "honest" and "respectable" pursuits of the elites.[77] This interclass tension, which scholars of Nigeria have grossly overlooked, appears obvious in another editorial titled "Night Club for Lagos," which called for the introduction of a "night club

Figure 1.3. Glover Memorial Hall in the early twentieth century, Lagos. Reproduced by courtesy of the National Archives Ibadan.

where decent folks can have a honest to goodness enjoyment, an ideal place where respectable youths can safely meet, make new friends . . . and those who like to dance do so in a congenial atmosphere."[78]

Competition for and pressure on social space is one manifestation of what I call selective modernity. If some elites of the nineteenth century tended to be culturally nationalistic by denouncing the imposition of Europeans' culture and version of Christianity, those of the 1920s through the 1950s accommodated Western values as an indispensable tool of modernization. Indeed, Lagosians were more Europeanized in the 1930s than in previous decades. Although the elites of the 1930s and 1940s tended to favor Western culture, they also criticized aspects that they believed were inimical to the well being of the people. They wanted Lagos to be a "modern" city but believed that not all aspects of European city culture should be emulated. An advocate of cinema censorship recognized the usefulness of the cinema as a "medium of interpreting the Western way of life," but expressed the feeling that to act like famous European and American superstars like Greta Garbo, Joan Crawford, or George Raft or to attempt to reproduce the actions depicted in Hollywood gangster films was detrimental to the "mental outlook" of many members of the jobless youth population.[79] Aspects of European culture deemed "positive," some reformists believed, should be copied to the letter.

Men dominated the rhetoric of selective modernity because they outnumbered women as editors and columnists of the leading newspapers, which attempted to shape ideas of social decency in conformity with their own "enlightened" fixations.[80] However, the few women editors also dedicated quality writing to the subject. Miss Silva, one of the 1940s' most influential female columnists and pseudonymous editor of the *West African Pilot*'s women's column (Milady's Bower), reacted to the "uncivilized" ballroom behavior of some ladies: "I have no objection," she wrote, "to a lady refusing to dance when she is in reality 'exhausted' but I am opposed to the idea of a female dancer just shunning one 'unknown' dancer to make way for favourite."[81] In another entry, she decried the "immoral dancing" in vogue as "scandalous," "nefarious," and "demoralizing . . . a sight of which can make a spectator shudder." "The speed with which several women cultivate vice" while wearing revealing dresses, she continued, "is alarming."[82] Miss Silva was not alone in criticizing the dancing for its lack of etiquette. B. A. Tagoe, the principal of Lagos Tricity Academy of Dancing, besides believing that "it [was] a privilege and not a right" for ladies to be offered drinks in parties, agreed with Miss Silva that "it [was] against the ballroom etiquette to dance with one's favourite all the time and snubbing others." Neither Miss Silva nor other decriers gave a clear picture of what constituted "iniquitous" dance. They also did not illustrate the so-called provocative dresses, probably to avoid being accused of promoting a social malady they themselves were criticizing. But other sources give a glimpse.

Gumbe, a popular dance believed to be of Sierra Leonean origin, involved "the woman shaking her hips in front of a man," while *pandero*, whose origin was traced to Brazil, featured seminude dancing that some educated elements believed was fit only for the "unenlightened" rural setting.[83] Ekwensi gives a vivid picture of the revealing dresses that were being rebuked: Aina, one of Sango's lovers, wore "big-sleeved velvet blouses . . . so loose, so carelessly revealing . . . clinging to the body curves so intimately that the nipples of the breasts showed through. Certainly not the most comfortable sight to confront a young bachelor on a morning when he had just made noble resolutions."[84] In all, smoking and drinking by women, "boisterousness and vociferousness" in the cinema, "painting lips," and wearing "roasted and charred" hair were among the "excessive" aspects of Westernization that moralists condemned as they attempted to prescribe decent city life.[85]

No groups were more "guilty" of "excessive" partying than the ethnic associations called "tribal" unions. Through "dances" and "shows," occasionally used for raising funds for scholarships and development programs in their native homes, the unions helped members to socialize, share drinks and food, and expand the horizons of recreation.[86] Social space in Lagos became more ethnicized as the population of each ethnic group grew in response to the many real and imagined benefits of living in the colonial state's capital. Although membership of the unions included men and women, some like the Efik Ladies Union admitted only females from the Efik ethnic group.[87] As the one-stop arena for individuals who sought spouses or relationships with fellow ethnic citizens, the unions facilitated intra-ethnic relations while maintaining their primary agenda of diasporic self-help and hometown community development. During the era of decolonization starting in the 1940s, they would play a significant role in urban politics and diversify party membership. Rivalry for the gains of living abroad within the ethnic association was easily grafted onto the rhetoric of maintaining the "cultural integrity" of the homeland, as the unions navigated the stereotype of running the Lagos prostitution network. During the serious crackdown on prostitution from the 1940s, the unions became defensive and contested authorities' labeling of their activities as supportive of sexual immorality.

Criticism of moral degeneration went hand in hand with attacks on uncontrolled immigration. Indeed, the elite popularly assumed they could promote a serene Lagos by discouraging provincial Nigerians from leaving for the city because of its "materialism and comparative modernism and fineries" or from seeking "refuge from the alleged Native Administration persecution."[88] The gulf in development between Lagos and the provinces was so wide that "Lagos is to the average rural Native of Nigeria as London is to the average Lagosian."[89] A newspaper editorial narrates the typical experience of some frustrated immigrants after being drawn into the colonial capital: "Lagos soon loses its

40 CHAPTER I

charm and he is embarrassed as to how to get bread even if unbuttered."[90] When unemployment and crime began to increase starting in the 1920s, the elites blamed the conditions on uncontrolled immigration.[91] Another newspaper editorial advised provincial Nigerians that the "employment outlook in Lagos is not as rosy as they seem to feel."[92] Titled "Exodus into Lagos Capital," this editorial expressed the belief that the provinces were not as bereft of employment opportunities as was widely assumed: "But what we cannot understand is men having to pay their passage all the way down to seek for a labourer's job when so many avenues exist in the provinces for such employment."[93] Not all immigrants came either to work or to enjoy the splendor of the city. Some, especially from the north, came to beg for alms, which by the 1930s had been officially recognized as a profitable venture.[94] The "army" of northerners with physical disabilities plying the roads to beg regularly attracted public denunciation and frequent calls for their repatriation. After narrating the experience of a Hausa immigrant beggar arrested by the police for faking blindness, a critic wrote, "Those who are planning to come to Lagos with no defined end, we sound the note of warning citing the plight of this Hausa youth, if another could benefit from the sufferings of another."[95]

"No Nigerian Is a Foreigner in Lagos"

Although the ethnic composition of Lagos was diverse from 1861 when immigrants from outside Nigeria began to move into the city in increasing numbers, nineteenth-century racial heterogeneity appeared to have been simply collapsed into two groups: Africans and Europeans. The European populations were predominantly from Britain, France, and Greece. Some non-Europeans, including the Lebanese, were generally identified as "Europeans."[96] Yet, all African residents of Lagos, regardless of ethnicity, were simply identified as "Lagosians"—at least from the 1890s or earlier. The first reference to the term "Lagosian" that I have come across is in a column by Janus titled "Lagosian on Dits," which appeared regularly in the 1890s in the *Lagos Standard*. It would appear that the nationalists of that era were more concerned about creating a united African front for contesting the ills of imperialism since the African population, regardless of social class, ethnic origin, and religion, among other points of difference, experienced similar forms of oppression. For instance, in 1906 the Lagos press led a strong campaign against the sequestration of the Hausa quarters, which was founded around 1865 by soldiers of the West African Frontier Force.[97] Flipping through the pages of such leading newspapers as the *Lagos Weekly Records* and *Lagos Standard* from the 1890s and early 1900s, one sees that intra-African conflicts were drawn not so much along lines of ethnic difference, but were generated by the ideological polarization between the "collaborators" (i.e., groups that supported the British or subscribed to their ideal of civilization) and the cultural nationalists who campaigned vigorously against the implantation of Eurocentric culture. Another major source of tension appeared to be between those who supported Christian marriage and their rivals who believed that it was un-African.[98] I am not suggesting that there was no conflict within the ranks of the African population—there were frictions between the indigenous Yoruba Lagosians and the Saro and Aguda—but it appears that ideological ferment regarding the best path to progress (whether traditional or modern) took precedence over ethnicity.

But from the first and second decades of the twentieth century, the various Nigerian groups began to be fully identified by their places of origin or ethnicity. This shift in identity formation owed much to the increase in the representation of each group and the consolidation of their activities. If the emergence of Lagos as the capital of southern Nigeria and of the Nigerian state in 1906 and 1914, respectively, facilitated the influx of people into the city, it nevertheless created a new regime of social identity and otherness. Although all Lagos residents were generally called Lagosians, not everyone was a Lagos "citizen." Only Yoruba whose ancestors were from Lagos and those of the hinterland that migrated there, along with the Saro and Aguda and their descendants like Macaulay, received citizenship. The construction of citizenship not only determined the protection each ethnic group received under the colonial state; it also influenced levels of political participation and access to the instruments of power. Hence, most of the few elective offices held by Africans in Lagos went to the "citizens," particularly the Saros and their descendants.[99] Although this is not surprising given that they had a lead in education through their contact with missionaries, it is obvious that non-Yoruba or those who did not have a strong economic and professional pedigree were barred from actively participating in politics.

The city ordinance that empowered the Lagos Town Council (LTC) to repatriate "foreigners" to their native homes for offenses ranging from prostitution to public disorder is probably the most important signifier of the dichotomy between the "indigene" and the "foreigner." In addition, newspaper reports of criminal activities also contributed to molding public perceptions toward ethnic dissimilarity by clearly establishing the ethnicity of those accused or convicted.[100] In Lagos as in other colonial centers in Africa, the "indigenes" stereotypically viewed the "foreigners" as the source of social problems, such as violent crime, theft, and prostitution. Successful immigrants were most likely to be envied, as the hosts worked to delimit their access to the often-scarce resources and opportunities provided by the colonial state. Although the tension between the "indigenes" and "foreigners" appeared to be as old as the history of colonial Lagos, it first became worrisome in the second decade of the twentieth century—a period characterized by the rise of unemployment.

One excellent example of this anti-immigration sentiment is a two-part 1933 editorial in the *Lagos Daily News* titled "Unemployed Warri Men and Women in Lagos."[101] The editorial acknowledged the deep-rooted social menace that people from Calabar, Warri, Owerri, and Ogoja Provinces constituted, but singled out Warri as the most notorious. It gave a brief background to the moral nuisance perpetrated by Warri women by recounting how Chief Dore of Warri, during his visit to Lagos in the early 1910s, pleaded with Sir Walter Egerton to help him repatriate the "undesirables." The editorial laments that the largest percentage of Warri men, "the unit which makes up the mighty army of white men's cooks and stewards, by reason of their aversion to become labourers, scavengers," were left jobless as a result of the retrenchment of their white masters during the Great Depression. But instead of returning to their original homelands, these men allegedly engaged in all manner of vice, ranging from "burglary" and "illicit spirit distilling" to "broad day light stealing, *wayo* [fraud], gambling and trafficking in mamies [child prostitutes]." Moreover, their womenfolk, "with the one desire of getting rich in silks and gold without toil, come to Lagos because—apart from the licence they enjoy through the flexibility and vagaries of the law, the freedom from the tyranny of avaricious Chiefs and the cruelties of barbarous husbands."[102]

This editorial viewpoint clearly mirrors the politics of nativism that Herbert Macaulay, the publisher of the *Lagos Daily News*, extolled throughout his lifetime. Macaulay advocated traditional Yoruba customs in the wake of enormous cultural erosion accentuated by alien rule. Although Yoruba Lagosians could bitterly complain about the activities of the "foreigners," they could not expel them without the order of the LTC. This reality is not unique to Lagos but was common to the entirety of Nigeria. During the 1940s, Ibadan chiefs did repatriate non-Yoruba for prostitution.[103] Also in the north the emir embarked on large-scale repatriation of all immigrant women believed to be living on "immoral earning."[104] The repatriation power vested in local authorities exposed a major contradiction in the Pax Britannica: although all Nigerians could live peacefully wherever they liked, the native authorities or town council could establish a segregated neighborhood (widely known as *sabon gari*: meaning new town, or strangers' quarters) for strangers and could repatriate "undesirables" in the interest of public safety.[105] But the main ramification of repatriation laws on intergroup relations was that it promoted the British divide-and-rule policy that consistently placed Nigerian ethnicities in opposition. It was not until the end of colonial rule that this distinction between "aliens" and "foreigners" snowballed into major violence in certain parts of the country and became a major challenge to the creation of a united Nigeria.

The undue distinction between the "indigenes" and the "foreigners" did not go unchallenged by leading nationalists. From 1941, when Dr. Nnamdi Azikiwe, one of the founding fathers of independent Nigeria, lost a bid to become the president of the NYM, owing to "tribalism," the Igbo elements in

Figure 1.4. Broad Street, Lagos. Reproduced by courtesy of the National Archives Ibadan.

Lagos became more assertive in opposing political and social exclusion and alleged discrimination in all facets of urban life.[106] Indeed, the 1941 episode, the "first major manifestation of a tribal tension," would greatly impact subsequent efforts to achieve national cohesion.[107] No media outlet registered the tense political quagmire of the era better than the *West African Pilot*, the flagship of Azikiwe's press empire, and the *Daily Service* of the NYM. Powerful editorials with such headlines as "Citizenship of Lagos," "Lagos for Lagosians?" and "Quit Lagos Conference?" among others, exposed the alleged ploy of the Yoruba Lagosians to expel all the Igbo from Lagos. Through satire and graphic political cartoons by the pioneering cartoonist Akinola Lasekan, the *West African Pilot* lambasted the NYM for advocating "Pakistanism"—that is, the breakup of the Nigerian state—while the *Daily Service* accused Azikiwe of promoting an exclusive Igbo agenda in a multicultural Nigeria. Not surprisingly, the various newspaper contributors to the debate argued from the perspective of their own ethnic groups while attempting to disguise themselves as supporters of a united Nigeria as the road to self-determination became clearer. Comprehensive articles with headings like "No Nigerian Is a Foreigner in Lagos" by Mazi Mbonu Ojike, an Igbo and a frontline politician and cultural nationalist, which was written in the wake of the rumored expulsion of non-Yoruba from Lagos, sought to ridicule the political capital of some Yoruba elites, especially the Saro descendants: "Those who claim ownership of Lagos are not by tradition and history indigenes. They are mere naturalized aliens. If anyone should be driven out of Lagos, they and whites only will be expelled."[108]

Race and Racial Relations in the Colony

The exploration of the social, political, and economic character of Lagos is incomplete without a discussion of race and racial relations. Unlike South Africa, Zimbabwe, and Kenya, Lagos was not a settler colony, but it had a sizable European population. Most of the earliest European immigrants were merchants and expatriates who were lured into the city through the promise of international commerce, which rose steadily through the British imperial presence. The population of the administrative class increased astronomically from the second half of the nineteenth century as the British gradually solidified their presence—politically and economically. The European population would have been higher still but for high mortality. Of the estimated 150 Europeans in Lagos in 1894, 31 died of malaria. The 1931 population census estimated that 1,124 British, German, and French citizens lived in Lagos.[109] But this figure excluded unregistered aliens and occasional visitors, mostly including seamen, merchants, and expatriates. Authorities regularly conceded their inability to monitor the immigration of Europeans into the colony; during the 1940s, non-Africans between the ages of 16 and 60 were compelled to register with the commissioner of the colony or face a fine of £1,000 or imprisonment. Lagos, being the capital of the colonial state and location of most European firms, had the largest percentage of Europeans living in Nigeria throughout the colonial period—43 and 60 percent in 1921 and 1951, respectively.[110]

Race relations were at times harmonious but also discordant. The Africans (especially the elites) and Europeans occasionally socialized when situations or circumstances permitted. Indeed, nineteenth-century elite culture, which borrowed extensively from the European and Pan-African culture of refreshment, took firm root partly because of the regular social contact between African and European residents. Moreover, many of the African elites, especially the Saro and Aguda, had gone through European or missionary education systems either in Africa or in Europe and seemed to appreciate the values of Western culture. But racial conflict arising from discrimination was inevitable, not mainly because race played a significant role in the colonization of Nigeria, as with other African colonies, but because European officers would not treat Africans as equals. One of the first elements of open racial conflict took the form of trade competition. African merchants traditionally saw the Europeans, who had more economic resources and the support of their home governments, as economic predators. By forming limited liability companies, European trading firms and merchants fared much better than their African counterparts with marginal capital. In the colonial civil service, few Africans occupied significant positions of authority up to the 1890s. By 1900, only Dr. Henry Carr, the inspector of schools and assistant colonial secretary, held a position comparable to that of a European.[111]

The paucity of Europeans in the colonial civil service should not be taken to mean that Africans were not qualified. Rather, most of the very qualified Africans resigned their positions or refused to join the colonial service due to prejudice in matters of promotion and remuneration. Dr. Obadiah Johnson and Dr. John K. Randle, two of the earliest African medical doctors, resigned their positions due to disagreement with their white surgeon counterparts.[112] Macaulay resigned from the colonial service when his white superiors accused him of using his official position to his personal ends, soon after being appointed as surveyor of the Crown Grant in 1893.[113] Most educated Africans were frustrated that the Europeans would not treat them as equals despite their having learned to dress, eat, talk, and behave like Europeans. In fact, those who believed that acquisition of Western education would raise them to the status of whites were soon disappointed because of being discriminated against after receiving training in some of the most prestigious professions of the era, such as medicine and law.[114]

Aside from refusing to join or resigning from the colonial service, the educated elites also adopted cultural nationalism as another response to racism. From the 1880s or earlier, the elites began to attack European culture and advocate for a return to African cultural roots. Through newspapers like the *Lagos Weekly News*, attacks were launched against "negrophobia" (racial discrimination) and exposés publicized the ills of Western culture. Some of the leading cultural nationalists denounced their English names and adopted African names: David Vincent became Mojola Agbebi, Reverend S. H. Samuel became Adegboyega Edun, and George William Johnson became Tejumade Osholake Johnson. They abandoned European dress for African clothing, even when they visited Europe. Because they knew the Bible inside out, they were able to differentiate between actual scriptural provisions and doctrines that did not have any biblical sanction but were merely Europeanized notions of the white missionaries. They condemned monogamous marriage, claiming its roots were not in Christianity, but in European culture. They also established African churches from the 1880s, thus giving African Christianity a boost.[115]

But to view racism mainly through the lens of relations between Europeans and the few educated elites is to miss its full entrenchment in virtually all spheres of the society and across multiple social classes. The cultural geography of racism and its intensity expanded tremendously in the first half of the twentieth century when Lagos became a truly Nigerian city and as colonialism established itself as a strong force for social change. Racism was not an open official policy of the colonialists, but the British established a society that was very much divided along racial lines by making proof of income and evidence of taxes paid criteria for admission into various professional associations and social and sports clubs.[116] This policy automatically barred Africans from participating in many social functions and from socializing in the best restaurants and bars because they made far less than most Europeans. In order to safeguard the health of Europeans, racial segregation of residential districts, recreational facilities, and hospitals was introduced.[117] Indeed, Europeans had specialist clinics for such ailments as VD despite the fact that the incidence of gonorrhea and syphilis was reported to be higher among Nigerians. As we will see, the introduction and implementation of anti-prostitution laws were drawn along racial lines as the criminal justice system traditionally let European offenders of prostitution laws off the hook.

During the 1930s and 1940s, Lagos newspapers built on the efforts of their predecessors by committing adequate energy to fighting racial discrimination and allowing people who experienced the humiliating color bar to publish unedited protest letters.[118] As one editorial titled "Jim Crow Hospitals" remarked, "It is the existence of such institutions [segregated hospitals] we are fighting to remove from the face of the earth."[119] When the LTC rejected the application of Ayodeji Ajayi, the owner of Hotel Wayfarers, to operate a cinema on his hotel premises on Broad Street on the grounds that the property did not pass city safety codes, the print media seized the opportunity to further lambast authorities for attempting to undermine the African entrepreneurial spirit in order to safeguard the economic interests of two European cinemas (Royal and Capitol) located just a few blocks from the proposed African cinema.[120] Similarly, in April 1944 the chairman of the Hotel Association of Nigeria criticized European firms for discriminating against African hoteliers by not supplying them enough beer: "Whereas European owned hotel obtains as much as 20 or 30 cases [of beer], the highest that an African hotel can get is about three."[121] Although no hotel was permitted to serve whisky and gin, in accordance with wartime defense regulations, hard liquor "pour[ed] freely into a certain European-owned hotel." This discrimination in matters of alcoholic beverages was, in Ajayi's conviction, a "systematic and studied attempt to oust Africans from the hotel market" since access to liquor boosted hotel patronage.[122]

But no case of white privilege in the post–World War II era embarrassed the colonialists more than the Bristol Hotel scandal of February 1947. Ivor Cummings, a black British and senior officer of the Colonial Office who was on an official visit to Nigeria, was denied lodging in the Bristol Hotel, even though the government had reserved a room for him. Nothing seems more racially scandalous than an officer of the imperial government being denied accommodation in the best hotel in the capital of one of Britain's most prosperous colonies because of the color of his skin. As one would expect, Lagos newspapers capitalized on the event to further register their disdain for racism.[123] The leading nationalist parties of the era, the National Council of Nigeria and the Cameroons (NCNC) and the NYM, temporarily abandoned their ideological differences to mount a common front, the "United Front Committee," to end all forms of discrimination.[124] By the time the political wrangling subsided, the governor general had been compelled to issue a public apology and directive forbidding all forms of racial segregation and white privilege. Appropriately titled "Racial Discrimination," the circular addressed to European officers reiterated that racism was not an official policy of the government and demanded the elimination of "all possible grounds of suspicion for [racism]."[125]

The Bristol Hotel case marked a turning point in the history of race and racial relations as Lagosians became more verbally assertive against racism and vigilant about the growing population of Europeans in the city. Critics of European immigration like the Nigerian Association of African Importers and Exporters asked the government to check the influx of Italians and Greeks, "whose supreme and only aim is the expropriation of the country's natural wealth and the strangulation of the indigenous enterprise."[126] Reports and "rumors" about the growing economic influence and immigration after the Bristol Hotel incidence served the intended purpose of sensitizing the public to the projected consequences of the colonialist agenda to transform Lagos into another South Africa or Australia.[127] Meanwhile, the road to a more racially integrated society became wider when Ikoyi, a Europeans-only neighborhood, was officially desegregated by making income, not race, the criterion for residency.[128] Lagosians took advantage of this new policy. By 1951, some of Nigeria's highest-ranked professionals, including Ben Enwonwu (artist), Oladele Ajose (academic), Samuel Manuwa (physician), and Olumuyiwa Jibowu (magistrate), lived in Ikoyi.[129] In addition, membership in the Ikoyi Club, "a European Club and a bastion of expatriate superiority," was opened to Africans in 1953.[130] This positive progression toward racial harmony did not signal an end to racial discrimination, however. Until the end of colonial rule in 1960 the attitude of the British toward Nigerians "was very much that of a benevolent colonial master."[131]

Conclusion

Lagos was a true cosmopolitan city. A combination of geographical, economic, and political factors at both the global and the local levels contributed to its becoming one of Africa's most culturally heterogeneous cities. People made the city, but the city also transformed lives through its infrastructure and the opportunities it presented for economic and social mobility. Thus the people were the city, and the city was the people. While the British were mostly responsible for the major physical infrastructure (electricity, roads, public water, ports), they did not dictate or monopolize the accompanying social outlook that emerged out of Lagosians' quest to mold the city to their own taste. The impacts of erecting huge physical infrastructure were predictable, but the concomitant social changes and continuities were hard to foresee. Indeed, city life entailed maintaining a balance in the ways people lived their lives; the kinds of music they enjoyed; and how they socialized, dressed, and conducted themselves as they sought to maximize the benefits of colonial capitalism. This chapter has introduced the environment under which prostitution flourished and the main characters in the sexuality debate, as well as the ethnic, gendered, and racial composition of Lagos, all of which would play diverse roles in shaping the events to come.

CHAPTER 2

"THE VULGAR AND OBSCENE LANGUAGE"
Prostitution, Criminality, and Immorality

> It is a plain truth and well-known fact that prostitutes and
> criminals go together. Without the prostitutes, there can be no home
> for those who live solely on crime. The two are a disgraceful pair
> and in order to clear any community of the menace of one the other
> also must be given similar attention . . . We are not here to tell the
> police what to do nor are we trying to teach them their job. We
> know they are aware of the presence of these undesirable elements
> in our society. [We want] them [the police] to take action in time so
> that honest citizens may be protected . . . The honest woman and
> trader are entitled to the fullest of police protection.
> —Editorial: "Prostitutes and Criminals,"
>   *Southern Nigeria Defender*, November 29, 1950

The above epigraph summarily captures dominant ideas about one of the major dangers of prostitution: crime. The world over, during the twentieth century, the quest to police prostitution was traditionally informed by its perceived role in promoting public disorder—hence the interrelatedness of sex work and criminality transcended place, ethnicity, race, and power relations.[1] What seems different in the case of Lagos and some colonial sites is that sexual and moral degeneration were normally coded in the rhetoric of the negative impact of colonialism or the failure of imperialism to achieve its widely professed civilizing mission. Unlike most colonial societies where the colonialists monopolized the debate over dissident sexuality, African men and women in Lagos were at the arrowhead of prostitution prohibition. They moralized and Africanized their protest against prostitution because they wanted a colonial society that was free from some of the vices in European cities. As a critic claimed, "The progress of Lagos on the plane of civilization is being done at the expense of imitation of the worst forms of the social mores of a section of the Western communities."[2] The elites' exposure to Western culture provided a comparative lens for viewing the immediate and future impact of unregulated sexuality and how a responsible regime should address it. They consistently but paradoxically referenced the manner in which prostitution was policed in London: on the one hand, the incidence of prostitution was higher in the metropole than in Lagos; on the other hand, the British government's policy of prohibition was intended to "sanitize" the mother country. The parallel that Lagosians drew between London and Lagos was informed by the imperial philosophy that the colony should follow the metropole's path of civility. Therefore, the agitation of the era had a paternalistic slant.[3]

Lagos elites and nationalists pictured sexual laxity as one of the numerous social ills that must be tackled as they envisioned an end to colonial domination and a pathway to nation-building. It was their conviction that unregulated sexuality "tends to have a deleterious effect on the race. The racial stock becomes considerably degenerated."[4] Criminal activities intensified urban insecurity, which negatively impacted colonial economic prosperity, while venereal disease undermined the procreative capacities, allowing the state to lose "some of our ablest men and women too rapidly."[5] Sexual immorality, the "king of all sins" in the moralists' imagination, created social corruption and prevented an individual from making the wise choices needed to live a healthy and productive life. The "problem" of illicit sex transcended isolated behaviors of men and women that traditionally took place behind closed doors, thereby extending the power of the private to produce outcomes of public interest. The interrelatedness of private and public existence not only informed the centrality of sex to mainstream ideas of modernization but also reinforced the ability of the "outlawed" women and men to receive the attention of the colonial state, which was mainly elitist and selective in its approach to matters of the public good. The ultimate goal of the nationalistic campaign against social problems was the "need for prolonging our lives in order to enable us to battle successfully the problems which face us from day to day."[6]

In this first of three chapters that place prostitution within the broader context of colonial progress, respectability, and, by extension, nation-building, I examine the interplay between sex work, immorality, and crime within the framework of the rapid social changes and continuities during the first half of the twentieth century. My focus here is adult prostitution, or "prostitution proper." In the view of moralists, adult prostitutes represented a different category of women believed to be in firm control of their sexuality, the financial resources they accrued from their activities, and how that money was spent. Hence, both colonialists and Lagosians understood the sexualities of adult and child prostitution divergently. Instead of focusing attention entirely on prostitutes, I engage the sexual identities of men of diverse social backgrounds, ethnicities, and races who patronized the sex market. Scholars' narrative focus mainly on women as prostitutes or on men as moralists—as we have seen in most existing works on prostitution—tends to downplay the identity of men who bought sex. It is by inserting into the narrative the involvement of men in casual sex work—as landlords, brothel owners, customers, pimps, and corrupt policemen who took bribes in order to allow prostitutes to work, among other identities—that we can fully come to terms with the multiplier effect of casual sex work and decenter the dominant perspectives of women's criminality and victimhood. Prostitution is therefore about men as much as it is about women.

If the moralists, both Lagosian and British, claimed that women destabilized the "traditional" socio-sexual order when they sold sex, there were many others who would not genuinely press for the criminalization of prostitution: men who claimed to derive their strength to work hard for the colonial state by spending their free time with prostitutes, landlords who received rent from women sex workers, family members who were able to meet important financial needs from the proceeds from sex work, the coterie of married and "respectable" Lagosian men who cheated on their wives when they visited prostitutes, European seamen who depended almost solely on prostitution to ease the boredom of seafaring, and brothel and bar operators whose sales increased as men and women congregated to exchange pleasure for cash. Certainly the *boma* boys and *jaguda* boys, delinquent youth who helped maintain the underground sex tourism business, would lose a substantial part of their income. And there is also little expectation that corrupt policemen who collected "security" fees and granted "illegal permits" to streetwalkers would genuinely want prostitution proscribed.

Unveiling the *Akunakuna*

Prostitutes were unable to construct their own image in the public gaze—not for lack of desire to do so, but because dominant narratives about their work and bodies were already being constructed by the moralists. Whether in court records or in newspaper reports, prostitutes were regularly depicted as criminally minded women who deserted their homes in search of "easy wealth" in the city. This well-entrenched portrayal satisfied the colonial society that consistently adopted a "puritanical" approach while establishing double standards of morality for men and women, blacks and white, elites and commoners. Moralists' reading of a prostitute's body and identity was influenced by the assumption that the sex worker contravened "conventional" codes of sexual respectability.[7] She was viewed as poor because of the notion that only poverty could drive a woman into sex work; as a criminal because she associated herself with *boma* and *jaguda* boys; as uneducated because it was assumed that education enhanced upward social mobility and obviated prostitution as a lifestyle choice. From the beginning of the twentieth century, moralists had established a rigid binary between the roles of men and women in prostitution. Men, though indispensable partners in the culture of sexual vice, were traditionally pictured as the victims of women's irresistible lure.

As prejudiced as the moralists' records are, we do know that women who practiced prostitution were involved in production and reproduction. One oral history of 1940s Lagos recalled the story of a popular prostitute, Asabi Olowo Abe (Asabi the owner of bottom money), who acquired the capital to start a successful textile business from prostitution.[8] She was well known among Lagos's Muslim community for her philanthropy, which disturbed the prevailing patriarchal configuration, as she became more popular than several influential men of her generation. But it was in the provinces that the impact of prostitution on social structure and gender relations was felt most.[9] "It is an open fact," L. A. Esien Offiong, the secretary of Calabar Council, pontificated in January 1944, "that some incorrigible harlots would return to Calabar and display their fineries and fortunes made from prostitution, and like the emissaries of Satan they would succeed in enticing other unthinking women to do the same."[10] When prostitutes acquired property or fulfilled financial responsibilities ordinarily considered to be the preserve of men, they created a backlash, typically condensed into the language of sin, immorality, and cultural blasphemy.[11] This is particularly true in the case of Ruth, a native of Warri who returned home after practicing prostitution in Lagos for five years. She used her earnings to offset the marriage expenses of two of her brothers. Her estranged husband made an official complaint to the district officer demanding that she should not be allowed to return to Lagos after the ceremony.[12] Indeed, so important was prostitution to the domestic economy of Ogoja and Calabar Provinces that colonial officers and native authorities clamored for the introduction of a new tax regime specifically for returnee prostitutes.[13]

One of the most detailed written sources about the life and times of a Lagos prostitute is the autobiography of Segilola, titled *Itan Igbesi-Aiye Emi 'Segilola Eleyinju Ege, Elegberun Oko L 'Aiye* (The Life History of Me Segilola Endowed with Fascinating Eyes, the Sweetheart of a Thousand and One Men).[14] Initially serialized into thirty chapters in *Akede Eko* (*Lagos Herald*), a leading bilingual newspaper, in 1929–30, published as the first Yoruba novel, and later translated into English, this autobiography tells the story of a popular Lagos prostitute and her clientele, which cuts across ethnicity, social class, nationality, and race.[15] Indeed, in narrating her experiences as a beautiful prostitute much adored by "thousands" of men, Segilola unveiled a great deal of core information that has proved helpful in mapping out the enormous transformation in the social and cultural landscape of Lagos in the first three decades of the twentieth century. Her autobiography is not an orthodox piece of writing—it remains a tour de force in Nigeria's history of print culture and a major contribution to the evolution of contemporary Yoruba writing. Although critics claimed that the autobiography was fiction and doubted Segilola's true identity, most contemporaries believed that her account was real and a genuine representation of social and sexual patterns of the first three decades of the twentieth century.[16]

Figure 2.1. Advertisement of the novel *Life History of Segilola Eleyinju Ege* in *Akede Eko* (*Lagos Herald*), July 5, 1930.

Critics like the *Nigerian Daily Times* appeared to be jealous of the success of the rival *Akede Eko*, which grew in popularity through Segilola's story. Thus, what appeared to be just an interesting story of a prostitute created a "press war"—a competition for readership. Segilola's story appears credible when cross-examined by comparison with other contemporary historical sources about the social life of Lagos.

Born into an "excellent" Yoruba family in Lagos in September 1882, Segilola was the only surviving child of six children. Her father died shortly after her first birthday, leaving only her mother with the task of raising her. After losing her virginity to an herbalist whom she had contacted to help her make love juju (charm) to entice men, Segilola lived an active sex life and courted men across generations. One of them, a famous European businessman, became financially distressed and had to be rescued by his fellow Europeans, who raised money for his fare back home. Her story defied occasional male-centric or colonialist depictions of prostitutes as victims or hapless elements compelled to suffer at the whims and caprice of men. Rather, she was in firm control of her body and resources, not only because she suavely made them do her wishes, but because she possessed "a radiantly fair beauty" that left men "soakingly wet" whenever they saw her walk by. [17] Segilola provided very sketchy information about what she did with men behind closed doors. She probably did not reveal too much about sexual intercourse in order to retain the attention of her weekly audience who could be discouraged with explicit sexual contents. But such phrases as "enjoy sweet pleasure-time" and "enjoy the pleasures of the world" used to describe the time she spent with men in the bedroom suggested that she enjoyed a great sex life. [18] In another part of her autobiography, she asserted that men exclaimed, "Ah can a woman be that beautiful?" when they saw her, but "it was only the surface layer of the palm oil they were looking at!" [19] The metaphorical "surface layer of palm oil" suggests that she was "sweeter," "sexier," and even more "valuable" than she appeared to men's gaze—as they would find out if they got to know her better. In Yoruba culinary culture from where she adapted the metaphor, the upper layer of palm oil (*ogere*), though reddish and attractive, was not as "concentrated" and "valuable" as the *ogidi* (the bottom layer). The *ogere*, though attractive, was a facade, covering the *ogidi*, the real value. Hence, the authentic Segilola was not the physically charming lady that everyone saw, but the sexy persona that only those few men who courted her could see.

Lagos prostitutes like Segilola were variously called *akunakuna, ashewo, karuwa, asape*, and Marina girls, among other epithets. These designations reflected the ethnic diversity of prostitutes as well as the physical geography of transactional sex. For instance, *ashewo*, which appeared in Lagos newspapers as early as the 1930s, is probably of Yoruba origin.[20] It literally translates as "someone who breaks money" (i.e., into smaller dominations). Prostitutes probably assumed this name because they usually had cash to help people make change. Akunakuna was the name of a town in Ogoja Province where a majority of Lagos prostitutes were believed to have come from.[21] Marina, a densely populated neighborhood and one of the economic nerve centers of Lagos, was a major red-light zone where prostitutes from diverse ethnic groups solicited. The ethnic composition of the prostitute corps appeared to have undergone a transformation as Lagos expanded. Before the second decade of the twentieth century, when Lagos emerged as the capital of the Nigerian state and a truly heterogeneous city, women who practiced prostitution were mostly Yoruba. The mass immigration in the early 1900s led to a diversification of sex work as women from other regions of Nigeria began to partake in colonial capitalism in increasing numbers. It also pushed Yoruba prostitution to the margins. One of the earliest reports about the ethnic background of immigrant prostitutes in Lagos dating to the first decade of the twentieth century identified Warri women as the most populous group.[22] Under conflicting situations, moralists blamed Akunakuna, Calabar, Efik, Edo, and Igbo women as the pollutants of the moral serenity of Lagos during the 1930s and 1940s.[23]

But this conclusion is flawed because it was not based on any coordinated census; rather, it derived from petitions and convictions of women accused of child trafficking, both in Nigeria and the Gold Coast.[24] Moreover, it was not unusual for prostitutes to lie about their ethnic origins in order to retain anonymity or undermine legal and repatriation proceedings. During the early 1940s, Calabar native authorities protested against the repatriation of non-Calabrians to their communities.[25] It would appear that estimations of the ethnic composition and numerical strength of prostitutes were based on the demographics of male immigrants from each ethnic group. Men patronized prostitutes from their own ethnic group because, apart from sex, prostitutes provided other services including companionship that could be better enhanced among people of the same ethnicity. Yet, Lagos prostitutes (with the exception of Hausa) sold sex to men across ethnic and racial lines.

Hausa prostitutes (*karuwai*) lived predominantly in the *sabon gari*.[26] The Hausa had a longer history of being an established community in Lagos than did most other Nigerian ethnic groups. Indeed, the first visible Hausa quarters in Lagos were founded in 1865 by Hausa soldiers who comprised the main stock of the Lagos Constabulary, a colonial military force that would later become the Nigeria Regiment of the West African Frontier Force (WAFF), later the Royal West African Frontier Force (RWAFF).[27] Generally speaking, the Hausa form of prostitution was quite different from the "conventional" type practiced by other Nigerians in terms of patronage, method of solicitation, legality, and acceptability/normalization. While Hausa prostitutes were largely patronized by Hausa men who lived mostly in the *sabon gari*, non-Hausa prostitutes were largely patronized by non-Hausa men and served diverse groups of Africans and non-Africans alike.[28] While Hausa prostitutes solicited mainly in the *sabon gari*, waiting inside or in front of their rooms for men to come to them, rarely engaging in streetwalking, non-Hausa prostitutes solicited in major points of social rendezvous and in the streets of Marina.[29] *Karuwanci* (prostitution) can be likened to the Malaya form found in Nairobi, Kenya.[30] The method of solicitation not only determined the income of prostitutes, the risk involved in the sale of sex, and the identity of clients and ethnicity but also perceptions of criminality. Thus, *karuwanci* did not attract the form of criminality associated with the conventional prostitution found among other Nigerian groups because its geographical confinement to the *sabon gari* allowed it to be unnoticed and unsanctioned by administrators.

Beyond the physical and cultural geography of sex work, normalization was another factor. *Karuwanci* was considered a "socially acceptable" practice among the Hausa of the *sabon gari* partly because the high rate of divorce created a pool of both single and unattached males and females. Hausa migratory culture supported short- and only occasionally long-term relationships within the enclaves.[31] While Lagosians of other ethnicities wrote petitions accusing their own people of prostitution, I have not come across any petitions from *sabon gari* residents about the activities of the *karuwai*. Indeed, the Colony Welfare Office (CWO) did not deal with any cases of child prostitution in the *sabon gari* throughout the 1940s and 1950s. Hausa leaders, unlike other "tribal" leaders and associations, neither worked with the CWO against the menace of prostitution nor helped the government establish criminal charges against their countrymen and women accused of breaking anti-prostitution laws.[32] Chieftaincy disputes within the Lagos Hausa community were the most dominant theme in their relations with the Lagos authorities from the 1930s to the 1950s.[33]

Not all women who practiced prostitution were Nigerian nationals—some were from the neighboring countries of the Gold Coast (modern-day Ghana) and Dahomey (modern-day Benin). Porto Novo Market Street, one of the main red-light streets in Lagos, had large concentrations of non-Nigerians, especially Dahomeans, who were believed to have settled the community, first as a trading center. However, this group was numerically insignificant. Unlike Johannesburg, where white women practiced prostitution, I have not come across any information pointing to the presence of white prostitutes in Lagos.[34] One should not be surprised by this since most European women in colonial Nigeria, as Helen Callaway has shown, were either wives of colonial administrators, or professionals/expatriates, or both.[35]

Colonial records are silent about the ages of adult prostitutes. But oral history provides a glimpse: most of Lagos's 1940s adult prostitutes were in their twenties and thirties.[36] When a woman started and stopped engaging in prostitution depended on when she decided to be a prostitute, the resources she accrued, and such family factors as the decision whether to get married. Segilola practiced prostitution for about 25 years, stopping at age 47. Prostitutes' marital status varied widely—they included singles/unmarried, married, separated, divorcées, and widows. H. E. Coker, a *West African Pilot* editor and author of a pamphlet on prostitution titled *Surplus Women* (1948), which was praised by Mazi Mbonu Ojike as the "boldest" attempt to engage a subject "many have feared to discuss," identified three categories of adult prostitutes based on marital and economic status: "working class unmarried, the non-working class unmarried women and the class of women who commit prostitution either for economic reasons or sexual laxity."[37] Marriage did not necessarily end prostitution—Segilola, for instance, practiced prostitution before and during marriage. On August 31, 1943, Selina Omif, whose husband was described as a "thoroughly bred gentleman," pleaded guilty to converting her family's rented room into a brothel.[38] It is unclear whether her husband consented to this, but some married men did pimp their wives and use their private residences for prostitution. On other occasions, married women practiced prostitution without the approval of their husbands, causing men to report them to authorities. In June 1944, Bernard of No. 18 Taiwo Street wrote a petition against his wife, Office Udugba, for prostitution. Described as "becoming worse day after day," Office was well known by welfare authorities for girl trafficking.[39] One could read men's motives for reporting their wives as beyond mere attempts to be "law-abiding" citizens, as they normally claimed to be. Domestic matters occasionally degenerated into "public crime," with men accusing their wives of prostitution in order to gain leverage.

Most Lagos prostitutes operated from brothels, known variously as "houses of *akunakuna*" and "houses of ill fame." In 1946 the government marked out the following nine streets as hotspots for brothels: Broad, Breadfruit, John, Labinjo, Market, Martins, Porto Novo Market, Taiwo, and Williams.[40] A midsize brothel in the 1940s had up to fifteen rooms.[41] While some brothel owners leased out rooms to prostitutes on a monthly basis, others, like the famous Round-Up Hotel and Havana Inn, both in Marina, provided hourly lodging for prostitutes and their male customers. Owned mostly by men and retired prostitutes or madams who also acted as pimps, most brothels had a bar and a dancing space.[42] In legal terms, any residence used for prostitution (whether a conventional fifteen-bedroom property that housed prostitutes on Market Street or a single room leased to a prostitute in a purely residential area) was a brothel. Legal officers and the Nigeria Police Force (NPF) gave an expanded definition to a brothel in order to broaden the implementation of anti-prostitution law since many Lagos prostitutes operated from their rented rooms but solicited in popular rendezvous spots such as the Race Course, Apapa, and Marina. The presence of military barracks in Ikeja boosted the sex market in that part of the city.

What is the monetary worth of prostitution? Sex work belonged to the off-the-books sector of the imperial treasury, hence its value did not appear in the annual income of the colonial state. However, the multiplier effect of the business of sexual pleasure was mostly reflected in the increasing number of brothels, bars, and people (prostitutes, brothel owners, and *boma* and *jaguda* boys, among others) who derived their means of livelihood from it, or in the investments of prostitutes and other members of the prostitution subculture in landed property or their families' education, businesses, and purchases of items for daily needs. Prostitutes' incomes varied widely, depending on method of solicitation, day and time of the week, type of prostitution practiced, length of service rendered, and even ethnicity. The quickest and most inexpensive sexual service would be one or two rounds of sex in either a brothel or a rented home. In the first half of the 1940s, a round of sex went for 1s. to 2s. If a prostitute entertained three men in a day (a scenario possible for those operating from popular brothels on weekends), she could make about 6s. in a day, between £6 and £9 in a month, and from £72 to £108 per annum.[43] Since prostitutes also made more money when they danced with men, shared drinks, or cooked for them, this estimate is definitely on the low side. Their age and the makeup of their clientele also determined the income of prostitutes. Ojike noted that younger prostitutes made more money than older ones, especially those over 25 whose "physical youthfulness [had begun] to fade away" and who began to "lose their many he callers-in."[44] One of Segilola's lovers promised to give her "pocket money" of £10 every month. Another, identified simply as La-bode, spent about £30 on her within three months in the 1910s or 1920s.[45] She claimed she made "vast amounts of money" because she only kept "very exclusive, distinguished gentlemen."[46] In addition to using her body, Segilola, a self-proclaimed "woman among women" and "Iyalode of them all," made more from prostitution because she was "armed with knowledge of medicines and charms" and a "magical herbal potion" that she used in manipulating men.[47]

To put this in the broader perspective of the wage labor system, the lowest-earning prostitute's estimated annual income, as given above, doubled or tripled the government's annual minimum wage of £36.[48] Using the cost-of-living index in Lagos compiled by the government in 1942 as a yardstick, prostitutes would apparently fare very well with such a projected income—in spite of the rise in the cost of living of 50 to 75 percent between 1939 and 1942.[49] Average monthly expenses for a household of four on food and rent (which consumed the largest proportion of Lagosians' income) were £4 and 13s., respectively.[50] A prostitute who lived by herself (most of them did) and made between £6 and £9 in a month would have enough to save, remit to the family, or invest in landed property, after paying rent and bribes to the police. Some prostitutes combined sex work with other businesses that yielded additional resources to augment their income from prostitution, which fluctuated from time to time. Madam Comfort Abes, in addition to prostitution, also ran the "Holly Wood Bar" located at 7 Harbour Road, Apapa.[51] A petition against Madam Afiong Bassey of 9 Onibudu Lane, who was accused of girl trafficking, stated that she claimed to be a seamstress "just to deceive the general public and the authority whereas she [was] a notorious harlot."[52]

As mentioned in the introduction, sexual networking in Lagos was very diverse, making prostitution only one of the numerous aspects of sex work. Some women at various stages in their lives sold sex either for direct monetary gain or to enhance their private businesses. Fento, a corrupt court clerk in Cyprian Ekwensi's *People of the City*, offered this stereotypical description of a woman who accosted him for help to secure a market stall:

> How can you prove she does not maintain herself and her children on the earnings of her body? True she has a stall in the market where she sells imported European foods, but that may just be eye-wash to fool the police. She's come to me to help her get a stall licence. I know she has no money to bribe me, but I like her. If I make a demand, she has either to accept or refuse. If she accepts, she will not need to go on a waiting list like others; the licence will be hers in a week instead of a year. So much for the licence . . . the clerk is young, and she is in need. And so it goes on. She doesn't mind. Five years of that and you'll be counting her among the richest women in the city.[53]

Yet, the popular stereotype that women always used their bodies for material gain promoted sexism and to large extent social exclusion.

The *Oko Ashewo* and the John Bulls

Without *oko ashewo* (prostitutes' husbands, or, in Yoruba, men who patronized prostitutes), sex would not take place. Indeed, men's appetite for sexual pleasure provided the demand for female sexual labor. The African clientele of casual sex workers cut across social class, ethnic, and generational boundaries. Why men visited or kept prostitutes has remained a significant historiographical question for historians of sexuality. But what seems apparent in the case of

Lagos and other colonial African locations is that transactional prostitution was the most guaranteed avenue for satisfying sexual desires for the majority of immigrants and the "indigenes" (both married and unmarried) who capitalized on the moral tolerance of the urban environment to experiment with new forms of sexual socialization that were rarely permissible in the rural settings. The wage labor and cash economy that the city had to offer facilitated the exchange of money for pleasure. Unlike southern Africa, where mining activities led to the ubiquity of prostitution, in Lagos the economy revolved around massive private and government investment in physical infrastructure, the civil service, international commerce, and military service. Lagos was a youthful city—67.3 percent of its entire population in 1950 was under 30 years of age. Although the male population was higher than the female population (124,858 to 105,398, respectively), the popularization of transactional sex cannot, unlike in the masculinized mining settlements, be blamed on the "scarcity" of women.[54] Rather, it should be seen as a core component of urban life, its youth-centeredness, and its economic opportunities.

Prostitution filled the void of the loneliness of bachelorhood, which was prolonged for many Nigerian men as bride-price and other marriage payments soared and as men failed to meet financial expectations due to the unstable colonial economy. Even for the married, it guaranteed a secretive and less expensive opportunity to engage in an extramarital affair with limited or no emotional commitment. Some of Segilola's clientele included single and married men whom she described variously as "young bloods with money to burn" and "people of substance and standing."[55] Although records of coition are rare, rumors of sexual behavior were legion. For instance, during the 1940s, men's demand for Efik women was high because of the assumption that they were better in bed than women of other ethnic groups.[56] However, the ease of buying sex with cash did not wholly explain the ubiquity of prostitution. Indeed, to link sex directly with money or other gratification is to underestimate the complexity of human sexuality, thought, and action. Obviously, coition was gratifying to varying extents in the relations between a prostitute and her clientele, but it was not always the most important benefit that either derived. Men also "bought" women's time when they danced with them in the clubs, shared drinks in the bar, or "hired" their beauty to show them off to their friends. "If they [prostitutes] are all sent back to their respective towns," an antagonist of the criminalization of prostitution who identified himself simply as a "soldier" wrote in affirmation, "men would have no ladies to dance with in halls."[57] The more money men were willing to spend, the more time and attention they received from women.

As we can see, sexual desire represented only one component of the entire relationship between men and women; ethnicity also influenced the pattern of patronage. Segilola, in addition to providing sex, also cooked for her lovers.

She wrote that she "robbed" many women of their husbands "by means of delicious food."[58] The following statement gives a clearer insight into the kinds of food she prepared for men: "I Segilola used to fry ripe plantain in palm oil for a man, and would fry a whole piece of dried fish, about five-shilling's worth, in pepper sauce to put on top of the fried plantain."[59] Men also sought accommodations with prostitutes, often living semi-permanently and on occasion even permanently with them. One of the most guaranteed accommodations for a new male immigrant was a brothel. He could stay with the prostitute as long as he wanted, provided he could pay for the time better spent with other men. Indirectly, prostitution supplied the resources that augmented, complemented, and facilitated the colonial state's quest to create a city of competitively cheap male labor. Some men even made prostitutes their "confidantes" and "banks."[60] Hausa men preferred *karuwai* to women of other ethnicities partly because they believed they were "honest" and could be trusted with their secrets and money. In all, what started as a mere "transient" attraction could lead to a long and well-sustained relationship—and some men even married prostitutes or established lifetime relationships with them.

Among the African men who patronized prostitutes, soldiers stood out prominently. Indeed, they were one of the most clearly identifiable demographics of consumers of sexual pleasure. As chapter 4 further attests, the quest to control the sexual recklessness of soldiers ushered in new regimes that accorded separate approaches to the regulation of VD among the military and the civilian populations. The soldiers' reputation for sexual recklessness was promoted by the prevailing army culture that overtly and covertly encouraged military prostitution under the pretext that soldiers' sexual perversion could not be successfully tamed.[61] Before the late 1940s, when military authorities began to encourage "family-centered living," the African rank-and-file were officially treated as single, unattached men—though some of them lived with their wives in the barracks during peacetime.[62] For singles mostly under age 30, frequent transfers militated against opportunities to contract long-term relationships and marriage.[63] Prostitution was the certain means of satisfying sexual desires for this class of men who had enough disposable income to buy sex in uncommitted relationships.[64] The military did not allow brothels within the barracks. But conventional brothels of varying sizes and other premises used for prostitution dotted every part of the island and mainland (especially Ikeja) where military bases were sited during peacetime and wartime.

African men were not, of course, the only clientele of prostitutes; European colonial administrators, military officers, expatriates, and seamen (nicknamed John Bulls and Jimmies in the prostitution subculture), among other classes, also paid for sex. Given that Nigeria was a culturally, economically, and linguistically diverse place, one should hardly expect the sexual behaviors of its invaders to be homogeneous. Contrary to the assertion by Ronald Hyam that "sexual . . . expression is likely to have been generally less exploitative than the records suggest," evidence from Nigeria clearly shows that Europeans saw the colony as a site of sexual adventure and opportunity.[65] Several of the Colonial Office's policies on marriage indirectly encouraged the promiscuity of officers in the colonies. For instance, the Colonial Office did not grant permission for officers to relocate with their wives if facilities to support a decent family life were unavailable.[66] Indeed, up to the 1920s Nigeria was still considered "no place for a white woman," due to the absence of modern conveniences comparable to Europe.[67] The Colonial Office made bachelorhood a criterion for certain jobs: up until 1939, British military officers to be posted to West Africa had to be between 23 and 30 years of age and unmarried.[68]

Information about the sexual liaisons between colonial masters and Lagos women is scanty. This is probably because European administrators in Lagos lived segregated private lives, hidden from the surveillance of the public. Reference to sex in the memoirs and biographies of colonial officers is also very sketchy.[69] The secret sex lives of colonial officers became even more hidden from public view after 1909 with the issuance of a confidential circular by Lord Crewe, the secretary of state for the colonies. Known variously across the British Empire as the "concubine circular," the "immoral relations memo," the "moral dispatch," and "the Crewe circular," the memo forbad concubinage and all forms of sexual relations between colonial officers and native women.[70] This two-part circular (part A for officers joining the service and part B for those already serving) was prompted by a serious sex scandal involving Hubert Silberrad, assistant district commissioner at Nyeri in central Kenya, and a 12- or 13-year-old native girl named Nyakayena in February 1908.[71] It expressed the impact of sexual misconduct with natives on the British civilizing mission thus: "It is not possible for any member of the administration to countenance such practices without lowering himself in the eyes of the natives, diminishing his authority to an extent which will seriously impair his capacity for useful work in the Service in which it is his duty to strive to set an honourable example to all with whom he comes in contact."[72] The tone of this circular is clear: colonial officers were in the colonies primarily for imperial business and could not mix sexual pleasure with administrative duty. Moreover, it revealed a sexuality angle to Britain's paternalistic posture by insisting that sex carried a burden of moral responsibility, especially when indulged in with the "primitive" population who required civilizing. As bold as this attempt at policing sexual boundaries sounded, it nonetheless exposed one of the contradictions in colonial policy: spousal living was not encouraged, yet administrators were expected to be sexually disciplined.

I have not come across any documents detailing the reactions of Nigerian administrators to this circular. The closest document I have found, titled "Marriage of British Subjects in Foreign Dependencies," is completely silent about

Crewe's circular.[73] However, the Crewe circular apparently did not repress interracial sexual liaisons but only redefined the prostitute-client relationship and further removed it from the public gaze. A 1919 report by Principal Medical Officer E. E. Maples on VD among European officers clearly reveals that the Crewe circular did not constrain administrators' sexual behavior.[74] Maples reported that he had treated VD among every class of European and that married and unmarried men "eminently" preferred to keep a "mistress" to a "stray" woman in order to reduce the chances of contracting VD and avoid the embarrassment an interracial affair could create if it became public. He affirmed that administrators tended to be watchful when contracting interracial sexual liaisons because native women could use sex to blackmail them. He observed further that except for the missionaries, "practically no class of European at every stage of their career in West Africa, live continent lives" (i.e., practice sexual abstinence).[75] His comment that "it should not, in my opinion, be expected that the European in West Africa will remain free from sexual intercourse" would have embarrassed some "decent and married" colonial officers and undermined the authorities' quest to police sexual boundaries.[76]

No doubt, Maples's distinction between a "mistress" and a "stray" woman was imported from Britain where men's socio-sexual relations reflected their status. According to Victorian social and sexual norms, a "common prostitute" or "stray" woman was constructed as a "poor," "uneducated," "dirty whore," while a "mistress" assumed the identity of a "polished, "clean," and "special" woman.[77] While imperial and metropolitan elite culture looked down at the visiting of prostitutes in a brothel, a man's having a mistress received some degree of social approval (especially in the nineteenth century) in a society struggling to reconcile its double standard on sexual morality. However, sexual affairs—whether with a "mistress" in such a morally less damaging arrangement as "concubinage" or in a "degrading" circumstance like "prostitution"—carried the tone of power. In other words, although the politics of nomenclature influenced the social implications of sexual behavior, keeping a "prostitute" or a "mistress" each involved exchange of sex for money, favors, or countless other forms of gratification.

Although Maples's affirmation that he had treated VD among all classes of Europeans was in direct conflict with official policy toward interracial sex and could have implicated his colleagues in a way they probably would not have wanted, he also absolved them of inherent immorality by blaming the tropical climate for its "excitant effect upon sexual desires" and the availability of women who "for all practical purpose . . . are mere goods and chattels." The practice of attributing imperial failure to Africa's climate and backward culture satisfied the prevailing philosophy that viewed colonialism as a rescue mission. Maples did not state if his European clients contracted VD in Nigeria or were infected in Europe or other colonial sites before being posted to Nigeria, but we do know that military and government personnel had to pass a medi-cal test before being posted to Nigeria. It was during one such pre-departure test that a medical officer at Royal Herbert Hospital at Woolwich discovered that Captain F. C. W. Brown of the WAFF had catarrhal inflammation of the urethra caused by gonorrhea. The confidential medical report on the 30-year-old officer attributed his sickness to "illicit sexual intercourse," but did not state if he contracted VD in France, where he visited between February and November 1920, or in Britain.[78] Yet, those already in the colonial service who went home to Britain on leave also had to pass a VD test before returning to the colony. The return of F. Rolfe, the district stationmaster of the Nigerian Railway, was delayed for two months because his Wassermann test (used for diagnosing syphilis) was positive.[79] In his case, like that of Captain Brown, the medical report did not state where he had contracted VD. The pre-departure test reinforced Maples's pronouncement that European officers contracted VD from Nigerian women and helped establish that sexual affairs between Nigerian and European officers were common, though discreet.

Maples's report is the most comprehensive information about administrators' sexuality that I have come across. There is a probability that interracial affairs increased as more colonial officers were posted to Nigeria. After narrating a short tale of adultery between a European wife of a trader and a bachelor government officer in Lagos around 1934, Sir Rex Niven, a colonial officer who served in Nigeria for forty years, remarked that "in practice, the general standard of sexual morals between white people was high, in spite of the attractiveness of many individuals" but that "many white men had black mistresses."[80] Lieutenant Colonel F. H. G. Higgins and Brigadier R. M. Allen, who served in Nigeria in the 1930s, mentioned that British officers "kept women in their quarters" and that it was easy to find "black sleeping partners."[81] Another British military officer, Major General G. F. Upjohn, who also served in the 1930s, was more explicit about the sexual conduct of his comrades: "Everybody knew that it went on . . . There were certain people who did and certain people who didn't."[82] None of these military and civil officers revealed the identity of any European's Nigerian "sleeping partners." This is consistent with their tendency to minimize the guilt of sexual waywardness by not referring to lovers as "prostitutes" or "whores" but as "concubines" or "sleeping partners"—terms that carried lesser culpability of sexual responsibility. Meanwhile, the paucity of mixed-race persons in Lagos and Nigeria as a whole suggests that pleasurable affairs between Nigerian women and colonial officers were transient, non-committed, and mostly transactional.

From the foregoing, the social class of men and the position they occupied in the colonial project largely determined how their sexual conduct was discussed in the colonial records. While "mistresses" were the sexual partners of colonial officers, "prostitutes" were what other classes of Europeans, especially the seamen, consorted with. The sexual escapades of colonial officers were discreet, whereas those of seamen, most of whom came to Lagos on the Elder Dempster Shipping Line, which monopolized maritime trade between Britain and West Africa from 1900, were visible.[83] The records of the CWO and newspaper accounts are replete with the involvement of sailors in prostitution and the refusal of the criminal justice system to prosecute them.[84] Although colonial officers (both civil and military) could be sanctioned for sexual recklessness because they occupied elite positions in the colonial hierarchy and, as such, could not officially have sexual relations with native women, seamen were treated as "foreigners" whose conduct carried little or no moral implications for either the colonial establishment or their employers. Unlike colonial officers who represented the governments of the metropole and were symbols of colonial paternalism and civilization, seamen were temporary visitors whose mission was purely economic and who were treated as outside the reach of imperial administration. The latter's appetite for sex abetted the activities of criminals like the *boma* and *jaguda* boys, who served as prostitutes' pimps. So high was the incidence of VD among seamen that a VD clinic was established solely for them in 1921, about twenty-four years before the residents of Lagos received one.

Social class and whiteness determined not only the identities of European seekers of sexual pleasure and their lovers but also the domain where sexual activities took place. Whereas most African patrons of prostitutes visited brothels or rented prostitutes' rooms, the European clientele hosted prostitutes in their private lodgings in first-class hotels—the Grand Hotel (operated by a Briton named Efeller and his wife and staffed with Italians, Spaniards, and Africans), the Bristol Hotel, Hotel Metropole, and the Ritz Hotel.[85] Of these, the Grand Hotel was arguably the most famous because it was located on Broad Street and surrounded by several European bars and businesses. A survey of Lagos hotels described it as "really a first class for this country [Nigeria]."[86] The white, three-storied property housed a ladies shop and was "equipped with the most up-to-date cushion chairs . . . luxurious dining hall and very well supplied with [a] nice mess-set."[87] Any visitor, the survey asserted, "will surely have a very good impression" of the hotel's excellent organization, which testified to the European origins of its managers.[88]

The differing legal and social definitions of a brothel conveniently permitted the Grand Hotel and other five-star hotels to assume contradictory identities as "first-class hotels" and, simultaneously, "brothels." In strictly social terms, the Grand Hotel was truly a "first-class" hotel because its guests did not include the poor, lower-class Lagosians. It epitomized colonial modernity by offering service comparable to that of the developed Western world. Although the guests of the hotel were upper-middle-class Lagosians and visiting Europeans, its outer premises were surrounded by "unsavory elements" willing to help seamen and sex tourists locate prostitutes and unlock the "authentic" nightlife of Lagos at the eastern end of the Broad Street, in Marina, on Porto Novo Market Street, and on Labinjo Street, among other red-light regions.[89] However, the Grand Hotel was also a brothel because it fit into the legal definition of brothel as "any premises or room or set of rooms in any premises kept for purpose of prostitution."[90] The moralists did not publicly label the Grand Hotel a "brothel," however, because it defied the general profile of "houses of ill fame" that operated mostly under the cover of darkness and anonymity and were located in densely populated, poorly maintained neighborhoods.

The "Dirty" Language of Sex

If prostitution remained a private matter between consenting male and female adults and if it did not involve public solicitation, moralists would have little or no case against it. However, prostitution could not be confined strictly to the four corners of a room at Porto Novo Market Street. Both men's search for sex and women's solicitation of prospective customers had to be conducted in places observable by individuals and groups whose ideology toward sex work varied from moderate to die-hard prohibitionist. The term "sexual immorality," which moralists deployed in condemning prostitution, though vague sounding, had a well-ascribed and commonly accepted connotation. It included references to sex in popular music and in public conversation, flirtation in public space, nudity, and other acts that facilitated the sale of sexual favors. A popular *asiko* song of the interwar years titled "Sawa Sawa" (meaning prostitute) described the conduct of prostitutes in hotels and bars along the Lagos Marina and included the line "If you didn't sleep there, how you come about gonorrhea?"[91] Tijani Omoyele, who played the *apala* genre, released a 1932 album titled *Ashewo/Omo jaguda* (Prostitutes/Criminals) to great fanfare.[92] In addition, Irewole Denge, an Ijebu Yoruba and the first to record palm wine music, titled his 1937 album *Orin Asape Eko* (Song of Prostitution in Lagos).[93] These talented artists apparently thought they had the poetic license to highlight this dominant aspect of city life through music they believed the majority of socialites would enjoy: the moralists, however, thought their exhibitionism worsened the moral climate by publicizing degenerate acts that were not only disgraceful but supposed to be secret.

The first concerted effort to prohibit prostitution came not from the British colonialists but from Lagosians. And women, not men, led it. In October 1923 the Lagos Ladies League (later the Lagos Women's League, or LWL), led by Charlotte Olajumoke Obasa, petitioned Governor Hugh Clifford of Nigeria, asking his government to look into "the vulgar and obscene language on the streets of Lagos, and the lewd songs, pernicious newspaper literature, indecent behavior"; they decried "the want of action to discourage prostitutes from other parts of

Nigeria openly making this town [Lagos] their headquarters," asserting that the sad result of all this immorality was "an effect for much evil on growing children which ends in making them become criminals."[94] The women also blamed prostitutes for the spread of VD. In his response to the LWL's "moral crusade," the governor through Secretary Donald Cameron did not deny "that prostitution exists in Lagos, as it does in all other seaport towns in all parts of the world." However, he claimed that "every possible effort is being made by the Colony police to keep them [the prostitutes] within bounds."[95] He asserted further that "any prostitute who becomes a nuisance to the general public is recommended to the Town Council for deportation forthwith." Cameron further replied that the LWL's "sweeping generalization as to the degeneracy of the people of Lagos is not confirmed by police report."[96] And he went on to challenge Obasa "to indicate the newspaper literature circulating in Lagos which they regard as being pernicious to the morals of the population." He admitted that "it is impossible to take action on such vague generalizations."[97]

In their counterargument, the elite women, who also identified themselves as the "Women of Lagos," contended that the failure of the NPF to report the ubiquity of obscene newspaper literature and vulgar street language was a manifestation of poor policing of the city.[98] Unsatisfied with the government's policy of tolerating prostitution, the LWL reaffirmed its position in 1924 and 1926 through follow-up petitions that asked the government to initiate measures "to repatriate those [prostitutes] already in town to their homes and to prevent others from coming in, as their example is a source of great danger."[99] It is hard to tell why the women throughout the 1920s declined to provide evidence of "pernicious" literature. Presumably, they felt that the obscene words were too offensive to put to paper. In colonial civic culture, the rendering of sexual organs in print was considered too vulgar for the small but highly influential Lagos elites. In addition, they probably did not want to be quoted since well-known pro-British personalities like Sir Kitoyi Ajasa, anti-establishmentarians like Herbert Macaulay, and cultural nationalists like I. B. Thomas were the publishers of some of Lagos's newspapers—such as the *Nigerian Pioneer*, the *Lagos Daily News*, and *Akede Eko* (*Lagos Herald*), respectively, which carried advertisements for VD medicine.

During the 1930s newspapers, notably the *Comet*, the *Lagos Daily News*, and the *West African Pilot*, dedicated critical editorials toward the government for its ineptitude in policing prostitution.[100] The public conduct of prostitutes, according to one newspaper critic, amounted to "social pathology" and a dent on colonial civilization.[101] A *West African Pilot* editorial of December 17, 1937, titled "Red Light District," clearly portrayed the interrelatedness of prostitution and sexual explicitness:

> Professions vary in their tastes, earnings, social importance, etc., but what is known
> in literary and Bohemian circles as the oldest profession in the world, is evidence

of social pathology and deserves Police vigilance, occasionally to prevent the practitioners of this art making a nuisance of themselves and their profession to the
danger of the public and safety of the State. We do not quarrel with the right of
any person to earn a livelihood, but when the means adopted encourages shouting
heehaws, street fights, debates as to terms, abusive languages, among the women
and their namby-pamby who visit these slums, and also outrage the peaceful section of the community, by disturbing their sleep and rest, then we feel that it is
time the Police co-operated in eradicating this social evil in our community life.
Live and let live must not be interpreted to imply licentiousness, irrespective of
the rights of others.[102]

Another editorial differentiated between the "inevitable street noise" characteristic of urban life and the "loose immoral talk by nocturnal adventurers"
on Porto Novo Market Street, and the "endless squabbles, midnight revelries,
and pugilistic display."[103] Neither such editorials nor petitions succeeded in
stimulating the government to launch a coordinated attack against prostitution.
The inaction of the British throughout the interwar years firmly established the
prevailing official policy of tolerating prostitution as long as it did not create
considerable public disorder. Indeed, there was no tangible solid machinery
for policing prostitution. This "policy of toleration" was also informed by the
institutionalized principle of colonial policing. Imperial police in Nigeria, as
elsewhere in Africa, were established not to protect the colonized but to guard
the symbols and infrastructure of imperialism such as the ports, railways,
mines, and colonial administration.[104] Before World War II, prostitution did
not have a legal definition, and it was not unlawful for children to be trafficked
for sexual exploitation. However, despite the absence of a well-defined legal
statute, prostitutes were prosecuted discretionarily, using an array of public
order laws. On April 20, 1938, Ajayi Macaulay, who was under the influence
of alcohol, pleaded guilty to three charges of "idling, unlawfully damaging and
misbehavior" while soliciting sex from French seamen in front of the Bristol
Hotel.[105] In December of the same year, Mary Adagbe, Mary Uto, and Jane
Warri were charged for solicitation in their rented abode. After she initially
pled not guilty, the court found Mary Adagbe guilty of running a brothel and
sentenced her to three months in prison and acquitted the two other accused
women.[106]

Juvenile Delinquency, Crime, and Imperial Security

A turn of events during the World War II years would compel the government to
abandon toleration and adopt a prohibitory stance toward prostitution. While
the criticism of prostitution during the interwar years centered heavily on such
esoteric charges as "immorality," vulgarity, and public nudity, the outbreak of
another global catastrophe made crime committed by young male juveniles the
centerpiece of public anxiety. This new development is explicable in terms of

the economic, structural, and demographic transformation that started from the early 1930s and reached its peak a decade later. In the first place, the Great Depression increased immigration into Lagos of men and women seeking refuge from rural poverty. As unemployment, which was first noticed in the 1920s, soared, so did the consolidation of poverty and criminal behavior perpetrated by juveniles and young adults. At the outbreak of World War II, a delinquent youth culture that epitomized the reality of urban poverty and vagrancy had become well established. Among the various youth gangs of the era, *jaguda* and *boma* boys stood out clearly for their numerical strength and criminal methods.[107] Administrators and welfare officers presented conflicting accounts of the origins of these delinquent youths, most of whom were between the ages of 12 and 18. While the governor of Nigeria Bernard Bourdillon traced the origins of the word *boma* boy to East Africa, Major Akinwande Jones, a probation officer of the Salvation Army, which operated a nongovernmental reformatory for boys, believed it had a root in the seafaring culture of Sierra Leone, a neighboring West African country.[108] Speaking in 1941, Dr. Henry Carr, a renowned educationist and the highest-ranking African colonial administrator, who was derogatorily labeled as a "collaborator" for his pro-British stance on several issues, attributed the origin of the *boma* boys phenomenon to the impact of the Great Depression: "After the war [World War I], there was a boom, and people found themselves with unusually large sums of money with the result that they got into the habit [of] spending money recklessly. But the boom was soon followed by a slump which necessitated relentless retrenchment by Government, as a result of which a large number of people was thrown out of employment. But as many of these had become accustomed to spending money recklessly, they had to find money by any possible means, and this led to an outbreak of burglaries and brigandage."[109]

Juvenile delinquency might have external or internal causes, but it was on the streets of Lagos that it grew into a full-blown threat to public safety. The *boma* and *jaguda* boys led an existence that epitomized a countercultural street life, committing crimes such as pickpocketing and currency counterfeiting, and creating an atmosphere of public insecurity.[110] They moved about in gangs and could be found in major bus and train terminals and markets like Idumagbo and Ereko. The newspapers labeled them as local terrorists whose conduct the locals could not report to the police for fear of reprisal. Such activities as illegal street gambling presided over by these delinquent youth not only created significant public disorder, but robbed the government of resources accrued from a state-managed lottery system.[111] When some *boma* boys attacked and wounded a police constable at Oshodi, a *West African Pilot* editorial submitted that public insecurity is "hardly complimentary to a progressive capital like Lagos," and contended that the audacity of the criminals "transcended the limit by making even Police Officers insecure."[112]

Public knowledge of *boma* and *jaguda* boys oscillated between sensational-istic newspaper accounts of their criminal exploits to well-defined "scientific" explanations by British and Lagos physicians, correction officers, and com-mentators.[113] Indeed, the gangs were practically turned into a human laboratory for studying vice. The interrelated problems of lack of education, disintegration of the household, vagrancy, poverty, imitation of Western gangsterism, and un-controlled immigration were among some of the leading environment-centered explanations. So complex were the propounded causes of delinquency that Dr. Kofoworola Abayomi, a leading physician and member of the Nigerian Youth Movement (NYM), in his public lecture titled "Problems Confronting the Nigerian Boy," warned, "There are no mathematical formulae with ready answers" for juvenile delinquency.[114] If all the "theories" of delinquency re-vealed anything, it was that colonialists and Lagosians alike were far behind in their focus on youth vagrancy. As varied as the experts' explanations were, they all agreed that solutions must be systemic and policy driven. The lifecycle or the process of degeneration of juveniles not only sounded scientific, it also made colonialists aware of the long-term implications of unregulated juvenile disorder, as this fact-finding report revealed:

> We identified a boma boy as one who acts as a guise or a tout for houses of ill-fame. We saw him at different stages of development. At the first stage he is a simple unsophisticated out-of-work, introduced to the trade by a friend, a casual guide without an arrangement with a particular house. He has not the experience to make the work very remunerative, so he sleeps outside and leads rather a meager existence. When he becomes more experienced and by his glib tongue and polite manner can get more customers he lives in a house, dresses well and feeds well. He may earn upwards of £2 per month. He probably has a definite arrangement with special harlots or particular houses . . . He is gradually deteriorating morally and eventually becomes a sophisticated cynical youth, up to all the tricks of the trade, lazy and immoral, perhaps acting as a master to a group of younger boys. He may now be working as a master to a group of younger boma boys. He may now be working on a percentage basis as an important partner of an organized trade.[115]

Prostitution and juvenile delinquency were mutually constitutive and sym-biotic. Prostitutes and *boma* and *jaguda* boys shared the same public space—they lived and congregated in Marina, Porto Novo Market Street, Balogun, and other districts of Lagos Island where prostitutes solicited.[116] Thus, con-demnation of the notoriety of the *boma* boys touched heavily on that of the prostitutes and vice versa. The *boma* and *jaguda* boys carried out two major functions in the Lagos prostitution network. As pimps, they sometimes served as "brokers," connecting men with prostitutes, and also provided security by serving as prostitutes' guards. Because the Lagos red-light districts were underpoliced, they formed themselves into a quasi-security outfit, ensuring that socialites conducted themselves in a manner appropriate to the social conditions of the nightlife and prostitution subculture. Drunken men who behaved in a disorderly way and other unruly male customers were mugged, extorted, and readily removed from the premises. Unlike in Western societies, where pimps also supplied prostitutes with drugs, I have not come across any evidence pointing to the use of narcotic drugs among Lagos prostitutes.

The activities of the delinquent juveniles affected different segments of the community in different ways. Lagosians decried the impact of their notoriety on public safety and prostitution. For some, *boma* boys eroded African pride and gave foreigners a negative impression of the core values of Nigerian society, as gleaned from one commentator's (Olatunji Otusanya) admission that "the average sailor must leave Lagos with the impression that Nigeria is full of a lot of 'Niggers,' whose life is spent in prostitution, touting for brothels and molesting strangers."[117] Even an editorial in the *Nigerian Daily Times*, criticized by Obafemi Awolowo, one of the founding fathers of independent Nigeria, for lacking "animation, pungency and nationalist favour," believed that the streets of Lagos "stink in the nostrils of our visitors" because the *boma* boys gave the city a bad name "as a place where venereal disease is most startlingly rife."[118] For their part, the colonialists were concerned about the safety of seamen, foreign expatriates, and tourists, who often needed *boma* boys to navigate the red-light districts of Lagos for "immoral objectives which are certainly not in the best interest of the populace."[119] Although the *jaguda* and *boma* boys derived their living from several illegal activities, they probably made more money serving as "unauthorized" guides of seamen and sex tourists who had disposable income to spend on sex.[120] Lagos sex tourism developed in the wake of the globalization of prostitution occasioned by the integration of African economies into the blossoming Industrial Revolution through the railway and the sea. In the early 1940s seamen paid an average of 10s. to *boma* boys in addition to the cost of transportation. They also paid for drinks and food if they met the *boma* boys in hotels or bars. The *boma* boys' indispensability as the conduit for seamen's sexual desires was made inevitable by the port authorities' policy of barring women from the ships and the limited options of sexual socialization around the wharves, the combination of which compelled the seamen to venture into the heart of the city.

The illegal transactions between *boma* boys and European visitors tradition-ally went smoothly, but on a number of occasions they degenerated into open frays that caught the attention of the public. Two *boma* boys—Michael and Adekunle—"exchanged cuffs" at Taiwo Street as they vied to secure a prosti-tute for a seaman in 1938.[121] On other occasions, the seamen themselves were victims of their collaborators. Edward Salt, a sailor with the Elder Dempster Shipping Line, was reportedly beaten at a bar in Marina. In his statement to the police, he narrated that he paid a *boma* boy to take him to a brothel, but instead of doing the job for which he was paid, the boy took him to a hideout where he was mercilessly beaten and robbed of his personal effects.[122] According to an account in a local newspaper (*African Mirror*), *boma* boys would guide seamen to "sordid and disreputable places, and when the victims are drunk they 'bomb' them by relieving them of what money they have in their pockets."[123] The press's melodramatic rendition of violence against seamen was ambivalent, however—the fact that the seamen's desire for illicit sexual pleasure fueled the *boma* boys' activities did not mean that they should be victims of assault and theft.[124]

Delinquent boys remained largely faceless until they were apprehended by the police or admitted into the Salvation Army reformatory and the Boys' Hostel managed by the CWO. Their life histories, queried during legal proceedings, revealed the intersections of immigration, lack of education, and the unavailability of social services for Nigerian children in need of help. By 1942, 15-year-old Victor, who first came to Lagos in 1937 to "learn cookery" from his uncle who worked at the sailors' restaurant in Apapa, had been arrested five times (four times for pimping and once for theft). According to his uncle, he left the home they both shared because he was becoming "hard to control" and was attracted to the "plenty" money supposedly being made by serving as an illegal guide for sex tourists.[125] During his trial for defrauding a sailor named David Bremner of 10s. at a hotel, John Thomas (alias Lamino) testified that he was a tailor but became a *boma* boy because of poverty.[126] When social welfare officers and the police wrote about delinquent juveniles, they also attempted to measure the degree of the youths' "intelligence" in relation to the possibility of redemption through rehabilitation. While 14-year-old R. Ayo (aka Jack Morris), who lived permanently with a prostitute at 7 Porto Novo Market Street, was described as someone who "did not want to work" and "unintelligent," his counterpart, 16-year-old Felix Bolaji, received the accolades of being an "outstanding boy" who spoke "very good English" and deserved more education to achieve his dream of becoming a mechanic.[127]

Conclusion

This chapter has unveiled the men and women who sold and bought sex and has detailed how unregulated sexuality impacted urban security and notions of immorality. Sexual immorality was codified as a threat to nation-building—obscene literature, the language of sex on the street, public nudity, and disorderliness all represented cultural backwardness. Moralists among both the colonialists and the Lagosian elite were clear and consistent in their opposition to prostitution: sex work unleashed a vicious process, creating opportunities for criminal behavior to thrive. The boundary between "legitimate" and "illegitimate" socialization was blurred because the prostitution subculture was managed by men and women whose activities were considered unlawful. Before the outbreak of World War II, the colonialists did not take criminal activities perpetrated by delinquent youth seriously because they did not pose any serious threat to imperialism. The colonialists declined all petitions from elite women and men to tame sex work. But the outbreak of the war radically transformed their posture, creating a series of deliberations on the need to ensure that domestic insecurity did not undermine Britain's Win-the-War efforts. If the colonialists thought mainly in security terms, Lagosians' concern went beyond public order. They pictured the immoral behavior of fellow citizens as a dent in the project of modernizing a state they envisioned ruling after the anticipated demise of imperialism.

This chapter is also about prostitution proper—that is, adult prostitution. Adult prostitutes represented a different category of pleasure givers who were considered to be in firm control of their bodies, their sexuality, and the resources that accrued from prostitution. The vocabulary of sexual exploitation does not really apply to adult prostitution, despite the fact that prostitutes were usually exploited and harassed by police. But what made prostitution more problematic was not only the indecent talk and the criminal exploits of the *boma* boys, but the involvement of children who required adults' protection because of their defenselessness and passivity. As the following chapter explicates, child prostitution occupied a special position in the thought and imagination of moralists because it was wholly constructed as a sex crime against girls—one of the most defenseless demographics in the colonial state.

CHAPTER 3

CHILDHOOD INNOCENCE, ADULT CRIMINALITY

Child Prostitution and Moral Anxiety

> If they [child prostitutes] are brazen and unscrupulous, can it be
> wondered at? They were introduced to sex-relations before nature
> had prepared them for it. Their experiences have developed in them
> contempt and hatred for man and marriage institutions and so
> they spend their time getting as much as they can from any foolish
> men who allow themselves to their clutches. No pity is felt for the
> children introduced to this sordid business [prostitution] because
> they were themselves hardened at an early age.
> —Donald Faulkner, "Child Welfare:
>   Prostitution and Child Marriage," May 1943[1]

> This is a complaint against 3 minor girls by age 9–10–12 old that
> were under a certain old woman named Madam Ogoudi at 41
> Taiwo Street Lagos . . . I went there a certain evening by 7.30 pm.
> I heard a girl voice was crying in the room and to my observation,
> I discovered that a girl not up to the age of haven to do with man
> is in room with certain seaman . . . I have to appeal to your highly
> suppervision as to inspect the place and have such action be seized
> by transporting those three girls away otherwise it will no longer
> course their death.
> —Informant to the Colony Welfare Office, July 10, 1943[2]

The early 1940s remains a significant era in the history of childhood in Nigeria
for two main reasons. First, the decade ushered in the establishment of the
Colony Welfare Office (CWO)—the first government-sponsored institution for
addressing child and juvenile delinquency—and the appointment of Donald
Faulkner as its head. Second and more important, the colonial state through
Faulkner and his assistant, Alison Izzett, became intimately involved in policing

girlhood sexuality as a component of its larger project of modernization. Although Lagosians' moral indignation from the 1920s criticized the colonialists for falling behind in their paternalistic responsibility toward children of the empire, the adoption of endangered girlhood sexuality as an imperial project, the invention of a crude science of childhood, and the idea of the erotic and psychosocial child all began to take consistent shape from 1941. The moral panic among both the colonialists and the Lagosian elites over endangered girlhood sexuality mirrored a much larger anxiety over the transformation of colonial social and economic structures, generational conflict, and the tussle between the overlapping categories of "new" and "old," "modern" and "traditional," "urban" and "rural" lifestyles. Lagosians could only attempt to set the standard of sexual morality or complain about child prostitution, as the second epigraph above illustrates. They did not possess the machinery of the state required to institutionalize reform.

The deployment of a spectrum of categories—child prostitutes, neglected girls, girls in moral danger, and child wives, among others—to describe sexual danger pivoted toward the creation of institutional structures for safeguarding girls' sexuality from criminally minded adults and the dreadful delights of the city. Although all these categories constituted moral endangerments and received the attention of the CWO in varying proportions, the most worrisome was child prostitution in that it was constructed as the end product of all forms of sexual danger. In other words, illegal guardianships, abandonment, and child marriage set in motion a process, as the CWO believed, that finally culminated in child prostitution. The moral panic over imperiled girlhood sexuality in particular and children's welfare in general renders useful entry into the broader and intricate politics of class, agency, gender, and race in colonial Nigeria.[3] It reflects the divergent postures held by both the colonialists and the British government about the best means of protecting children from the scourge of moral danger that threatened the security of the colony and future generations of Nigerians.[4]

My main argument in this chapter is that the colonialists as well as the Lagosian elites from the 1920s constructed a rigid contrast between adult and girl-child sexualities hinged on the notion of childhood innocence and the criminality of the adults who lured them into sex work. Underage girls, both Lagosians and the CWO contended, were not physically, emotionally, and psychologically mature enough to engage in consensual sexual activities. All forms of prostitution and methods of solicitation damaged the image of Lagos as the bastion of West African colonial civility. But child prostitution meant more than moral degeneration. It epitomized the failure of "responsible" adults and the machinery of a modern colonial state to protect future generations of Nigerian mothers and wives. Adults' dangerous sexuality, in the colonialists' imagination, owed much to the distinctiveness of African sexualities that were not only profane but excessive. However, self-driven sexual pathology did not manifest in children until they reached adulthood. Put differently, unlike adults' reckless sexuality that was coded as a product of pathological differences, the colonialists believed that the traits of sexual perversion did not develop until the child reached adulthood. But the foundation could be laid, as the first epigraph suggests, at childhood through early sexual encounter and manifest at adulthood—producing strong psychosexual problems such as hatred for marriage and for healthy heterosexuality. The colonialists' framing of psychosexual development was therefore age specific.

Identifying and Defining a Child Prostitute

Childhood, like gender, is a social construction or category. It is also biologically, historically, and culturally specific. Hence, there is no universal notion of a child or childhood. Rather, at various times, and under myriads of competing circumstances, societies have defined and redefined childhood to satisfy particular sociocultural purposes and indeed imaginations.[5] This was particularly evident in colonial Lagos, where legal and social construction coalesced to create contradictory interpretations of the place of a child within the judicial system and the larger society. While the legal construction included the definition of a child as contained in colonial law books, which tended to tie childhood to chronological age, the social construction was the fixation of the public/society based mostly on status and social role. Both the legal and social definitions featured some elements of dependency as they placed adults in a supervisory position for children. Before 1958, the age of consent in Nigeria was 13, meaning that an individual legally ceased to be a child at this age. Criminal liability could not be brought against an individual for defiling or having carnal knowledge of a 13-year-old. But this was not an absolute legal definition of a child. Various sections of the criminal code gave conflicting definitions of a child for different purposes. For instance, the Venereal Diseases Ordinance (VDO, 1943) and the Children and Young Persons Ordinance (CYPO, 1943) defined a child as someone under the age of 14. Yet an individual could not be prosecuted as an adult for violent crimes like murder if he or she was under 16. In the wake of the socioeconomic exploitation of children through pawnship, the colonial government in 1927 made it illegal for children under 16 to be pawned for debt or other purposes.[6] Explicitly, this pawnship law established that a child was an individual under 16.

If the legal construction of a child was rigid, the social definition, which dominantly shaped moralists' understanding of sexual vice, was flexible. The social constructionist posture saw childhood more in terms of rites of passage—progression from childhood to adolescent to adult—and the corresponding identity and social roles, not age. The print media, which played an active role in socially framing childhood, also relied on physiological and morphological appearance (not the age of consent) as a yardstick for identifying child prostitutes. Indeed, such observable physical attributes as height, body structure, dress, mannerisms, and the power relations of the prostitution underclass supplied the language for identifying a child in terms of sexual activity. The newspapers' petitioners rarely mentioned the ages of the "pleasure girls" because most of the former did not establish direct contact with them since prostitution usually took place in the red-light districts, entry into which was considered "unethical" for the "enlightened" or "law-abiding" citizen. And when ages were given, the girl prostitutes were identified as between the ages of 10 and 15.

A more definite age of child prostitutes appeared in colonial records through the activities of the CWO, which documented their life stories in order to press for institutional reforms and bring procurers to book. Most of the girls rescued by the CWO (as table 3.1 shows) ranged from the age of 5 to 13. Several were above 15 but not over 20. If the CWO used the legal definition (i.e., the age of consent) as its guiding principle, it would not extend its supervisory and rehabilitative activities to girls over 13. Girl prostitutes like Dinah (13) and Agnes (15), who were repatriated to Kwale District in 1943, should have been arraigned as adults before a regular (magistrate) court for breaking anti-prostitution law since they were legally adults.[7] So why, then, did the CWO repatriate these girls and not prosecute them? One straightforward answer is that the CWO believed that all females under the age of 16 were intellectually or emotionally too immature to consent to sexual intercourse and that all forms of sexual relations (whether under a properly consummated marriage or the disgraceful prostitution) was a sex crime against minors. The term "child marriage" was literally and intrinsically defined by the CWO as marriage involving a girl under 16 years of age. Faulkner and Izzett believed that psychological maturity comes much later than physiological maturity. Hence, the fact that a girl appeared physiologically mature at 13 did not mean that she was psychologically capable of giving sexual consent.

When girls could not tell their own ages, the CWO relied on the attainment of puberty and medical screening. But this method had its own limitations: nutrition and genetic variation could delay physio-sexual development. This implies that an 18-year-old girl could have been inaccurately categorized as a child by the CWO. Traveling to the provinces from where most of the girls were trafficked and interviewing parents and guardians who, in the absence of formal birth records, could use established traditional methods of dating would have been the most authentic manner of establishing ages of the girls. But this procedure would have certainly delayed or undermined the effectiveness of the CWO's propaganda. In addition, procurers and some girl prostitutes lied about their place of origin in order to frustrate criminal prosecution for child trafficking.

The application of the age-of-consent law in prosecuting sex crime produced a host of complications, not because the law was not explicit enough but because of the difficulty of determining the exact ages of girls. On July 30, 1938, William Nugojobo was arraigned at Ebute Metta Police Magistrate Court "before an enormous crowd of expectant onlookers" for abducting an underage girl named Rebecca Ayenidejo. Although the medical report ordered for the case revealed that Rebecca was 17 years old, the presiding judge strongly contended that "there was no definite proof of the girl's age." Neither Rebecca nor her guardian, Johnson Eguakun, who worked with the prison service, knew her exact age. Nugojobo would have been guilty of sex crime if the police prosecutor could prove beyond doubt that Rebecca was under 13. Instead of relying on age in dismissing the case, the magistrate relied on Rebecca's physical appearance and her own testimony that William "was not the first husband she had ever lived with." This case is similar to that of Madam Folly, who was accused of prostituting Tunu to European seamen. The police prosecution invoked section 222A of the criminal code, which punished "unlawful carnal knowledge" of an underage girl (under 13). But Tunu testified that she was 16, not 12 as claimed by the police, and that she had been "seeing men" before following Madam Folly to Lagos in 1940. The case was subsequently dismissed.[8] If these two cases reveal anything, it is that the law and science alone could not proffer answers to the complex question of age, especially in determining criminal liability. The social interpretation—the circumstances and character of the individuals involved—seemed to override the legal one.

However, it was outside the courtroom that the controversy over age produced the greatest impact. Although Faulkner was confident that it would be easy to implement a township law that banned hawking by girls under 14—because it exposed them to prostitution and sexual exploitation—Lagosians queried the arrest of girls over this age. Even Faulkner's superiors, like Commissioner of the Colony J. G. C. Allen, doubted the exact ages of girls arrested when he asserted that "in this country age is always a doubtful quantity."[9] Yet, the terms "grown-up" and "little girls" deployed as markers of maturity or vulnerability are ill-defined and vague. As complicated as the question of age was, both Lagosians and the CWO believed that girls under 16 qualified to be categorized as a "child" or "underage" and deserved state paternalism through the institutionalized welfare system. In broader terms, what seems more important was not the age of a girl per se but the relationship between her and other members of the prostitution subculture. As a general rule, the CWO and the Lagosian elites believed that all girls found in brothels or in the company of known prostitutes or *boma* boys, and caught up in other forms of sexual exploitation, required state protection.

Table 3.1. Social Welfare Office Case Data on Juvenile Delinquency, 1944

Cases	Number of Victims	Remarks
Raped	1	—
Unlawfully carnally known	2	One of them, age 5, had venereal disease
Child prostitutes	34	Formally in custody of adult prostitutes
Runaways from maltreatment by guardian	13	Nine of them had venereal disease
Beyond parental control	3	One of them, age 13, had venereal disease
Girls in moral danger	2	One of them, age 13, was found to be pregnant
Girl hawkers	1	One of them, age 11, was found not to be a virgin

Source: NAI, COMCOL 1, 2600 vol. 2, "Social Welfare, General Questions, Establishment of Social Welfare Department," 1942–45.

Becoming a Child Prostitute

One of the earliest recognized "gateways" to child prostitution was hawking, or street vending that relies on the seller's calling out. A traditional aspect of raising children, it provided a means of helping to support the household and to pass skills from generation to generation. Hawking was central to the domestic economy in both precolonial and colonial times as it was one of the means of distributing items across and within communities. Although men and women, as well as boys and girls, engaged in hawking, the practice from early on was feminized probably because women monopolized the domestic markets and distribution system.[10] As with most economic activities, the establishment of colonial rule over Lagos did not put an end to hawking. By the 1920s or earlier, hawking would receive administrative attention. Sylvia Leith-Ross, a colonial officer and anthropologist, famous for her book on Igbo women, remarked in her memoir that the file labeled "child hawkers" was "growing heavier day by day . . . It was one I was to see again and again all down the long years, its rival in size, labeled 'Disposal of Nightsoil.'"[11] Hawkers were accused of depriving the government of income accruing from the allocation of stalls or market space since they did not require a permit to sell their wares. They were also blamed for traffic congestion. Some commentators argued against hawking from the point of view of sanitation and health, claiming that the foods the children hawked were unhygienic.[12]

But for moralists like the Lagos Women's League (LWL), the danger of hawking included sexual exploitation. In a 1926 petition, the women asked the government to prohibit hawking by girls under 16 in order to check the immorality they were exposed to on a daily basis.[13] Four years later, an editorial in the *Nigerian Daily Times* lamented "the long standing problem of the girl-hawkers who have become such hopeless prey to traffickers in prostitution."[14] Throughout the 1930s, Lagos newspapers continued to publish stories and letters written by "concerned" citizens about hawking, the escalating menace of child prostitution, and girl-child delinquency in general.[15] In September and October 1935 in the pages of the *Comet*, published by Duse Mohammed Ali, a frontline Egyptian Pan-Africanist who adopted Nigeria as his home, there appeared under such headlines as "Save the Future Mothers" and "Girl Hawkers Morals" reports and polemics that added a new tone to the existing anxiety over the security of underage girls. They noted that not all the girl hawkers were innocently lured into prostitution—some acted independently, selling their bodies but disguising as vendors.[16]

This blurred boundary between coercion and consent did not attract much debate, even though it contravened the dominant notion of girlhood innocence and passivity. However, attempts to "ethnicize" or "religionize" sexual vice and suggestions for stemming its tide divided the moralists. When Sodigi, one of the commentators, stated that "hawking prostitution" was rampant among Muslim girls, another, Kabiboy, immediately gave a rebuttal: "The morals of our Mohammedan girls are not worse than the morals of our Christian girls."[17] While not exonerating Muslim girls from the moral degeneration of the era, Kabiboy asserted that "if Sogidi can get twenty virgins out of every hundred Christian girls, he had scored a very high number—in fact it is impossible."[18] Another contributor (C. O. O.) to the debate in the *Comet* who supported Kabiboy, argued: "It had nothing to do with religious belief of any hawker . . . Girl hawkers are of every religious belief and of every tribe."[19] C. O. O. demanded that religion be separated from morality: "The matter must be dealt with from the moral stand point."[20] Kabiboy disagreed with another commentator (a Muslim) and others who called for the criminalization of hawking by looking at the wider implications of such a move: "When hawking is prohibited at Lagos," Kabiboy noted, "we shall not have promoted the morals of our Mohammedan or Christian girls in the least but rather shall have greatly cut off the means of living of many old women who largely depend on the help of their daughters by way of hawking."[21] If these debates reveal anything, it is that moralists were not united about the modus operandi of sexual immorality and the best method for addressing it. It also establishes that the print media was alive to its primary goal of serving as the watchdog of the ills of imperialism and contributed immensely to shaping the public's perception of the moral panic of the era.

The world of the girl hawkers traversed multiple tragedies—in addition to being raped and recruited into the Lagos prostitution network they were regular victims of ritualists and tricksters and some were even murdered. On June 8, 1932, Samuel Wahehe (alias John Loko), who had eight previous convictions, was sentenced to twelve months in jail for using juju (charm) to abduct a

12-year-old yam hawker, Oluremi, whom he planned to sell for rituals for £3.[22] The plight of Mulu, another girl hawker, received front-page coverage in the *West African Pilot* of August 18, 1938. Mulu was accosted by a male currency counterfeiter on Moloney Bridge who gave her a fake 4s. and collected the 3s. 4 ½d. that she made plying the major streets of Lagos Island. Although Mulu did not realize that she received fake currency until she returned home, most girls who found themselves in this awkward but common situation and those who recorded poor sales rarely returned home because of the fear of being punished by their parents or guardians. Instead, they roamed around begging for the rest of the money—a condition that exposed them to sexual advances and violence.[23]

When the colonial government began to take juvenile delinquency seriously from the early 1940s, welfare officers not only relied on the information supplied by the public through the print media but collected their own by actively interviewing girls rescued from their procurers. Whereas most moralists who wrote in the newspapers relied on public observation of the urban subculture for evidence of declining morality, Faulkner and his staff had direct interaction with the victims of prostitution, which allowed them to systematically gather information about hawking prostitution. Moreover, the incidence of hawking prostitution increased as urban poverty soared in the wake of unprecedented immigration from the provinces and the breakdown of public order accentuated by wartime austerity and emergency regulations. In convincing the Lagos Town Council (LTC) to introduce an anti-prostitution law in 1941, Faulkner relied on police reports that affirmed that "from time to time . . . many of the children who are procured for prostitution exist under the guise of hawkers."[24] In one of her reports, Izzett concluded: "Girl hawkers are often sent out late at night to solicit and lead men to adult prostitutes." She approvingly declared that "all my female staff unanimously agreed that girl hawkers are frequently used for prostitution."[25] Other well-acknowledged dangers of street hawking such as rape intensified in the wake of public insecurity. The rape and murder of 10-year-old Badiaran, whose lifeless body was recovered from the Race Course on March 13, 1945, sent a significant shock of grief through the Lagos community.[26] The *West African Pilot* described this homicide as "one of the biggest sensations of the year."[27] Lagosians felt further anguish when the corpse of 11-year-old Olawunmi Olusanya, which showed signs of assault, was recovered from a park called Dig for Victory Garden. She had been sent out the previous day at 8:00 p.m. to hawk a local food called *fufu*.[28] The fact that these murder cases were not resolved made Lagosians aware of the presence of dangerous men hiding under the cover of urban facelessness to perpetrate heinous crimes against defenseless children. Yet, the reported cases likely were only a fraction of the actual incidence of sexual violence against the children of Lagos—we will never know the full extent.

Although public narratives generally regretted the failure of the state to protect its endangered girls, the complex issue at stake bordered on the change and continuity of hawking between the precolonial and colonial periods. Hawking was not an entirely safe practice even in the precolonial setting where communal parenting and stricter observance of moral regulatory codes helped protect girls against assault. Indeed, child hawkers could have been easy prey of kidnappers and even slave raiders.[29] What colonialism did was to increase the degree of danger that hawkers faced. The transformation of Lagos from a backwater small settlement of five thousand inhabitants in 1800 to a quarter million in 1950, and its exalted position as the capital of the colonial state, brought massive transformation to virtually every aspect of the society.[30] The epileptic character of the colonial economy created a cycle of poverty and increased the incorporation of children into the urban workforce as hawkers, movers, and haulers. As the Pax Britannica facilitated massive immigration into Lagos, the city's ethnic heterogeneity that resulted created anonymity, allowing practices that rarely took place in the precolonial setting to flourish. Violence against girls and their recruitment into prostitution through hawking was supported and sustained by urban poverty and the underground subculture of vice, vagrancy, and delinquency. Lagos of the 1930s and 1940s could not guarantee the safety of adults, much less that of children.

Hawking was dangerous, not just because it exposed girls to sexual exploitation, but also because it allowed them to be highly sexualized. The sight of partially naked girls on the major streets of the colonial capital was considered a drawback for a society advancing rapidly on the scale of modernity and a reminder of the "barbarous" living conditions in the remote villages, far from the breath of "civilization." Several critics lamented the sexual assault of girls by men acting under the pretext of buying items from them. After recounting how young men stole from girl hawkers while pretending to be patronizing them, a May 27, 1932, editorial in the *Lagos Daily News* claimed that they "play[ed] indecently with them in the streets as they would with grown-up girls."[31] Street life also corrupted girls by exposing them to "dirty" language, "immoral" music, and "bad" mannerisms. In painting the erotic child, moralists drew a parallel relationship between the girls' economic activities and the urban popular culture that was capable of inducing sexual violence against them.

At a public meeting organized by the Women's Welfare (WWC) Council, R. Timson, one of the speakers, described how *apala* (a popular genre of Yoruba music) corrupted girls: "The very sound of an 'Apala' drum was sufficient to send girls of low morals crazy. Girl hawkers would put down their wares pull their resources and engage drummers in order to dance to the 'Apala' tune. They would then start turning, twisting, rolling and rocking to all forms of disgraceful contortions."[32] *Apala*, according to her, was "opposed to the pristine delicacy and grace associated with womanhood."[33] She went on to recommend the banning of the "curious" and "shameful" dance, calling it "a curse on the people."[34] Another critic made a connection between vulgarity, illicit sexuality, and the escalating incidence of VD: "How many a time are not passers-by outraged with the handling, the indecent and obscene languages they [girl hawkers] utter? How will not the morals of the community be tainted and corrupted? Is it in this way that the serious allegations of Government and private medical practitioners about the prevalence of diseases will be remedied?"[35]

While hawking prostitution attracted moralists' attention from the early 1920s, it was in the early 1940s that Lagos authorities (the CWO in particular) began to draw correlations between prostitution and betrothal. While the dangers of rape and the murder of hawkers were publicly visible to Lagosians and to Faulkner and his staff, betrothed girls prostituted in brothels were hidden from their "supervisory eyes."[36] In precolonial and colonial times, betrothal served as a tool for fostering inter- and intra-ethnic friendship. It involved elaborate rituals and ceremonies that were not only procedural but lasted for years until the final marriage ceremony was conducted.[37] Marriage payments (mostly in agricultural products and cattle) and services were entirely symbolic and representative of the spiritual approval of the gods and goddesses. However, the cash economy introduced through colonialism significantly transformed traditional marriage practices—not only in Nigeria but in most parts of Africa—as marriage payments had to be made in cash.[38] The new era of this "commercialization of marriage" compelled some young men to leave for the city or mines—or to pawn themselves to the elites, as Olatunji Ojo has shown in the case of the Ekiti region of Yorubaland—to raise marriage payments, which could vary from £50 to £300 during the 1930s and 1940s.[39] The commercialization of marriage not only delayed marriage—some potential grooms worked for ten years or more to raise money—but created tensions between the junior men (young urban workers) and the senior men (rural patriarchs) who were accused of "bride-price racketeering."[40]

By the late 1930s, some urban men discovered they could circumvent the marriage rituals and marry "cheaply" by "proxy"—sending money to the village and having family members or friends bring new "wives" to town.[41] However, as cases II and IV in table 3.2 show, traffickers capitalized on proxy marriage by posing to help secure husbands for young girls in Lagos. Social welfare reports of the early 1940s indicate that parents and guardians were giving their daughters in marriage to men they had never met after collecting lump sums of money as bride-price. The untraditional manner in which proxy marriages were conducted made differentiating between men who married "genuinely" by proxy because they could not raise the marriage payment and those whose motive was sexual exploitation difficult to establish. Moreover, most of these men were in low-paying jobs and had little or no public agency.

Table 3.2. Sample of Betrothal Cases

Case No.	Description
I	"There lives in a one-roomed house in the corner of my compound a man with 2 wives. One wife is an adult woman, the other a child of between 11–13 years of age, in the pre-pubertal stage of development. The man states that his marriage to the girl will be consummated in 4 years time, and that, until then, she is undergoing training. Having already paid £8 as dowry, he will pay a further £7 when she actually becomes his wife."
II	"A woman of notorious character was found harbouring a girl of 15 in circumstances strongly suggestive of prostitution. The girl was said to be the wife of her brother and £13 was said to have been paid as dowry. Repeated requests to see the alleged husband produced no result although ample time was given. As the woman raised no objection to the repatriation of the girl, and in fact arranged and paid for it herself, it was assumed that the foregoing story was untrue."
III	"A well-known boma boy heard of the death of his uncle and, remembering that there was a young girl left fatherless, went to the home and persuaded the girl to come to Lagos on the promise that there was a husband waiting for her. She was brought to Lagos, kept in close confinement and prostituted to European sailors. Eventually, she escaped from the man and reported to the police."
IV	"A woman of known bad character went to the Urhobo country and so she says paid £10 dowry for a girl to be the wife of a soldier in Lagos. The girl was found living in the woman's house. She proved to be about 12 years of age, with little pubertal development. A soldier appeared and corroborated the woman's story."

Source: NAI, COMCOL 1, 2844, "Child Welfare—Prostitution and Child Marriage," May 1943.

In October 1943, Ayekumeh Izebuno of Fugar in Kukuruku Division sent Osheke home to help him "fetch" a "wife." Ajala, the "child wife" in question, was an orphan who confessed that she had not met Ayekumeh at all and that customary marriage rites had not been carried out. Except for a distant relative who admitted collecting bride-price, no one else in the family or village was aware of the arrangement.[42] Ayekumeh's proxy marriage raised a red flag because he was a steward working for European soldiers. The CWO believed his motive was to prostitute the girl to his European employers.[43]

It would appear that neither parents nor guardians knew the fate of their girls once they were removed from the village. In March 1946 a petitioner from Okitipupa Division pleaded with the CWO to help him return his daughter who was betrothed to an office clerk in 1945 but was sighted working as a prostitute in Porto Novo Market Street, one of the busiest red-light districts in Lagos. The following month Ogbo Abuyola from the same community wrote a petition to the CWO asking "if the order was gave to Madam Ogudu, 41 Taiwo street Lagos to trade with girls."[44] She claimed Madam Ogudu frequently came to her area to "pack all the girls to Lagos" and that one of them "died of sickness" after being repatriated.[45] Yet in some places, fictitious betrothals followed a well-established pattern—encouraged and supported by the parents and the entire community. After enumerating his approaches for preventing marriage by proxy, the district officer of Kukuruku Division promised the CWO that he would not allow girls to be taken to Lagos, but added the phrase "if I can help it," which suggests that the situation was beyond his control. He continued: "I am getting them to take the attitude that if the marriage is genuine, the intending husband must come and marry the girl in her own native village in front of all." He then stated the plausible next line of action he could not stop: "If she and her parents then consent for her to go to Lagos with him that is purely their affair. If the case is genuine this can always be managed."[46]

The danger girls faced went beyond fictitious marriage. Cases of child stealing and "wife" abduction had huge implications for the welfare of the underaged because an "unapproved" or "illegal" union was highly susceptible to exploitation, which then led to absconding and vulnerability to recruitment into prostitution.[47] On September 13, 1938, Joaqium Okpoko was arraigned for having "unlawfully taken away" Rosa Egbuehe, a girl under age 15, from her guardian.[48] Two months later, another man named Lamina Alabi was bound over for twelve months for abducting Awesetu "without her mother's consent."[49] Similarly, in September 1943 Stella Thomas, West Africa's first female solicitor, who later became a magistrate, sentenced 34-year-old Amos Olu to 6 months in prison or a £25 fine for using juju (charm) to entice Eunice Njoku, a schoolgirl under the age of 16. Amos, a native doctor who was asked to treat the sick Eunice, instead used "voodooism" and "a bogus god called Tanda to win the girl's heart."[50] Most of the abducted girls were moved to a different location within Lagos; however, in some instances, they were moved to other parts of Nigeria or even elsewhere in West Africa. This is true in the particular case of Amudatu Anike, a girl under 16 years of age who was abducted by Jibo Amusu and trafficked into neighboring Dahomey (Benin). Amusu, who was Anike's neighbor, abducted her on her way to running an errand for her sick guardian.[51] It would appear that not all cases of wife-abduction were initiated by men. In May 1943 a Lagos newspaper reported, under the sensational headline "13-Year-Old Hawker Plants Self in Man's Home as His Wife," that "huge fun was created" in Santa Anna Court when Salami Agbaje was arraigned for abducting 13-year-old Memunotu Ashake.[52] In his defense, Agbaje testified that he reported Memunotu—who had absconded from home to escape her parents' cruelty—to the police when he returned from work to find her in his home.

The Child Prostitutes at Work

Child prostitutes shared the same ambience with their adult counterparts. They solicited in the same brothels and popular red-light districts like Market and Taiwo Streets and were occasionally employed as bar attendants in order to bring them close to male customers or reduce the risk (such as of violent crime and theft) of streetwalking. The case of Madam Comfort Abes vividly illuminates the coexistence of adult and child sex work. An undercover police report filed by Lance Corporal E. Ogbe against Madam Abes, who owned the "Holly Wood Bar" located at Harbour Road Apapa, accused her of pimping Raleigh, a child prostitute. Lance Corporal Ogbe gave an account of the bar and of the personalities like the *boma* boys who frequented the place. After serving beer to some police on patrol, Madam Abes, who probably knew she was being monitored, reportedly said "there would be no offence that she would commit that would warrant Apapa policemen to take action against her."[53] During Ogbe's short stay, no male customers came for Raleigh, who was helping Abes as a bar attendant. However, Madam Abes frequently went into a room with a "Congo man" named Thomas and returned with money, which she openly displayed, in a manner suggesting that she had just returned from having sexual intercourse. A later police report confirmed that both Madam Abes and Raleigh were prostitutes. The multiple identity of bar owner and prostitute was not unique to Madam Abes. Prostitutes sometimes combined sex work with other activities that either facilitated solicitation or provided extra income.

Another note submitted by two European men who went undercover for the CWO provides better insight into the relationship between adults and child prostitutes. The men moved from one brothel to another taking note of the extent of child prostitution in four different locations. The first location was the Seven Seas Hotel, where they met a woman who had some child prostitutes under her control. In the room provided for the men were two beds, placed on the floor and surrounded by several child prostitutes. On request, they were presented with two child prostitutes aged 14 or 15. The second location was a traveler's inn with 12 girls, ranging in ages from 15 to 24. In a journalistic manner, the researchers wrote: "Two of the youngest girls immediately came forward to sit on men's knees and had obviously been trained how to behave."[54] The men asked for two virgins and the woman in charge promised to make them available the following day. The third location was a house located behind the Seven Seas Hotel. They met a woman of about 30 years of age and asked for a 14-year-old girl prostitute. The woman answered that two young virgins would be available for the following day as they had to be fetched from another location. The last location was the Crystal Garden Club, where they saw numerous adult prostitutes. When the men asked a taxi driver if he would take them to a place where they could get *piccin* (child prostitutes), he answered yes—"and immediately others came forward offering to take us to where we can get small *piccin* as late as twelve midnight."[55] The Europeans submitted: "No man would have any difficulty in being provided with a girl of any age, virgin if desired. The young girls all undressed to show the men their breasts to prove their age. Some of the girls appeared passive: others enjoyed themselves and were evidently used to being given money and cigarettes. The usual price appears to be about 10/- [10s.] and more for a virgin. These places are patronized by European Seamen."[56]

As previously noted, power relations within the prostitution subculture portrayed child prostitutes as docile and hapless victims subject to the whims and caprice of their madams. This aspect of economic and sexual exploitation, among others, distinctively differentiated adult from child prostitutes. Some moralists even believed the girls could die from sexual intercourse that took the form of rape. But child prostitutes' own testimony of sexual violence, more than that of the moralists, gives real-life examples of the unequal power dynamics within the prostitution subculture. After recounting how Madam Alice Etovbodia lured her from her parents under the guise of apprenticeship and prostituted her to European seamen, Rose Ojenughe, a child prostitute, requested, "I do not claim for all the pounds that I have foolishly worked for her. I want £10 only from her and the three pounds [as] my virgin fee all £13.0.0d."[57] The last two sentences of her long petition show she was conscious of her identity and rights: "Please sir, ask me and I will tell you how I, a little girl like this will be force[d] to keep three oversea soldiers at a time . . . I am not a slave sir, I cannot go home without my money."[58] Rose had previously been repatriated and reunited with her mother in Okitipupa Division but returned to Lagos disguised as the wife of an office clerk in order to recover her money from her formal madam by enlisting the sympathy of the CWO.[59] Rose's was not, by any means, an isolated case. Child prostitutes after being repatriated often returned to Lagos under different names to continue to work as prostitutes.[60]

Like forms of legitimate vocational training, child prostitution introduced girls to various aspects of the trade procedurally. During the interwar years madams did allow child prostitutes to solicit along with them. However, the massive police crackdown on prostitution from the 1940s forced them to keep prostitutes in the brothels, disguise them as domestic helpers, and rely on taxi drivers and *boma* boys to bring prospective customers. There is limited information about when child prostitutes "graduated" or received their freedom. Available information such as this comment by Faulkner made a link between age, income, and the changing identity of prostitutes: "At first, being fresh and virginal she [the child prostitute] fetches a good price but gradually she ages, venereal disease leaves its mark and she becomes the hardened harlot, who in a few years will be bringing young girls herself to Lagos."[61]

There is more to the economic and sexual exploitation of children than the preceding analyses suggest. During the early 1940s, both colonial and African moralists gave wide publicity to the established myth that sex with virgins or underage girls was capable of helping to cure VD.[62] In 1944 Dr. A. B. I. Olorun-nimbe, a University of Glasgow–trained physician who would later become the first mayor of Lagos, opined thus: "Let that erroneous idea that

Table 3.3. Girls' Hostel Cases, 1945–46

Case Description	1946 (no.)	Remark
Hawkers	10	"Where enquiry shows unsuitable home condition"
Lost children	40	"Children who run away from their homes, parents, or guardians, through ill-treatment. With one exception these have all been Yorubas, and have frequently been interfered with by men"
Rescued from prostitution	82	
Prostitutes	42	"Cases definitely known to be prostituted by adults; or girls of 14–17 who have their own rooms and live entirely by prostitution"
Moral danger	40	"Girls found in Brothels who have not yet been used for prostitution; girls living a promiscuous life; children with guardians not exercising proper control so that the children are no longer virgin though about 10 years of age"
Beyond parental control	15	"Usually on sexual grounds"
Absconding from husbands	5	"Young girls who have been forced into marriage at a very early age"
Criminal offenses against girls	9	Seduction, rape, abduction, indecent assault, etc.
Mentally deranged	1	
Theft, assaults	4	Court cases
Detention	17	"Suspected prostitutes sometimes en route for Gold Coast"

Source: NAI, COMCOL 1, 2600, "Social Welfare: General Questions; Establishment of Welfare Department."

to cure gonorrhea, a man must have relations with a girl under 14 be abolished immediately."[63] Two years later, in 1946, Izzett expressed that the proposition was common among the Igbo: "There is a belief, common among men of the Eastern Provinces, that men can be cured of venereal disease by sexual intercourse with a virgin."[64] Statistics collected by the CWO are in tandem with the prevailing myth. As table 3.4 further illuminates, the CWO reported that 68 girls with ages ranging from 3 to 15 were treated for VD. Child prostitution reached its peak in the World War II years when anxiety over VD among European military officers and seamen as well as African soldiers reached an all-time high.[65] Coincidentally, demand for child prostitutes was higher among these demographic groups, which probably preferred child prostitutes to adults because the former were easier to exploit, economically and sexually, than the latter. Because the CWO and the moralists were mostly concerned with girl-child delinquency, and not the sexual waywardness of their male clients, it is difficult to account for clients' motivation beyond the conventional explanation of sexual desire. Some male patrons of child prostitutes could have been pedophiles.

Table 3.4. Incidence of Venereal Disease among the Girls in Moral Danger

Cases	Number of Victims	Ages
Seduced	46	3–11
Treated for venereal disease	21	3–11
Criminally assaulted	46	3–11
Seduced	59	11–15
Treated for venereal disease	47	11–15

Source: "Mr. Faulkner Lectures on Social Welfare and Its Relations to Church," *Daily Service,* November 21, 1944.

Racial Science, Cultural Backwardness, and Environmental Determinism

Although moralists of all stripes, regardless of social class, race, and affiliation, agreed that the sexual exploitation of girls was a crime that must be halted, they did not agree on the motivation and methods for ameliorating it. Some Lagosians, such as Major Akinwande Jones (Salvation Army), Charlotte Obasa (LWL), Oyinkan Abayomi (Nigerian Women's Party, or NWP), and H. Millicent Douglas (WWC), believed that hawking and betrothal were not entirely bad practices, and that it was the very nature of the colonial economy and the realities of urban living that exposed girls to danger. The educationist Dr. Henry Carr advocated for the "adjustment" of education policy to focus more strongly on girls' education.[66] Although the positions held by Lagosians changed over time and were often contradictory—for instance, the stance of elite women shifted from prohibition to regulation of hawking between the 1920s and 1946—they were consistent about a long-term proposal of structural changes that centered on increased colonial investment in public education, implementation of policies to empower women, and reduction of urban poverty. Immediate goals included effective policing of red-light districts and removal of girls from the brothels for rehabilitation and reuniting with their "legitimate" guardians or parents. Although Lagos was a modernizing society where contrasting ideas of modernity and tradition mirrored the diverse social and education statuses of its residents, most Lagosians did not support the criminalization of native marriage or betrothal.

The colonialists' proposed solution targeted crime and public insecurity, where the immediate impact of prostitution and delinquency was felt the most. Theirs was not a systemic proposal that involved increasing girls' access to education and empowering families to be able to better care for them. This is not surprising—the colonial state was not a welfarist one. The CWO believed strongly in the power of the criminal justice system to solve the problems of delinquency and attempted to transform cultural practices that were suppos-edly facilitating the exploitation of children. For instance, Faulkner made little exception for altruistic guardianship, but placed more emphasis on sexual exploitation when he declared: "There are few people so charitable that they will go hundreds of miles to bring a girl to Lagos to give her free training of the right sort. It is obvious to us, but perhaps not to the parents, that such people's only interest is in the sex of the girl."[67] After living in Lagos for about two years, Faulkner would confidently remark in 1943 that "there are no husbands for provincial girls in Lagos" and that men who wanted to marry "legitimately" tended to go to the provinces, perform the required traditional rites, and bring their new brides to Lagos.[68] Men, he believed, tended to maltreat wives mar-ried by proxy because they paid a high bride-price and did not undergo the required traditional rite. When child wives were maltreated, they ran away and, with time, were coerced by adults into prostitution. He often used such terminology as "child wives" and "child marriage" to redefine girlhood and delegitimize sex and marriage for girls under 16.

Aside from suggesting that betrothal be criminalized, Faulkner and Izzett insisted that the age of consent be raised from 13 to 16 in order to give legal protection to girlhood sexuality. They were also convinced that their proposal would extend childhood and enhance the physical maturity needed to resist unwanted intercourse. Meanwhile, protecting girls went beyond extending childhood and seeking legal protection. It also involved inquiry into psycho-sexual development and comparative racial science. Nigerian girls, according to Faulkner in a 1942 report, might mature at an earlier age than their European counterparts but "it is a fallacy that they are generally speaking, developed for child-bearing at the age of 13."[69] Later in 1946 Izzett would contradict her boss: "In fact, the average English working-class girl matures much earlier than these girls." But the two welfare officers both seemed to agree that African girls' early attainment of adolescence did not translate into an ability to make consensual decisions about sex and marriage and that European girls were more intelligent than African girls of the same age. W. W. Llewellin, a British administrator who visited Nigeria in 1951 to conduct a supervisory survey of the progress of the CWO, reconciled the relationship between childhood, sexual maturity, and intelligence: "Those with long experience of West Africans agree that adolescence starts at an earlier age than amongst Europeans, but they also agree that adolescence on the physical side is a longer process and that Africans are not fully mature intellectually until they are around 21."[70] It is interesting to see how the idea of intellectual inferiority, one of the core components of racial prejudice, was extended to the "science" of girlhood sexuality.

Faulkner concluded one of his most comprehensive reports, titled "Child Welfare: Prostitution and Child Marriage," by urging his superiors to treat child prostitution like cannibalism, ritual murder, and the domestic slave trade—all of which had attracted strong administrative attention from the nineteenth century. Like most colonial administrators, he often demonstrated his ignorance of African customs. Not only did he think that marriage under native law did not require a formal ceremony; he also held that hawking was not a Yoruba custom but "has evolved under the peculiar circumstances of life and trade in a metropolitan area."[71] In another report he claimed that the "Yoruba people are rather averse to bringing up their own children" because of the fear of "spoiling" them.[72] These comments, among several others, pointedly show the disconnection between the colonialist's explanations of social problems and the realities at stake. Apparently he had limited genuine knowledge of the culture of the peoples he was working with.

Unlike in Europe where a comprehensive science of childhood was introduced to deal with social vice, the CWO gave Nigeria crude British-styled scientific methods of identifying social aberration but placed heavy blame on African marriage customs and the morally corrosive effects of the city for socio-sexual pathology.[73] What seems "scientific" or modern about the activities of the CWO was an environment-centered explanation of delinquency; the realization of delinquency as a problem that must be tackled in childhood and be properly documented; and the introduction of child- and juvenile-specific laws, hostels, reformatories, and juvenile courts. Three plausible reasons explain why the British did not adopt comprehensive scientific methods of addressing child delinquency.

First, the paucity of trained personnel and the underdevelopment of colonial science left limited room for assessing vice from a holistic point of view, although the CWO did not explicitly state this as the reason for its African-centered interpretation of vice. Over the years 1941–46 Faulkner was primarily responsible for producing nearly all the policy-driven reports for a city of 150,000-plus inhabitants. Second, although the CWO attempted to deal with each case of child prostitution independent of the rest, blaming individual girls for deviance would not earn the desired public and institutional attention as much as blaming indigenous marriage customs as a whole. Third, it would have contradicted racial otherness and pathology, which was central to the idea of Africa's racial inferiority. The African root of delinquency satisfied the colonialists' well-entrenched assumption that Nigerians needed Western civilization to advance on the ladder of modernity. While the practice of blaming the slow pace of their civilization on remnants of "backward" customs dates back to the nineteenth century, the 1940s witnessed the indexing of child prostitution as one of those numerous problems accentuated by cultural savagery.

I am not suggesting that Western scientific explanations of sexual deviance can fully decode or should be used to examine the African situation—indeed, the attempt to use science to explain Africa's biological, morphological, and physiological distinctiveness from the nineteenth century produced devastating racist conclusions. Rather, I contend that in order to sustain the established notion of Africa's otherness, European models, institutions, and practices associated with modernity and progress were selectively deployed in Africa. Traits of Western-style scientific conclusions, whenever introduced, were used to justify the supposed inferiority of African girls to their European counterparts. It would appear that the familiar rhetoric of African cultural backwardness sounded more appropriate in explaining the problems confronting the people of the "dark continent" than sophisticated scientific theories of human behavior, which the British believed were only applicable to their advanced and "civilized" race. By neglecting other plausible causes of socio-sexual deviance in favor of the alleged cultural backwardness of Africans, the CWO justified anew colonial domination during the 1940s, when the momentum of nationalism and anticolonial sentiments was reaching new heights. As it turned out, the debate over girlhood sexuality presented critics of African culture another opportunity to register their disdain of cultural backwardness and to further legitimize imperialism.

Conclusion

This chapter has examined the moral panic over underage prostitution as a significant site of state paternalism and the modernization of childhood welfare. For the first time in Nigerian history, the colonialists began to be deeply involved in child-rearing practices relating to girls (heretofore a purely private family matter) in their quest to ameliorate the public disorder and criminal activity facilitated by sex work. Believing that child prostitutes were likely to become adult prostitutes, madams, and girl traffickers, the colonial welfare officers Faulkner and Izzett became convinced that ensuring that girls were rehabilitated was the best and most inexpensive solution to urban vice. In the imaginations of both the CWO and the Lagosian elites, all types of prostitution were immoral, but the fact of child prostitution signified more than moral degeneration. It denoted the failure of the colonial state to protect the sexuality of endangered girls and to combat the criminality of adults who exploited children economically and sexually. Child prostitution was coded as a sex crime against children because girls were presumed to be lured and forced into sexual affairs against their will. Another major consideration of the era was the idea of psychosexual development. At what age was a female intellectually mature enough to consent to sexual intercourse? There was no single or simple answer to this question. In the first place, most Nigerian ethnic groups defined childhood and adulthood not solely in terms of chronological age but relative to the fulfillment of core traditions associated with rites of passage and other aspects of culture. The idea of defining childhood in terms of chronological age was a colonialist import not in consonance with most local cultural practices.

The CWO did not monopolize the rhetoric of sexual endangerment of girls. Before the 1940s, Lagos elites and the press gave wide publicity to the ineptitude of the colonial government in protecting endangered young women. Both African and British agencies attributed sexual danger to environmental and cultural factors—the resilience of old practices like hawking and betrothal that served as a ruse for sex trafficking, amid urban poverty and crime. However, neither could agree on the best methods for dealing with the problem. Lagosians wanted reform that centered on social and economic transformation. The CWO pushed for the complete criminalization of betrothal, "illegal guardianship," and street hawking. This divergence of ideological approaches would take on a vociferous dimension once the government passed child prostitution laws that Lagosians believed were either poorly implemented or negatively impacted the social and economic activities of the entire population. In the following chapter, I adjust the focus of my inquiry to another major site of sexual politics: sexually transmitted diseases.

CHAPTER 4

The Sexual Scourge
of Imperial Order
Race, the Medicalization of Sex,
and Colonial Security

> This may sound like a gospel of despair, but it is the truth. An
> African human nature being what it is, castration is the only
> certain method by which venereal infections can be banished from
> amongst the soldiery. Such practice is hardly practicable: it is true
> that Narses [a sixth-century Roman eunuch and general] provides
> a precedent for it; but the colleague of Belisarius [another Roman
> general] was not one of the African rank-and-file.
> —Senior sanitary officer, 1918[1]

The preceding statement is excerpted from correspondence generated by the
senior sanitary officer (SSO), a military doctor, about the challenges of controlling venereal disease among the African rank-and-file of the Nigerian colonial
army known as the West African Frontier Force (WAFF), later the Royal West
African Frontier Force (RWAFF). The well-entrenched idea among British civil
and military authorities in Nigeria was that VD was inherently and distinctively
an "African-soldier problem." This notion contradicted established knowledge
about soldiery and sexual conduct. Indeed, military prostitution and VD were
major noncombatant threats to military institutions the world over during the
nineteenth and twentieth centuries.[2] The Contagious Diseases Acts (CDAs),
arguably the most repressive VD legislation in modern British history, which
also sparked reactions from feminists worldwide from the 1860s, were aimed
at combating the high incidence of VD in the British army by criminalizing
women believed to be the purveyors of sexually transmitted diseases.[3] I contend
that by treating VD as exclusively a "soldiers' problem," colonial administrators created an Africanized vocabulary of sexual otherness for a problem
that transcended racial, ethnic, and geographical boundaries. African soldiers'

sexuality was judged by the color of their skin, not by the prevailing military culture that openly and tacitly promoted sexual impropriety.

Any critical analysis of VD in the colonial context must recognize the primacy of race and the notion of "civilization" in molding imperial attitudes toward its epidemiology. In theory and reality, VD was a "colorblind" disease—any individual, regardless of race, social class, gender, or ethnicity could contract it. However, in the colonial context, the color of VD was black, as it was construed as both the symptom and the manifestation of African cultural backwardness and primitivity in the rhetoric of the day that featured prominently in Europeans' justification for colonizing the continent.[4] For the imperialists, VD was the visible manifestation of pathological and physiological differences between the "superior" (white) and "inferior" (black) races because, unlike most other ailments, it was associated with immorality, sin, and sexual laxity. Stereotypes of sexual recklessness on the part of women who sold sex and men who paid for it were directly linked to savagery, physiological mutation, and the inability of Africans to develop into sophisticated humans.[5] Although the colonialists occasionally encountered difficulties in justifying the introduction of legislation that exploited Africans or restricted their choices, it was relatively easy for them to establish the need for VD laws on the grounds of sin, immorality, and concerns for the "extinction" of the African race.

The relationship between the construction of VD as a medico-moral ailment and biomedicine was simply that of "problem" and "solution." Indeed, the moralization of sex and pathologization of the African body as the vessel of VD justified colonialists' and missionaries' investment in biomedicine. As an integral arm of imperial order, Western biomedicine supplied the scientific language of cause and effect of VD, paving the way for regimes that policed and criminalized African bodies—particularly females'. From what follows, the interrelatedness of VD and race on the one hand, and Western biomedicine on the other, is an integral component of Africa's experience under colonial rule.[6] It is a history that resonates in many spheres of African engagement with alien rule—from gender, social order, and migration to labor, urbanization, and public health. But to fully comprehend the variegated character of VD in colonial Africa, it is important to stress that it was approached essentially as an issue of political economy. Because VD negatively impacted the health of the colonial subject, its control was significant to the economic prosperity of the colonies.

This chapter engages the medicalization of sex through the prisms of prostitution and VD. It expands the historiography of African military history—which has focused mainly on themes around recruitment of soldiers, military episodes, war generals, security, law and order, and the contributions of ex-servicemen to nationalism—by bringing in perspectives on VD and sexuality.[7] Unlike existing studies on the racialization of sex that concentrate wholly on the civilian population, which focus in particular on the criminalization of the African woman's body as the abode of disease, this chapter broadens the scope of investigation by bringing in perspectives on the military. I argue that in order to fully appreciate the entrenchment of VD in colonial ordering, we need to realize that the colonialists constructed its menace in a class-specific manner. Using a civil-military approach, and straddling the axes of gender, class, and race, I hope to explicate how the British gave separate and unequal attention to VD among soldiers and civilians because they pictured their role or position in the colonial project differently.

If the soldiers were seen as the guardians of the empire, the civilians were perceived as producers and reproducers, whose procreative and economic activities were required for sustaining alien rule and fed imperial capitalism. Although soldiers did have families and children, their primary purpose was to secure the empire. This divergent socio-sexual ordering also informed the approaches adopted for combating VD. Unlike in most parts of Africa where campaigns against VD in the civilian population led to the introduction and institutionalization of venereology from the late nineteenth and early twentieth centuries, in Lagos and Nigeria as a whole, the medical, material, and security implications of VD among the military outweighed concern for the civilian population. This should not be taken to mean that the colonialists did not worry about the impact of VD on civilians; rather, for the obvious military exigency of upholding imperial hegemony, the impact of VD on the army received greater attention.

While sexual recklessness and prostitution were tolerated among the soldiers, their civilian counterparts, in the colonialists' conviction, had to be sexually disciplined in order to be modern or to maximize the gains of imperialism—civilization. Prevailing policies were also coded in the language of difference between the "enlightened" military population composed exclusively of men and the "backward" native population of civilians. All Nigerians were racially backward, in the colonialists' view; however, the rank-and-file military, by virtue of their training and apprenticeship under white officers, were considered to be advancing more rapidly on the ladder of civilization than the teeming population of natives who still clung to their ancient "barbaric" ways.

The Colonial Army and Sexualized Masculinity

Britain had dealt with the problem of VD in its overseas armies in India and Hong Kong before experiencing it in Nigeria. Hence, the British did not have troubles deploying the racially stereotypical terminologies to depict native soldiers as sexual other. Although references to VD in the WAFF date back to the first half of the 1900s, it was only toward the end of World War I that they began to appear in consistent and coherent format. Among the more informative materials is a series of 1918 correspondences involving the following highly ranked civil and military officers: the senior sanitary officer (SSO), the commandant of the WAFF, the director of medical and sanitary services (DMSS), and the chief central secretary.[8] Their writings portrayed the social and sexual conduct of African soldiers, including their psychological disposition to contract VD and institutionalized means of controlling it.[9] The DMSS commented that African soldiers considered VD "a trivial matter,"[10] while the SSO believed they saw it as a "glorifying symbol of tribal life."[11] As the introductory epigraph suggests, African soldiers were perceived as stubborn, undisciplined, and sexually unrestrained. The prevailing debate went beyond the notion of sexual laxity to question the religious standing of the predominantly Hausa-Fulani Muslim soldiers: "Most of them are Mohammedans—at least, they profess Islam, after a fashion; few or no Mohammedans will consent to keep their genuine wives in such a state of publicity as residence in barracks involves; their women are, consequently, well high universally, ammunition wives [prostitutes], the rule of whose lives is promiscuity."[12]

Racialization of African sexuality was just one of the numerous elements of prejudice in the colonial army—itself one of the strongholds of colonial racism. The African rank-and-file faced discrimination in promotion, remuneration, and enforcement of discipline.[13] The highest position they could aspire to was battalion sergeant-major, and they were paid far less than their white counterparts.[14] Besides, they were required to stand at attention to British soldiers (regardless of rank), salute all white civilians, and march barefooted unless on the battlefield.[15] While corporal punishment was inflicted on African soldiers, their white counterparts escaped sanctions for such common offenses as drunkenness and were not punished for contracting VD.[16] No African received a commission as an officer until 1948, when Lieutenant L. V. Ugboma was commissioned.[17] This meant that between 1863, when the WAFF came into existence, and 1948, Nigerian soldiers did not occupy important positions of military authority.

How was VD controlled in the force? This question is best illustrated by first noting that the military was considered to be a separate edifice from the entire colonial structure. Although it was funded by the resources generated by the civilians, it had a chain of command that allowed it to take significant decisions with little or no directive from civil administrators in Nigeria. The anti-VD campaign in the WAFF was rooted in the long history of the British imperial army. Hence, templates existed for such biomedical undertakings. Nevertheless, military authorities, some of whom were also physicians, were flexible enough to make recommendations and adopt procedures in accordance with circumstances unique to Nigeria. In other words, although the imperial army had its own peculiar manner of dealing with VD, decisions taken were mostly influenced by circumstances obtainable in each imperial site. The 1920s afforded military doctors the opportunity to experiment with new policies as they abandoned practices that had failed in other imperial sites or had become anachronistic to the imperial military culture of the era.

Administrators deliberated on two approaches: demanding sexual responsibility from the soldiers or promoting a family-centered military culture.[18] The former entailed policing prostitutes accused of giving soldiers VD, punishing those soldiers who contracted the disease but concealed it, and detecting concealment by enforcing the monthly examination of penises, known in military culture as "cock-pulling."[19] The family-centered approach involved encouraging single, unmarried soldiers to get married and building family-friendly infrastructure on the military bases.[20] The SSO, who sponsored this proposal, recognized that the barracks were not a family-friendly environment, and affirmed that more soldiers would get married if two- or three-bedroom flats were built for them. "We cannot enforce sexual discipline," the SSO noted, "in a situation where most men share rooms."[21] He offered this "predictable" outcome of such arrangements to encourage marriage: reduction of multiple sexual liaisons and thus lower chances of contracting VD.[22] The SSO was not proposing an entirely new scheme—women and children of soldiers had always lived on the military bases. He was only calling for official recognition and financial commitment to marriage and family-centered living arrangements in the barracks.

The SSO simplified soldiers' patterns of sexual behavior by assuming that marriage would automatically stop soldiers from visiting prostitutes and thus decrease the risk of contracting VD. In addition, he did not acknowledge sexual diversity; instead, he upheld prevailing heteronormativity. While not all soldiers were heterosexual, there were very few documented cases of homosexual behavior. In a 1921 report on discipline and compliance authorities recorded that two soldiers were dismissed for "sodomy . . . They were seen penetrating each other."[23] Military and civil records are generally silent about homoeroticism. But this is not surprising. Sex, whether constructed as "natural" or "unnatural," became an administrative issue and thus documented only when performed under circumstances or at a frequency that contravened Eurocentric fixations on normative sexuality or that threatened the established order of moral decency. Soldiers' so-called reckless sexuality came under the moralists' lens because it increased their risk of contracting VD and becoming ill, thus undermining the productivity of an institution cardinal to the sustenance of imperialism.

Figure 4.1. Soldiers of the West African Frontier Force. Reproduced by courtesy of the National Archives Ibadan.

Be that as it may, the "family-friendly" barracks proposal endorsed marriage and a more homebound lifestyle for soldiers. However, this seemed contradictory because African soldiers until the late 1940s were not expected to have strong family attachments or responsibilities that could militate against their productivity and geographical mobility. In disagreeing with the SSO's proposal, the commandant of the Lagos Island unit asserted that "a good African soldier cannot be a good family man."[24] He thought building family-friendly barracks would increase the cost of keeping the WAFF. For him, the government's benevolence of "rescuing men from the wilderness of tribal life" by enlisting them in the army should not be overstretched.[25]

Eventually, the SSO's recommendation was shelved.[26] Authorities finally settled on the first model—demanding sexual responsibility from soldiers—which hinged on their conviction that VD and prostitution were ineradicable in the WAFF.[27] Consequently, soldiers were required to report early symptoms of gonorrhea and syphilis promptly in order to nip in the bud the spread of the diseases and thus reduce the cost of treatment and sickbed leave.[28] Monthly cock-pulling was enforced to detect concealment, while a fine of 6d. per day was imposed on soldiers who could not work due to VD-related illness. But soldiers who voluntarily reported early symptoms received pay while on a sickbed. Base commandants were given discretionary power to implement "any method deemed appropriate."[29] In 1920 the commandant of Apapa barracks set aside enforcing the "no work no pay" policy and instead flogged soldiers found in violation.[30] Cock-pulling and "no work no pay" were not popular among all administrators. The chief central secretary believed the cock-pulling procedure was more "disgusting even than the term."[31] He contended that the fine of 6d. per day imposed on soldiers was not enough to deter them "from answering the call of nature" because African soldiers "have not been trained to self-restraint."[32] In 1925 a more medically assertive step was taken: early-treatment centers were opened in all Lagos barracks. Prior to this period, soldiers who had VD were referred to the government hospital for Africans on Lagos Island. In addition, free treatment was offered to encourage soldiers to seek prompt care, on the assumption that making them pay for medical expenses incurred in the government hospitals encouraged them to conceal VD and/or patronize the "inefficacious" native/quack alternatives.[33]

Throughout the 1910s up to the early 1940s, authorities treated military prostitution as an inevitable aspect of military culture.[34] They believed that prohibiting it could cause mutiny, criminalize soldiers, and expand the casual sex market beyond the military zones.[35] Moreover, they believed it would be easier to monitor soldiers' movements if prostitution was tolerated rather than completely outlawed.[36] This official policy of tolerating prostitution also benefited prostitutes who were neither screened for VD nor prevented from providing sexual services to the military. In summary, during the interwar years, the prevailing approach was curative rather than preventive. It was also army-centered rather than civilian-centered as authorities tacitly encouraged soldiers' promiscuity.

It was not until the 1940s that military prostitution and VD became a major crisis of imperial security. In response to the outbreak of another global conflict in 1939, the strength of the WAFF would grow from about 14,000 during World War I to 130,000 during World War II.[37] In addition to numerous buildings, which housed the WAFF, Lagos had seven major military bases at Surulere, Apapa, Ikeja, Lagos Island, Ijora, Ikoyi, and Yaba during the war.[38] Because Lagos was the political and administrative capital of the country, the effective defense of the city from external invasion was significant for both Nigeria and the entirety of British West Africa. The early fall of France in June 1940 intensified the panic over the future of imperialism in British West Africa, surrounded as it was by close to a dozen French colonies. To make matters worse, VD infections continued to rise as the strength of the army swelled in response to the war. In 1942 the yearly percentage of new infections was put at 43.2 percent, a figure higher than other common ailments such as malaria.[39] In the same year, the West African Conference of Governors released a report affirming that nearly half of the force was at one time or another rendered unfit for active service on account of VD.[40] The figures for the whole of British

West Africa, as table 4.1 shows, may be higher since they were derived from government hospital statistics. And since infected soldiers tended to seek undocumented non-Western remedies, the cases reported were definitely lower than the actual rate of infection.

Rumors about the connection between VD and heart disease also caused considerable fear. Confirming the popularity of this rumor, Colonel Bingham (assistant director of medical services—military) reported that the assumption that the African type of gonorrhea was more deadly than its Western type because it caused "a cold in the heart" should not be discarded by medical authorities.[41] He also decried the financial strain resulting from venereal disease, lamenting that it cost the military £125 to purchase M & B 693, a gonorrhea medicine, for the month of May 1941 alone. In July of the same year, the total cost of treating VD was put at £1,760.[42] It soon dawned on both civil and military authorities that Britain could not win the war if its troops were not physically and medically fit. Fighting VD suddenly became an integral part of the Win-the-War efforts and strategies.

Authorities were compelled to revisit old (peacetime) policies and deliberate on new ones.[43] Cock-pulling was discontinued because it conflicted with troops' assignments. Military prostitution continued to be tolerated in order to keep the soldiers on the base, while sick soldiers who reported early symptoms received free treatment. A host of highly unpopular suggestions and anticolonial ideas surfaced and prompted vociferous debates. For instance, Financial Secretary G. F. T. Colby argued that sick soldiers, not the government, should offset medical bills since Lagosians did not receive free treatment from government. Bingham expressed unpopular ideas about the impact of colonialism on Africans.[44] He decried the contradictory approaches adopted for combating VD and ameliorating the impact of STDs on the civilian population: "I feel that our policy with regard to V.D. is almost entirely negative . . . The present policy can only lead to wastage of manpower and clogging of medical service in the event of active operations . . . *In addition, we will have to face the distressing fact that we will leave Nigeria worse than we found it as regards Venereal Disease.* Personally, I can see no difference in principle from a moral

Table 4.1. Venereal Disease among African Troops

Colony	Average Monthly Percentage with Fresh Infection	Average Yearly Percentage with Fresh Infection
Nigeria	3.6	43.2
Gold Coast	3.25	39.0
Sierra Leone	2.9	34.8
The Gambia	1.7	20.4

Source: NAI, MH (Fed) 1/1 5021 (Confidential), "West African Governors' Conference," March 1942.

point of view between the issue of E.T. Packets [which contained condoms] and the establishment of supervision over harlots."[45]

The proposal for the establishment of "controlled" (variously called "legalized," "unofficial," and "soldier-only") brothels also divided military and civilian authorities. Military authorities believed that "controlled" brothels, in vogue in parts of Europe, Asia, and the Middle East, where soldiers could patronize VD-screened prostitutes, would promote safe sex and reduce the cost of VD treatment. For Attorney General G. L. Howl, who had a better understanding of colonial bureaucracy and Africans' response to imperial policies, the idea of "controlled" brothels would foster a bad image for Britain's "civilizing" mission in Nigeria because it would implicate administrators as proponents of immorality—given the fact that it was a controversial means of dealing with VD even in "civilized" nations of the world.[46] Howl was writing against the backdrop of the global fight against forced prostitution, also known as the "white slave traffic," and of Nigeria's policy of not officially recognizing brothels in order not to be accused of promoting trafficking in women and girls.[47]

Civilians and Racialized Sexuality

It was among the civilians, rather than the military, that the medicalization of VD and its consequences for racial ordering manifested most. The civilians represented the "real" natives—individuals and groups that required civilization in order to move up the ladder of progress and modernity. Indeed, the colonialists were not in Nigeria purposely to create armies; rather, they came primarily for the natives, the so-called barbarians whose labor and resources were required for maximizing the economic motives of imperialism. The army was only a child of necessity—an institution erected for upholding imperial hegemony. The British designed the army as a citadel of state paternalism. European officers were expected to, and did, behave like "fathers" to the African soldiers whom they thought to be capable of being civilized, disciplined, and loyal to the empire. Colonial paternalism therefore took stronger root in the army than among the civilian population. In fact, the idea of the colonial army as a "disciplined" sphere had a major impact on civil-military relations. Soldiers' violence against and impunity vis-à-vis often defenseless civilians was informed almost entirely by the indoctrinated ideology that they were more "civilized" and enlightened than the civilians.[48]

The colonial medics' notion of civilian sexual primitivity was not homogeneous—location, gender, and ethnicity impacted their multitudinous writings, thoughts, and actions. It was also not static; it kept changing in accordance with time, audience, and the politics of relevance between and among various arms of the colonial establishment. In terms of location, contradictory expositions about the difference between urban and rural sexualities swayed anti-VD campaigns. On the one hand, the sexuality of Lagosians was framed as faceless and reckless, while that of rural natives received the derogatory compliment of being "pure," "traditional," and "close to nature." When VD assumed epidemic proportions in the rural communities, the medics blamed it on urbanites, polygamy, and their preference for native medicine over "efficacious" Western therapies. Although Lagos's urban environment was modern, its sexuality was still treated as "primitive" in that it bred untamed sexual liaisons of myriad types. Generally, all Nigerians, regardless of location, were considered promiscuous in the medics' gaze. Genderwise, although both men and women were considered sexually reckless, women were viewed as more sexually dangerous than men because of the reinforcing stereotypes of being "female" and being "black."

The incidence of VD among the civilians was computed in annual returns of the medical department from the early years of the twentieth century. In 1919 the first comprehensive body of reports appeared. This new interest in documenting VD among civilians, like several other issues in the British Empire, was initiated by the Colonial Office. On November 18, 1919, the Colonial Office dispatch inquired from Nigerian Governor Huge Clifford "whether a comprehensive anti-venereal campaign is likely to produce fruitful results and whether you are in favour of the creation of a special department to deal with these diseases."[49] This dispatch demanded detailed information about the prevalence of VD, its impact on Britain's civilizing mission, and the cost of establishing and running VD clinics.[50] The relationship between VD and reproduction seemed to be the main concern of the Colonial Office, which was apparently aware of the long battle to prevent the "extinction" of the African race in East Africa.

The Nigerian government treated this dispatch with the utmost secrecy—the file generated in response to it was marked confidential and access was restricted to European medical and civil officers. One should not be surprised by this. Issues around VD and sexuality were central to the colonial project of modernization, which could aggravate the tense racial relations in the colonial medical service that included some African physicians on its staff.[51] Beyond official secrecy, the dispatch produced unexpected outcomes by repositioning colonial medics as a strong arm of imperialism. Political authorities like the chief secretary to the government did not contest the medics' expertise on VD. For example, in one memorandum he admitted that "it is obvious that I cannot advise the government on the subject until I am acquainted with the views of my colleagues—PMOs [principal medical officers], SSOs, and Medical Officers generally—and put in possession of the facts which they alone can supply."[52] The chief secretary demanded that future correspondence on VD should be addressed directly to his medical counterparts. For their part, the medics did not underestimate their exalted and newly reinforced position. First, being asked to advise the government on matters that appeared important to the British Empire highlighted their elitist role as "saviors" of African sexual primitivity. To be sure, colonial medics, prior to this period, had played a significant role in molding official positions on public health. For instance, they influenced the criminalization of various cultural practices—such as the worship of deities like *sopona* (the Yoruba god of smallpox)—and of native medicine and framed institutional perceptions toward social hygiene and sanitation by supplying the "scientific" evidence that galvanized support for such racist policies as residential segregation.[53] However, the 1919 dispatch added a new "honor" to their established reputation by including "dissident" sexuality in the long list of backward behavior that needed to be tamed. More important, their new task afforded them the opportunity to demand the improvement of the colonial medical service, which for the most part was underserving the natives in both preventive and curative biomedicine.

In their search for the causes of VD prevalence, medics relied not only on the accepted pseudoscience of sexual difference, but also on the people's perceptions. In their view, the lines between sin and shame were blurred because of civilians' normalization of VD and all its medico-moral connotations. Dr. E. E. Maples, a PMO of Lagos, stated that the Yoruba believed that "a man who has not gonorrhea in him does not breed" and a "woman who is not capable of getting gonorrhea is not a breeding woman."[54] Although Dr. Maples, like most of his colleagues, did not state the source of his information about the "permissiveness" and "shamelessness" of Yoruba sexuality, he probably derived this information from the street language of sex, which as one would expect was profane, "modern," and "excessive." During the first half of the twentieth century, unscientific rumors about sexuality and VD were rampant among the people to the point that leading Lagos doctors had to make public pronouncements denouncing such beliefs that sex with underage girls was capable of curing VD.[55] The notion that the Yorubas (like other Nigerians) tolerated sexual excesses is flawed when one considers the wide range of well-documented practices used for regulating sexuality in both precolonial and colonial times.[56] European physicians frequently deplored isolated and purely unscientific evidence of sexual misconduct to reinforce prevailing notions of sexual pathology and the importance of biomedicine as the solution to barbarism.

Although the medics' proposals for combating VD varied widely, they all agreed that prostitution must be prohibited. Their proposals were therefore completely different from the military's. As seen earlier, military doctors wanted regimentation, a system of prostitution regulation to allow soldiers to patronize "clean" and registered prostitutes who would undertake regular VD screening and receive authorization to work within the military base. On the contrary, civil doctors like PMO Dr. W. Best believed that prohibition of prostitution "should be officially accepted as an effective measure for the reduction of Venereal Diseases."[57] The conflicting stances on prostitutes as vectors of VD unveiled the inherent challenges of medicalizing sex—indeed, it was not unusual for medics to change their positions on major issues within a short time frame. For instance, Maples, who had previously commented on the need to police prostitutes, would later remark, "The professional Jekri or Sobo harlot is frequently a 'clean' woman. She is trained in her calling from an early age and knows how to keep herself clean."[58] He believed that non-prostitutes were the main carriers of VD. As unusual as this statement sounded because it did not blame prostitutes for VD, it had a broader implication for gender relations in that it labeled all women as prostitutes. While the idea of the "oversexed" African woman had gained currency prior to 1919, the portrayal of prostitutes as "clean" sounded odd. Dr. Best made another unpopular statement when he asserted that VD remained a big problem in Europe despite technological advancement and the "heroic" attempts by both governmental and nongovernmental institutions.[59] Such statements defied the prevailing notion that VD was distinctively an African problem because of Africans' inherent promiscuity.

When the medics wrote about VD and sexuality, they substantively compared and contrasted African and European sexualities. European sexual mores served as a yardstick for measuring the extent of deviation of the natives from a healthy heterosexual life and as a prescription for all-around human wellness. While not denying observable cases of VD among the European residents who supposedly refused to "live a continent life"—to practice sexual abstinence— the medics believed that European sufferers themselves should not be blamed for sexual misconduct, but rather the overlapping geographical and social factors peculiar to the tropics. The tropical climate, Dr. Maples asserted, had an "excitant" effect on European men, who could easily secure African women, most of whom were, however, diseased. Maples contended that Europeans could teach Nigerians how to report symptoms of VD and undergo a treatment regimen. "When it comes to treatment," he remarked, "the European gives intelligent assistance to the doctor; it is comparatively easy. A European having sexual intercourse with a native woman (or women as the case may be) is always on the look-out for venereal disease. He discovers it early and he comes to the doctor promptly for treatment. He follows out the course of treatment faithfully and with intelligence."[60] Words like "intelligence" used for describing the manner a European undergoing VD treatment contrasts with such terms as "idiotic" used of African patients. Maples expressed satisfaction in "social" solutions to VD among Europeans, such as encouraging them to marry or relocate with their wives. He even advocated for employers to increase their salaries in order to help them acquire the resources to start a family. This "social" solution for the Europeans contrasts with proposals for Africans, whose problem was seen as pathological—marriage would not solve the problem of VD among them because it would not deter them from patronizing prostitutes. Rather, Western education, biomedicine, and Christianity would civilize Africans and allow them to live decent sexual lives. The power of Western civilization to cure sexual pathology was considered evident in the behavior of the few educated elites whose sexual lives were purportedly "healthy" compared to the teeming populace of uneducated natives.

Data on VD infections represent another significant component of the medics' reports. Annual returns of cases, to a large extent, were significant indexes for advocating for a government-sponsored venereology scheme. As affirmative as the medics sounded on the importance of controlling prostitutes and VD, they could not present "actual" data on the incidence of VD due to a number of interrelated factors, including the living conditions of the vast majority of the civilians, the state of Western biomedicine, and the perceptions of the people toward therapy. First, while confinement within the barracks and the entire military culture of coercion gave military doctors the liberty to police African soldiers' sexual lives, thus enabling them to come up with relatively reliable data on infections, the civilians lived an unconfined existence and were not subjected to compulsory activities (such as cock-pulling) that could reveal their VD status. Second, Western biomedicine, despite its professed civilizing mission, was underserving Lagosians, to say nothing of the millions of Nigerians living in the remotest parts of the colony. The efficacy of native therapies, including their accessibility and affordability, made them more popular than their Western counterparts, thus inhibiting the compilation of data on rates of infection. More worrisome was the gulf between the reported cases of infection and the medics' affirmation about the ubiquity of VD. Although only 2.3 percent of all cases at Lagos government hospitals in 1919 were diagnosed as VD, Dr. Maples claimed, "I am certain there is a large amount of [undocumented cases of] venereal disease."[61] He noted further that a number of serious disabilities, such as orchitis, optic atrophy, osteitis, arthritis, chronic urethritis, salpingitis, and sterility, among others, that were not classified as VD infections in the annual returns were in fact attributable to gonorrhea and syphilis. Dr. Best made a similar speculation when he concluded, "I am unable to give a definite figure though I regard this [incidence] as very high." He estimated that about 50 percent of the population of southern Nigeria (about 3 million people) "have been infected at some time or other of their lives—congenital or acquired."[62]

Medics did highlight the implications of the contradiction between the actual cases of VD as derived from annual medical returns and speculations about the epidemic of the disease. One could argue that they probably exaggerated the rate of VD infection in order to pressure the government to increase funding for the medical service. Moreover, claiming that VD was not an epidemic would have challenged the firmly established proposition about sexual otherness and undermined the colonial project and Western biomedicine as a vehicle of civilization. Nigeria could not be an exception to the general rule that the Africans and other colonial subjects in the British Empire needed sexual discipline in order to climb up the ladder of civilization. Nor did arguments over major gray areas in imperial venereology surface. For instance, the medics were uncritical about the challenges of differentiating between venereal syphilis and non-venereal treponemal infections such as yaws transmitted by skin contact and saliva. By the 1920s, it was already well established in colonial venereology that the symptoms of non-venereal syphilis were practically indistinguishable from venereal ones.[63]

Nigeria's First Venereology Scheme

In January 1920, after two months of an intense exchange of ideas, the medics yielded to the Colonial Office directive by devising Nigeria's first venereology scheme, anchored on two broad approaches to combating VD: medical (establishment of VD clinics) and social (regulation of prostitution and publication of health propaganda). As table 4.2 shows, it would cost the colonial government close to £6,000 to start a full VD clinic for both inpatients and outpatients and to fulfill the medical component of the venereology project. Estimated annual recurring expenditures were about 90 percent of the initial cost of establishment. The cost of establishing six locations in southern Nigeria was estimated at more than £30,000 and double that amount for twelve locations

Table 4.2. Estimated Cost of Establishing a VD/Urology Clinic at One Location

Labor and Equipment	Cost (£)
Annual salary of one European medical officer	255.8.
Annual salary of 17 African staff:	557.7.6
1 second-class clerk	
1 second-class dispenser	
2 first-class nurses	
4 second-class nurses	
2 laboratory attendants	
7 support staff (cook, laundryman,	
gatekeeper, and laborers)	
Medicines and druggist sundries	4,250
Surgical instruments and appliances	200
Microscopes	100
Diets, provisions, and necessaries	200
Antigen and ambroceptor	50
Clothing, beddings, and equipment	250
Medical library	10
Uniform of native staff	25
Medical comforts	10
Total	5,907.15.6

Source: NAI, COMCOL 1, 894 vol. 1, "Principal Medical Officer of Lagos to the Director of Medical and Sanitary Service," January 28, 1920.

nationwide. World-class diagnostic techniques such as the Wassermann test (named after its inventor, the German bacteriologist August Paul von Wassermann) were scientifically praised for their ability to detect syphilis infection easily. New medical personnel (including urologists and pathologists) were to be trained in the United Kingdom. The social aspect of the scheme involved coercion—controlling the movements of prostitutes and ensuring that both inpatients and outpatients completed their cycle of treatment. Other social programs of attitudinal change included promoting monogamy and discouraging polygamy. Although authorities admitted that new legislation would be required to implement such suggestions as imposing restrictions on prostitutes, they thought that convincing the public about seeking "modern" medical help would yield immediate positive results.

As highly elaborate and promising as Nigeria's first venereology project appeared on paper, it was not implemented. VD was not declared a notifiable disease as proposed by the medics, and prostitution was not prohibited. Medical authorities could only make recommendations; they could not force the civil authorities who managed the imperial treasury to fund a project that they considered to be irrelevant, untimely, or expensive. Although the records are silent about why the medics' report was not implemented, one could provide plausible guesses drawing on demographics, race, and colonial economics.

First, while the medics highlighted the impact of VD on procreation, there was no verifiable evidence that gonorrhea and syphilis were causing death at alarming rates. With a population of about 100,000 in 1921, Lagos and indeed the whole of Nigeria had adequate human resources to service the colonial economy; therefore, fear of a labor shortage attributable to death from VD could be dismissed. Indeed, unemployment and underemployment, a direct effect of superfluous immigration, began to surface in Lagos as early as the 1920s.[64] Second, the cost of establishing VD clinics was deemed too high. Funds for the new project were to be generated internally, even though the Colonial Office instigated the investigation into VD. The medical authorities may have expected their proposal would require expansion of the colonial medical service, but their political counterparts who ran the state probably felt doing so would overstretch the unstable post–World War I budgetary constraints. Moreover, Lagos was arguably the most expensive part of Nigeria to maintain in terms of public health. While data establishing the impact of VD on demography did not exist, those pointing to the effects of malaria, dysentery, plague, and influenza, among the public health challenges arising from poor sanitation, were abundant.[65] For instance, between the 1870s and 1920s, mortality attributed to malaria dropped from about 80 and 100 to 13 and 40 per 1,000 among European and Africans, respectively.[66]

This declining mortality rate owed much to the massive expenditures on anti-malaria campaigns, swamp reclamation, public sewage/latrine construction, and the erection of European segregated neighborhoods in order to safeguard the health of the European population from the unceasing impact of malaria.[67] If not for improvements in public health, the population of the city would not have exploded during the first half of the twentieth century. Indeed, it would not have emerged as the economic center of the colonial state, the most culturally heterogeneous region of the country, and the colonial state capital. The British were largely successful in their bold attempt to improve the health of both the African and European populations in order to maximize the economic gains of imperialism.[68] However, the massive investment in public health did not make the city the healthiest part of Nigeria to live in—pandemics like influenza consistently threatened the overpopulated environs. What it did was to create a livable city attractive to both Africans and Europeans. It is evident from the foregoing that the colonialists mainly invested in the areas of public health that had a visible and verifiable impact on the population. They took the impact of sanitation-related diseases more seriously because their consequences were more visible, accountable, and verifiable than that of VD, which was mainly speculative.

Third, unlike their counterparts in other settler colonies (especially South Africa), Nigerian administrators' anti-prostitution campaigns did not find expression in the need to uphold the "sanctity" of whiteness.[69] In actual fact, interracial sex never prompted a state of anxiety over mixed-race children and the idea of the "purity" of the white race. For the most part, throughout the 1920s, both the civil and medical authorities put the issue of VD to rest. Even the aspects of the venereology report such as policing of prostitution that did not involve capital expenditure were not implemented. Women were not subjected to compulsory screening for VD or prevented from moving to certain parts of the city.[70]

Obscene Literature, Dangerous Sexuality

Ten years would pass before medical and civil authorities seriously put VD on the administrative agenda. As was the case with the 1919–20 venereology report, this new interest had external rather than internal origins. The dispatch/circular of March 8, 1930, issued by Lord Passfield, the secretary of state for the colonies, triggered a new investigation into the "Customs Calculated to Impair the Health and Progress of the Less Civilized Population in Certain Parts of the [British] Empire."[71] This inquiry was aimed at assessing the progress of Britain's "civilizing" mission in its worldwide colonies and the extent to which "barbaric" cultures were still impeding "civilization." In July of the same year, Nigerian colonial administrators submitted an elaborate thirty-two-paragraph report titled "Abolition of Customs Which Are Detrimental to Native Welfare and Economic Prosperity," detailing the frustration they were encountering in civilizing Nigerians.[72] Filled with familiar language of racial and cultural otherness, this report regretted the refusal of a large segment of the Nigerian populace to embrace Western culture and biomedicine, as well as the popularity of old backward customs. In explaining the prevalence of VD and the ubiquity of aphrodisiacs, the report, which was signed by Deputy Governor A. Burns, gave a sexualized portrayal of Yoruba culture similar to the one Dr. Maples gave ten years earlier: "Among the unenlightened Yorubas there is a belief that a man cannot reproduce his species unless he has had gonorrhea."[73] The following is an excerpt from a long list of herbal preparations that the report believed encouraged sexual promiscuity:

1. *Egbo igi* [herb]; for strengthening the nerves of the penis for connection with women 5/ [5s.]
2. Golden female tonic no. 1: Splendid remedy for female disease 10/6 [10s. 6d.]
3. Young Ladies' Tonic: This medicine removes diseases from the generative organs of young ladies and thereby prevents serious diseases and barrenness after marriage. Every young lady ought to use at least one bottle every month 5/- [5s.]
4. Golden Male Tonic: This medicine cures weakness of erection, lack of semen, insufficiency of semen, watery semen, impure semen, and other diseases which prevent breeding in men 5/- [5s.].[74]

The administrative report initiated a new probe into the proliferation of "pernicious" newspaper literature on VD drugs and advertisements, which the Lagos Women's League (LWL) (as mentioned in chapter 2) had petitioned against in 1923, which petition was denied by the government. Similarly, medical authorities were worried that a pharmaceutical company (E. C. Jones & Co.) operating from Hamburg was sending literature about "many vaunted" VD medicines and aphrodisiacs to "Nigerian school-boys." They would later conclude that the "unprecedented" incidence of reported cases of gonorrhea in Lagos was attributable to consumption of aphrodisiacs, which supposedly stimulated "undue" sexual desire, thus increasing the patronage of prostitutes and the spread of VD, and the consumption of "fake" VD drugs. The panic of the period was pictured as a vicious circle: the fact that African healers and apothecaries who made aphrodisiacs also recommended VD drugs informed the government of the existence of a "notorious cabal" that exploited people's ignorance. Newspaper proprietors received their share of the blame for encouraging the spread of knowledge about dangerous drugs capable of harming Lagosians' health. The following advertisement paid for by Nigerian Medicine Stores, a leading apothecary, appeared regularly in Herbert Macaulay's *Lagos Daily News*:

DIBIL Masculine:

Indications: Functional and endocrine impotence, premature senility, sexual neurasthenia, sexual abuses, nervous state, mental and physical disinclination, frigidity, abuse of narcotics;

DIBIL Feminine:

Indications: Premature ageing, climacteric disorders, troubles of menstruation and all other diseases peculiar to women;

The most carefully devised composition of the restorative DIBIL offers an enormous advantage over other remedies which are recommended for sexual life, mostly acting by means of high doses of Yohimbe detrimental to the orgasm and thus being unable of having any other effect but to incite the sexual functions, the remaining part of the body, however remains averaged and thus a dangerous disproportion is often created between artificially stirred up sexual life and bodily construction. "Dibil" improves both is multaneously in a harmonious way well adapted to the organic system of the body and their common task; it does not stimulate the sexual part function only, but it rejuvenates the entire body. The excellency of the preparation is also clearly demonstrated by the fact that the small dose of one tablet three times a day is sufficient in order to obtain the desired effect; the regular and normal use of the restorative Dibil will produce the surest result. A cure with "Dibil" is far less a costly matter, for one standard packing is sufficient for a month, and you will notice its interesting influence on the circulation of the blood.[75]

Unlike the 1919–20 reports on the incidence of VD, which were speculative, the medics' affirmation of the connection between VD and drugs and aphrodisiacs was beyond just a scientific guess. One of the physicians narrated how a man who had an erection that lasted for more than seven hours was rushed to the Lagos Island African Hospital for treatment. Further diagnosis, according to him, revealed that the patient also had gonorrhea.[76] Unlike other deliberations about VD that took place only among high-ranking British medics, the aphrodisiac debates were opened to African physicians. Whereas African medical doctors and colonial medical authorities were always at loggerheads over racially motivated prejudices in the areas of wages, promotion, and professional competence, they appeared to have set aside what Adell Patton termed "intraprofessional conflict" in order to reach a conclusion about the danger of fake VD drugs and aphrodisiacs and the need to legislate against them.[77] Indeed, correspondence over the issue of VD drugs reveals the inappropriateness of using a rigid binary of "collaborators" and "resisters" to explain the responses of Africans to colonial rule. The African medical doctors, who had agitated against racism, suddenly became collaborators in order to safeguard their craft from the encroaching herbalists and apothecaries. It seems inevitable that the African doctors would support the colonialists in this matter because the former were faced with two challenges: (1) racial prejudice in the government medical establishment, and (2) competition from alternative curative medicines offered by traditional healers.[78]

Figure 4.2. Advertisements of aphrodisiacs and VD medicines in *Lagos Daily News* and *Akede Eko* (Lagos Herald), 1929–30.

Conclusion

VD and prostitution were constructed as bedfellows. In colonialists' framing, VD was the "wage of sin," the punishment for indulging in reckless sexual behavior. But beyond its depiction as an ailment, it was appropriated as one of the numerous problems confronting the African race that needed to be tackled in order to firmly establish civilization. Hence, VD and prostitution were synonymous with such categories as "savage," "pathological otherness," and "primitivity" that stood at the center of the imperial project. Looking beyond the African littoral, it is apparent that the color of VD was not black, but neutral. Anyone, regardless of color, gender, or ethnicity, could contract gonorrhea or syphilis. But the British "Africanized" VD by insisting that it was distinctively an "African" problem. The idea of creating an African-centered meaning of VD served the colonialists' imagination of using both the prevalence of disease (whether venereal or non-venereal) and Western biomedicine as tools of imperialism.

The varied and unequal attention given to VD among civilians and the military reflected the professed significance of the disease to the colonial project. The British made VD an exclusively military affair, despite the fact that physicians held (though in the absence of credible data) that it was primarily a public health problem among the civilian population. For the authorities, the wellness of the army was more important than that of the civilians since Lagos and Nigeria as a whole had an adequately productive population to service the colonial economy. This situation runs contrary to what obtained in parts of East Africa (Uganda, for instance), where authorities feared the impact of VD on procreation, "extinction of the African race," and by extension reduction in the availability of labor needed to sustain capitalism.[79] Furthermore, civil authorities did not take VD seriously among the civilians because Lagos, unlike Zimbabwe and South Africa, was not a settler colony. The racialization of VD in South Africa and the institutionalization of approaches against it were informed by the need to safeguard the public health of the white population. The cost of institutionalizing venereology was another factor. It was far more costly to institute a venereology program among civilians than among soldiers. As it played out, the British put their money, time, and resources where it mattered most to them.

The 1919–20 debate over the institutionalization of venereology revealed that the colonialists were never united about the best methods of combating VD. Their identity, profession, and authority within the colonial system principally dictated the kinds of recommendations they gave. While the medics claimed that VD among the civilians was a public health problem and advocated for the establishment of VD clinics, their counterparts in the civil administration focused their attention on other pressing public health challenges such as sanitation, which seemed to have a graver impact on the population and the stability of the colonial capital. While the military authorities favored "controlled" brothels because of the assumption that military prostitution was ineradicable, their civilian counterparts, who were far more informed about the politics of sexual immorality in the British Empire, believed that tolerating prostitution would not go well with the critics of imperialism who associated prostitution with backwardness. Although medical authorities felt that their proposed venereology project would stem the tide of VD and help expand the medical service, their civil counterparts, who had better knowledge of the financial state of the economy, would shelve their proposal.

CHAPTER 5

SEXUALIZED LAWS, CRIMINALIZED BODIES

Anti-prostitution Law and the Making of a New Socio-Sexual Order

The three preceding chapters have engaged the colonialists' and Lagosians' concerns over the medico-moral and security implications of prostitution in relation to the wider issues of colonial progress, modernity, respectability, and civilization. Beginning in 1941, after decades of tolerating prostitution, the colonialists began to take a prohibitory stance toward casual sex work.[1] The fact that prostitution was taken seriously during World War II when budgetary constraints inhibited the colonial administration's ability to fulfill its budgetary commitment firmly established the cardinal position that casual sex work occupied in the history of the sustenance of imperial rule. In fact, the British were waging two wars: one was foreign (against Nazi Germany) and the other domestic (against prostitution). The passing of laws represented only one component of a prohibitionist agenda—implementing them was the most important. Legislation cost little to draft and pass, but it was far more expensive to implement because it added to the long list of orders the overstretched Nigeria Police Force (NPF) was expected to enforce. Yet, all the anti-prostitution laws were designed for, and implemented only in, Lagos because the menace of VD and prostitution-related crime was reported to be higher in the port city than in any other parts of the country; moreover, its place in Britain's Win-the-War efforts and in the security of the entire colony was of key significance.

Generally, colonial laws remain a useful prism to the mapping of social change and to the shifting relationship between the colonizers and the colonized. Indeed, colonialism, through its imported legal system, "sought to impose a new moral as well as political order, founded on loyalty to metropolitan and colonial states and on discipline, order, and regularity in work, leisure and bodily habits."[2] Yet, anti-prostitution laws were distinct from most colonial laws in terms of their scope, implementation, and projected outcome. While most colonial laws were motivated by explicit political and economic considerations, anti-prostitution laws tended to have far-reaching and broader implicit undertones—political, economic, military, medico-moral, racial, and social.[3] The overwhelming attention given to VD laws in the current literature has seriously downplayed how legalistic assumptions interfaced with numerous domains of people's encounter with imperialism. In other words, VD laws should be considered as a fraction of a range of anti-prostitution laws aimed at addressing sexual danger for the purpose of prolonging the life of the empire.

By engaging anti-prostitution laws through the perspectives of gender, class, and ethnicity, I hope to demonstrate that the colonialists' interventions in the lives of the colonized found strong expression in the conviction that the criminal justice system was the best institution for promoting a moral society free from the menace of criminality and disease. The fact that anti-prostitution laws were age specific introduced another important yet provoking layer of thought about the changing meaning of childhood and adulthood in a colonial state struggling to reconcile the contradictions between African and Western cultures. Child prostitution laws not only defined childhood in strictly legal terms, they also drew parallel connections between physical bodily development and psychological progression and made the idea of an erotic child a component of state paternalism. The state's intervention in children's lives through legislation inserted their experience into the legal record and marked them clearly as a sexually endangered population, not only passive but also subjective. Childhood innocence contrasted with adults' independence. Hence, adult prostitution laws treated women as "criminals"—individuals who voluntarily engaged in prostitution as a means of undermining the colonial state's infrastructure of decency, respectability, and public order. Yet, the laws' racial dimension informs the intersection of power, sexuality, and racial ordering. The introduction of anti-prostitution laws specifically to protect Europeans together with their prejudiced implementation within racial confines is important for understanding the double-standard posture of the colonialists. In terms of class, the colonialists introduced separate anti-prostitution laws among the civilians and the military because of their differing perceptions of the danger each group posed to the imperial status quo.

The procedures for passing anti-prostitution laws were not different from other categories of laws. The Colony Welfare Office (CWO) and the NPF worked with the attorney general to draft a bill, which was then presented to the Legislative Council of Nigeria (LCN), the apex legislative body of the colonial state, introduced, among other reasons, to give Nigerians some voice in the imperial administration.[4] Unlike most economic and political bills that went through a series of debates before they were eventually passed into law, anti-prostitution legislation encountered limited opposition.[5] This is not surprising. Few would argue against legislation to protect girls from sexual exploitation, to remove criminals from the streets, or to eradicate VD. Even when Nigerian members of the LCN disagreed with a bill (whether related to prostitution or something else), they did not have the political weight to stop it because they were in the minority and were all unofficial members.[6] As Margery Perham has noted, the LCN was essentially British-centered as it was established to "satisfy their own principles and to obtain, in the central exercise of their power, as much local advice and opinion as could be evoked."[7] Anti-prostitution bills, once passed, were divulged to the public through official government publications and the newspaper press, which added streams of editorial comments and letters from readers, mostly praising the British for taking the right step.[8] However, it would be wrong to think that the majority of Lagosians knew these government publications existed because they had limited circulation and were mostly available only in government offices. Not all Lagosians could afford the newspapers or were literate in English. The *West African Pilot*, the top-selling newspaper in the whole of Nigeria (population 20 million-plus) had a daily circulation of just 20,000 in the mid-1940s.[9] Moreover, very few people could afford the price tag of 2s. to 3s. for most of the dailies.

Adult Prostitution and Vagrancy Laws

Anti-prostitution laws first appeared in Nigerian legal books in 1916. The first set of laws prohibited such activities as public soliciting by prostitutes and brothel keeping. There is no evidence to suggest that they were passed because authorities were worried about prostitution—though sex work had already become a dominant feature of urban life at this period. Rather, it would appear that the British considered it an integral component of "civilization" needed to put Nigeria on the path of social progress. H. F. Morris has noted that colonial legal officers demonstrated their legalistic brilliance and dedication to the colonial service by encouraging the importation of English laws, even if they were irrelevant to the conditions obtainable in the colonies.[10] From 1916 through the early 1940s, anti-prostitution laws were erratically implemented, and very few people were prosecuted for violating them. Indeed, the police effectively followed the official policy of tolerating prostitution by only arresting prostitutes who conducted themselves in a "disorderly" manner. Also the scope and definitions of various prostitution-related activities were vague, thereby inhibiting the initiation of legal actions against prostitutes. For instance, up to 1944, prostitution and brothel keeping did not yet have any ascribed legal meaning.

During the LCN debate on the Unlicensed Guide (Prohibition) Ordinance (UGPO) in 1941, the first anti-prostitution law of the World War II years, all members agreed that "in any civilized country, the need for licensed guides for seamen and tourists could not be denied."[11] However, Honorable Rhodes, representing Rivers Division, criticized the bill for "not providing a remedy against prostitution" and advocated for employment of girls to prevent them from drifting into vice.[12] His criticism was fruitless as the bill was passed unanimously and later praised by the press.[13] Known publicly or informally as the "loitering law," the UGPO targeted the *boma* and *jaguda* boys with the purpose of disrupting the chain of contact between European sex tourists and prostitutes. Yet it also reflected the assumption that the visible threat these delinquent children and juveniles posed to the public at large would lessen if their activities were criminalized, even though it was explicit in its goal of protecting only the European population. The law formalized the tourist guide system by laying down the procedures for becoming a licensed guide. A licensed guide was expected to renew his permit on a yearly basis and carry a government-issued photo identification when conducting business. In remolding how taxi drivers should conduct themselves, the UGPO made it illegal to "speak, or call out to, any tourist, make any noise or sound any instrument" in order to seek their attention. It also established a new law enforcement outfit, the "Anti-Vice Squad (AVS)" (a detachment of the NPF known among Lagos taxi drivers as *onlotinrin*—a Yorubaized word meaning loitering). Section 11 applied to prostitutes in strong terms: "Any common prostitute: wandering in any public way and behaving riotously or indecently loitering and persistently importuning or soliciting tourists for the purpose of prostitution shall be guilty of an offence and on summary conviction shall be liable for a first and second offence to a fine not exceeding five pounds or to imprisonment for a term not exceeding two months."[14]

A major amendment was made to this law within a year of its enactment. Legal authorities deracialized it by repealing the term "tourist" and replacing it with "wayfarer." While a tourist was popularly designated as European and a foreigner, a wayfarer could be an individual of any race or nationality.[15] The deracialization of the UGPO, a move to cover its originally overt racial undertone, did not change the mode of enforcement as the AVS gave protection only to European visitors, not Lagosians. The UGPO was the only anti-prostitution ordinance that explicitly protected European visitors and expatriates. As we saw in chapter 1, racial prejudice existed in various spheres of Lagos society. The need to guarantee the safety of Europeans went beyond the general ideology of their racial and intellectual superiority—danger to the lives of sailors jeopardized the maritime industry, which like the military was needed to bring the war to a conclusion. In enforcing the UGPO, the AVS frequently patrolled the red-light districts and the hotels where Europeans lodged in search of prostitutes and *boma* and *jaguda* boys. One such raid in July 1943, as shown in table 5.1, led to the arrest of twenty-five *boma* boys, ranging in age from 9 to 15. Twenty of them were convicted.

The criminal justice system normalized sexual deviance among Europeans by covertly recognizing their involvement in prostitution as a "treat," not a "crime," and treating them as "victims" of prostitutes' and *boma* boys' "criminality." While the UGPO punished *boma* boys for offering to take foreign visi-

Table 5.1. *Boma* Boy Menace in Lagos, July 1943

Number of Accused	Offense
12	Caught acting as unlicensed guides—that is, guiding Europeans to houses of prostitution
10	Loitering in and about hotels, street corners, places of amusement, and other suspicious places
2	Disorderly behavior in public
1	Stole 12s. 4d.

Source: NAI, COMCOL 1, 2471, "(1) Juvenile Delinquency in Lagos; (2) Juvenile Court, Lagos."

tors to prostitutes, it was not a crime for the Europeans to buy or solicit sex. Indeed, the UGPO sought to put in place a system that allowed foreigners to have access to prostitutes through "credible" guides who had been prescreened and were known by police authorities. However, the racial prejudice in the administration of this anti-prostitution law should not be taken to mean that Europeans were above the law in all respects. Indeed, there is vast information about their prosecution for such offenses as assaults on Africans (especially the police) and theft.[16] According to a November 21, 1941, issue of the *West African Pilot*, an "unusual scene of spectators" witnessed the Ebute Metta Police Court proceedings in which four seamen (Thomas Moloney, Carold Deen, James Robbinson, and Albert Field) were convicted for assaulting Police Constable Julius Fejoku while he attempted to arrest them for being in unlawful possession of illicit gin.[17] They were each sentenced to five weeks' imprisonment with an option of a £5 fine; they opted for the fine. In another case, Willy Ulleland, a French sailor with Elder Dempster Shipping Line, was fined £17 10s. for assaulting Police Constable Abayomi Shobande by "dragging him about, [tearing] his cloths, while thrashing him soundly."[18] Even British military personnel who were expected to be more "disciplined" than the seamen frequently assaulted the police. In one instance, George Baxter, attached to the Royal Air Force, was fined £25 for assaulting Lance Corporal I. Egbona.[19] Very few cases of assault between Europeans and civilians were prosecuted partly because of the fear of retribution. In one rare case, C. S. Fowler, assistant manager at the Public Works Department, was fined £12 for calling his junior African worker, Emmanuel Lawrence, an "African Nigger." Lawrence passed out when Fowler kicked his scrotum.[20] The victim was able to secure justice because he hired a lawyer (Olatunji Martins) and initiated a legal suit after enduring two previous incidents of workplace violence.

Europeans' assaults against the police were highly influenced by the racial assumption of their presumed legal invincibility. Indeed, the criminal justice system seemed to have drawn a rigid boundary between crime against the state and crime against morality for Europeans. While public assault (especially against the police) appeared to have been treated as an offense against the state, soliciting for sex contravened morality law, which was never prosecuted. Indeed, so prejudiced was the implementation of prostitution laws that un-authorized passage of seamen from their ship carried more punishment than prostitution offenses. Kaleo Martins, a seaman from Ceylon who had VD, was sentenced to twelve weeks' imprisonment without the option of a fine for leaving his post. Martins was given thirty tablets of M & B for his sickness, but reportedly he sold them. The captain of his ship accused him of "go[ing] ashore in many cases in company of women."[21]

Three years after the UGPO became law, the government overhauled its criminal code on prostitution and codified it as "Offences against Morality." Not only did the new amendments define prostitution and brothels, they also criminalized activities such as pimping and public solicitation by men. The 1916 law only punished women for solicitation. Solicitation was central to the policing of prostitution because in legal and social understandings, without it, prostitution could not take place. Prostitution, "with its grammatical variations and cognate expressions," was defined as the "offering by a female of her body commonly for acts of lewdness for payments."[22] Aside from making prostitu-tion a female-specific offense by not mentioning "male," this definition also indicated that a female must offer her body for sexual liaison for an act legally defined as prostitution to take place. People could be charged for "living on immoral earnings" if they derived their means of livelihood from casual sex work as brothel owners, pimps, and families of prostitutes. Consequently, some of the offenses against morality laws were gender neutral: sections 225A(3 & 4) affirmed that both men and women could be pimps, madams, or procur-ers who "exercised control, direction, or influence over the movements of a prostitute."[23] If found guilty, a first offender could serve up to six months in prison and/or pay a £50 fine. Second and subsequent convictions increased punishment to one year in prison and/or a £150 fine. Corporal punishment was also reserved for second and subsequent male offenders.[24]

It is quite obvious that the British legal officers who authored anti-prostitu-tion laws knew the difficulties of establishing criminal charges against casual sex work, not only because sex was traditionally performed behind closed doors and hidden from the public gaze, but also because it was difficult to establish the motives of such associations. Prostitution itself, they realized, was not policeable, but activities connected with it such as solicitation, lewdness, and brothel keeping were. Therefore attempts were made to widen the scope of detecting and prosecuting prostitution offenses in order to intensify the grip on prostitutes and their clients. In fact, when the criminal code on prostitution was first introduced to the LCN for debate, it contained a section that empowered the police to arrest a woman if "she was seen to address three or more persons within one hour."[25] But some African members of the council—Honorables

Jubril Martin and Ernest Egbuna—readily kicked against it. For Martin "it gave the prosecution wide powers . . . to accept such presumptive evidence would have the effect of jeopardizing the liberty of the subject." Egbuna believed that it was "inconsistent with the generally accepted principle" of English criminal procedure and law.[26] Egbuna's criticism was based on the impact the law would have in reordering the ways people conducted themselves publicly. "In a community such as Nigeria," he remarked, "people are used to addressing each other regularly in public places, and to read into such addresses what this amendment to the criminal code implied was a danger which one should be guarded against."[27] Martin's and Egbuna's criticisms were strong enough to compel the attorney general to drop that section of the criminal code. Yet, if the British truly wanted this section of the law, they would have passed it, regardless of the nationalists' criticism.

But authorities got away with several measures in the adult anti-prostitution law that violated individuals' freedom of movement and gathering. Two examples suffice. The definition of prostitution overtly criminalized erotic behavior as lewdness, flirting, and licentious acts, not the actual sex act that took place (typically) in secret. By making flirting and lewdness an offense under prostitution law, the government pathologized all women and extended the geography of policing prostitution beyond the famous red-light districts to virtually any domain. It also meant that sexual intercourse did not have to take place for a woman to be arrested for prostitution. On a number of occasions, women categorized as "unescorted" (i.e., those attending nightclubs and bars without male company) were arrested and prosecuted for breaking anti-prostitution laws. Such categories as "unattached" and "unescorted" women were loosely used to stigmatize women as prostitutes and served as strong weapons for policing women's movement outside the red-light streets. Indeed, the implementation of anti-prostitution laws tended to masculinize nightclubs by exposing "unescorted" women to legal insecurity and aided police corruption. Delivering his judgment in a case involving "forty hotel girls" arrested for loitering and solicitation, Magistrate E.A.S. Ogunmuyiwa sentenced all the accused to one month in prison or a fine of £5 (each) and advised them to "find jobs or get married."[28] Court proceedings did not establish that the "hotel girls" were all prostitutes. They could have been partygoers. But their presence in a hotel was taken to mean that they were there to solicit sex.

Another component of the criminal code that infringed on Lagosians' rights included the expanded definition of a brothel as "any premises or room or set of rooms in any premises kept for the purpose of prostitution." Unlike in some parts of North America and Western Europe where a brothel had a more definitive meaning (geographically, architecturally, and socially) because of the existence of policies like regimentation that decriminalized prostitution in tolerated zones, in Lagos a brothel had a more esoteric meaning. The

Figure 5.1. Court House, Tinubu Square, Lagos. Reproduced by courtesy of the National Archives Ibadan.

brothel law made all buildings and premises potential brothels and landlords or their owners potentially guilty of "living on immoral earnings." Although only legal officers or the NPF could legally determine if a place passed for a brothel, citizens could report women who frequently brought men to their rooms (mostly this was done by cotenants). This is true in the case of John Iloma (male landlord) and Adejoke Oshinlaja (female), decided at Sant Anna Police Court on August 16, 1944. While Iloma was prosecuted for keeping a brothel, Oshinlaja was tried for prostitution. Their premises at Odo Street, Obalende, was legally defined as a brothel because the police established that Oshinlaja used her room for "immoral purposes," and saw a male customer (who escaped arrest) during the raid. The two were sentenced to six months in prison each.[29] But unlike Iloma and Oshinlaja, whose premises was not a brothel in a social but in the legal sense, James Market ran a conventional brothel at Idowu Street that housed ten prostitutes.[30]

Child Prostitutes and the Criminal Justice System

Prohibiting child prostitution went beyond passing and implementing legislation—it involved establishing child and juvenile services, called the Colony

Welfare Office, in 1941.[31] Policing sexual violence against girls formed an integral component of the institutionalization of child and juvenile welfare service because Faulkner, the pioneering head of the CWO, had a development-oriented philosophy about vice and the future of delinquent children and youth. *Jaguda* and *boma* boys, according to welfare officers' predictions, would become hardened adult criminals, while child prostitutes would take the almost certain route of becoming adult prostitutes or criminally minded madams who recruited young girls into prostitution. "The surest way of insuring against heavy increase of crime in the next twenty years," remarked Alexander Paterson, a British officer who was invited to Nigeria to study crime and the prison system, in his 1944 report, "is to pay more attention to the young offenders of today."[32] Paterson pointed out that, although most Nigerian prison inmates were in their twenties and thirties, based on criminal statistics the majority of these adult inmates had been convicted at ages ranging from 10 to 15.[33]

The CWO development approach to vice explained why children and juvenile delinquency laws were futuristically oriented. They were also gendered in the sense that they sought to address socio-sexual aberrations like prostitution (among girls) and crime (among boys) by establishing separate legal and rehabilitation procedures that centered on the perceived danger posed to each gender. By allowing boys and girls to undergo separate and unequal rehabilitation programs, the CWO, not unlike schools and churches, played a significant role in framing the notion of separate boyhood and girlhood experiences.

More than 90 percent of child prostitution laws were contained in the CWO-sponsored Children and Young Persons Ordinance, or CYPO, of 1943, an adaptation of Britain's Children and Young Persons Act of 1933.[34] The CYPO was introduced after nearly two decades of administrative denial of the impact of juvenile delinquency on the colonial state.[35] The remainder is contained in the various sections of the criminal code ordinance (such as sections 22A and B) that criminalized child prostitution and carnal knowledge and indecent assault of an underage girl.[36] In addition, the street trading law titled Regulations to Prevent Children Trading in the Streets, which banned hawking by girls under 14, was targeted at reducing sex crime against girls and prostitution.[37] Girls over 14 but under 16 could only hawk for their parents or guardians appointed by the court. All girls under 16, regardless of whom they hawked for, were prevented from hawking after 6:30 p.m.[38]

The CYPO detailed the reformatory procedures for dealing with a child (an individual under 14) and a young person (over 14 but under 17).[39] The age of consent remained 13. The law established juvenile courts, remand homes, a probation service, and vocational institutions, while outlawing the imprisonment of children under 14. Before 1943 children and adults were tried in the same (magistrate) courts and kept in the same prisons.[40] The CYPO established a framework for cooperation between the CWO, on the one hand, and the commissioner of the colony, legal officers, police, courts, and the prison system, on the other hand. However, the CYPO and CWO were not a child protective law and service per se—their scope (at least during the 1940s) did not extend to ensuring that children lived in safe family environments or to taking custody of orphans or children of broken homes—even though part V of the CYPO established that children found to be destitute, wandering, or neglected and those whose parents were incarcerated should be taken into custody.[41] It was mainly interested in girls being kept in sexually exploitative situations and vagrant boys exposed to the vices of street life. However, on very rare occasions, the CWO did take custody of children from broken homes. A case in point was that of a soldier's three children (ages ranging from 4 to 10) who were admitted into the girls' hostel when their mother absconded for "mere fancy for another man."[42] The CWO took custody of the children probably because their father was a soldier involved in military operations and did not have relatives in Lagos. It could also have been an attempt to prevent the eldest of the children from slipping into the hands of a procurer.

Anti-child prostitution laws were about both children and adults. In establishing the prime responsibility of adults as protectors of children, the laws also held them responsible for sex crimes.[43] Adults' dual identity as "protectors" and as "criminals" had a major implication for the criminal justice system: in order to reduce the incidence of child prostitution, procurers or madams had to be brought to book. But the loophole in the criminal justice system created a counterproductive situation. Most adults accused of child trafficking circumvented the corrupt criminal justice system by bribing the police or staff of the CWO, as seen in the case of Ayodele Potts-Johnson. Most of those repatriated for breaking anti-prostitution laws by the Lagos Town Council (LTC) soon returned under a new identity and to a different part of Lagos to continue their trade. More worrisome is the fact that punishments for sex crimes against children were not stern enough to serve as a deterrent. Before 1960, the maximum punishment for defiling and having unlawful carnal knowledge of a girl under 13 was two years' imprisonment.[44] The 1960 amendment increased the punishment to life in prison.[45] Indeed, very few adults prosecuted for trafficking or rape served prison sentences because they were given the option of paying a fine.

It would appear that payment of a fine in place of a prison sentence favored the government, which sought to decongest its overcrowded prisons in the wake of the soaring lawlessness and public disorder of the World War II years. Paterson reinforced this unofficial policy when he asserted that "it should however be remembered that a fine paid in lieu of a sentence served a double financial gain to the Government. It is a sum of cash paid into revenue instead of the expense of an extra prisoner paid out of revenue. A hundred such cases will pay for the salaries of several additional clerks."[46] This statement is compelling on several counts. It underscored the political economy of crime and punishment. Indeed, it is not out of place to argue that policing prostitution served a dual goal of reducing crime and swelling the imperial treasury. A fine of £50 imposed on a convicted prostitute was more than the annual minimum wage of a government employee. A fine of £150 on a second and subsequent conviction would hire several low-cadre clerks and a senior administrative officer. If reducing crime was the initial intention of passing anti-prostitution laws, it nevertheless produced "positive" outcomes through the payment of fines that augmented the treasury during one of its most financially distressing times. The fact that prostitutes' fines contributed revenue to the treasury meant that the government itself, ironically, was guilty of violating its own law by "living on immoral earnings."

The CYPO's establishment of a dichotomy between a child and a young person, aside from legitimizing the protection of children and punishing adults for prostitution, also introduced the science of childhood development. It defined childhood in purely legal terms by insisting that adulthood did not come until age 17. At this age, the CWO believed, an individual was mentally, physiologically, and emotionally competent to stand trial for offenses. Legally, a child (someone under 14) or a young person (at least 14 but under 17) who practiced prostitution voluntarily was an "offender" who violated section 249(a-i & ii) of the criminal code that made solicitation an offense.[47] However, the difference between the status of either and that of an adult (someone over 17) was that while an adult prostitute would most likely be prosecuted in a regular (magistrate) court and be imprisoned or fined for violating anti-prostitution laws, a child or young prostitute who acted on her own volition would be tried in a juvenile court and sent to a remand home.[48] Even when girls under 17 worked voluntarily as prostitutes, the CWO believed that they were innocent, betrayed by the society and cultural practices that did not protect them. Moreover, the boundary between forced and voluntary prostitution was easily blurred in situations where prostitution networks were maintained by powerful brothel owners, madams, and pimps. Although the law differentiated between a child and a young person, the CWO generally treated any girl under 16 or 17 as a "child" and "underage."

The CWO was conceived as and in reality was another arm of law enforcement. Its supervisors responded to information and petitions from "concerned" citizens about sexual exploitation by visiting brothels allegedly housing child prostitutes, taking possession of the girls, and providing evidence for the prosecution in court. Faulkner and Izzett personally carried out or authorized several actions—such as policing the train stations and preventing girls between 14 and 16 from coming into Lagos from the provinces—that appeared not to have any legal backing. They also attempted to work with shipping lines to prevent immigration through the port and combed premises in search of child prostitutes—a task traditionally reserved for the NPF—without police escort or warrant.[49] Indeed, the government gave Faulkner and Izzett power to take any actions deemed "appropriate." In order to determine if the girls had been prostituted, the CWO performed virginity and VD tests. Positive testing for VD and/or lack of virginity, as seen in the cases of Alice Kpodame (16), Agnes Johnson (16), and Anibe Alice (14), was taken as evidence of prostitution and was presented to the court in prosecuting alleged procurers.[50]

After examining individual cases, the CYPO empowered the CWO to decide whether to repatriate the girls to their homes in the provinces, reunite them with their parents or "lawful" guardians (if they lived in Lagos), or send them to the juvenile court. Generally, the manner in which each case was approached was determined by many factors including but not limited to where the girl was taken into custody; the criminal records of her procurers; and her life history, age, and place of origin. Girls taken from brothels received greater attention than their counterparts living "under conditions suggestive of sexual exploitation."[51] The flexibility of procedures and the extensive authority given to Faulkner and Izzett reflected the complication of policing sex and the difficulty of having all actions backed by the law—a situation that would have delayed administrative action or created legal controversy among colonial officers who often held different positions on children's welfare. While the CYPO created the structure for the operation of the CWO, social interpretations of situations took precedence over the legal ones. Although Faulkner and his staff complained that child traffickers were escaping punishment because of the loophole in the criminal justice system, they did record some success. On June 24, 1946, they secured a punishment of six months in prison—through Justice Adetokunbo Ademola—for Toro Edefuge convicted for "exercising control over the movement" of a 15-year-old girl.[52] Faulkner then directed the public relations officer to publicize this case in the local newspaper in order to serve as deterrent to other madams.[53]

It did not take long for the CWO to realize that policing child prostitution in Lagos required maintaining streams of information and cooperation with administrative officers in the provinces—since evidence abounded that most Lagos child prostitutes were recruited from outside the port city.[54] In fact, by 1944 most of the southern provincial offices kept files on child prostitution, including correspondence between them and the CWO.[55] Faulkner and Izzett gathered information about the life histories of girls from their colleagues in the provinces and ensured that repatriates arrived in their respective communities.[56] In addition, they occasionally toured some provinces and districts, met with the locals, and sensitized them to the ills of allowing their female children to be taken to Lagos. A communiqué of forty-two paragraphs was issued after one such visit to Warri Province, which took the form of a town hall meeting attended by the chiefs and locals.[57] Provincial officers not only pledged to prevent the emigration of girls from their communities; some actually took unpopular decisions, which in some cases violated the free movement of people. The district officer of Kukuruku in Auchi compelled citizens taking girls out of his jurisdiction to apply in writing and receive his approval before embarking on their journey.[58] But procurers appeared to have devised other methods of circumventing this procedure. In October 1943 the district officer stopped four girls from being removed when he discovered the following contradictions in the application of their so-called husbands: two of the different writers posing as husbands had one Lagos address; all letters were written on September 24 and 25; and three out of the four letters had consecutive registration slips.[59]

The CWO succeeded in getting all its sponsored laws passed partly because its jurisdiction was confined mainly to Lagos. Faulkner and Izzett's colleagues in the offices of the attorney general and commissioner of the colony recognized their expertise and practically rubber-stamped their every legal suggestion. Lagos did not have a native authority; hence, Faulkner did not require the approval of the *oba* (king) and chiefs of Lagos for any of its laws and administrative actions. However, an exception was a piece of legislation titled Native Authority Child Betrothal Order, or NACBO, of 1943, which was influenced by Faulkner's conviction that girls were being recruited into the Lagos prostitution network under fictitious marriages and illegal guardianship.[60] This proposed bill criminalized "child" marriage, betrothal of girls under 17, or their removal from their parents or legal guardian; it also reduced bride-price and made registration of all marriages (whether under native or English law) mandatory. Unlike other child prostitution laws that were enforced only in Lagos, the NACBO jurisdictionally covered the entire country of more than 20 million inhabitants. In addition, multiple bureaucratic hurdles—from the highest officeholder (i.e., the governor) to the chiefs in the big cities and remote villages alike—had to be overcome.

In drafting the NACBO, Faulkner and the attorney general realized that their biggest challenge was using age as a basis for defining "carnal knowledge." Thus, the bill probably avoided using the term "carnal knowledge" to reduce opposition, and no justification was given as to why the bill needed to be introduced. But implicitly, the bill would regulate sexuality by delaying marriage and criminalizing sex with girls until age 17. Although the bill was silent about carnal knowledge, the cover letter by the chief secretary to the government of Nigeria attached to it and sent to all the resident officers explicitly established the intersection between carnal knowledge, betrothal, child marriage, and prostitution:

> The expression husband and wife without further qualification includes a man and woman married in accordance with native law and custom and it is therefore a defence, even in the case of a child of ten, if the man alleges and the prosecution cannot disprove that he is the husband by native law and custom of the child. I am to request that the question of the protection of young girls from premature sexual intercourse may be discussed at Chiefs conference and that Resident and District Officers may be instructed to discuss it with the people and that His Honour's [the governor] views, whether the evil of child prostitution and the carnal knowledge of children under the cloak of marriage by native law and custom may be controlled.[61]

The NACBO was not the first attempt to regulate traditional marriage and by extension sexuality. Before 1943 traditional marriage practices had come under attack by the colonialists, who believed that such practices as polygamy and "indissolubility" of marriage were uncivilized. The legalization of divorce by the British not only undermined traditional Nigerian male authority by enhancing women's control over their reproductive and productive capabilities, it also contributed revenue to the native authorities' coffers through court charges.[62] However, the NACBO was the boldest attempt since the late nineteenth century to overhaul native marriage (nationwide) to suit the British project of protecting endangered girlhood sexuality. Had it passed, the bill would have undermined the power that traditional agency had over native marriage and over junior, unmarried, urban wage earners.

I have previously indicated that the colonial government did not create social welfare institutions purely out of concern for Nigeria's children but in an attempt to prevent delinquent children from growing into hardened prostitutes and criminals. But a related dimension to this development approach to criminality was the escalating cost of running the criminal justice system and maintaining incarcerated adults. Police and prison authorities were convinced that it was more expensive to attempt to prevent crime committed by adults and maintain the prison system than to remove delinquent girls and boys off the streets. Commissioner of the Colony G. B. Williams, one of the most vocal exponents of this idea, asserted that "money spent on these young potential criminals will save much greater expenditure later on."[63] Paterson also advised that in order to reduce the prison population of 40,000 inmates and the cost of maintaining a total of 134 prisons, it was "far more economical for the government" to invest in the treatment of juvenile delinquency.[64] Although adult criminals outnumbered their younger counterparts, Paterson argued that since most adult criminals had been prosecuted as children and juvenile offenders, the government should consider decongesting its prisons by focusing on young offenders.

Venereal Disease, Biomedicine, and the Law

As chapter 4 explicates, colonial medics believed that the rise in venereal disease was attributable to the proliferation of information about and consumption of aphrodisiacs, which heightened sexual desire, thereby increasing the patronage of prostitutes, and in turn the use of "fake" VD remedies offered by African herbalists, druggists, and apothecaries. The proposal of the director of medical and sanitary services (DMSS) for the introduction of the Undesirable Advertisement Ordinance (UAO), Nigeria's first anti-VD law, received the blessing of the chief secretary to the government and attorney general and was subsequently presented to the LCN in June 1932. Codified under chapter 130 of the Custom Ordinance, the final version of the UAO was formally introduced to the public in August 1932 and was expected to take effect three months later. Section 3 of the law criminalized "the importation into Nigeria of such advertisements, notices, announcements, papers, and handbills recommending to the public preparations as medicines or medicaments for the prevention, cure or relief of any VD or as aphrodisiacs."[65] It also criminalized the advertisement both in the newspapers and through other outlets such as posters, catalogs, pamphlets, and handbills of "medicines or medicaments for the prevention, cure or relief of any VD and aphrodisiacs."[66] Section 5 banned "any packet, box, phial, or other enclosure containing any preparation, affixed to or delivered with which there is or are any label or words written or printed, holding out or recommending to the public such preparation as medicine or medicaments for the prevention, cure, or relief of any VD or as an aphrodisiac."[67]

The UAO, like other anti-prostitution laws, was replete with inconsistencies, which mirrored the general colonialist approach to issues precipitated by real and imagined anxiety. The law neither stopped local herbalists and apothecaries from producing aphrodisiacs and VD drugs nor prevented the public from buying them. It only forbade their advertisement and recommendation through any media channels and E. C. Jones & Co. from selling its aphrodisiac in Nigeria. A careful scrutiny of correspondence among British medical doctors clearly reveals the economic origins of the UAO and why it was passed in 1932, not earlier. First, the fact that it was placed under the Custom Ordinance, not under the Infectious Diseases Ordinance, which controlled the spread of dangerous public health diseases like smallpox, tuberculosis, malaria, and leprosy, among others, meant that it was economically driven. The law would have been a better fit in chapter 21 of the Criminal Code Ordinance (Offenses against Morality) where most morality- and sexuality-oriented legislation appeared. Second, with the Great Depression upturning virtually every sphere of the colonial economy, Nigeria was compelled to introduce several fiscal policies to safeguard metropolitan producers since E. C Jones & Co.'s aphrodisiac and those produced locally were competing with another brand of aphrodisiac called "Overbeck Rejuvenator," imported from the United Kingdom. Indeed, Britain was consistently forced to abandon its widely professed "free trade/ open door" economic policy during periods of crisis like the 1930s Depression. In short, the UAO was not public health legislation per se but an economic subsidy camouflaged in the language of sin and medico-morality.

But looking beyond the law's narrow target of VD remedies and aphrodisiacs, one sees other larger issues at stake. Since most, if not all, aphrodisiacs and VD medicines prepared by herbalists and apothecaries claimed to cure common ailments like insomnia, malaria, indigestion, pneumonia, body and head aches, and typhoid, to mention but a few maladies, the campaign against VD drugs indirectly targeted the entire edifice of non-Western therapy.[68] But authorities were smart enough to realize that it would be difficult to legislate against malaria or typhoid herbs but easy to convince the educated elites (both the collaborators and the resisters) that a law on dangerous aphrodisiacs was needed to safeguard Lagosians' health. In a correspondence to the secretary of state for the colonies, Sir Philip Cunliffe-Lister, justifying the UAO, G. Hemmant, the officer administering the government of Nigeria, described the expanded goal and projected outcome of the UAO: "It is considered that by forbidding the advertisement of aphrodisiacs, the public would at the same time be protected from such other undesirable quack medicines for which separate legislations could not easily be devised."[69]

Having established the economic undertone of the UAO, let us consider what the government should have done under a genuine circumstance to help promote sexual health in the civilian population. Ideally, a law aimed at truly combating VD should have established VD clinics and increased access to the so-called superior treatments offered in government hospitals. Medics should have resuscitated the 1919–20 proposed venereology scheme that was shelved due to financial constraints. Instead, authorities devised what they believed to be a creative and inexpensive solution to VD by censoring information channels that created awareness of "fake" remedies. Race and class also influenced the attention the colonialists gave to VD. The only government VD clinic in Lagos, and in any part of Nigeria up to the mid-1940s, was a facility for European seamen located at Apapa Wharf. This clinic served only the foreign sailors who were universally notorious for their sexual recklessness and high incidence of VD. International maritime standards mandated VD clinics in all seaports. In addition, an early treatment center was established for the African rank-and-file of the West African Frontier Force (WAFF) during the 1920s. However, this facility was not opened to African civilians. Apparently, the colonialists only invested in the groups that mattered most to colonial capitalism and security. Other West African colonies—the Gold Coast, Sierra Leone, The

Gambia, and Liberia—all had VD hospitals for Africans dating back to the early 1920s.[70] When Nigeria was advised in 1926 to emulate these colonies, the DMSS responded that Nigeria should wait and evaluate the success of the VD campaigns in those places before embarking on its own. He suggested a nonmedical solution: "It is highly probable that education by publicity and other propaganda may be needed."[71]

There was no other anti-VD law until 1943, when the Venereal Diseases Ordinance (VDO) was passed because of the presumption that gonorrhea and syphilis spread by prostitutes could jeopardize Britain's Win-the-War efforts. The popular assumption among civil and military authorities was that controlling VD among the civilians was the best means of safeguarding the health of the soldiers. Unlike the UAO, which neither established VD clinics nor laid down any procedures for the treatment or prosecution of infected people, the VDO criminalized Lagosians by empowering "qualified" medical practitioners to subject women to VD screening and treatment. An adaptation of the notorious Contagious Diseases Acts (CDAs) passed in Britain in 1864, 1866, and 1869 for the purpose of combating the high incidence of VD among the British armed forces, the metropolitan version empowered plainclothes police to detain and subject women to compulsory medical checkups in any garrison or seaport identified as a danger zone for VD. Unlike the CDAs, which were designed to deal with VD and prostitution in military areas (attempts to extend it to the north of England and civilian areas met with hostility), the Nigerian VDO jurisdictionally covered the entire civilian population of Lagos but empowered the governor to apply it to any region of the country as deemed necessary. Section 4(2) of the ordinance empowered "medical officers" and "qualified medical practitioners" to initiate criminal charges against anyone whom he or she "[knew] or [had] reason to believe [was] suffering from a venereal disease in a communicable form and [was] not under treatment therefore [was] not attending regularly for such treatment."[72] "Qualified medical practitioner" meant someone trained in Western medicine, not an African or a so-called native or quack doctor. Aside from empowering them to prevent sufferers of VD from contracting marriage until they were certified healthy, the VDO also punished medical practitioners who failed to comply with its provisions. Indeed, the VDO made medical practitioners another arm of colonial agency like the NPF to police and regulate sexuality.

In addition, under the VDO, it was an offense to employ infected persons in such responsibilities as child rearing, food preparation, or any other task that involved direct contact with people. It was also illegal for a suspected carrier to refuse treatment. Other sections of the VDO provided guidelines for treating infected persons and the procedure for establishing criminal charges against defaulters. Defaulters were liable to a fine of £100 or six months in prison or both.[73] But the most important section of the law, which had the greatest ramifications for public health and gender relations, was section 3, which made VD a *notifiable* disease—an ailment that had to be reported to medical authorities. By equating the gravity of VD with such highly epidemic diseases as smallpox and tuberculosis, the government sought to police the private existence of the colonized while publicly stigmatizing "unattached women"—the so-called purveyors of VD. Any sufferer from VD was a potential offender under the VDO. It basically criminalized the activities of druggists, pharmacists, the apothecaries, and the native doctors who recommended and offered treatment for VD since they were by law expected to report their patients or clients to the medical authorities.

To enhance the effective implementation of the VDO, the government established three VD clinics in Lagos: two in the civilian-populated region of Lagos Island and one at Ikeja, a military base. One of the two Lagos Island clinics was located close to Porto Novo Market Street to bring therapy closer to the prostitutes. The DMSS even sponsored newspaper advertisement publicizing free treatment for VD, including the locations and daily schedules of the new clinics.[74] Drawing from the original venereology scheme designed in 1920 but shelved for financial reasons, each of the new clinics was staffed with a pathologist, a bacteriologist, and a military doctor. Their mode of operations was similar to those of the notorious lock hospitals used almost a century earlier in Britain for implementing the CDAs in that it empowered doctors to detain patients until they were satisfactorily healed. Thus, the clinics operated like detention camps. Like other prostitution laws, the VDO was highly flawed. Racewise, the VDO did not apply to seamen, who were predominantly males and whites and who, like the African soldiers, were a high-risk population.[75] And like the African soldiers, they were another conspicuous class of individuals who should have been prosecuted under section 7, which empowered physicians to compel perceived sufferers of VD to be screened.

Ethnicity and the Politics of Sex

Policing prostitution also took on an ethnic dimension because women and men accused of breaking anti-prostitution laws were from diverse ethnic backgrounds. In devising anti-prostitution laws, the British did not specifically "ethnicize" legislation by directing it at a particular ethnic group. However, the CWO and the NPF did stigmatize non-Yoruba (labeled as "foreigners") as the prime moral pollutants of Lagos. Realizing the difficulty of policing the "foreigners," Lagos authorities informally enlisted their ethnic or hometown associations, otherwise called the "tribal" unions. This method seemed inexpensive since most, if not all, "foreigners" were members of ethnic unions, which received their certificate of operation from the government. In August 1942 Faulkner sent out a memo to the unions giving them an ultimatum of a month to address girl trafficking. In response to the authorities' order, not only did the unions constitute themselves into a quasi-law enforcement agency by facilitating the repatriation of "erring" female members accused of prostitution, they also enacted laws to punish members for "immoral" practices. Chapter 51 of the Owerri Union's constitution, titled "Indolence and Prostitution," states: "Any member who shall be discovered to be incurably indolent and disorderly and who shall engage solely and disgracefully in prostitution and shall thereby become undesirable shall be sent home with sanction of the authorities."[76] The Owerri Union even had laws on adultery. Chapter 49 states that "any member discovered guilty of adultry with another's wife whether marriage was contracted under native or European law shall be fined a sum not less than one pound."[77] In order to monitor the criminal activities of its members, the Owerri Union decreed that only the president or head of a family association was permitted to secure bail for members arrested for any offenses. Like former colonial laws, the rules of ethnic associations were authored by men who tended to extend rural patriarchy to the urban space. Although the city created avenues to experiment with new modes of socialization rarely permissible in the villages, components of rural life considered "useful" were selectively deployed to satisfy the interest of the men who had agency.

Like those controlled by men, the very few females-only ethnic associations also attempted to police the sexuality of their members through their bylaws. Chapter 7(d) of the constitution of the Efik Ladies Union stated that "any member who disgraces herself outside or in any function being a member of the Efik Ladies Union who practices prostitution must understand that she disgraces our native land and such a member is liable to dismissal."[78] Chapter 2 of the Warri Women's Society's constitution fined members accused of prostitution £2, while the Calabar Ladies Union did not extend membership to convicted prostitutes.[79] The reason for the women's associations' quest to regulate the activities of their members is self-evident: they were usually accused of harboring prostitutes or managing the underground prostitution ring. The very idea of women-only associations also challenged the dominant paradigm of the city as a male-centered arena.

Ethnic associations' activities did not stop with making laws on prostitution and facilitating repatriation of "disgraced" members. They assumed a broader responsibility as informants on the activities of their members. A case in point was Madam Affiong, who was accused of brothel keeping. Because the NPF could not establish any case against her after sending undercover police to her home, which she allegedly used as a brothel on several occasions, they approached the leaders of the Calabar Improvement League demanding information about her means of livelihood.[80] Other information supplied by the ethnic associations included determinations of how girls were trafficked, as seen in the case of 10- or 11-year-old Bassey Etim, who according to the Calabar Ladies Union was probably abducted from Calabar around 1939.[81]

Other examples of cooperation between the colonial government and ethnic unions abound. When police arrested two Urhobo girls for contravening the anti-prostitution law, O. O. Okoro, the honorable secretary of the Urhobo Progress Union, pleaded that Faulkner should allow his association to deal with the case.[82] He then convened an emergency meeting requesting that members "bring all women and girls."[83] The case of Alice Samuel (age 9) can be used to further illustrate the kind of alliance and cooperation between the ethnic unions and the CWO. Alice, whose father hailed from Warri Province, was living with a female guardian at No. 14 Richards Lane (in Lagos). In the reports filed by Faulkner, "although the child appears to be in some moral danger, she is well looked after."[84] The Urhobo Progress Union convened an "Emergency General Meeting," and concluded that Alice was in "supposed moral bankruptcy" and should be repatriated to the compound of Chief Ogagbe, the head of the family, in Ovie Town, Warri Province.[85]

While I do not attempt to disprove that the unions truly wanted their members to live crime-free lives, I contend that their disposition toward the alleged criminality of their members was informed largely by the need to prevent sanctions from the government. The commissioner of the colony and the LTC reserved the right to dissolve any association that did not comply with authorities' regulations or cooperate with them on matters of public safety. Proscription had strong implications. Not only would association members be unable to gather as a group and create the machinery for self-help; they would also not be able to give back to their homeland by sponsoring development programs like scholarships and schools. Thus, in the calculation of these unions, it paid to facilitate the repatriations of a few "delinquent" members and put up a good image, to avoid having their association proscribed by the government. The case of John Effiong also sheds light on the unions' sexual politics. Effiong, who was suspected of prostituting his niece named Deborah to soldiers and seamen, was asked to return the girl to Obubra Division. Effiong denied this allegation and claimed that Deborah was an orphan who would suffer if repatriated from Lagos. But when the CWO rejected his appeal to keep Deborah in Lagos, Effiong turned to his association (the Obubra Improvement Union), which declined to help.[86] In other instances, it would appear that the ethnic unions refused to help their members, not because they did not want to, but because the accused refused to cooperate with investigation. In 1943 the CWO accused Madam Idola Aparis of child prostitution and approached the Okpe Union for information about the true identity of the girl found with her. In their response, the Union advised Faulkner to "deal with the case as you may deem fit" because Madam Aparis did not cooperate with them in ascertaining the relationship between her and the girl.[87] They ended their letter assuring the CWO of assistance "at all times."[88]

What is more, jealousy within the ranks of the association was easily appropriated into the politics of sexuality regulation—members even reported their detractors to the police, accusing them of breaking anti-prostitution laws in order to get rid of competition in business and the workplace. The politics of the proliferation of intra-ethnic associations also took some vociferous turns. Writing against the emergence of a new splinter association (the Efik Women's Society), the Efik Ladies Union wrote the commissioner of the colony affirming that it was the "only proper Efik Ladies Union in Lagos" and that all matters related to Efik women "should first of all be rendered to us before your final judgment."[89] And when Faulkner noticed a conflict between the Efik Ladies Union and the Calabar Improvement League over the agency to be contacted for prostitution matters, he arranged a "peace" meeting with the leaders of the two associations in January 1944 to "draw up concrete proposals for a closer co-operation in the interest and welfare of Calabar."[90] Even this meeting did not end the political squabble over legitimacy. Writing three months later, Faulkner praised the Efik Ladies Union for helping in "spotting out culprits" of child prostitution, and regretted the impact of the "feeling, [and] spirit of rivalry and petty jealousies" between the two associations in the war against illicit sexuality.

Conclusion

On paper the barrage of anti-prostitution legislation appeared to contain good measures against the menace of sex work. However, they were erratically and inconsistently implemented. The impact of prostitution on certain spheres of colonial society determined the extent of the implementation of anti-prostitution laws. Thus, the well-implemented ordinances were those that were presumed to have a greater impact on the colonial political economy, public order and health, and security. For instance, the UAO was successfully implemented, during the first few years of its passing because it involved international trade protectionism and a spirited fight to kill the indigenous alternatives to VD cures. Some newspapers, like the *Lagos Daily News*, stopped carrying VD adverts when the draft of the UAO was publicized in March 1932, while *The Daily Telegraph* waited until August 1932, barely three months before it came into effect.[91] Although the UAO remained in the law books throughout the colonial period, it was erratically enforced. Unlike the pre-1932 period when adverts featured such "offensive" words as "impotence" and "orgasm," new adverts were less explicit. A November 1938 advert in the *West African Pilot* described two brands of drugs, "Methexin Pills" and "Kawasot Tablet," as the "leading German preparation for the rapid cure of all ACUTE and CHRONIC Disease of the urinary organs."

The UGPO established the AVS but was a gross failure, as the following chapter fully shows. By and large, laws related to child prostitution were the only category of legislation that appeared to have been enforced to a greater extent. Apart from being the most elaborate single body of law, these laws were overseen by the CWO and resulted in a sort of "Save the Child" crusade. The CWO had virtually all the power of the NPF other than the fact that it could not directly arrest offenders. Nevertheless, it could not successfully eradicate child prostitution. Interestingly, while World War II initiated institutional attention to prostitution, it would also be remembered for starting a process that could not be brought to a logical conclusion.

CHAPTER 6

MEN, MASCULINITIES, AND THE POLITICS OF SEXUAL CONTROL

One would expect opposition to anti-prostitution legislation to come from men and women who derived their means of economic survival and social relevance from the business of sexual pleasure. Surprisingly, moralists who initially pressured the government to legislate against sex work would become the most vocal antagonists of anti-prostitution laws. Though directed mainly at the "enemies" of sexual morality (i.e., prostitutes, African male customers, and *boma* boys), anti-prostitution legislation had unanticipated impacts on the general public, creating new notions of respectability and honor. Indeed, the laws tended to reconfigure social relations, public conduct, practices of socialization, and people's everyday interactions within the colonial state. Moreover, individuals and groups interpreted them to satisfy circumstances appropriate to their existence. A law targeted at an "underclass" minority would become a burden to the entire population.

This penultimate chapter—one of two that focus on the reactions of Lagosians to prostitution legislation—deals with men. The final chapter explores the dispositions of women. Gender is a useful tool for dissecting the reaction of Lagosians to anti-prostitution laws because men and women had divergent and often conflicting perspectives on the policing of sexuality. Reactions or responses were also influenced by social class and its corresponding features, such as income level, educational attainment, and marital status. If the colonialists who devised laws to criminalize prostitution drew them along class lines, it is logical that those affected by the laws do not constitute a monolithic block identity. Different contours of masculinities informed by location and by political and economic power influenced the degree of condemnation of or support for anti-prostitution laws. Men's reactions also differed depending on the age of prostitutes (i.e., whether child or adult).

A question that seemed relevant for this discussion of men's sexual politics is what it might take for moralists to become defenders of prostitutes' rights.

The change of identity from being a moralist to an advocate for prostitutes' rights underscores the fluidity of debates about prostitution and the shifting positions of moralists. In "defending" prostitutes' rights against the injustice of the colonial state, men deployed the vocabularies of political and cultural nationalism, as they highlighted the integrity of "traditional" customs or criticized the British for imperial failure. With time, prostitution became another strong factor in Nigeria's history of decolonization, as nationalists focused on it as one aspect of social decadence that would end with the attainment of independence. What started as a war against sexual immorality later found expression in the rhetoric of political self-determination.

The Print Media, Racial Politics, and Anti-Prostitution Laws

The newspaper press had protested against the government's regulationist agenda before the outbreak of World War II. Voices called for the proper implementation of the 1916 criminal code that criminalized public solicitation by prostitutes. Newspapers were also critical of the impact that such activities as hawking were having on the security of girls.[1] Although the police did prosecute some prostitutes for solicitation, most men believed that outright prohibition was the best method of dealing with sexual immorality. From 1916 up to the outbreak of World War II, the print media did not condemn indiscriminate arrests of "innocent" people for prostitution, probably because the police prosecuted their main targets (prostitutes and criminals) or because unlawful arrests were uncommon. But the pattern of protest changed after 1941, when the British launched their prohibitionist agenda.

When the Unlicensed Guide (Prohibition) Ordinance (UGPO) of 1941 came into effect, the Lagos press commended the government and expressed optimism that it would help ameliorate the danger of illicit sexuality.[2] Indeed, a newspaper editorial viewed the importance of the law beyond social control when it claimed that it would prevent *boma* boys from leaking secrets capable of jeopardizing Britain's war strategies to foreign spies and enemies of the British Empire.[3] However, it is one thing to pass a law; it is another to implement it effectively. And like all other colonial laws, the UGPO did not come without major problems of interpretation. For instance, by institutionalizing the tourist guide system, the law prevented "an average respectable" Lagosian from showing foreign friends around the town without first obtaining a permit from the police.[4] Since the elites (mostly merchants, professionals, and politicians) had foreign friends who visited the city, the UGPO targeted the underclass, indirectly affecting the crème de la crème of the colonial society. Moreover, several "law-abiding" people (like "wait-and-get" photographers) who derived their means of livelihood from the tourist industry came under unprovoked police harassment.[5] Eight months after it came into effect, it appeared that the UGPO was not achieving its objective. Critics began blaming the Anti-Vice Squad (AVS) for not effectively policing prostitution. The *boma* boys, observed a September 1941 editorial in the *West African Pilot*, "have been going from strength to strength as anyone would confirm who happens to move about in the nights and see them guiding visitors."[6] Speaking of prostitutes, the editorial remarked, "this menace has assumed an alarming proportion . . . The roads to hotels and cinemas are lined at nights with young women busy touting in the most unashamed manner for clients."[7] Two years after it was passed, another editorial criticized the government for not carrying out effective background checks on the licensed guides who, like the much-outlawed *boma* boys, were not only leading European visitors to brothels, but also "perpetrating daring acts of hooliganism apparently and regardless of the law."[8]

But the problem the UGPO posed transcended poor implementation and the creativity of prostitutes and *boma* boys in outmaneuvering it. Indeed, the AVS was persistently accused of arresting "innocent" and "law-abiding" citizens in lieu of prostitutes.[9] This criticism would be one of the most intense of all the agitation directed against those policing prostitution. As it turned out, Lagos men committed more energy to fighting the police over indiscriminate arrests than they did encouraging them to intensify their watch over the main targets of the law. A *Daily Service* editorial of November 1944 admonished the police to "separate the wheat from the chaff." It affirmed that "not all women found alone in the Street are loiterers or persons of questionable character."[10] Another critic of the law captured the extent of Lagosians' susceptibility to arbitrary arrest in a poetic and mocking manner: "A casual walk at any hour of the day along such places as Marina and Tinubu Square may lead one into the clutch of a policeman, who might, to all purposes look like any personage between a Roman Catholic priest in his snow-white Soutans and an aristocratic northerner in flowing gown and turban."[11] Similarly, at the monthly meeting of the traditional rulers of Lagos, one of the chiefs (Onikoyi) narrated the unlawful arrest of his son whom he had sent on an errand.[12]

Editorial criticism served its main goal of calling the attention of the public to police injustice and intensifying the campaign against illegal arrest. Letters from victims of unlawful arrest put a human face on injustice, while comments by prominent lawyers gave a legal backing to the public outcry. In an article titled "Is Everybody Equal before the Law?" F. R. A. Williams gave a brief history of the UGPO and affirmed that many of the accused "really ought not to have been brought [to the court] at all." He pointed out that illegal arrests overcrowded the court and added to the work of the already overburdened magistrates.[13] Even judges like Adebiyi Desalu and E. J. Alex Taylor expressed the opinion that many of the accused brought before them should not have been arrested, much less prosecuted.[14] According to a law clerk, the average number of cases tried under the UGPO in each magistrate court on a daily basis was between fifteen and twenty.[15] But most of these illegal arraignments did not lead to convictions since the accused could justify that they were not prostitutes or *boma* boys, but "law-abiding," "responsible" citizens with "legitimate" means of livelihood.[16] Justice Desalu was reported to have dismissed charges brought against "a respectable gentleman," and an employee of the Lagos Town Council (LTC) who was apprehended on his way home from Victoria Beach.[17]

The illegal arrest of "innocent" citizens went beyond ordinary mischief by the police alone. Indeed, the public in collaboration with the Nigeria Police Force (NPF) exploited the law to satisfy financial and other motives by serving as fake informants and precipitating arrests of estranged lovers or wives. It was not unusual for potential offenders like *boma* boys (interested in protecting their means of livelihood) to lead police to the homes of "alleged" prostitutes. In addition, competition for financial resources and social relevance among diverse groups of Lagosians produced enmity and the labeling of successful women and men as "prostitutes" or "brothel keepers." Editorial headlines such as "Manufactured Prostitutes?" "False Informants," and "Are All Idlers and Loiterers?" exposed the shady relationship between Lagos men and the police in what the press vividly painted as an elaborate illegal-arrest racket.[18] However, few such accusations led to prosecution because the "accused" could easily secure "bail" on the spot by bribing the police or staff of the Colony Welfare Office (CWO). Women were highly prone to give bribes to avoid being labeled as prostitutes; this largely explains why they were so often targeted by the police. What is more, anti-prostitution laws ended up creating additional opportunities for police to exploit Lagosians rather than reducing the alleged medical, security, and social impacts of sex work.

However, the crisis of corruption and policing prostitution could not be laid on the authentic members of the NPF. Police impersonation was on the rise as some Lagosians discovered it was a good way to exploit fellow citizens. On November 21, 1944, Jonathan Robinson, a Gambian national with nine previous convictions, was sentenced to two years in prison for impersonating an AVS officer when he "arrested" Lasisi Aremu, an apprentice bus conductor.[19] Private security outfits variously called "vigilantes" and "irregular forces," whose uniforms resembled those of the NPF, were frequently accused of impersonating the authentic police. The Ashogbon Police Force, one of the most controversial irregular police outfits, was established in 1941 to help the overstretched NPF with the escalating wave of robberies.[20] But it would later outlive its importance in the wake of complaints about excesses that included harassment of Lagosians.[21] This situation prompted J. G. C. Allen, the acting commissioner of the colony, to declare that he would "not tolerate the existence of any force which is likely to be confused in any way with the official police" and went on to disband the Ashogbon Police Force.[22] Although Allen's order was lauded by the press, it did not stop the privatization of security in Lagos—vigilantes or night guards continued to exist throughout the 1940s and 1950s.[23] For Allen, the refusal to comply with the government order was an indication that "these young hooligans [e.g., the Ashogbon Police] had been making a good thing out of it for years."[24]

The NPF and other law enforcement agencies' failure to effectively police prostitution and avoid wrongfully arresting citizens reflected the entrenchment of corruption in virtually all spheres of Nigerian society during the 1940s. Wartime emergency regulations (such as food price controls) not only criminalized many people but also intensified poverty and greed across the board.[25] In January and February 1944, the *West African Pilot* ran a series of powerful and controversial editorials on bribery that, more than any newspaper sources I have seen, revealed the deep-rooted crisis of corruption that permeated all sections of colonial society.[26] The police were on the receiving end of corruption criticism because as the "upholders" of the law they were expected to not be corrupt. Although police corruption was not unknown in the interwar years, the social and economic mutations accentuated by World War II intensified the degree of corruption among the rank-and-file of the NPF. Prosecutions of police for collecting bribes not only were the subjects of press sensationalism but also revealed the degree of the breakdown of law and order.[27] In one case, Police Constable Flavian Opara swallowed a bribe of £5 to escape arrest by his colleagues.[28] A Lagos high court later sentenced him to six months in prison. "Policing the police," a phrase that gained currency in the press, registered effectively the public's frustration in getting the NPF to perform its responsibility in the wake of the increasing cases of corruption brought against policemen in the courts.[29] It also touched on the identity and class of people enlisted in the force and on levels of remuneration. A critic blamed police ineptitude and corruption on poor pay and lack of a union, which kept "intelligent young men" from enlisting in the NPF.[30] Another went so far as to suggest that police constables were recruited from the same class to which *boma* boys belonged.[31]

If the crises of policing prostitution revealed anything, it is that the problem of regulating illicit sexuality cannot be laid on the colonialists alone or be isolated from the wider challenges of running a modern colonial state. Indeed, one editorial titled "Bribery, Prostitution & Theft" captured well the thought of most contributors to the debate over prostitution regulations: "Bribery is very often the outcome of low wages, and prostitution and theft the upshot of poverty and unemployment . . . Were Nigeria's immense resources developed, and the realisations devoted to the welfare and wellbeing of the people, so that unemployment was eradicated, and every man and woman had sufficiently remunerative work to do, there would be little cause for theft or prostitution."[32] Other literary sources also affirmed the popular understanding of the relationship between bribery and theft. In Cyprian Ekwensi's *People of the City*, Fento, a court clerk, confesses to being corrupt during his conversation with Amusa Sango, the main character of the novel, affirming that "bribery is like prostitution: a private thing between a giver and a taker." He goes on to state the difficulties of establishing criminal liability between the two: "Nobody knows about it, nobody can prove it, nobody is hurt."[33]

Public outcry against anti-prostitution laws also took on a racial dimension, not only because Lagosians were all too familiar with discrimination along color lines but also because some anti-prostitution laws like the UGPO were specifically designed to protect European visitors and tourists. Critics like T. Babs F. Opayemi queried why European solicitors were not prosecuted while Lagosians continued to be unjustly punished. Some even believed that such Europeans should be repatriated from Lagos, like prostitutes.[34] A *Daily Service* editorial under the heading "Law and Prostitution" not only called for the prosecution of European consumers of sex work but redefined prostitution in an unpopular manner: "Equity is the essence of law," the editorial begins. "Women found wandering about especially at night with European visitors, now so common in Lagos, are arrested by the police and charged for an offence. We wonder why the women are invariably punished and the men are allowed to go free." The editorial sounded pro-prostitution when it asserted, "This is unfair to the hostesses of the romantic visitors. If both are guilty of the same vice, why should one party be dragged to court and the other unscathed? We detest prostitution no less in men than in women. Let the law apply its punitive measure to all irrespective of race and sex."[35] Another editorial called for racial neutrality in the implementation of the UGPO: "Sailors and foreign visitors are entitled to protection, but not at the expense of the innocent citizens of Nigeria."[36] Racial discrimination in the implementation of prostitution laws increased after the Bristol Hotel scandal. Indeed, the nationalists began to appear paternalistic in their defense of interracial sexual relations by accusing European tourists of not only creating demand for prostitutes but also perpetrating acts amounting to "abuse of the very dignity of African womanhood."[37] One antagonist called for the protection of girls against "uncultured Europeans" and "foreign irresponsibles who, with money and drinks, allure them into vehicles that convey them into questionable cubicles and hotels."[38]

Between Prohibition and Regulation

As men decried the failures in the policing of prostitution, two major contentious positions surfaced: Should prostitution be regulated or prohibited?[39]

These rigid and often overlapping and conflicting stances carried significant moral and sociopolitical implications. Although they did not emerge into a well-organized ideological movement, those who favored a regulatory approach thought decriminalizing prostitution would formally recognize sex work as a legitimate trade and bring regimentation to associated activities such as loitering and public soliciting. Such an approach, they believed, would help increase police surveillance since the NPF would only have to concentrate on a manageable section of the city and offer protection to socialites. In turn, prostitutes would pay taxes and conduct themselves in an orderly fashion. There is an element of parallel modernity in the suggestion of regimentation or "legal" brothels. Proponents of this view, some of whom had probably visited Europe or read about the popular "comfort zone" where prostitution was decriminalized, believed that the "oldest profession" could not be eradicated, and so should be regulated or modernized in the interest of public safety. Not all Lagosians framed regulation in strictly medical and public security terms. Critics of child prostitution such as Oged Macaulay (the son of Herbert Macaulay) called for the introduction of licensed "private or public brothels" to allow the police to monitor the activities of procurers.[40] Generally, regulation was considered to be economically wise, given that prohibition had been a failure and expensive. Moreover, the policy of repatriating prostitutes to their homes in the provinces was, to many, an ethnically discriminatory policy, and one that put a dent in the unity of multiethnic Nigeria. Repatriation was not only ethnically discriminatory—it categorized some Lagosians as "foreigners" and labeled them as "undesirables"—but it also promoted a militant nativism in a city that was built by both "indigenes" and "foreigners." What is more, it supposedly facilitated the spread of VD to the provinces since authorities there did not conduct VD screening on repatriates.[41]

It is important to note that the civilians' idea of regulation was different from the military's. While the Royal West African Frontier Force's (RWAFF) proposal was framed as a solution to VD among a small demographic group (i.e., the African rank-and-file of the army) and as an imperial security issue, civilians viewed it from the perspectives of public health, reproduction, and law and order. Nonetheless, it is misleading to think that the protagonists of decriminalization were strictly altruistic. Some may have thought that decriminalization would enhance their access to casual sex work and protection from *boma* boys who terrorized the red-light districts, and reduce or totally eliminate harassment by both the authentic and "fake" police that extorted male customers under the guise of policing prostitution. Although newspaper reports do not establish the marital status or social identity of regulationists, they were probably singles who depended on prostitution for their sexual needs. One advocate of regulation who identified himself simply as a "soldier" asserted that "young men who are yet to marry cannot do without prostitutes."[42]

Aside from the issue of policing red-light districts and child prostitution, another aspect of regulationists' criticism touched on the disagreement over the credibility of African or Christian/European marriage. Although controversy over these two types of marriage custom dates back to the second half of the nineteenth century (and has formed the basis of excellent works, such as Kristin Mann's *Marrying Well*), the 1940s saw a new wave of politics that tied marriage closely to the politics of prostitution regulation. In advocating for the legalization of prostitution, regulationists blamed monogamy as the root cause of prostitution. Polygamy, they contended, had helped to reduce or eliminate prostitution in precolonial times by guaranteeing marriage for every woman.[43] They cited the impact of human catastrophes such as World Wars on men's demography and pointed out that men "die[d] sooner than women."[44] Dennis Osadebay, a lawyer and founding member of the National Council of Nigeria and the Cameroons (NCNC), who would later become the premier of the Mid-Western Region, almost turned the debate over regulation into a "scientific discourse" when he drew a parallel between "sex drive" and "economic security."[45] Writing to criticize the Nigerian branch of the World Affairs Group (nicknamed the "Brain Trust"), which recommended job creation as the solution to prostitution, Osadebay contended that polygamy was the "only natural" solution to sex work. He believed economic security would not eradicate prostitution because all women were "entitled to the loving embrace and the protection of a man." Apparently referring to Dr. Elizabeth Akerele and Magistrate Stella Thomas (two of the highest-ranked African female professionals), Osadebay gave an analogy that if they could leave the "dignity and economic security" of the operating room and the court for the "loving arms of a man," thus doing the "natural thing" and the "will of the Great First Cause," then this would prove that economic empowerment was not as important as sex drive.[46] So well received was Osadebay's rebuttal of the "Brain Trust" that a *West African Pilot* editorial exaggeratedly described his as a "pragmatic" position that "typifies the present day outlook of every thinking and serious African."[47] A more elaborate proposal for polygamy as the solution to prostitution was given in a pamphlet on prostitution titled *The Surplus Women* authored by Increase H. E. Coker, a *West African Pilot* journalist who would later assume "godfather" status in the Nigerian print media. In his endorsement of Coker's pamphlet, Mazi Mbonu Ojike, a leading nationalist, asserted that monogamy left fifty women without husbands, and since "these fifty women" cannot be denied sexual satisfaction, "prostitution or polygamy is the only natural and sincere solution to their problem."[48]

Prohibition is the opposite of regulation or legalization. Prohibitionists generally invoked male authority and the language of sin in condemning official legitimization of prostitution. Some even believed that sex work was a curse, foreign, and un-African. "To face the stubborn fact," one critic wrote, "prostitution is not a Native of this country."[49] In supporting continued criminalization, prohibitionists occasionally historicized sexuality by spotlighting the difference between precolonial and colonial sexualities. In a public lecture sponsored by the Araromi Baptist Church titled "Men, Women, and Divorce," S. L. A. Akintola, the managing editor of the *Daily Service*, who would later become premier of the Western Region, asserted, "In the good old African society prostitution was an anathema."[50] He went on to draw a parallel correlation between divorce and sexual immorality, and asserted that the "life of a nation" depended on a strong institution of marriage. Carefully read, this lecture straddles the line between the discourse of a modern society looking forward to taking its rightful place in the comity of nations and a decaying one that is fast losing some of the prime values of the "novel" precolonial social life that once derived its strength from sexual chastity and the indissolubility of the household. "The widespread prostitution," according to Akintola, "can be partly traced to the waning influence of the paterfamilias." He went on to blame divorce for prostitution: "The newly discovered liberty accentuated by Rousseau's individualism has intoxicated women. Consequently there are those among them (and their number is not inconsiderable) who prefer treading 'the red light street' to rearing sons and daughters in the good old ways of their mothers. They want for themselves the best things of this life, and determine to get them by all means, fair or foul. This leads to trafficking in divorce."[51] Akintola was not alone in espousing a relationship between divorce and prostitution. Prohibitionists' sentiments were generally subsumed in the hysteria of unprecedented rage for divorce across social classes and the growing "army of free women" who desert their "poor" husbands to search for "easy wealth."

To establish the profundity of their positions, prohibitionists and regulationists alike occasionally used abusive words against each other while painting hypothetical situations aimed at highlighting the moral implications of their positions. A man named Olu Adeyemi called the suggestion for legalization by Sergeant Chuks Jian a "sheer absurdity." He gibed, "Tomorrow, a notorious pick-pocket might come forward and ask that since the Police failed to wipe out pick pocketing completely it must become a legalized trade in the country."[52] The practice of drawing a correlation between prostitution and theft was a common one, as seen earlier. Generally, Lagosians and British colonialists considered "light" crimes (like theft) perpetrated by *boma* boys and prostitution as birds of a feather. When a contributor wrote to the *Daily Service* in support of regulation, the editor not only refused to publish the letter but also composed an editorial that adequately represented the stance of Lagos elites' on this controversial issue:

> We are shocked by a letter addressed to us by a correspondent appealing to the Government to legalize prostitution. Should we grant license to rogues and housebreakers on the ground that stealing is one of the oldest and most stubborn evils

mankind has ever been called upon to battle? . . . Rationalization of evil can only lead to its perpetration. Can any government worth its salt, whose duty it is to uphold the moral standard of the people under its control condone, encourage, or legalize an evil the ultimate result of which would be disastrous to the progress of some people? If prostitution cannot be wholly exterminated in Nigeria, it can be considerably reduced with the introduction of a new industrial policy broad and generous enough to accord to womanhood the position befitting it. We warn our youth against the importation into this country of a system which has nothing but pernicious effects on the country where it is in practice.[53]

In the absence of any official or unofficial polls, it is difficult to measure the extent of support for or against prohibition and regulation of prostitution. Our knowledge of the issue is determined largely by the ideology of the editors of the various nationalist newspapers and the access they granted to protagonists and antagonists. For instance, the *Daily Service*, the official organ of the Nigerian Youth Movement (NYM), was openly prohibitionist. Its financiers—which included the famous Dr. Kofoworola Abayomi, F. R. A. Williams, Ernest Ikoli, and Hezekiah Oladipo Davies, among others—and "educated" readership probably considered themselves too "civilized" to read stories advocating regulation. As the party that sought to position itself for possible postcolonial leadership, the NYM no doubt had an anticolonial agenda that included prostitution as an issue of social degradation to be combated. Indeed, the NYM's stance on domestic and transnational prostitution was officially recognized by the government—the party played a prominent role in the criminalization of a notorious West African prostitution network when the activities of Nigerian prostitutes in what is now Ghana reached the point where "the Gold Coast men and women who have not travelled farther than their area believe that all the Nigerian women are harlots, and that it is a recognized custom in Nigeria."[54]

Unlike the *Daily Service*, which maintained a rigid conservative stance against regulation, Dr. Nnamdi Azikiwe's (Zik) newspapers—the *West African Pilot*, the *Southern Nigeria Defender*, the *Nigerian Spokesman*, and the *Daily Comet*—were liberal and tended to entertain opposing views.[55] Indeed, Zik, a member of NYM until 1941, when a leadership crisis prompted him to abandon the group, monopolized the newspaper industry throughout the 1940s to the first decade of independent Nigeria.[56] But Zik's popularity went beyond his monopoly of the print media. Unlike the *Daily Service*, which represented the voice of elite and upper-class Lagosians, Zik's newspapers propagated his "populist" ideology that was trendy among the middle-class (so-called third-class) clerks who seemed closer to the realities of the social revolution accentuated by colonial rule. Zik, who introduced into Nigerian print media American-style "sensational journalism," carried more pro-regulationist stories than any other Nigerian newspaper operators and seemed to have capitalized on the melodrama of prostitution stories to facilitate readership and sales.

Zik himself was neither openly prohibitionist nor regulationist. But his position tended to maintain a balance between the discussions of sex that were "useful" and those that were "injurious" to the state. This fence-sitting dovetailed with the nationalists' selective modernity that hinged on the appropriation of some elements of Western sexual culture but not others. Indeed, it is only in the pages of the *West African Pilot* that one could read articles on such issues as the importance of sex education in the development of a virile nationhood or editorials advising the school system to integrate sex education into the curriculum in order to stem the tide of "premature" sexual encounter, prostitution, and the increasing wave of VD.[57] Zik even wrote an interesting piece titled "Sexology," in which he challenged the silencing of sex in the public square.[58] "I do not want to give the impression that I am vulgar nor do I claim to be sanctimonious," he told his audience, "but I want to discuss a very delicate subject within the bounds of propriety and decency." He gave a brief definition of sexology as the "scientific understanding of sexual factors" in the society and argued that despite Africans' advancement, "we [Africans] are deplorably ignorant on the factors of sex." He suggested that the African drive toward modernity must recognize and emulate the Western societies where teenagers receive sex education in schools. While some conservatives may not have liked Zik's mentioning of the physiology of male and female sexual organs, or his frank discussion of the different functions each performed, or his willingness to turn a scientific discussion of sex into a subject for public consumption, they would have liked how he ended his piece by tying sexuality to larger issues of public health and nation-building. He recommended sex education for prospective brides and grooms because "the basic cause of maladjustment in married life is sexual." For him, Africans' "ignorance of sexology" accounted for the high rates of divorce and VD incidence that were detrimental to the emergence of a virile state. Zik's sex education article and others could have been "sexually liberating" because they were outside the conventional purview of the impact of dangerous sexualities like prostitution on the state.

Child Prostitution and the
Age of Consent Controversy

Child prostitution laws, like those concerning adults, also came under vehement criticism. For instance, critics accused the police of unjustly arresting child hawkers over 16 years of age. However, the problem of policing child hawkers went beyond police mischief to encompass the challenges of using age as a parameter for enforcing law, as one editorial in the *Nigerian Daily Times* pontificated: "We appreciate fully that the police cannot be expected to be exact in determining the age of an alleged girl offender especially when she is an up country girl."[59] In a confidential, handwritten memo responding to a newspaper criticism on the indiscriminate arrest of girls, Commissioner of the Colony J. G. C. Allen admitted seeing "some adults and grown-up girls chased around Balogun Square."[60] Another problem was how to reconcile the contradiction of hawking as a form of apprenticeship that prepared children for adult roles, augmented household income, and helped transmit skills from generation to generation, and as a "backward" custom that was anachronistic in the face of rapid urbanization and immense urban insecurity. Two polemics appeared on the hawking debate: the neotraditionalist view (that hawking was useful in the constantly unstable economic situation of Lagos that created poverty) and the modernist view (that such practices had outlived their precolonial relevance).[61] Although these opposing views date back to the 1930s, it was during the 1940s when street trading laws came into firm effect that the polarization assumed a vociferous dimension on the pages of the newspapers. The street trading laws, like other prostitution and child protective laws, had been passed without consultation with the public whom it affected. Parents decried the fines imposed on children and the incessant police harassment.

However, no child prostitution law created controversy like the proposed Native Authority Child Betrothal Order, or NACBO, of 1943. As noted in chapter 5, this bill—expected to be passed and implemented in the provinces because of the government's conviction that most Lagos child prostitutes were from outside the city—raised the age of consent and betrothal to 17 and criminalized carnal knowledge of girls under this age. When it came up for deliberation at the meeting of the Ibadan Native Authority Inner Council on March 20, 1944, the council defended the credibility of betrothal by arguing that their girls lived with their parents until the time when full marriage arrangements and rites (*igbeyawo*) were made.[62] "Passing a law to forbid the practice [betrothal] in Ibadan," the council concluded, "was unnecessary."[63] The district officer of the Ibadan Northern Districts communicated the outcome of the native authority's deliberation on the matter to the Lagos authority not only by denying the trafficking of girls from the region but also by attempting to educate the government about the process of native marriage: "The normal procedure throughout this area is that parents do not allow their daughters to marry until they are at least sixteen years of age and seventeen or eighteen is more usual . . . Betrothal of young children still takes place but is rapidly dying out as it becomes generally known that girls cannot be forced to marry against their wishes. In general the men leave young girls alone until they become of marriageable age and cases of offences against young girls are in the Courts." On a final note, the district officer submitted: "I do not consider any legislation necessary in the circumstances."[64] A similar statement was issued after the meeting of the native authorities in Ijebu Province.[65] The NACBO was also condemned by the Islamic authorities in the north. Unlike their southern counterparts who denied betrothal of girls or claimed that girls were not given in marriage until 16 or 17, the northern clerics, according to M. H. Varvill, the secretary of the Northern Provinces, argued that betrothal was the only way to maintain a girl's chastity "in the present atmosphere of sexual promiscuity."[66] In a confidential memo to the resident of Kano Province, Varvill pointed out that the NACBO met stiff opposition because the term "unlawful carnal knowledge" was interpreted to mean sexual intercourse between husband and wife, if the wife was younger than 15. This, according to him, "was regarded as an unacceptable interference with Moslem marriage custom."[67]

The CWO and other sponsors of the NACBO encountered stiff opposition because they presented their agenda without any sensitivity to native marriage customs. Terms like "child marriage" were of Western derivation and were obviously absent from most if not all Nigerian customary laws.[68] The CWO attempt to impose a unitary age of consent on hundreds of ethnic groups contravened traditional marriage practices that rarely considered chronological age as a marker of attainment of adulthood or readiness for marriage but instead considered the satisfaction of social responsibilities and participation in rites of passages. Moreover, child prostitution was predominantly an urban phenomenon, and girls were not trafficked from all Nigerian towns and villages. Indeed, some native authorities claimed they were not aware of such inhuman activities as underage prostitution. Yet, the hike in bride-price that critics believed contributed to trafficking did not affect the entire country uniformly. Indeed, in the 1940s marriage customs in several parts of southern Nigeria and the north continued to be conducted in a manner similar to the precolonial and pre-monetization eras when bride-price was paid in agricultural products and cash payments were symbolic not transactional. It is unclear why the CWO did not restrict the NACBO to certain parts of southern Nigeria where most of the child prostitutes came from. Probably, it would have passed in places like Kukuruku Division, where the district officer's unpopular decision to prevent girls from leaving his jurisdiction appeared to have worked, or in Owerri, where the district officer helped the CWO to stop Elizabeth Nwannena, "a reputed prostitute," from removing 13-year-old Akuigbo Ibejianya from his jurisdiction under the pretext of betrothal.[69] The bill was bound to fail given the Nigeria-wide outlook on which it was based and the uncritical or prejudiced British stance on marriage, one of the core components of traditional existence.

As it turned out, controversy over the NACBO brought cultural nationalism into the realm of sexuality regulation. The native authorities strongly guarded the regulation of marriage because as senior men they received honor and respect, in part, through the possession of a harem of young wives. By criminalizing carnal knowledge of girls under 17, the bill made them potential offenders. Moreover, it undermined the authority they wielded over the junior unmarried men since bride-price augmented their income and by extension that of the larger community. The earlier a girl was betrothed, the longer the duration of premarital obligations, which included the transfer of gifts, money, and social responsibilities from one family to another. Beyond its impact on the political economy of marriage, the NACBO would have negatively revolutionized the pattern of social and communal relations that to a large extent was facilitated through marriage. In addition, marriage was traditionally considered a private family matter, outside the jurisdiction of the state. For many, the forces of rapid urbanization, monetization, and the legalization of divorce were already undermining Nigerian male authority; they saw the NACBO as another potential crisis.

The age of women also determined the reactions of the native authorities to both the proposed NACBO and several other marriage laws that came before it. While all the native authorities condemned the NACBO, they encouraged the government, in several instances, to pass laws forbidding adult women's migration to Lagos and other cities. Thus, the native authorities in various parts of the country were selective in approving or disapproving marriage laws in accordance with demography and age. For some native authorities (especially in rural areas), the local economy suffered setbacks when wives who contributed to the domestic economy as traders, agriculturists, and artisans left for the city.[70] Control over their productive and reproductive rights and capabilities—publicly couched in the vocabulary of preserving the sanctity of African culture—targeted women's growing influence in the society. A petition by the chiefs of Agwagwune Town in Obubra Division of Ogoja Province sheds adequate light on the power of women's labor and the impact of prostitution on the community:

> Because of harlotism the population of our village is diminishing. Our taxable males are few and for that sake our taxable money is so little that it does not suffice for use for general improvement of the town . . . Owing to our small population, it is difficult for us to maintain our school. Owing to lack of population we cannot do anything to improve our town . . . Because our women cannot marry or live at home to produce children, the shortage of labour is acute in our town so much that we are compelled to employ labour from other villages. It is practically impossible to count all the havoc done to any village, town, or nation in which harlotism prevails.[71]

Another factor was the challenge to established hierarchies posed by returnee adult prostitutes when they invested their income in property considered to be the preserve of men.[72] Men feared that the wealth displayed by returnee prostitutes could discourage young girls from marrying and jeopardize the prospect of receiving bride-price. However, it would appear that the attitude of the chiefs toward casual sex work varied from place to place and was shaped by the impact of women's emigration on local economies. It seems that the men who protested migratory prostitution were those who did not benefit from remittances.

VD Laws, Nationalism, and the Politics of Economic Survival

As one would expect, the Undesirable Advertisement Ordinance, or UAO, even before it came into effect, encountered vehement criticism by pharmacists and apothecaries who believed it undermined their profession and means of livelihood. The Nigerian Pharmaceutical Society (NPS) and the Nigerian Apothecary Society (NAS), a unionized body of apothecaries permitted under the Poisons and Pharmacy Ordinance to "mix, compound, prepare, dispense and sell drugs," were among the first Lagosians to resist the UAO.[73] Although they were not trained physicians, the apothecaries and pharmacists advised and recommended Western medicines for the treatment of various illnesses. Because their fees were moderate, they enjoyed patronage from middle-class, Western-educated Lagosians who could not afford the charges of government hospitals and private practitioners and did not have access to, or disliked, the "uncivilized" herbalist remedies.[74] A NAS petition dated May 30, 1932, and signed by five representatives (C. Ayo Savage, A. Babatunde King, V. Ayo Taiwo, Fred. Mobolaji Benson, and J. O. Akin Allen), lamented that the UAO would further limit their income.[75] They itemized the contradictions inherent in a law that did not prevent them from preparing drugs but criminalized their advertisement. "Are we to infer that we could so prepare a medicine without advertising it or providing direction for use?"[76]

Although it did not challenge the government's observation on the ubiquity of VD advertisement and the danger it could pose to the medical well-being of Lagosians, the NAS came up with a creative way to negotiate its economic survival while enhancing social control. It asked the government to declare that all literature and advertisements for drugs be distributed through them. "In the interest of trade," it asserted, "we are of the opinion that it is only fair for the government to allow the circulation through the proper channel only, namely, the Chemists and Druggists and selling Dispensers and their Agents."[77] This proposal, while preserving the economic interest of the NAS, would have turned them into another arm of social control. In addition, it would also have given the group economic leverage against recalcitrant members and nonmembers who defied the society's rules. The government declined this proposal, insisting that it reserved the sole right to ensure that its subjects were protected from "dangerous" medicines.

When the NAS discovered that authorities would not yield to this request, it lobbied to repeal the UAO through Dr. C. C. Adeniyi-Jones, one of the Lagos members of the Legislative Council of Nigeria (LCN). Adeniyi-Jones, a physician trained at the Universities of Durham and Dublin, was also a founding member (with Macaulay) of the Nigerian National Democratic Party (NNDP), which held political sway in Lagos from 1923 until 1938.[78] Adeniyi-Jones confessed to having supported the ordinance when it was brought before the council for deliberation because he felt that the promiscuous patronage of fake remedies was out of hand. The rhetoric of the danger of VD drugs and literature might have appealed to the judgment of Adeniyi-Jones, who was well known for promoting African business. The NPS and the NAS, however, were able to pressure him to change his position on the UAO by resisting legislation he had earlier supported. Adeniyi-Jones probably feared losing political relevance, especially with the rise of a young and vibrant generation of nationalists who had founded the Lagos Youth Movement in 1934 (later the NYM). Adeniyi-Jones was putting the cart before the horse when he asked the director of medical and sanitary service (DMSS) to provide him with the following data he was supposed to have requested before the UAO was passed:

> a. To ask whether Government will give an indication of the incidence of venereal diseases, and their effects, in the seaport towns of Lagos, Port Harcourt and Calabar for the ten years ended December 1933;
> b. A comparison with that of the previous ten years;
> c. If the comparison suggests an increasing prevalence of the complaint, what measures are in operation to arrest its spread and alleviate its effects?[79]

In his response, the DMSS replied that because VD was not a notifiable disease, there was no record of its incidence.[80] He mentioned also that there was "no evidence that VD [had] increased in prevalence during the past ten years." And according to him, the only VD clinic in Nigeria was established on the Apapa Wharf "specifically for the benefit of the seamen."[81] Probably not convinced that the present arrangement was adequate for dealing with VD among Africans and unhappy that only the European seamen had a VD clinic, Adeniyi-Jones composed a proposal suggesting the establishment of a VD clinic at the African Hospital on Lagos Island.[82] The DMSS replied that one section of the Outpatient Department at the African Hospital was already planned for conversion to a VD clinic and "[could] be opened shortly if funds [could] be found."[83] In any event, the DMSS did not embark on the immediate establishment of a VD clinic in the African Hospital and Lagosians did not get a VD clinic until 1945. The response of the DMSS firmly established official policy toward venereal disease and, as mentioned earlier, the overwhelming role that economic factors played in the formulating of the UAO—legislation passed without concrete documented evidence of any increase in the cases of VD over time.

Of all the antagonists of the UAO, the African healers were the most unpopular with colonial administrators. Indeed, the tension between the healers and authorities dates back to the early days of colonial administration when the latter expressed the belief that the former's profession/activities impeded colonial civilization. The healers were frequently blamed for deliberately spreading epidemic diseases like smallpox and accusing innocent people of witchcraft in order to extort patients. Indeed, the African healing system faced both local and foreign opposition. While local opposition came from African doctors trained in Western medicine, foreign opponents included European medical authorities and Christian missionaries. With the exception of Dr. Oguntola Odunbaku Sapara, the most influential traditional medical practitioner and one of colonial Nigeria's frontline cultural nationalists, nearly all the African medical doctors, especially the famous Dr. Kofoworola Abayomi, worked against the local healers' trade.[84] Sapara, who trained at the Universities of Glasgow and Edinburgh and was inducted into the Royal Institute of Public Health in 1895, believed that African and Western medicine could coexist successfully.[85] After collaborating with the British in breaking the ranks of the *Sopona* (Yoruba god of smallpox) cult and facilitating the promulgation of the Witchcraft and Juju Ordinance, Sapara became the best ally of the native healers, helping them in their quest to legitimize and professionalize their occupation.[86] He organized them into guilds and facilitated their registration under the Companies Ordinance of 1922. These associations, including the Nigerian Association of Medical Herbalists, the Native Medical Society, and the Lagos Doctor's Society of Shangodeyi's House, set up rules and regulations that members were expected to abide by.[87]

Already popular among both political and medical authorities as the mouthpiece of the African healers, Sapara roundly condemned the UAO. In a February 1933 letter to the DMSS, he contended that the native healers were not responsible for the rise in cases of VD; instead, he blamed the lax sexual behavior of modern Lagos.[88] He extolled the healers for their selfless work in improving the health of Lagosians and decried the poor state of infrastructure in the government hospitals. No Lagosian knew the state of government medical facilities as did Sapara, who was the longest-serving Nigerian colonial surgeon of his time—he served for thirty-two years.[89] He used the UAO controversy to further his agitation for the government to formally accept and incorporate native medicine into the medical department. When his request that the law be repealed was not granted, he followed up with two other petitions in June 1933 and August 1934. As in his February 1933 petition, Sapara reiterated the need to stop the implementation of the UAO but added a new component.[90] He believed that criminalizing the advertisement of the VD drugs and aphrodisiacs would only create an underground market for medicine and endanger the health of Lagosians. Advertisement in the public domain, according to him, would allow authorities to monitor medical providers and prosecute them for illegal practices.[91] The August 1934 petition would be Sapara's final critique of the UAO, as he fell sick and later died in June 1935 of prostate enlargement. His demise created a major vacuum in the African healers' politics of legitimacy and mobilization against the UAO and their occupation in general. However, the healers were quick to realize the need to move ahead with their struggle. They wrote at least five petitions to the government between 1936 and 1943. A November 1941 petition by the Lagos Doctor's Society of Shangodeyi's House, thumb-printed by 121 registered herbalists, reiterated its concern over enforcement of the UAO and demanded that the government stop police harassment.

Just as the herbalists were working to decriminalize the advertising of VD drugs and aphrodisiacs, African medical doctors continued to publicly denounce traditional medicine. At a public lecture titled "Venereal Disease as a Social Problem," delivered in March 1945, Dr. Abayomi lambasted the healers for promoting sexual recklessness by selling aphrodisiacs.[92] When asked about his take on *magun*, a spiritual charm professed to have the power to regulate/prohibit promiscuity by killing adulterous men and women, Abayomi added another element to the long list of controversies on Yoruba medicine when he claimed that it was a superstition.[93] He pointed out that the instant death presumed to be caused by *magun* was attributable to "bursting of the heart or some blood vessels caused by the high blood pressure resulting from the excitement derived from sexual intercourse."[94] He tacitly withdrew his statement when more than a dozen healers volunteered to demonstrate the efficacy of *magun* before the public in exchange for his £50 bet.[95] This episode helps illustrate the confusion associated with the nationalists' construction of progress and their idea of modernity. Abayomi's vision of a modern and progressive Nigeria both under colonial rule and after independence contradicted the mainstream culture that was more receptive to native remedies. He was both a resister and a collaborator, as his views on the "primitivity" of native medicines concurred with those of the imperialists.

Lagosians and the VD Clinic

The announcement of the Venereal Diseases Ordinance (VDO) in 1943 was popular in the press, partly because it was not aimed primarily at controlling venereal disease in the army but also targeted the civilian population.[96] The *West African Pilot* applauded what it called the "unsilencing" of VD and went on to state that "the sense of reserve which used to be maintained in dealing with this human ailment has been found to be nothing short of false modesty . . . Much life could be saved and many more salvaged by its application."[97] For the *Daily Service*, the importance of the VDO transcended public health to include nation-building: "Our readers would readily understand how distressingly serious is the incidence of venereal disease in this country today. Venereal disease more than any other malady precedes virile, robust and radiant manhood, without which no nation can hope to achieve great things and command the respect of its neighbours. It is therefore a national danger of more serious type against which we cannot be too vigilant."[98] Moreover, the *Nigerian Daily*

Times, known for its pro-British orientation, expressed optimism in the projected outcome of the VDO: "We hope that the VD law will do something to check this dangerous scourge."[99]

Unfortunately, the VDO did not produce the anticipated outcome, partly because of stereotyping of VD victims and misinterpretations of certain sections of the ordinance. Dr. Kofoworola Abayomi, in his lecture on "Venereal Disease as a Social Problem," stated categorically that "the sowers of VD are prostitutes."[100] Another Lagos physician, Dr. A. B. I. Olorun-nimbe also blamed prostitutes for spreading VD.[101] Even the influential artist Akinola Lasekan produced works that reinforced the assertions of the physicians. In one of his cartoons published in 1944, Lasekan rendered a visual representation of the relationship between prostitution and VD.[102] These pronouncements by influential personalities discouraged VD sufferers from attending government clinics so as to avoid being labeled as "prostitutes."[103] As table 6.1 shows, attendance at the Ikeja clinic did not correspond with the alleged gravity of VD in a city of about 250,000 people in 1950. The fact that more men than women attended the Ikeja clinic suggests that the former were more likely to accommodate the stereotype of VD than the latter. Furthermore, Lagosians misinterpreted section 4(2) of the VDO, which empowered physicians to notify the police if a patient

Table 6.1. Monthly Returns of Venereal Disease, November 1945
Males

VD types	Cured	Under Treatment	Absconders
Gonorrhea	3	11	4
Complications of gonorrhea	—	—	2
Syphilis	—	2	1
Complications of syphilis	—	—	—
Chancroid	3	—	—
Disease other than venereal (Yaw)	—	5	5
Total	6	18	12

Females

VD types	Cured	Under Treatment	Absconders
Gonorrhea	7	4	—
Complications of gonorrhea	3	—	—
Syphilis	—	1	2
Complications of syphilis	—	—	—
Chancroid	—	—	—
Disease other than venereal (Yaw)	—	1	3
Total	10	6	5

Source: NAI, (Fed) 1/1 6304A, "Venereal Disease Clinic Ikeja: Return of Cases."

refused to comply with a treatment regimen. They thought patients would be arrested after completing their treatment.[104] This communication gap reinforced the lack of trust in colonial administration. Lagosians saw the VD clinic as another ill-conceived project of public sanitation, which punished "innocent" citizens in lieu of the "undesirables" (i.e., criminals and prostitutes).

The popularity of native remedies for VD continued to grow in spite of the free treatment given at the VD clinics.[105] While the African alternative healers guaranteed anonymity of patients, the government VD clinics documented information about social and sexual history, which patients were reluctant to divulge. The admission form for both inpatients and outpatients contained such fields as marital status, occupation, number of past and present sex partners, and so on.[106] The Ikeja clinic demanded that patients attend appointments with their spouses or partners, a decision that most people found unacceptable.[107] Military Doctor M. Taylor, who operated the Ikeja clinic, realized that patients were reluctant to give information that could help him administer appropriate treatment, and was discouraged by the low attendance.[108] He suggested to the DMSS that clinics should protect a patient's privacy by not collecting personal information.[109] For the DMSS, medical records were an integral component of modern medical practice and the basis of funding the clinic.[110] Throughout the 1940s, attendance at each of the three clinics did not exceed three hundred during a given year. On the whole, the project of increasing Lagosians' access to Western remedies for VD in order to safeguard the health of the military fell short as the military continued to look inward in dealing with VD by establishing early-treatment centers in the barracks and enforcing disciplinary measures for concealment.

Conclusion

The reactions of Lagos men to anti-prostitution laws revealed that the moralists' perceptions of sexual immorality were not static but continued to change in accordance with the issues involved. Also, men's identity and social status tended to influence where they stood. If Lagos men did not speak with one voice about prostitution, it was because sexual immorality did not have a "unitary" definition and did not impact the entire male population in the same manner. An occasionally blurred distinction existed between those who wanted prostitution to be regulated and those who advocated prohibition. The upper class tended to be prohibitionists probably because advocating for regulation could undermine their elitist status as politicians, public intellectuals, and leading professionals of the era. Regardless of the position taken by various categories of men, the challenges of policing prostitution exemplified the broader problems confronting the colonial state. Social instability and poverty were blamed for both the increasing rate of prostitution and the government's failed attempt to effectively police it. The activities of *boma* boys were on the rise as World War II emergency regulations inhibited the internal security of the colony. Their impact paralleled that of prostitution, which also increased in response to escalating demand created by the presence of troops and massive immigration of men from the provinces. By the end of World War II, anti-prostitution laws, instead of serving the purposes for which they had been enacted, redefined the landscape of sexuality as prostitutes, their patrons, and other members of the underclass adopted new methods of solicitation to protect a trade that guaranteed their livelihood and protected or enhanced their social status.

Lagos was the main scene of most of the controversy over sexuality regulation. However, the debate over the introduction of the NACBO took sexual politics to the villages and native authorities as the chiefs defended the "integrity" of native marriage in order to safeguard their socioeconomic interests. The ordinance was not on par with most native marriage practices because its aim was to fix bride-price, age of betrothal, and the definition of carnal knowledge. The NACBO also enhanced government intervention in marriage, which most believed was strictly a family matter. In defending against this encroachment, the chiefs denied that guardianship, apprenticeship, and betrothal facilitated girl trafficking. But age largely determined the disposition of the native authorities to the British attempt to regulate marriage. While they tended to condemn the emigration of women to the city and sometimes enlisted the British in policing the mobility of their women, they condemned girls-oriented laws.

To better understand why men contested anti-prostitution laws, we must first acknowledge that the colonial state's understanding of the impact of vice did not correspond with the facilities necessary to tackle it. The failure of anti-prostitution laws was not due to a lack of motivation on the British side; indeed, the British believed that the laws would ameliorate the real and imagined threat prostitution posed to imperial interests in Nigeria. Instead, the failure can best be explained as the result of poor implementation on the part of both the colonial masters and their Nigerian staff, including but not limited to the NPF and the CWO. Racial and gender bias and a lack of sensitivity to cultural variations among the myriad of Nigerian ethnic groups were only a few of the reasons anti-prostitution laws did not achieve their desired results. The adoption of a short-term approach to controlling vice meant that the colonialists were merely attacking the superficial aspects of the "problem of prostitution."

CHAPTER 7

LAGOS ELITE WOMEN
AND THE STRUGGLE
FOR LEGITIMACY

Men in Nigeria (both the colonized and the colonizers) did not monopolize the tenor of sexual politics. Indeed, Lagos elite women, dating back to the early 1920s, were the first to insert illicit sexuality into their long list of projects aimed at improving women's sociopolitical and economic visibility. Like the male nationalists, they expressed optimism that the 1940s prohibitionist regime would help curb the menace of prostitution, especially the trafficking of girls. For instance, when the Unlicensed Guide (Prohibition) Ordinance (UGPO) was passed in 1941, Charlotte Obasa sent a congratulatory message to the chief secretary to the government for honoring the decades-long call of the Lagos Women's League (LWL) for "sweeping Lagos of the bad and dangerous elements of decency."[1] With time, the elite women would be disappointed by the paradoxical situation resulting from anti-prostitution laws: on the one hand, they fulfilled the demand for policing prostitutes and controlling the influx of girls into Lagos, but on the other hand, they opened up new arenas for the violation of women's rights.

But sexual politics between the colonialists and elite women went beyond the criticism of the poor implementation of anti-prostitution laws—Obasa, Oyinkan Abayomi, H. Millicent Douglas, among other prominent members of the LWL, the Nigerian Women's Party (NWP), and the Women's Welfare Council (WWC) began to change their position on major aspects of sex crime against girls and worked to undermine the colonialists' rehabilitation projects. This ideological transition reflects one of the core arguments of this book— that illicit sexuality constituted different forms of danger to the ideas and projects of the various classes within the colonial system in terms of power relations. Because each group within the colonialist and Lagosian hierarchy interpreted sexual vice from a different perspective, they were bound to view solutions through a diverse lens. Controversy over the implementation of anti-prostitution legislation fully brings to the fore the division between the elite women and the government over which institution should be responsible for regulating prostitution and added a new dimension to the longstanding heated politics of race and the question of the employment of African women in government service. From the 1940s, the movement to rescue girls from the "moral scourge" of prostitution became a new site of struggle over the unresolved conflict arising from the notion of the inferiority of African women, popular among British colonial administrators. As it turned out, the elite women were fighting not only to establish their ability to help stop the trafficking of girls but to reposition themselves within the racist and sexist colonial structure that sidelined them. Illicit sexuality became a battleground of contestation over gendered colonialism.

Market women and the uneducated groups played a very limited role in shaping sexual politics, which reflected the differential in the kinds of challenges women across social classes faced and how they mobilized to address them. In the 1940s, more than in previous decades, market women were confronted with a bigger crisis of economic survival because they were on the receiving end of numerous harsh economic policies during the war, which aside from impoverishing them also criminalized them for selling items above price levels fixed by the government.[2] While educated women spent time meeting with top government officers about such matters as the improper implementation of anti-prostitution statutes, market women led by Alimotu Pelewura, by contrast, were marching on the government house to demand the release of women arrested for profiteering.[3] At times they closed the markets until their demands were met and engaged in anticolonial activities, some of which undermined Britain's Win-the-War effort.[4] I am not suggesting that the market women did not oppose sex crime against girl hawkers and other categories of often defenseless girls. But they committed far more energy to fighting adverse economic policies that were more relevant to their economic survival than to campaigns against anti-prostitution legislation. It is a truism that the elite women were supportive of some of the activities of market women.[5] For instance, the LWL helped the market women compose an eight-paragraph petition against the negative socioeconomic impact of food price controls in 1943.[6] However, when examined in a broader context, it is apparent that the anticolonial activities of each class of women reflected their construction of personal and collective progress under colonialism. For the uneducated market women, progress would mean freedom from negative economic policies that prevented them from fulfilling desired social and financial obligations in their families and community. For the educated, most of whom were upper-class, "wealthy" persons, it meant helping to position Nigeria as a modern state through increased access for women to Western education and elimination of male-centered policies that exploited women. Although sexual politics manifested in the confluence and divergence of ideas of normalcy and respectability espoused by diverse groups operating from different levels, it was essentially an elitist project.

The Elite Women
and Their Prohibitionist Agenda

Unlike the African men whose stance on prostitution from the 1940s revealed polarization across class, location, and agency, the elite women constituted a single ideological bloc. Even the creation of the WWC and the NWP, in 1942 and 1944, respectively, did not polarize their agenda. This contrast is to be expected. Men outnumbered women in weighty positions of authority and in terms of public visibility—as newspaper editors, politicians, native authorities, professionals, and public commentators.[7] The NWP, LWL, and WWC viewed regulationist policies as politically and morally unacceptable probably because to support them would brand them as advocates of immorality. As we will see later, although they did revise some of their positions, they remained adamant that prostitution must be prohibited. And while the British from the early 1940s treated child prostitution and juvenile delinquency as threats to colonial security, elite women focused on their impact on their project of modern African womanhood. The modern African womanhood project involved increasing women's access to the positive gains of Western civilization (especially education) while doing away with African and British sociocultural obstacles that inhibited upward mobility. The women eloquently espoused this idea in several of their communications, one of which was Abayomi's article "Modern Womanhood."[8] Another article by Kofoworola Ademola titled "Miss Kofo Moore Defends Her Sex" was serialized in the *West African Pilot.*[9] Elite women envisioned political independence and believed that women would play important roles in the life of the newly independent state of Nigeria.[10]

The constructed dichotomy between underage and adult sexualities principally informed the elite women's position on criminalization. While they viewed adult prostitutes as inherently irredeemable, they believed that the girls in moral danger could still be removed from the streets and brothels and rehabilitated for their good and the good of society.[11] Hence, their development approach to vice mirrored that of the Colony Welfare Office (CWO). And like the CWO they believed that girls' sexual deviance was attributable to the criminality of adults. While they demanded that the government establish hostels where delinquent girls could be rehabilitated and increase funding for girls' education, they neither worked to rehabilitate adult prostitutes convicted of breaking anti-prostitution statutes nor believed that repatriating the women to the provinces would create any problems. Whereas they protested against VD and the virginity screening of underage girls, they did not contest such sexist laws as the Venereal Diseases Ordinance (VDO) (1943).[12] The elite women did not generally protest against the gender-biased nature of anti-prostitution laws, which prosecuted prostitutes but excluded European seamen, sex tourists, and soldiers—the customers of prostitutes.[13] For them, wayward adult women did not qualify for their political protection because they were agents of immorality and disease.

The women's pre–World War II prohibitionist agenda was reflected mostly in petitions sent to authorities; during the 1940s, however, they would, in addition to petitions, organize lectures featuring highly respected professional women who were also public intellectuals. The lectures, which were open to the public, clearly unveiled their agenda and popularized their activities, especially when the proceedings were also published in the newspapers.[14] Even minutes of their meetings with administrators appeared in the papers and stimulated editorial and public commentary.[15] A typical public lecture (as table 7.1 illustrates) tended to be well structured, allowing speakers to dwell on specific aspects of moral danger. This approach dovetailed into the women's strong conviction that any solution to sexual immorality must be systemic and grounded in the colonial state's radical transformation of some of its core gender values, which saw women as "inferior."

Nativism, influenced by the politics of place, was another potent element of the women's response to anti-prostitution legislation. Before the early 1940s, they localized their agitation against sexual vice by insisting that Lagos should not be made the "headquarters" of prostitutes and did not petition for the stamping out of sex work in the provinces because they identified themselves first as Lagosians and then as British subjects of Nigeria. Most of the women had been born in Lagos during the last quarter of the nineteenth century and lived their entire lives there (except when they traveled abroad to receive education or for other purposes). But the government's new prohibitionist

Table 7.1. Proceedings of a Public Meeting Organized by the Women's Welfare Council on Girls' Moral Danger

Speakers	Title of Lecture
Mrs. Oyinkan Abayomi	"Effect of Prostitution on the Womanhood of This Country"
Mrs. Ajose	"Influence of the Home on Girl Prostitution"
Mrs. R. Timson	"Apala Dancing—a Moral Danger"
Mrs. C.E.N. Cadle	"Prostitution among Girl Hawkers"
Mr. S.L.A. Akintola	"The Pioneer Women in Industry—Their Moral Danger"
Dr. A.B.I. Olorun-nimbe	"Venereal Disease—A Moral Danger"

Sources: "Mrs Abayomi Attributes Prostitution to Laziness, Undue Gaiety, and Unemployment," West African Pilot, August 10, 1944; "Women's Welfare League's Protest Meeting against Moral Danger Proves a Big Success," Daily Service, August 10, 1944.

regime in the 1940s and the founding of the WWC and the NWP broadened the geographical reach of their agitation, from its initial "Lagos-centeredness" to "Pan-Nigerian" coverage. They began to actively participate in the fight against the trafficking of girls from the provinces by writing colonial officers and maintaining a stream of correspondence with them. Members of the NWP, which initially was named the Lagos Women's Party, toured the provinces and attempted to create a common ground for dealing with problems confronting Nigerian women and girls.[16]

The Police Women Controversy

Besides criticizing the unlawful arrest of "innocent" women for violations of anti-prostitution law, elite women recommended the enlistment of women in the Nigeria Police Force (NPF). Believing that prostitution was a female-specific crime, they thought it could best be policed by women who could go "into nooks and corners to ferret out these girls."[17] In October and December 1944, the NWP met and presented their women police proposal to three high-ranking officers—the secretary of the Lagos Town Council (LTC), A. Martin; Superintendent of the Police Mitchelin; and the chief secretary to the government of Nigeria, Hoskyns Abrahall.[18] In their meeting with the first official, they clearly established their knowledge of the racial origin of the UGPO and its intended goal to protect European sex visitors and sex tourists. But this objective, according to them, "has been carried too far and people of unquestionable character have been arrested without necessary caution."[19] They recommended that "unless in cases of questionable character and known prostitutes and 'Boma boys,' intending arrests should be carefully undertaken."[20] When they met with Superintendent Mitchelin, they narrated how a member of the NWP described as "middle aged and educated" was arrested for "loitering" in front of her own house, only to be released "after a lot of begging and some tipping."[21] Their meeting with Chief Secretary Abrahall appeared to be the most decisive. Represented by its Political and Social Committee (Abayomi, T. Dedeke, A. Manuwa, Ekemode, A. Coker, B. Oyediran, L. Timson, and E. Kuti-Okoya), the NWP went beyond proposing the mere introduction of women police to specifying the ages of the women to be so employed: between 40 and 50.[22] It is unclear why the NWP recommended women of a particular age range. It may be that they believed women in their forties were mature wives and mothers, who would also be strong enough to undertake police work.

Public opinion was divided over the employment of women as police. One commentator, Miss Silva, the editor of the Women's Column of the *West African Pilot*, believed it would help reduce child prostitution; others thought that policing the red-light district with women would not end the systemic moral decadence that caused it.[23] If the public was divided over the use of women police, authorities were firmly united—in opposition. In his response to the NWP's demand, Commissioner of Police W. C. C. King rejected the proposal outright, claiming that civilians did not understand "how difficult a Policeman's job is."[24] His condemnation of the enrollment of women in the NPF touched on the lawlessness of the red-light districts, ethnicity and public disorder, women's physical and intellectual inferiority, and women's inability to police the dangerous streets of Lagos. Portions of his three-page memo are worth quoting:

> I find it quite impossible to visualise women police in action in Lagos. They may patrol along the Marina or round the Race Course, where prostitutes wait for their victims, but I cannot see that they will do any better than the Police do at present. The only other places are low-class bars or so-called "hotels" and the "red light" areas where, as soon as there is trouble or interferences with "clients" a free fight ensues and the scene is then certainly no place for any woman. Successful Police work generally depends on the skill and experience of the officer engaged, not only in one particular class of offence but in all forms of crime which have brought him in contact with people drawn from all classes of society. The same would apply to a woman constable dealing with any Police case of a delicate nature—and those connected with prostitution, brothels, solicitation etc. call for a high degree of tact and skill in handling, securing evidence and prosecution, and are usually entrusted to officers of experience . . . To sum up, I am definitely opposed to the appointment of women constables in Lagos. I cannot visualise them dealing with the screaming and swearing prostitutes, drunken merchants, seamen of all nationalities, pimps, boma boys, touts and the rest of the unsavoury fraternities.[25]

King wanted Lagos to depend on parents, teachers, and the church in dealing with prostitution. For him, if women were not qualified to police prostitutes in some parts of Britain, the Nigerian demand was simply unrealistic. He presented the popular position among British policemen that "only women of exceptional physique and possessed of special qualities of intelligence, tact and courage are qualified to undertake Police duties . . . The PC's [police constable] job is essentially a man's job."[26] Therefore, if women of these qualities were rare in Great Britain, the tone of King's correspondence suggested, they would be rarer in Nigeria where women were supposedly less educated, intelligent, and energetic. But one must read King's posture between the lines. In the first place, the NWP's proposal challenged the Victorian notion of masculine superiority, especially in tasks that required intrepidity, intellect, and force. Hence, King saw women police's role not as complementary but as competitive—women would be not only vying for jobs with men, but also encroaching on a career considered the "natural" preserve of men. In sum, the excuse that "only women of exceptional physique" could deal with criminals functioned as a cover-up to preserve and extol male chauvinism and the institution of male authority in general.

As one would expect, King's response did not go over well with the elite women. In a protest letter to the governor of Nigeria, the elite women "felt embarrassed and insulted" by the assertion that women could not "stand the danger and technicality of policing prostitution." They mentioned that the government should allow them to present names of women who were highly educated and possessed "'the so-called physique' required for police-woman's job . . . well-known and respected ladies who are good mothers and would not tarnish the image of womanhood by encouraging immorality in our society."[27] Neither the governor nor his officials saw fit to reply to this counterargument.

No doubt the NWP's request was unusual for attempting to feminize the maintenance of law and order. But this was not the first time that the government was asked to revise its policies on recruitment into the NPF. For instance, during the debate over the control of *boma* boys and prostitutes in the Legislative Council of Nigeria (LCN) in 1941, Dr. Henry Carr attempted to ethnicize maintenance of law and order when he criticized the overrepresentation of easterners in the police force in Lagos. For him, they were not only "strangers" but also "did not understand either the language or the people themselves."[28] To curb the menace of *boma* boys and prostitution, Dr. Carr contended that more Yoruba men who understood the language of the delinquent criminals should be enlisted in the NPF. His request must be seen as more than a personal agitation by a Lagos elite, the highest-ranked African colonial bureaucrat of his time, and a member of the LCN. Rather, his position was representative of the nativist ideology shared by most Lagos politicians and professionals who became increasingly assertive against the growing political and economic influence of the Igbo in Lagos during the 1940s and 1950s. Dr. Carr's suggestion was never implemented, for obvious reasons. First, the ethnicity of criminality was diverse in that men and women who broke the law were not mainly Yoruba, but of varied ethnic roots. Second, it was in the best interests of the colonialists to post law enforcement officers away from their place of origin in order to enhance anonymity and brutally suppress opposition in the name of upholding the hegemonic status quo.

The idea of women police did not go away. In fact, in 1954 the first class of women was recruited into the NPF. They received no training in firearms and riot drills and were not given specific assignments to police prostitution; rather, they were confined predominantly to enforcement of traffic laws. In other words, the change of policy did not overturn the earlier bias that women were physically and mentally "unfit" to police the red-light streets. However, by 1956, they were permitted to police the red-light districts but not allowed to carry firearms. This prompted the press to criticize the government for exposing women police to "risks and danger." Like their male counterparts, women police were also accused of corruption, putting a dash to the hope that they would not compromise justice when dealing with female offenders. In September 1956, Crescentia Ifedira was arraigned for collecting a bribe of a wristwatch valued at about £2 from Clementina Taiwo.[29]

Although the government appeared to have yielded to the demands of the elite women, the enrollment of women in the NPF probably had more to do with international pressure than local influences. By the early 1950s, the practice of using women to police prostitution was common among the countries that subscribed to the UN's numerous conventions on trafficking of women and girls.[30] Nigeria, which did not subscribe to these conventions, was apparently embarrassed to repeatedly report its lack of police women in the UN's annual questionnaires aimed at sharing information about global trafficking of women and girls.[31]

The Politics of Rehabilitating Girls in Moral Danger

Another source of tension between elite women and the government manifested in the struggle over which institution or group should be responsible for rehabilitating child prostitutes and other girls in moral danger.[32] After initially promising the WWC that it would be in charge of the proposed girls' hostel, Donald Faulkner, the colony welfare officer, changed his mind, refused to communicate with the group regarding its official status, and went behind the backs of the WWC's representatives to approve Marble Hall as the girls' hostel.[33] This decision angered the WWC and the NWP, which began to criticize virtually all the procedures of the CWO.[34] Three of the CWO's major decisions—the choice of Marble Hall as the girls' hostel, the proposal to appoint a European woman as a lady welfare officer, and some sections of the Children and Young Persons Ordinance (CYPO)—came under attack. Regarding the first decision, the WWC pointed out that Marble Hall was located between a three-story building and a two-story building; such a location would be a distressing environment for the girls, who needed a serene environment for effective learning.[35] What is more, a hostel located opposite the notorious Grand Hotel, where people of shady character congregated, was not suitable for rehabilitating girls in moral danger, according to the WWC. The women of the WWC felt that "the language of crowds and taxi drivers who congregate in the street will be edifying to the children."[36] They regarded the Grand Hotel as "a den of iniquity."[37]

If the location of the hostel did not go over well with the WWC, the proposal made by Gladys Plummer, the European lady education officer, was even more of an offense. Plummer's assertion that a European lady should be employed as the lady welfare officer "because she knows of no woman of the African race who is competent" introduced racial prejudice into the already existing tension.[38] To be sure, elite women had long protested against the practice whereby European women, the majority of whom were expatriates and wives of colonial officers, were absorbed into government service in lieu of qualified

African women. The WWC disagreed with Plummer that a European lady must be appointed as lady welfare officer and that sending an African woman to the United Kingdom for training would be impossible because of war conditions.[39] They mentioned Aduke Alakija, who was "actually taking a course in Social Work" in the United Kingdom, as a likely candidate for the position.[40] The conclusion of the WWC's letter intimated that the government was not prepared to hire an African for the job: "In the meantime," the WWC asserted, "if government needs an experienced Social Worker of the African race, the Council would like it to be known that there is a member of This Body who can safely be recommended for such an appointment."[41] The government, later in 1946, would appoint a European woman, Alison Izzett, as the first female welfare officer.

Neither Faulkner nor Commissioner of the Colony G. B. Williams was apologetic about the choice of the girls' hostel. In correspondence that seems to have put the hostel controversy and the appointment of a lady welfare officer permanently to rest, Williams defended Faulkner's choice, arguing that the WWC must have misunderstood his officer since it was never the government's intention that the WWC or any other women's association would be in charge of the girls' hostel.[42] He went on to state that he did not agree with the women that the location was unsuitable and that the government was not prepared to employ a paid lady welfare officer "in the near future."[43] Sensing that the women would not be satisfied with his explanation, he closed his letter saying that he would like to meet with them for further clarification. When the WWC demanded that the governor of Nigeria appoint and officially recognize them as a visiting committee to the girls' hostel, Williams and Faulkner quickly recognized the women's plausible intent to constitute themselves as watchdogs of the reformatory activities of the hostel.[44] In a confidential handwritten memo to Williams, Faulkner lamented that "these people [the elite women] can be very troublesome" and expressed his opinion that they do not have "any clear motive for visiting the hostel."[45] Directed by Williams, Faulkner responded to the WWC by noting that the government appreciated their desire to help the Nigerian girls and that their request was under consideration.[46] However, the WWC request was never acted on. Instead, all attempts were made to ensure that the women did not have any supervisory or advisory role in the activities of the girls' hostel.

Not only did the government refuse to allow the elite women to be involved in its reformatory activities, it also frustrated their ambition to organize an "industrial centre" for women by not approving the use of either the old Officers' Mess at the Race Course or the old market stall on Freeman Street. Williams's excuses for not approving the use of the old Officers' Mess ranged from its proximity to motor roads, which "makes them unsuitable as regards for classes for young children," to the building's need for extensive repairs.[47] No excuse was given for disapproval of the use of the old market stall.[48] A close reading of the tone of the correspondence suggests that the commissioner was simply not disposed to allowing the women to use the building—a reflection of the authorities' decision to frustrate the elite women's activities and probably an act of revenge for their condemnation of the CWO's choice of Marble Hall and for the WWC's activities in general. But the government's lack of support did not stop the women from continuing their voluntary activities and working with girls and women, though there was a marked limit to what they could accomplish. They did not have legal power to institutionalize core welfare activities, nor did they have the resources to manage the enormous crisis of disempowerment confronting the thousands of Lagos girls.[49]

Another twist came when the CYPO, the most comprehensive body of legislation aimed at protecting and rehabilitating delinquent juveniles, came into effect on July 1, 1946. (The ordinance had been passed in 1943 but could not be fully implemented until 1946 due to World War II budgetary constraints.) Although the CYPO made elaborate provisions for the establishment of juvenile courts, remand homes, and modern institutions for addressing juvenile delinquency, some sections were deemed unacceptable by the WWC, the LWL, and the NWP.[50] The reactions of women's groups to this law established the extent to which they were willing to go to antagonize the CWO, even if it required changing their position on some of the fundamental problems confronting the girl-child. A June 1946 joint petition by the WWC, the LWL, and the NWP on behalf of "mothers in the community" intensely criticized the CYPO's section 25, which criminalized street trading by all girls under the age of 14, and those between 14 and 16, unless employed by their parents or by a guardian appointed by a court.[51] They held that girls contributed to the household economy through the proceeds from hawking and that government policy amounted to a "direct interference with the economic home life of the average African home." The women also condemned the practice of performing virginity and VD screening for girls without the approval of their parents, guardians, or a court, or without evidence that "they were from a brothel or have associations with it."[52] They considered medical examination as "unjust, indecent and a violation of the ordinary rights of a citizen." In addition, the women held that the CWO policy of policing the train station and returning girls between 14 and 16 coming into Lagos from the provinces violated their freedom of movement. The closing sentence of the long petition asked the CWO to focus on the major problem of prostitution instead of infringing on the girls' freedom: "We are surprised by the apathetic attitude of both the Welfare Department and the Police to take steps in removing the undesirables [prostitutes] at Ikeja [a military base] who are a moral danger to our sons [soldiers] returning from overseas service in spite of their attention being called to the menace by all our local press."[53] In sum, this detailed petition called for the abolition or amendment of some sections of the CYPO, including those on street trading and girls' immigration—measures that these very groups had demanded for more than two decades. The manner in which the women changed their position on these issues suggests that the polarized politics between them and the CWO had reached a stage beyond repair.

The CWO's reaction to the elite women's petition is partially reflected in a sketchy handwritten memo composed by Izzett and addressed to Faulkner. This brief memo vividly portrays the CWO's perception of the politics and personalities of the women and the extent of their apparent irreconcilable differences. "Unless forced to answer," Izzett wrote to Faulkner, "I think the best plan is to ignore it or one starts an acrimonious discussion in the press with all the corresponding publicity."[54] She continued, "The Women's Party are alone at the back of it and they have no sympathy with ill used children."[55] Izzett could not successfully persuade her boss to ignore the women's petition. Williams and Faulkner probably came to the conclusion that silence would cause more harm than good. Unsurprisingly, Izzett's response included all the points raised in her memo. She defended the CWO's VD and virginity screening, claiming that it conducted tests only when girls were removed from brothels and if the court and police required evidence of child prostitution for prosecuting procurers.[56] However, she was unapologetic about the policing of train stations and went on to highlight eight major reasons why the practice must continue, such as the luring of girls into prostitution under the pretext of betrothal or informal job training.

Understanding of the Politics of Rehabilitating Girls in Moral Danger

Thus far, I have not discussed the reason the CWO decided not to enlist elite women to help run the girls' hostel and to support the activities of the CWO. I contend that two closely related factors—the politics of sexuality and colonial security, and the politics of gender and race—best explain why the women were sidelined. The politics of sexuality and colonial security is explicable in terms of the ideological disparity between the colonialists and the women concerning the impact of illicit sexuality on colonial society. The women wanted to be in charge of girls' reformatory activities because they felt they understood the problems of African girl-children better than the British did. Their claim was supported by their voluntary activities and activism, which dated back to the second decade of the twentieth century, as well as by their biological gender and their cultural identity as African women. They deployed such language as "practical women of the world" to highlight their qualifications for running the girls' hostel.[57] The women felt that their project of promoting modern African women would be reinforced through government-funded institutions like the

CWO. They also believed that the understaffed CWO would need their help in running the establishment. Before 1946, when Izzett was hired, Faulkner was principally responsible for nearly all the policies of the CWO.

For the colonial authorities (from the 1940s) juvenile delinquency was a security issue that could not be entrusted to voluntary associations. This position was popular among high-ranking administrators, including Faulkner's superiors; Colonel Victor L. Mabb, the director of prisons, asserted, during the planning of the CWO, that "it would be a great mistake to commence work on the problem with a voluntary organization."[58] He contended that treatment of juvenile delinquency, "from whatever source it springs, is essentially a function of Government which should be directed and controlled by the Government."[59] The problem, Mabb wrote convincingly, "is far too difficult and serious to be left to the spasmodic efforts of voluntary workers who at the best can only devote their spare time to the work."[60]

The second factor—the politics of gender and race—cannot be divorced from the first because it also bordered on issues of colonial security. As a masculine-centered edifice, the colonial service rarely appointed European women, let alone African women, to positions that commanded power. Available evidence of mismanagement of funds by male administrators did not help matters. For instance, the government accused the Salvation Army, run by both African and European men, of mismanaging the £16,000 subvention given to it for rehabilitating delinquent boys between 1925 and 1941.[61] "When I think of what could have been accomplished with £16,000 under practical and common-sense management," Mabb regretted, "I grudge them over every penny of it."[62] If the colonialists felt that men were bad administrators, they held that African women, who were traditionally considered less educated and less "civilized," were certainly not capable. For the British, putting these elite women in charge of the girls' hostel would be like repeating their mistake with the Salvation Army.

Although the CWO painted the elite women as "troublemakers" and "selfish," the women's interest in salvaging girls in moral danger and future generations of African womanhood was altruistic and emphasized the genuine interests of the African girl. There is little doubt—or concrete evidence to the contrary—that any other African group, not even the male nationalists and politicians who represented Lagos in both the LCN and the LTC, placed greater emphasis on the protection of girls in moral danger than did these women.

Conclusion

A careful reading of the archives produced by the Lagos Women's League, the Women's Welfare Council, and the Nigerian Women's Party greatly aids in interpreting how social and educational status influenced attitudes toward casual sex work. First, the elite women viewed prostitution as a profession of uneducated, poor, and criminally minded women from the provinces. Although they decried the government's ineptitude regarding female education and worked to improve women's literacy by holding informal classes, they thought poverty should not motivate women to practice prostitution. Hence, they separated morality from social and economic circumstances. Second, they moralized about multiple sexual behaviors, using categories like "immoral," "unethical," and "dangerous" to provoke authorities to criminalize prostitution. Explicitly, Christianity and monogamous marriage, which the elite women practiced, supplied the moral and ethical vocabulary for condemning sexual practices outside holy matrimony. In this chapter I have addressed the following major questions about gender and class: What role did the LWL, the WWC, and the NWP play in the politics of sexual regulation? What was their pattern of political negotiation, and how they did mobilize to achieve their goals? Did the imported Eurocentric notion of female inferiority influence the political alignment of the period? How does the established knowledge of colonialism as a masculine project fit into the contestation between colonial masters and elite women over sexuality?

On the issue of who should be responsible for regulating prostitution, the elite women knew they could not arrogate the government's primary function of securing public order. Thus, they called on the government to police prostitution and recommended the enlistment of women into the NPF. Authorities kept the elite women out of the girls' reformatory institution because they felt that juvenile delinquency was a security problem that only the state could manage. As highly thoughtful as the women's agenda was, there was little they could do to change a colonial system dominated by white men who believed in the Victorian notion of female inferiority and subjectivity. With the exception of Abayomi, who was appointed as a member of the Lagos Town Council in 1944, the elite women did not have a strong political ally to influence public policy.[63] They were mostly private professionals who by the virtue of their family backgrounds and education were able to secure the attention of the colonial masters. Even the agitation by the print media controlled wholly by men did little to change the colonialist perceptions toward women's education.

The story of women's involvement in sexual politics provides a new perspective on established knowledge about colonialism as a male-centered institution, adding another compelling layer of interpretation to the narrative. The policies of not enrolling women in the NPF until 1954 and of preventing elite women from running the girls' hostel were informed by the Victorian practice of limiting women's political influence, especially in domains traditionally reserved for men. In another vein, the presence of an influential body of educated women, which could rarely be found in most parts of colonial Africa, facilitates a new site of inquiry into how social class informed the condemnation of sex work.

Although the elite women and the British had varied understandings of why prostitution should be policed, both groups wanted young girls to be protected. While the colonial authorities thought along the lines of public order and safety, elite women, in addition to holding concerns over the security of "innocent" citizens, injected moral and cultural tones that reflected largely on the future of women, as respectable wives, mothers, politicians, administrators, and law-abiding members of society. In summary, the colonialists' paternalism contrasted with the elite women's maternalist posture.

Prostitution and Trafficking
in the Age of HIV/AIDS

In 2003 the Nigerian National Assembly, the country's chief lawmaking body, passed the Trafficking in Persons (Prohibition) Law Enforcement and Administration Act (TPPLEAA), and established the National Agency for the Prohibition of Traffic in Persons (NAPTIP) to enforce it.[1] This law came exactly sixty years after the Children and Young Persons Ordinance (CYPO), the most comprehensive legislation for protecting and rehabilitating children and youth in colonial Nigeria, was enacted. The conditions that galvanized the passage of the TPPLEAA were akin to those underpinning the CYPO. The independent state, like its colonial precursor, believed that the criminal sexual exploitation of children needed to be policed and that these individuals required state protection. The TPPLEAA did not repeal the CYPO. Nor did it nullify the functions of the various ministries of youth and social welfare, at state and federal levels, that inherited the legacy of the Colony Welfare Office (CWO), which implemented the CYPO.

Another major feature of sexual politics in postcolonial Nigeria—aside from the passing of the TPPLEAA—is the reversal of the colonial policy of prohibition of prostitution. From the 1960s to the present, brothels of varying sizes have sprung up in various parts of Lagos and other Nigerian cities in defiance of existing law. Whenever the police raid brothels and arrest streetwalkers (while letting their male customers go), it is mostly because prostitutes and brothel operators refuse to pay the "protection" money that guarantees legal toleration.[2] Moreover, successive post-independence regimes have occasionally used the policing of prostitution to divert public attention from the main problems of mismanagement because sexual matters usually generate public attention. In short, policing domestic prostitution has not occupied a sustained and coherent place on the institutional agenda since the demise of colonial rule.[3] But what accounts for this situation? Why did the nationalists promise that social problems such as prostitution would be eradicated with the attainment of independence? Why did it take Nigeria forty-three years after independence to put the sexual exploitation of children at the center of state policy? How successful is NAPTIP in policing sex crime against children and prostitution?

In attempting to answer these questions and others, this epilogue engages the change and continuity in the politics of sex, focusing on how postcolonial sociopolitical and economic mutations have influenced a new definition of sexual danger. I posit that the postcolonial state's interest in policing sexuality has an international rather than a local impetus. The government pictures domestic and international prostitution separately and seeks to police each type in accordance with the threat it poses to global standards of law and order. If the government of the Fourth Republic (since 1999) has not been successful in taming the alleged moral and medical implications of sex work, it is because, like the colonial state, its definition of respectability takes precedence over any genuine and sustained transformatory project to empower the citizenry. Nongovernmental organizations and a new level of women's agency exemplified in the activities of the wives of politicians have replaced the elite women of the colonial era, ensuring that the debate over illicit sexuality has remained gendered in public politics. The idea of dangerous sexuality has also been subsumed into the HIV/AIDS pandemic.

From Prohibition to Toleration:
Reversing the Colonial Status Quo

Immediately after the demise of colonial rule, Nigeria, like most countries in Africa, began to experience political crises that permeated nearly all sectors of society, putting a strong end to the idea that self-determination would solve all the nation's problems (including prostitution). Incessant military coups, dictatorial rule, civil war (1967–70), and unabated corruption fractured the core structures of political engineering, making a mirage of the social advancement and welfare of the masses. The oil boom of the 1970s brought little improvement to the welfare of children and women, as oil revenues, if not stolen by the elites, were largely channeled into erecting poorly maintained physical infrastructure.

As previously mentioned, the government of post-independence Nigeria inherited the CWO, but poor funding and inadequate human resources combined to undermine its effective operation. Although the colonial state gave unequal attention to social "deviance" among boys and girls in the 1940s and 1950s, the welfare office from the 1960s erratically focused on the former and stopped policing child prostitution in general. Vagrant boys were not reclaimed from the streets. Rather, they continued to experience social marginalization and exclusion as the gulf between the rich and the poor widened. What is more, the activities of the social welfare offices at independence expanded from policing children and juvenile delinquency to other areas such as family and grassroots mobilization. Apparently, the welfare office bit off more than it could chew by assuming wider responsibilities that could have been delegated instead to other government establishments such as the Ministry of Information or Ministry of Education. With a budget of less than £60,000 (and half of that for payroll) for the whole of the Western Region and Lagos in the 1960s, the social welfare office could not adequately perform its functions.

What is more, Lagos, like most Nigerian cities, witnessed a demographic revolution in the postcolonial era. Its population jumped exponentially from 250,000 in 1952 to more than 10 million in 2006.[4] Although it lost its exalted position as the capital of the post-independence state when the seat of government was officially moved to Abuja in December 1991, Lagos remains the economic backbone of the country. Sex work has found a place in the post-colonial economic and social matrix by creating opportunity for women and men to make a living in an ever-youthful population. Well-designated brothels sprung up in the old colonial red-light districts, while several residential areas on Lagos Island degenerated into slums dotted with brothels as the government deliberately tolerated sex work. Ikeja's fame as a military base and hotspot for prostitution has been sustained in the post-independence era. Prostitutes, in addition to serving the military, now have an expanded economic opportunity of selling sex to civilians in such areas as the popular Allen Avenue and Oshodi, both on the mainland. Indeed, so well normalized is prostitution in Oshodi that one brothel (Makossa Hotel) stands just beside a mosque. Beach prostitution, which did not exist under colonial rule, is now a major feature of social life in such places as Kuramo Beach, where a mini shanty settlement, sprinkled with illegal structures, gives both temporary and permanent abode to men and women who live off the proceeds of the business of sexual pleasure.

Figure E.1. A brothel (Makossa Hotel) and mosque (Owoseni Mosque). Oshodi, Lagos. Photograph by author. June 2013.

Another visible feature of postcolonial prostitution is the involvement of female undergraduate students. Popularly called *aristo* girls, these prostitutes, who mostly live on college campuses, serve upper-class Nigerians and foreigners, and tend to be better paid than other categories of prostitutes because they are assumed to be "cleaner" and "educated."[5] Their clientele has also included the politicians and elites who were expected to legislate against "moral pestilence." In August 2011 the *Daily Times* reported that ten undergraduate students of Lagos institutions of higher learning were arraigned for breaking anti-prostitution laws.[6] Similarly, Professor Elizabeth Balogun of the University of Ilorin, in a public lecture titled "Prostitution on Our Campuses: Effects and Solutions," organized by the National Association of Nigerian Students to mark its thirty-first anniversary, affirmed that 80 percent of prostitutes in Ogun State are undergraduate students.[7] The involvement of foreign nationals (especially non-Africans) has also expanded the racial horizon of prostitution. Thus, the physical and ethnic geography of prostitution has adapted to the changing economic and social structure. In August 2012 *Punch* announced that the Nigerian Immigration Service arrested eleven Chinese teenage prostitutes in a residence at Emina Crescent in Ikeja.[8] But there may have been more to these arrests than a genuine effort by law enforcement to stop foreign nationals from breaking the country's laws. It appeared to be in retaliation for the much-publicized inhuman treatment of Nigerians living in China, or for China's refusal to accept Abuja's proposal to allow Nigerian prisoners in Chinese prisons to be extradited.

As in the colonial era, prostitutes have continued to share the same social space with delinquent boys and juveniles. Prostitutes' clienteles, both foreign and local, have continued to rely on them to navigate the often violent red-light districts. From the 1960s, the area boys and *agbero* (touts)—the "offspring" of the *boma* and *jaguda* boys—perfected the operations of their "ancestors" while adding fresh ones.[9] So ubiquitous were their activities that the Nigerian Nobel Laureate Wole Soyinka wrote a play titled *The Beatification of Area Boys* about them in 1995.[10] More problematic is the fact that hardened criminals who had threatened public safety in Lagos and other Nigerian centers were recruited from among the class of the area boys as urban crime took on a more violent dimension in the post–civil war era characterized by the increased weaponization of Nigerian society.[11] Whereas the colonialists did not see the *boma* boys as a tool for achieving political power or maintaining control, politicians and elites since independence have depended on the area boys to intimidate opponents in the struggle for power.

The toleration of prostitution in postcolonial Nigeria cannot be explained in terms of mismanagement of state resources, population boom, and the lackadaisical attention to juvenile welfare alone. The cardinal philosophy of policing has not changed since the colonial era. The independent state, like its colonial predecessor, uses the police mainly to suppress the real and imagined enemies of the state and only indirectly to protect the citizenry. Policing domestic prostitution is largely viewed by the government as unimportant, when compared to the need to forcefully hold the disunited nation together and protect the elites. In 2011 Parry Osayande, the chairman of the Police Service Commission, made a startling disclosure that more than 100,000 of the nation's 330,000 policemen and policewomen were attached to politicians, elites, and corporate firms as part of private security outfits, leaving the rest to police a country of more than 150 million people and stop such violent crimes as robbery, kidnapping, and terrorism.[12] Even the deployment of both the police and the military cannot check the incessant intra- and inter-ethnic violence that threatens the unity of the state.

Postcolonial print media continue with the established tradition of serving as the mouthpiece of "ordinary" Nigerians, who are divided over regulation and prohibition. Advances in printing technology and media have expanded reportage, with photographs and cartoons of red-light streets bringing the public closer to the prostitution culture. Unlike in the colonial era when men, because of their lead in Western education, dominated public debate over prostitution, the postcolonial period has witnessed increased participation by women. Like their male counterparts, women commentators blame prostitution for the male-centeredness of the modern Nigerian state. Although girls' school enrollment since the 1960s is higher than in the colonial era, Nigerian women still lack significant agency necessary to institute political change. Indeed, the independent state was built on the advantages men had over women in the acquisition of Western education and preparation for civic engagement. Even the increase in the representation of women in politics since the beginning of the Fourth Republic has not been marked by radical transformation of the core principles undergirding gender bias and male-dominated authority.

The representation of prostitution in popular music and other forms of expressive arts dates back to the 1930s or earlier. But the revolution in Nigeria's entertainment industry and the increasing public tolerance of sexually explicit lyrics have expanded it. In 2010 Chinedu Okoli (aka Flavor) released his hit musical video titled *Nwa Baby*, which reproduced the colonial representation of prostitutes as "Sawa Sawa."[13] A remix of Jim Rex Lawson's 1960s classic high-life song, titled "Sawale," the video version contains a scene of red-light streets and prostitutes soliciting for men. However, the most enduring portrayal of prostitution in contemporary Nigerian popular culture can be found in the country's movie industry (known as Nollywood). Indeed, one of the major films that helped place Nollywood on global map is *The Prostitutes*, directed by Fred Amata and released in 2001.[14] It is based on the "true-life" story of Ugonma, an ex-prostitute. This film, more than any other, portrays the violent life of a brothel, which includes death, infighting, and competition among prostitutes for male customers; the use of juju (charms); and the involvement of madams, criminals, and the law enforcement agencies. Omotola Jolade-Ekeinde, one of Africa's most influential movie stars and listed in "*Time*'s 100 Most Influential People in the World" (2013), plays the lead role as the prostitute Veno.

Veno's journey into prostitution mirrors the predominant notion that poverty pushed women into sex trade. When her family's financial problem is having a negative impact on her education, the teenage Veno decides to secure a job. But her prospective "employers" attempt to rape her, instead of getting her a job. She escapes rape by killing one of the men and is arrested and charged with murder. After escaping from sexual assault in police custody, the fugitive Veno flees to Lagos, lives on the street, and inevitably integrates into Lagos's brothel industry. Initially naïve, Veno receives core training from the experienced prostitutes and quickly becomes a hardened one. Like most of her colleagues, she practices prostitution "without emotions" until she meets Razor (played by Segun Arinze), "the only man [she has] ever loved," an armed robber, whom she describes as "mysterious" and "dangerous." After returning from a robbery operation with 250,000 naira ($1,500), Razor attempts to fulfill his promise to marry and take Veno out of the brothel. But the operation leaves a deadly trail. A gun duel with the police severely injures Razor. He becomes defenseless and falls into the hands of an angry mob that lynches him. Veno takes the 250,000 naira and returns to her village to reunite with her family and "start a new life." While this film achieved its core mission to entertain the audience, it ended with a moralistic tone common in most Nollywood films, "As unaware by many, most young girls fall into prostitution by no fault of theirs. This is a call for parents, teachers, and society at large to please help and assist such ladies who fall into such situation. Say no to prostitution."[15]

The Politics of Transnational Prostitution in the Fourth Republic

The politics of sexuality were significantly affected by Nigeria's reintroduction to democratic governance in 1999. This development was exemplified in the consolidation of international prostitution and its impact on the image of Nigeria abroad. While transnational prostitution dates back to the colonial era, it was during the post-independence period that it assumed an intercontinental dimension, becoming one of the foremost features of the new globalization.[16] From the mid-1980s or earlier, Nigerian women began to travel by the thousands to European countries—to Spain, France, and Italy, in particular—to sell sex.[17] They were even found in Saudi Arabia. Because of their involvement in global prostitution and trafficking, Nigerian women have attracted significant international attention. During the 1990s and early 2000s, an estimated

20,000 to 50,000 Nigerian women were reported to be working as prostitutes in Europe. In July 2000 Etim Okpoyo, the Nigerian ambassador to Italy, revealed that out of 40,000 Nigerians living in that country, one-fourth were prostitutes.[18] Admittedly, such figures are difficult to trust because they can be used as propaganda. However, it is clear that thousands of Nigerian women are caught up in an elaborate underground network that includes immigration and law enforcement officials, religious authorities, criminal gangs, and ordinary families. The explanations for transnational prostitution are legion—whereas some scholars have argued that the Structural Adjustment Programme (SAP) introduced by General Babangida's administration (1985–93) sparked the new global prostitution, others blame family problems, ignorance, lack of education, and greed.[19] Regardless of the root cause of transnational prostitution, what is certain is that after 1999 the government began to implement new policies aimed at checking its menace.

The first example of this new attention was the passage of the TPPLEAA following intensive lobbying by Titi Abubakar, the wife of Vice President Atiku Abubakar, who in 1999 formed a nongovernmental organization (NGO) called the Women Trafficking and Child Labour Eradication Foundation (WOTCLEF).[20] The TPPLEAA made provisions for establishing NAPTIP, which performed a role akin to that of the CWO. Headquartered in Abuja, NAPTIP has seven branch offices located in Lagos, Benin, Uyo, Enugu, Kano, Sokoto, and Maiduguri. It carries out "research" on cases of women and girl trafficking, provides temporary housing for repatriates, initiates criminal proceedings against procurers or traffickers, and attempts to sensitize the public on the ills of allowing girls to be removed from homes under the guise of education abroad. Unlike the CYPO, which pegged the age of consent at 13, the TPPLEAA defines a child as an individual under the age of 18 (while not, however, repealing existing legislation that defines a child as an individual under 16). Punishment for child prostitution is ten years in prison or a fine not to exceed 200,000 naira ($1,300).[21]

On paper, NAPTIP resembles a government establishment committed to a serious moral crusade. But upon examining its mode of operation and core origins, it appears to be just another "white elephant" project. First, the government could have strengthened the various departments of social welfare in each state of the country, which inherited the ruins of the CWO, to carry out anti-prostitution activities since that was part of their job, by law. A new organization for policing prostitution was therefore unnecessary. In fact, NAPTIP sought to lay a shaky new foundation without building on existing structures. What is more, as gleaned from its reports and procedures, NAPTIP officials seem unaware of preexisting anti-prostitution legislation—its Legal and Prosecution Department even claimed that "prior to 2003, there was no anti-trafficking in persons legislation in Nigeria."[22] But as we have seen in chapter 5, various sections of the Criminal Code Ordinance and CYPO contain elaborate legislation on prostitution and the sexual exploitation of children that remain on Nigerian law books and are still discretionarily deployed today. Well-defined sections of immigration ordinances that prohibit transnational prostitution were enacted in the 1940s and are still relevant for the postcolonial situation. By enacting new legislation without repealing or making reference to the existing laws, the government created legal confusion, which people accused of trafficking could exploit with the aid of savvy lawyers. For instance, the 1960 amendment of section 219 of the Criminal Code reserved a punishment of life in prison for unlawful carnal knowledge of an underage (someone under 16) or someone that aided it.[23] Yet, section 14-(1) of the TPPLEAA gives a punishment of ten years for the same offense.[24] The option of fines for imprisonment (which could serve as deterrent) means that very few convicts will serve prison sentences.

Second, NAPTIP was primarily established to promote a good foreign image for Nigeria. By the early 2000s, the general impression in Spain and Italy was that every black prostitute was a Nigerian, or that every black woman was a Nigerian and a prostitute.[25] The government became increasingly embarrassed by the reports of streams of Nigerian women on the streets of Palermo and other Italian cities. Added to this was the enormous pressure from other countries that sought to monitor global prostitution in the name of international security. In 2000 the United States passed the Victims of Trafficking and Violence Protection Act, which provided $94 million in aid to Nigeria and other countries.[26] The following year the U.S. State Department launched the *Trafficking in Persons Report*, "the most comprehensive resource of governmental anti-human trafficking efforts" that evinces "the U.S. Government's commitment to global leadership."[27] Also, in 2001 Italy gave Nigeria $2.5 million "to stop the illegal trafficking of Nigerian girls for international prostitution."[28] In short, Nigeria showed up regularly on the international radar for contributing the bulk of transnational African prostitutes. This explains why NAPTIP focused almost entirely on transnational trafficking in order to demonstrate the Nigerian government's commitment to the various international anti-trafficking agreements it joined.

At its inception, NAPTIP publicized widely reports of the repatriation of Nigerian girls and women from Europe and other parts of Africa. However, it did not police domestic prostitution. What is more, the government has failed to recognize that both domestic and transnational prostitution are sustained by the same underworld network. A genuine war on sex crime against children should have closed down brothels where internationally bound prostitutes were frequently recruited. In addition, most prostitutes repatriated from abroad returned to local brothels and streets where they arranged to return to where they had been repatriated from. Unlike the colonialists, who treated adult women who worked independently as prostitutes as criminals who violated the anti-prostitution status quo, NAPTIP tends to handle both child and adult prostitutes as victims of coercion and "slavery." There is no doubting the fact that children and adults have been lured into international prostitution against their will; however, the imposition of the language of victimization on all adult women who engage in transnational prostitution blurs personal agency by not recognizing that some women took the international voyage with prior knowledge of the risk. But what is more important, it positions the government as a moral crusader.

But NAPTIP is not the only institution in Nigeria "committed" to fighting transnational prostitution. Various NGOs such as Women Trafficking and Child Labour Eradication Foundation (WOTCLEF) and Idia Renaissance, which was founded in 1999 by Eki Igbinedion, the wife of Lucky Igbinedion (the governor of Edo State between 1999 and 2007), were established mostly with public funds and run as the "pet" project of politicians' wives claimed to be working to stop girl-child trafficking. Unlike the elite women of the colonial period who did not have strong economic power because their families did not have much political power, a handful of women beginning with Maryam Babangida, the wife of the dictator General Ibrahim Babangida, who made the office of first lady an established but unconstitutional arm of the government, have had enormous power to raise money for projects they believed would help empower women. It is public knowledge that the pet projects of such women created avenues to siphon public funds for transient regimes, most of which came to power through political fraud.[29] Those who head up these "pet" projects and NGOs alike generally exaggerate their activities and impact by claiming to "rehabilitate" repatriated prostitutes through vocational training.[30] In order to ensure that they serve the material needs of founders they operate as private or personal agencies, instead of being integrated into existing ministries of women's affairs at the state and federal levels. Hence, at the end of regimes, most of them not only fall apart, but are also converted into private property.[31] Like NAPTIP, Igbinedion's and Atiku's project did not police domestic prostitution and sexual exploitation of children in local brothels.

Prostitution and the HIV/AIDS Pandemic

Nigeria's first official HIV/AIDS diagnosis was reported in Lagos in 1985.[32] Like most Africans, Nigerians denied it at first as a mere superstition. By the 1990s, public perceptions began to change as the disease became publicly visible, even claiming the lives of public figures, notably Fela Anikulapo Kuti, one of Africa's most iconic artists, in 1997.[33] Government-sponsored research affirmed that HIV prevalence rose from 1.8 percent in 1991 to 4.6 percent in 2008.[34]

Concern over the impact of HIV/AIDS in postcolonial Nigeria mirrors that of syphilis and gonorrhea under colonial rule—Nigerian leaders, leading physicians, and policy makers believe that HIV/AIDS is a national security crisis, creating an unhealthy population needed for socioeconomic development. The history of state response to HIV/AIDS is also as old as the history of the discovery of the disease in Nigeria. In 1985 the Federal Ministry of Health formed the National Expert Advisory Committee on AIDS (NEACA) to track the epidemiology of the disease. Two years later with the aid of the World Health Organization, the government established nine HIV testing centers across the country, and a Medium-Term Plan, which replaced the initial Short-Term Plan for battling the disease was put in place. In 1988 the National AIDS Control Program replaced NEACA. But it was not until 1999, when democratic governance was reintroduced, that a serious institutional plan was established with the formation of the Presidential Committee on AIDS and National Agency for the Control of AIDS (NACA) by the Obasanjo administration.

The state response to HIV/AIDS is as important as the numerous theoretical explanations for its causation. Indeed, the demise of colonial rule and advancements in medical technology did not end Western racialization of Africans. North American and European academics and health workers resuscitated colonial stereotypes by attributing the spread of HIV/AIDS to African sexual permissiveness. At the 10th International AIDS Conference in Yokohama in 1994, Dr. Yuichi Shiokawa affirmed that "AIDS would be brought under control only if Africans restrain their sexual cravings."[35] Five years later, John C. Caldwell, an academic demographer, and his collaborators, Pat Caldwell and Pat Quiggin, published a study titled "The Social Context of AIDS in Sub-Saharan Africa," in which they attributed the soaring pandemic to the fact that African societies "do not regard most sexual relations as sinful or as central to morality and religion, and at the most have fairly easily evaded prohibitions even on female premarital or extramarital sex."[36] Apparently, the Western practice of Africanizing sexual immorality has not changed, but has assumed a new guise—just like old wine in a new bottle.

Studies from the 1990s, including those conducted by Nigerian academics, identified prostitutes as "the major reservoirs" of HIV infection.[37] Other high-risk populations included military personnel, soldiers, and truck drivers.[38] Professor I. O. Orubuloye, one of the earliest Nigerian sociologists to devote a career to the study of HIV/AIDS, in a study published in 1997 noted that "the industry [prostitution] constitutes the most dangerous sector of society for the spread of the disease and for creating a self-sustaining and expanding AIDS epidemic throughout the society."[39] A similar study was more explicit in tracking the increasing rate of HIV among Lagos prostitutes: from 2 percent in 1988–89 to 12 percent in 1990–91 to 70 percent in 1995–96.[40] Generally, this study and others claim to carry out interviews among prostitutes and to review the medical histories of people infected with HIV/AIDS, which reveal that they contracted the disease through transient sexual encounters. Funded mostly by international agencies, Nigerian academics tended to confirm their donors' preconceptions of heterosexual transmission of the scourge.

But the rigid distinction between civilian and military sexual behavior, which characterized colonial VD control, did not find strong expression in postcolonial Nigeria. This is not to suggest that the government did not establish separate programs for the HIV/AIDS campaign among the civilians and the military. Rather, while the British focused on the military and attempted to deal with gonorrhea and syphilis in the civilian population in order to improve the health of the military, post-independent policies took an approach that focused on both the civilian and military populations. Indeed, the first concerted efforts at dealing with the menace of HIV/AIDS were directed at the civilian population, not the military as we have seen under imperial rule. It was not until 2001 that the "first behavioural survey" on the spread of HIV/AIDS was conducted in the Nigerian Army, which inherited the Royal West African Frontier Force (RWAFF) after independence.[41] The national representative survey of 1,600 military personnel (out of more than 100,000) discovered that soldiers "find themselves in professional and personal situations" that increased their chances of contracting HIV/AIDS. Among the "professional and personal situations" was frequent posting and assignments that took soldiers away from their families and facilitated multiple sexual contacts. Other factors suggest that soldiers tended to contract HIV/AIDS because they view reckless sexual behavior as a component of the broader risk their job entails and had access to cash for buying sex.[42]

Interestingly, the idea that access to cash to purchase sex and willingness to risk diseases was responsible for increasing incidence of HIV/AIDS in the Nigerian Army resembles the colonial stance toward VD. However, while the colonial military and civil authorities believed that the control of civilian sexual behavior was the best means of combating VD, their postcolonial counterparts thought that military personnel "could serve as a potential core transmission group" for sexually transmitted diseases, within the larger population, because they are "more aware of HIV/AIDS than the general population."[43] Aside from this government-sponsored and -approved study, other academic research affirmed that the military is a high-risk population for HIV/AIDS.[44]

Although prostitution and sexual laxity have been consistently considered as the major factor in the spread of HIV/AIDS among both civilians and the military, some research has also focused on lack of education, poverty, poor medical facilities, and sociocultural problems. It is now public knowledge that HIV/AIDS can be transmitted through unsterilized medical equipment and blood transfusions. Perhaps no research goes so far to challenge the prevailing notion of prostitutes as the conduit of HIV/AIDS as that presented by the venereologist Professor Rasheed Bakare of the University of Ibadan. In his inaugural lecture delivered in April 2012 titled "Microbes and Morals—an Unlikely Love Affair," Professor Bakare states: "The identified prostitutes don't constitute health hazards to the society because of the care they undergo and the policy they make concerning their trade." He averred that the policy of "no condom no sex" among identified prostitutes does not make them a high-risk population. In all, he called for separation of disease and morality: "Venereal diseases should no longer be regarded as shameful, abhorrent evidence of an individual's degraded moral character . . . There is no romance and no love affair between the sexually transmitted infection and the victim's moral character."[45]

Conclusion

One of the main ideas that runs through this epilogue and entire study is that prostitution is central to core ideas about security, nationalism, respectability, and social stability. It is a significant aspect of colonial Nigerian history that historians have neglected. Crime and disease that prostitution purportedly promoted constituted a danger not only to an individual, but also to the larger society. Hence anti-prostitution laws and regulations targeted Nigerians' behavior and bodily habits as a site of institutionalized regulation. Time brings events and changes. At every period in Nigerian history, the major actors among the colonialists and in the Nigerian bloc defined and redefined their position on sexuality regulation or prohibition to reflect the changing danger that sex work posed to their framing of normality. Hence, while the immorality of prostitution seemed to have a "common" connotation across gender, class, and race, its impact and how to address it varied widely.

NOTES

INTRODUCTION: SEX AND SEXUALITY
IN AFRICAN COLONIAL ENCOUNTER

1. "Lady Welfare Officer Potts-Johnson and Tout Get 6 Months Each: Eager Crowds Fill Court Precincts," *Daily Service*, February 18, 1947.

2. Ibid.

3. See from the *Daily Service*: "5 Lawyers Appear for Mrs. Ayo Potts-Johnson in Corruption Case," January 21, 1947; "Submission in Case against Lady Welfare Office Overruled," February 4, 1947; "Decision Next Monday on Submissions in Mrs. Potts-Johnson's Corruption Case," January 28, 1947.

4. "5 Lawyers Appear for Mrs. Ayo Potts-Johnson in Corruption Case," *Daily Service*, January 21, 1947.

5. Ibid.

6. "Decision Next Monday on Submissions in Mrs. Potts-Johnson's Corruption Case," *Daily Service*, January 28, 1947.

7. "5 Lawyers Appear for Mrs. Ayo Potts-Johnson in Corruption Case," *Daily Service*, January 21, 1947.

8. Coleman, *Nigeria*, 218; Fakoyede, ed., *F. R. A. Williams*.

9. For more on Ademola, see Alao, *Statesmanship on the Bench*.

10. "Lady Welfare Officer Lodges Appeal against Conviction for Corruption," *Daily Service*, May 3, 1947; "Ayo Potts-Johnson (Appellant) and Commissioner of Police (Respondent), July 29," in *Selected Judgments of the West African Court of Appeal, 1946/1949* (Lagos: Crown Agent, 1956).

11. "Submission in Case against Lady Welfare Office Overruled," *Daily Service*, February 4, 1947.

12. This conclusion is based on a review of court cases in Lagos magistrate courts during the 1930s and 1940s.

13. Foucault, *The History of Sexuality*, vol. I.

14. For instance, Luise White adopts a labor history perspective. See White, *The Comforts of Home*, 154–58.

15. Ibid., 11–13; Akyeampong, "Sexuality and Prostitution among the Akan of the Gold Coast."

16. Little, *African Women in Towns*, 76–129.

17. For a good review of sex work and the politics of nomenclature, see Bell, *Reading, Writing, and Rewriting the Prostitute Body*, 73–98.

18. Ibid.

19. See, for instance, Naanen, "The Itinerant Gold Mines"; Akyeampong, "Sexuality and Prostitution among the Akan of the Gold Coast." There is an array of work that, while not examining prostitution specifically, presents interesting dynamics about sexuality regulation; see, among others, Allman, "Of 'Sprinters,' 'Concubines' and 'Wicked Women'"; Allman, "Rounding Up Spinsters"; Allman, "Adultery and the State in Asante"; Ray, "The 'White Wife Problem'"; Pierce, "Farmers and 'Prostitutes'"; Lovejoy, "Concubinage." The literature on prostitution has expanded at a slow rate since 2005; see, among others, Aderinto, "Of Gender, Race, and Class"; Ray, "Sex Trafficking, Prostitution, and the Law."

Tangential references to prostitution in colonial Nigeria can be found in the following works: Fourchard, "Lagos and the Invention of Juvenile Delinquency in Nigeria"; Chuku, *Igbo Women and Economic Transformation in Southeastern Nigeria*, 164–65, 217–18; Achebe, *The Female King of Colonial Nigeria*, 77–86.

20. Levine, *Prostitution, Race, and Politics*.

21. Bryder, "Sex, Race and Colonialism"; Pedersen, "National Bodies, Unspeakable Acts"; Summers, "Intimate Colonialism"; Glaser, "Managing the Sexuality of Urban Youth"; Tuck, "Venereal Disease, Sexuality and Society in Uganda."

22. Foucault, *History of Sexuality, Vol. I*, 103; Berger, "Imperialism and Sexual Exploitation"; Hyam, *Empire and Sexuality*; Harrison, *Public Health in British India*; Levine, *Prostitution, Race, and Politics*.

23. Hyam, *Empire and Sexuality*, 2; Levine, *Prostitution, Race, and Politics*, 227.

24. Gilman, *Difference and Pathology*, 101.

25. White, *The Comforts of Home*; Van Onselen, *Studies in the Social and Economic History of the Witwatersrand*, 1:103–62; Bujra, "Sexual Politics in Atu"; Vaughan, *Curing Their Ills*; Pedersen, "National Bodies, Unspeakable Acts"; Summers, "Intimate Colonialism"; Glaser, "Managing the Sexuality of Urban Youth"; Shaw, *Colonial Inscriptions*; Hay, "Queens, Prostitutes, and Peasants"; Pape, "Black and White"; Bryder, "Sex, Race and Colonialism"; Parpart, "'Where Is Your Mother?'"; Parpart, "Sexuality and Power on the Zambian Copperbelt"; Frederiksen, "Jomo Kenyatta, Marie Bonaparte and Bronislaw Malinowski on Clitoridectomy and Female Sexuality"; Lindsay, "A Tragic Romance, A Nationalist Symbol"; Bonner, *Desirable or Undesirable Sotho Women?*; Eales, *Rehabilitating the Body Politic*; Jeater, *Marriage, Perversion and Power*; Klausen, *Race, Maternity, and the Politics of Birth Control*; McCulloch, *Black Peril, White Virtue*; Kanogo, *African Womanhood in Colonial Kenya*; Kaler, *Running After Pills*; Magubane, *Bringing the Empire Home*; Musisi, "The Politics of Perception or Perception of Politics?"; Scully, "Rape, Race, and Colonial Culture"; Barnes, "The Fight for Control of Women's Mobility in Colonial Zimbabwe"; Barnes, *"We Women Worked So Hard"*; Schmidt, *Peasants, Traders, and Wives*; Schmidt, "Race, Sex, and Domestic Labor"; Epprecht, *Hungochani*; Epprecht, *Heterosexual Africa?*; Barrera,

"Colonial Affairs"; Cornwell, "George Webb Hardy's *The Black Peril*"; Etherington, "Natal's Black Rape Scare of the 1870s"; McClintock, *Imperial Leather*; Ross, "Oppression, Sexuality and Slavery"; White, "Miscegenation and Colonial Society in French West Africa."

26. Vaughan, *Curing Their Ills*, 130.

27. Jochelson, *The Colour of Disease*; McCurdy, "Urban Threats"; Jackson, "'When in the White Man's Town.'"

28. Parsons, "All Askaris Are Family Men."

29. See, among others, McCulloch, *Black Peril, White Virtue*; Jeater, *Marriage, Perversion and Power*; Pape, "Black and White"; Jochelson, *The Colour of Disease*; Musisi, "The Politics of Perception"; McCurdy, "Urban Threats"; Jackson, "'When in the White Man's Town.'"

30. Glaser, "Managing the Sexuality of Urban Youth"; Jochelson, *The Colour of Disease*.

31. McCulloch, *Black Peril, White Virtue*, 11.

32. The following are among the few works on race and gender in West Africa: Ray, "The 'White Wife Problem'"; Aderinto, "Of Gender, Race, and Class"; Phillips, "Heterogeneous Imperialism and the Regulation of Sexuality in British West Africa"; Lindsay, "A Tragic Romance."

33. In her seminal work, White dedicates just five pages to the discussion of underage sexuality. White, *The Comforts of Home*, 154–58.

34. Schmidt, *Peasants, Traders, and Wives*, 122–54; Frederiksen, "Jomo Kenyatta, Marie Bonaparte and Bronislaw Malinowski"; Denzer, "Domestic Science Training in Colonial Yorubaland, Nigeria."

35. Mosse, *Nationalism and Sexuality*; Parker et al., eds., *Nationalisms and Sexualities*.

36. See, among others, Allman, "Rounding up Spinsters"; Barnes, "The Fight for Control of Women's Mobility in Zimbabwe"; Jackson, "'When in the White Man's Town'"; Schmidt, *Peasants, Traders, and Wives*, 98–121.

37. Kanogo, *African Womanhood in Colonial Kenya*, 42–163.

38. Thomas, *The Politics of the Womb*.

39. Cooper, "Conflict and Connection."

40. On the Contagious Diseases Acts and politics in Britain and its empire, see Walkowitz, *Prostitution and Victorian Society*; Levine, *Prostitution, Race, and Politics*.

41. Coker, *Landmarks of the Nigerian Press*, 4.

42. For more on the emic/etic binary in oral interviews, see Albert, "The Emics and Etics."

CHAPTER I. "THIS IS A CITY OF BUBBLES"

1. Ekwensi, *People of the City*, 32.

2. Ibid., 15.

3. Ibid., 17.

4. "The Needs of Modern Lagos I: Steps towards Creating the City Beautify," *Nigerian Pioneer*, September 10, 1920.

5. Notable readings on precolonial and colonial Lagos include the following: Aderibigbe, ed., *Lagos*; Adefuye, Agiri, and Osuntokun, eds., *History of the Peoples of Lagos State*; Losi, *History of Lagos*; Mabogunje, *Urbanization in Nigeria*, 238–311; Mann, *Slavery and the Birth of an African City*, 23–83; Smith, *The Lagos Consulate*; Baker, *Urbanization and Political Change*; Barnes, *Patrons and Power*; Mann, *Marrying Well*.

6. Baker, *Urbanization and Political Change*, 17–21; Mann, *Slavery and the Birth of an African City*, 23–32.

7. Mabogunje, *Urbanization in Nigeria*, 239.

8. Mann, *Slavery and the Birth of an African City*, 27.

9. Baker, *Urbanization and Political Change*, 17.

10. Law, *The Oyo Empire*.

11. Mann, *Slavery and the Birth of an African City*, 25.

12. Baker, *Urbanization and Political Change*, 18.

13. Mann, *Slavery and the Birth of an African City*, 31–50.

14. On the Yoruba civil wars of the nineteenth century, see, among others, Akintoye, *Revolution and Power Politics in Yorubaland*.

15. Mann, *Slavery and the Birth of an African City*, 38.

16. A lot of political intrigues took place between when Lagos was bombarded in 1851 and when it officially became a British colony in 1861. For more on this, see Smith, *The Lagos Consulate*, 18–33.

17. Kopytoff, *A Preface to Modern Nigeria*; Ajayi, *Christian Missions in Nigeria*; Ayandele, *The Missionary Impact on Modern Nigeria*.

18. Mabogunje, *Urbanization in Nigeria*, 243; Lindsay, "'To Return to the Bosom of Their Fatherland.'"

19. Mabogunje, *Urbanization in Nigeria*, 243.

20. Adeloye, *African Pioneers of Modern Medicine*; Adewoye, *The Legal Profession in Nigeria*.

21. Barber, *Print Culture and the First Yoruba Novel*, 15.

22. For more on the careers of early Nigerian professionals and nationalists, see, among others, Adeloye, *African Pioneers of Modern Medicine*; Baronov, *The African Transformation of Western Medicine*.

23. For a precise analysis of the ethnic identity of some of the leading Lagos politicians from 1900 to 1960, see Baker, *Urbanization and Political Change*, 286–306.

24. Mabogunje, *Urbanization in Nigeria*, 259. The *Lagos Weekly Record* decried poor sanitation and high mortality during the 1890s Lagos; see "Cholera Epidemic," October 1, 1892; "Our Local Drain System," July 13, 1895; "The Vital Statistics of the Colony," July 20, 1895; "The Present Sanitary Condition of the Town," February 29, 1896.

25. Marris, *Family and Social Change in an African City*, 82–115.

26. Mabogunje, *Urbanization in Nigeria*, 244.

27. Olukoju, *Infrastructure Development and Urban Facilities in Lagos*.

28. Lindsay, *Working with Gender*, 31–52.

29. Olukoju, *Infrastructure Development and Urban Facilities in Lagos*.

30. Ibid.

31. Mabogunje, *Urbanization in Nigeria*, 248–59.

32. Barrett, "The Rank and File of the Colonial Army in Nigeria."

33. Ibid.

34. Fafunwa, *History of Education in Nigeria*, 92–165.

35. Adesina, "The Development of Western Education," 125.

36. Peil, *Lagos*, 11.

37. "Private Medical Practice," *West African Pilot*, June 1, 1939.

38. Barber, *Print Culture and the First Yoruba Novel*, 15.

39. Ajayi, *Christian Missions in Nigeria*.

40. See Cole, *Modern and Traditional Elites*, 45–72; Mann, *Marrying Well*, 11–34; Ajayi, *Christian Missions in Nigeria*.

41. "Salary of African Magistrates," *Daily Service*, October 28, 1944; "No Colour Discrimination?" *West African Pilot*, December 20, 1947; "African Civil Servants' Salaries," *Nigerian Daily Times*, January 28, 1941.

42. Falola and Aderinto, *Nigeria, Nationalism, and Writing History*, 115–28.

43. Quoted in Agiri, "Kola in Western Nigeria," 72.

44. Coker, *Landmarks of the Nigerian Press*.

45. Denzer, "Domestic Science Training in Yorubaland, Nigeria," 116–39.

46. Chuku, "'Crack Kernels, Crack Hitler.'"

47. NAI, Ondo Prof D.13, "A Report to His Excellency the Governor of Nigeria on Social Welfare in the Colony and Protectorate by Alexander Paterson, 1944."

48. Little, *African Women in Towns*, 15–74.

49. For biographies of some of these elite women, see, among others, Awe, ed., *Nigerian Women in Historical Perspective*; Mba, *Nigerian Women Mobilized*; Coker, *A Lady*; Rosiji, *Lady Ademola*.

50. I found Ademola's account of her Oxford experience interesting in its focus on her multiple identities as a woman and a black, educated British subject. See Moore, "The Story of Kofoworola Aina Moore."

51. "Miss Stella Jane Thomas Is Created a Police Magistrate," *West African Pilot*, August 22, 1942.

52. The designation "full-blooded Nigerian" was used in the newspaper press to differentiate between, on the one hand, Nigerians of Sierra Leonean, Liberian, and American descent and, on the other hand, those whose parents were both originally from Nigeria. "Dr. Elizabeth Akerele Returns from Medical Study in UK," *West African Pilot*, February 25, 1938; Zedomi, "Women in the Lagos Newspaper Press," 8–15.

53. For more on Douglas's experience in Nigeria, see Denzer, "Intersections."

54. NAI, COMCOL 1, 498, "Lagos Women's League to Hugh Clifford," October 24, 1923; NAI, COMCOL 1, 498, "Mrs. Obasa to the Honourable Chief Secretary to the Government," February 26, 1924; NAI, COMCOL 1, 498, "Olajumoke Obasa to the Resident of the Colony," August 6, 1926. One of the most highly articulate positions bordering on several aspects of women's engagement with the colonial state is Ademola's lengthy public lecture that was later serialized and published in the *West African Pilot* in its inaugural month. See "Miss Kofo Moore Defends Her Sex," *West African Pilot*, November 24, 25, 26, 29, 30, 1937.

55. See "Miss Kofo Moore Defends Her Sex," *West African Pilot*, November 24, 25, 26, 29, 30, and December 1, 1937.

56. See from the *West African Pilot*: "Mrs Abayomi Speaks," November 25, 1937; "Nigerian Women Petition for World Peace," November 29, 1937; "Dr. Akerele Gives Impressive Lecture on School Hygine [Hygiene]," March 28, 1938; "Lagos Women's League Appeal for Funds," May 9, 1938; "Ladies' League Holds Annual Exhibition and Sale of Work," December 16, 1938; "Ladies' League Will Stage Exhibition," August 3, 1939.

57. "Women's Party Holds Grand Meeting," *Daily Service*, August 24, 1944.

58. *Daily Service*, May 15 and 25, 1944.

59. "Women's Party," *Daily Service*, August 25, 1944.

60. I briefly engaged gendered politics between male and female nationalists over girl-child rearing in a work on children in Nigeria; see Aderinto, "Researching Colonial Childhoods."

61. "Are Our Ladies Progressive?" *West African Pilot*, May 3, 1941.

62. See from the *West African Pilot*: "Our Women Folk," December 29, 1937; "Our Women Leaders," February 19, 1938; "Our Women Folk," February 21, 1938; "Female Education," August 4, 1938; "Our Women Folk," January 14, 1939; "Female Education," April 22, 1939; "Our Women Graduates," August 5, 1939; "Work for Female Club," May 6, 1941; "Our Womenfolk," November 26, 1941; "Women's Welfare Council and Our Girls," March 2, 1944; "Female Gathering Charges Women's Party with Inaction and Decides to Meet Government," August 18, 1944; "Women's Political Party Is Warned of Mud-Slinging as Appendage of Politics," May 12, 1944; "Women Dabble in Lagos Politics," May 12, 1944.

63. See Mba, *Nigerian Women Mobilized*, 193–211.

64. NAI, COMCOL 1, 1257, "Crime in Lagos and Its District," 1928–47; NAI, COMCOL 1, 2481, "Kidnapping," 1945–57; NAI, COMCOL 1, 2690, "Gambling," 1942–56.

65. Alaja-Browne, "The Origin and Development of Juju Music."

66. "Cost of Living Report," *West African Pilot*, June 27, 1942; "Cost of Living Index," *West African Pilot*, September 14, 1945; Olukoju, "The Cost of Living in Lagos."

67. "Capitol Cinema," *West African Pilot*, September 17, 1945.

68. "Dancing at Ritz Hotel," *Daily Service*, September 2, 1944; oral interview, Mr. John Alade, June 9, 2012.

69. Waterman, *Juju*, 27–81.

70. "Pubs and Housing Problem," *West African Pilot*, December 10, 1942.

71. See the following news and editorials in the *West African Pilot*: "One Way of Solving the Rent Problem," November 15, 1943; "Lagos Rent Assessment Board," January 13, 1944; "The Unending House Racket," February 9, 1944; "Increased Cost of Living in Lagos," June 6, 1944; "The Rent Problem in Lagos," August 16, 1944; "Control of House Rents," April 17, 1943; "Lady Tenant Weeps as Rent Board Issues Ejectment Order," May 1, 1943; "Rents in Lagos," May 26, 1943.

72. "Glover Hall Bookings," *West African Pilot*, March 5, 1943.

73. "Nigeria Wants Night Club Reforms," *West African Pilot*, February 4, 1948.

74. McIntyre, "Commander Glover and the Colony of Lagos"; Miller, "Glover Hall, Old and New."

75. Tamuno, *Herbert Macaulay*, 35.

76. *Aso ebi* is identical dress people wore on important ceremonies like weddings, funerals, and festivals. See from the *West African Pilot*: "Lady Raises Loan on Borrowed 'Aso Ebi' and Lands in Court," May 18, 1943; "Aso Ebi on the Stage!" August 27, 1946.

77. NAI, COMCOL 1, "Lagos Club," 1926–36.

78. "Night Club for Lagos," *West African Pilot*, December 31, 1942.

79. "Censorship and the Cinema," *West African Pilot*, August 1, 1944.

80. See from the *West African Pilot*: "Moral Control (1)," April 13, 1939; "Undesirable Women," December 6, 1939; "Our Girls and Ball Room Etiquette," November 23, 1945; "Our Girls and Ball Room Etiquette," November 29, 1945.

81. "Our Girls and Ball Room Etiquette," *West African Pilot*, November 23, 1945.

82. "Girls and Immoral Dancing," *West African Pilot*, November 25, 1947.

83. Barber, *Print Culture and the First Yoruba Novel*, 101.

84. Ekwensi, *People of the City*, 13.

85. *West African Pilot*: "Moral Control," April 13, 1939; "Undesirable Women," December 6, 1939; "Unstable Women," July 5, 1939; "Female Drunkard," October 15, 1945; "Drunkenness among Women," May 28, 1942; "Our Girls and Ballroom Etiquette," November 23, 1945.

86. Little, *West African Urbanization*.

87. NAI, COMCOL 1/248/58, "Efik Ladies Union."

88. "Urbanisation," *West African Pilot*, March 10, 1938.

89. Ibid.

90. Ibid.

91. NAI, COMCOL 1, 69, "Unemployed and Paupers: Repatriation of," 1927; NAI, CSO 38322/S.193, "Union of Unemployed Men and Women of Nigeria," November 19, 1945.

92. "Exodus into Lagos Capital," *West African Pilot*, November 2, 1945; "Repatriation of the Unemployed," *West African Pilot*, June 21, 1945.

93. "Exodus into Lagos Capital," *West African Pilot*, November 2, 1945.

94. "Urbanisation," *West African Pilot*, March 10, 1938, and "Repatriation of Beggars," *Nigerian Daily Times*, June 28, 1941.

95. "Urbanisation," *West African Pilot*, March 10, 1938.

96. For more on the Lebanese presence in southern Nigeria, see Falola, "Lebanese Traders in Southwestern Nigeria."

97. "Petition of the Hausa Population," *Lagos Weekly Record*, September 1, 1906.

98. See Mann, *Marrying Well*.

99. For more on this, see Cole, *Modern and Traditional Elites*.

100. *West African Pilot*: "2 Hausa Murderers Are Found Guilty & Sentenced to Death," April 21, 1939; "Three Ibariba Murderers Get Death Sentence at High Court," April 25, 1939. "Hausa Man Receives 7 Years," *Nigerian Daily Times*, March 10, 1941.

101. "The Unemployed Warri Men and Women in Lagos—a Menace: Round Up Their Dens and Ship Them Home" (pts. I and II), *Lagos Daily News*, March 13 and 14, 1933.

102. Ibid.

103. NAI, Oyo Prof. 1, 3562, "Measures against Prostitution," 1944.

104. NAK (MLG/S/RGA), "Committee on Problems of Prostitution in Northern Nigeria, 1950–1965."

105. Olusanya, "The Sabon-Gari System."

106. See from the *West African Pilot*: "Ibos Banned from Glover Hall," April 8, 1949; "Glover Hall Hired Out Agreement," April 11, 1949.

107. Coleman, *Nigeria*, 227.

108. "No Nigerian Is a Foreigner in Lagos," *West African Pilot*, October 16, 1948. For more on Mbonu as a cultural nationalist and fervent supporter of NCNC, see Njoku, *African Cultural Values*, 103–37.

109. NAI, COMCOL 1, 1177/S.I, "Non-Native Civilians in Lagos and Colony District: Population Figures," 1943–56.

110. Coleman, *Nigeria*, 144.

111. Cole, *Modern and Traditional Elites*, 75.

112. Ibid., 76.

113. Ibid.

114. Williams, *Faces, Cases and Places*, 30.

115. See Webster, *The African Churches among the Yoruba*.

116. NAI, CSO/23610, "Complaints against Grand Hotel," 1931.

117. Olukoju, "The Segregation of Europeans and Africans in Colonial Nigeria," 263–86; NAI, COMCOL 1, 263, "Recreation Grounds for Lagos African Community," 1927–34; NAI, COMCOL 1, 1979, "Yoruba Tennis Club," 1937–38; NAI, COMCOL 1, "The Ebute Metta African Tennis Club," 1926.

118. See from the *West African Pilot*: "The African Hospital," July 12, 1943; "Lagos Hospital," May 14, 1943; "Exploiting Racial Differences in Nigeria," September 16, 1944.

119. "Jim Crow Hospitals," *West African Pilot*, March 26, 1943.

120. "Hotel Wayfarer and Our Town Council," *West African Pilot*, December 14, 1945.

121. "Hotel Owner States that African Hotels Have Poor Patronage for Want of Liquor," *West African Pilot*, April 11, 1944.

122. Ibid.

123. See from the *West African Pilot*: "Greek Proprietor Refuses African in Bristol Hotel," February 24, 1947; "Colour Bar in Bristol Hotel," February 24, 1947.

124. See from the *Daily Service*: "His Excellency Is Willing to Discuss Racial Issue with United Front Committee Delegation," March 8, 1947.

125. NAI, COMCOL 1, 2900, "Circular No. 25: Racial Discrimination," March 3, 1947.

126. "The Menace of Alien Immigration," *West African Pilot*, May 8, 1947.

127. A report claimed that one-third of Lagos's assets belonged to Europeans. See "One-Third of Lagos Owned by Foreigners," *West African Pilot*, December 21, 1948.

128. Olukoju, "The Segregation of Europeans and Africans in Colonial Nigeria," 283.

129. Williams, *Faces, Cases and Places*, 27.

130. Ibid., 30.

131. Ibid., 21.

CHAPTER 2. "THE VULGAR AND OBSCENE LANGUAGE"

1. Walkowitz, *City of Dreadful Delight*.

2. "Red Light District," *West African Pilot*, December 17, 1937.

3. See from the *West African Pilot*: "The 'Surplus' Women," October 20, 1945; "The Problem of 'Surplus Women,'" September 13, 1945; "Evil Practices Create 'Surplus Women,'" September 20, 1945; "The Question of Prostitution," July 6, 1946; "Menace at Demobilisation Centre," July 5, 1946; "Cause of Surplus Women," February 7, 1946; "The Prostitution Problem," October 22, 1946; "These Ikeja Undesirables," July 9, 1946; "Men and Girls' Prostitution," October 11, 1946; "Finding a Solution to Prostitution," August 7, 1946; "Prostitution: A Social Necessity," August 3, 1946; "Prostitution: A Social Necessity," August 6, 1946; "This Question of Prostitution," July 13, 1946; "Surplus Women," September 11, 1948; from the *Daily Service*: "License Prostitution," July 19, 1945; "Problems of Prostitution," July 27, 1946; "Prostitution—Enemy of Society," September 23, 1946; "Prostitution—Enemy of Society," September 24, 1946; "Prostitution—Enemy of Society," September 25, 1946; "Prostitution—Enemy of Society," September 26, 1946; "Prostitution—Enemy of the Society," September 27, 1946; "Prostitutes Are Repatriated to Appease the Rain God," July 8, 1949; "Prostitution: Six Women Gaoled," December 28, 1954; "Repatriate These Prostitutes," July 6, 1956; "20 Prostitutes to Be Repatriated," July 14, 1956; "Legalise Prostitution," January 28, 1958; "Prostitution Should Not Be Legalized," February 4, 1958; "Prostitution, Inevitable Social Evil," February 27, 1958; "Prostitutes Should Be Sent to Jail," January 31, 1959; "Prostitution Isn't African—Says Judge," October 22, 1959; "Women See Law against Prostitution," March 1, 1960; from the *Nigerian Spokesman*: "This Question of Prostitution," May 31, 1944; "Considering Prostitution," June 15, 1944; "About the Prostitutes," June 17 1944; "Encouraging Prostitution (1)," June 20, 1944; "Encouraging Prostitution (2)," June 21, 1944; "2 Undesirables Fail to Quit Township Jailed," May 22, 1952; "Prostitutes and the Nation," January 28, 1953; "Problems of Prostitution," January 30, 1953; "Prostitution and Our Nation," January 31, 1953; "Prostitution and Our Nation," February 13, 1953; "Clearing Prostitutes from the Township," June 10, 1953; "Problems of Prostitution," June 13, 1953; "Hotels or Brothels," November 6, 1953.

4. "Living to Live (2)," *West African Pilot*, March 1, 1938.

5. Ibid.

6. Ibid.

7. For more on the politics of reading prostitutes' bodies and work, see Bell, *Reading, Writing, and Rewriting the Prostitute Body*.

8. "Bottom" is a Yoruba euphemism for "virginal." Oral interview with Madam Anike Isola, Lagos, June 13, 2012.

9. NAI, COMCOL 1, 2844, "Child Prostitution in Lagos"; NAI, COMCOL 1, 2844, "Calabar Improvement League"; NAI, COMCOL 1, 248/76, "Urhobo Progress Union."

10. NAI, COMCOL 1, 2844, "Child Prostitution in Lagos," January 17, 1944.

11. NAE, AIDIST 2.1.373, "Egbisim Improvement Union to the District Officer, Obubra Division," April 3, 1948.

12. NAI, COMCOL 1, 2844, "Child Prostitution in Lagos," March 5, 1943.

13. NAI, CSO 26, 36005, "District Officer of Obubra Division to the Resident of Ogoja Province," February 7, 1941.

14. Barber, *Print Culture and the First Yoruba Novel.*

15. Ibid.

16. Ibid., 271–359.

17. Ibid., 211.

18. Ibid., 203.

19. Ibid., 211.

20. "The Unemployed Warri Men and Women in Lagos—a Menace: Round Up Their Dens and Ship Them Home" (pts. I and II), *Lagos Daily News*, March 13 and 14, 1933.

21. NAI, CSO 26, 36005, "District Officer of Obubra Division to the Resident of Ogoja Province," February 7, 1941.

22. "The Unemployed Warri Men and Women in Lagos—a Menace: Round Up Their Dens and Ship Them Home" (pts. I and II), *Lagos Daily News*, March 13 and 14, 1933.

23. See the various documents in NAI, COMCOL 1, 2844, "Child Prostitution in Lagos," 1941–48

24. NAI, COMCOL 1, 2844, "The Reporter to the Commissioner of the Colony," February 10, 1943; NAI, COMCOL 1, 2844, "District Officer of Kukuruku to the Colony Welfare Office," October 6, 1943; NAI, COMCOL 1, 2844, "Rose Daniel," December 12, 1943; NAI, COMCOL 1, 2844, "A Report against Prostitution," November 4, 1946; NAI, COMCOL 1, 2844, "Ogbo Abuyola to Colony Welfare," July 12, 1946; NAI, COMCOL 1, 2844, "Secretary of Calabar Council to the District Officer, Calabar," March 13, 1944; Aderinto, "Journey to Work."

25. NAE, OBUBDIST, 4.1.71, "Resident of Ogoja Province to the Chief Secretary to the Government Administering Nigeria," February 13, 1941.

26. Oral interview with Madam Oluseyi Falade, Lagos, June 20, 2008. For the story of *karuwanci* in Ibadan, see Cohen, *Custom and Politics in Urban Africa*, 51–70. *Karuwanci* was a traditional institution that dates back to early Hausa civilization. In precolonial times it served as a gateway for reintegrating divorcées into households through courtship and did not involve the commoditization of sex. However, from around the 1930s or earlier, both women who sold sex in brothels and those who practiced the old *karuwanci* were collectively called *karuwai* (prostitutes). More research is required to historicize the transformation of *karuwanci* since the precolonial period. For more on *karuwanci*, see Barkow, "The Institution of Courtesanship"; Smith, "The Hausa System of Social Status."

27. "Petition of the Hausa Population," *Lagos Weekly Record*, September 1, 1906.

28. Oral interview with Mr. Akanji Olanrewaju, Lagos, June 15, 2008.

29. Oral interview with Madam Hauwa, Lagos, June 17, 2008.

30. White, *The Comforts of Home*, 18–19.

31. This is not unique to Lagos. For similar findings in Ibadan, see Cohen, *Custom and Politics in Urban Africa*, 51–70.

32. NAI, COMCOL 1, 248/76, "Colony Welfare Officer to the Honourable Secretary, Urhobo Progress Union," October 2, 1943.

33. NAI, COMCOL 1, 1420, "Hausas in Lagos," 1932–56.

34. Van Onselen, *Studies in the Social and Economic History of the Witwatersrand*, 1:103–62.

35. Callaway, *Gender, Culture and Empire.*

36. Oral interview with Mr. Raufu Adisa, Lagos, June 1, 2012.

37. Mbonu Ojike, review of *Surplus Women*, *West African Pilot*, September 11, 1948.

38. "Woman Is Fined £5 in Court for Allowing Her House to Be Used for Questionable Purpose," *West African Pilot*, September 1, 1943.

39. NAI, COMCOL 1, 2844, "Petition Dated June 24, 1944."

40. NAI, COMCOL 1, 2844, "Streets Habitually Used for Prostitutes' Dwellings," August 14, 1946.

41. Oral interview with Mr. Taju Adisa in Lagos, June 3, 2012.

42. Ibid.

43. Ibid.

44. Ojike, review of *Surplus Women*, *West African Pilot*, September 11, 1948.

45. Barber, *Print Culture and the First Yoruba Novel*, 109.

46. Ibid., 239.

47. The *iyalode* was a female chief in Yorubaland and a representative of women in the central political system. She provided leadership especially among market women and kept her own court. For more on the *iyalode*, see, among others, Denzer, *The Iyalode in Ibadan Politics and Society*. Segilola used the term here to describe herself as the "first among equals" within the female ranks.

48. Report of the Cost of Living Committee Lagos, Nigeria (Lagos: Government Printer, 1942), 48.

49. Ibid., 73–76.

50. Ibid., 74.

51. NAI, COMCOL 1, "Police Report," November 26, 1946.

52. NAI, COMCOL 1, 2844, "The Reporter to the Commissioner of the Colony," October 1, 1943.

53. Ekwensi, *People of the City*, 40–41.

54. Mabogunje, *Urbanization in Nigeria*, 266.

55. Barber, *Print Culture and the First Yoruba Novel*, 177.

56. Oral interview with Mr. Salako Abass, Lagos, June 12, 2008.

57. "Repatriation of Prostitutes," *Nigerian Spokesman*, June 21, 1943.

58. Barber, *Print Culture and the First Yoruba Novel*, 215.

59. Ibid., 215.

60. Oral interview with Mr. Salako Abass.

61. Thompson, "Colonial Policy," 438; Buckley, *Slaves in Red Coats*, 125–26.

62. NAI, N 1088, "WAFF—General Affairs," April 1918.

63. Ibid.

64. Ibid.

65. For similar circumstances in other imperial sites, see Harrison, *Public Health in British India*.

66. NAI, CSO N105/1920, "European Staff: Application for Permission to Bring Out Their Wives," 1920.

67. Niven, *Nigerian Kaleidoscope*, 62.

68. Clayton and Killingray, *Khaki and Blue*, 150–51.

69. Flint, *Sir George Goldie and the Making of Nigeria*; Gann and Duignan, eds., *African Proconsuls, European Governors in Africa*; Hasting, *Nigerian Days*; Muffett, *Empire Builder Extraordinary Sir George Goldie*.

70. Hyam, "Concubinage and the Colonial Service," 171.

71. Ibid., 172–73.

72. Ibid., 183–84.

73. NAI, CSO/34911, "Marriage of British Subjects in Foreign Dependencies," 1938.

74. NAI, CSO 20/1–9, NC.18/1920, "Memorandum by Principal Medical Officer E. E. Maples," December 10, 1919.

75. Ibid.

76. Ibid.

77. See, among others, Mason, *The Making of Victorian Sexuality*; Barret-Ducrocq, *Love in the Time of Victoria*; Harrison, *The Dark Angel*.

78. NAI, CSO 20/1–9, NC.54/20, "Proceedings of a Medical Board: Officers and Nurses," August 26, 1920.

79. NAI, CSO 20/1–9, NC.54/20, "John Rose Bradford to the Under Secretary of State for the Colonies," August 3, 1920.

80. Niven, *Nigerian Kaleidoscope*, 136.

81. Quoted in Clayton and Killingray, *Khaki and Blue*, 157.

82. Ibid.

83. Olukoju, "Elder Dempster and the Shipping Trade of Nigeria."

84. See NAI, COMCOL 1, 2844, "Child Prostitution in Lagos," 1942–46.

85. "Lagos Hotels Are Described by Our Staff Reporter," *West African Pilot*, December 6, 1937; NAI, COMCOL 1, 2558, "Ritz Hotel, 1941"; NAI, COMCOL 1, 2490, "Grand Hotel, 1942"; NAI, CSO 23610/61, "Complaints against Grand Hotel."

86. "Lagos Hotels Are Described by Our Staff Reporter," *West African Pilot*, December 6, 1937.

87. Ibid.

88. Ibid.

89. For more on the description of the elements that congregated around the Grand Hotel, see NAI, COMCOL 1, 248/107, "Bankole-Wright to the Comcol."

90. Annual Volume of the Laws of Nigeria Containing All Legislation Enacted during the Year 1944 (Lagos: Government Printer, 1945), A53.

91. Waterman, *Juju*, 41.

92. "Parlophone Records: Ashewo/Omo Jaguda," *Lagos Daily News*, April 2, 1932.

93. Waterman, *Juju*, 50.

94. NAI, COMCOL 1, 498, "Lagos Women's League to Hugh Clifford," October 24, 1923.

95. NAI, COMCOL 1, 498, "The Governor to Mrs. Obasa," December 20, 1923.

96. Ibid.

97. Ibid.

98. NAI, COMCOL 1, 498, "Mrs. Obasa to the Honourable Chief Secretary to the Government," February 26, 1924; NAI, COMCOL 1, 498, "Olajumoke Obasa to the Resident of the Colony," August 6, 1926.

99. NAI, COMCOL 1, 498, "Olajumoke Obasa to the Resident of the Colony," August 6, 1926.

100. "Moral Degeneracy in Lagos," *Lagos Daily News*, May 10, 1929; Sogidi, "Save the Future Mothers," *Comet*, September 21, 1935; [a Muslim], "Save the Future Mothers," *Comet*, October 5, 1935; Kabiboy, "Girl Hawkers' Morals," *Comet*, October 19, 1935; C.O.O., "Girl Hawkers' Morals," *Comet*, October 26, 1935.

101. "Moral Degeneracy in Lagos," *Lagos Daily News*, May 10, 1929.

102. "Red Light District," *West African Pilot*, December 17, 1937.

103. "Street Noises," *West African Pilot*, November 25, 1937.

104. Ahire, *Imperial Policing*; Tamuno, *The Police in Modern Nigeria*, 1–40.

105. "Pretty Girl Arraigned on Charge of Idling," *West African Pilot*, April 21, 1938.

106. "Woman Sentenced to Prison: She Runs Akunakuna House," *West African Pilot*, December 24, 1937.

107. See from the *West African Pilot*: "Boma Boys Engage in Free Fight," November 24, 1937; "Boma Boys Vanish as Constable Visits," December 17, 1937; "Boma Boy Robs Seaman of Ten Shillings Note," February 21, 1938; "Children and Crime," March 21, 1938; "The Jaguda Boys," April 21, 1938; "Hungry Jaguda Boys Rob Girl Hawker of Her Fish," September 21, 1938; "This Assault Menace," September 28, 1938.

108. Major Akinwade Jones, "Social Problems in Lagos (1)," *West African Pilot*, July 4, 1941.

109. "Leg. Co. Adjourns Sin Die: Bill against 'Boma Boys' Passed: Dr. Carr Advocates Adjustment of Educational Policy," *Nigerian Daily Times*, January 16, 1941.

110. See from the *West African Pilot*: "Stop the Hooliganism," October 31, 1939; "European Special Constables Arrest a Boma Boy and He Is Sentenced to Imprisonment for a Month," August 10, 1940; "Six Boma Boys Are Arraigned for Idling and Are Fined 40s or One Month," November 26, 1940.

111. NAI, COMCOL 1, 2690, "Street Gambling," 1942–56; "50 Gamblers Are Arrested around Race Course and Fined 10/- [10 shillings] Each," *Daily Service*, August 11, 1942.

112. "This Assault Menace." See also from *African Mirror*: Wizard, "Deadly Facts," June 20, 1940; "'Boma Boy' Dealt Police Constable Nasty Blows," July 13, 1940; "Boma Boy Who Beat Police Officer Sentenced by Magistrate," July 16, 1940.

113. See from the *West African Pilot*: "European Special Constables Arrest a Boma Boy and He Is Sentenced to Imprisonment for a Month," August 10, 1940; "Six Boma Boys Are Arraigned for Idling and Are Fined 40s or One Month," November 26, 1940; "Major A. Jones Exhaustively Discusses 'Boma Boy' Problem," August 13, 1940; Major Akinwande Jones, "Social Problems in Lagos (1)" and "Social Problems in Lagos (2)," July 5, 1941; Dr. K. A. Abayomi, "The Nigerian Boy of Today," November 30, 1942; "Functions of Committee for Juvenile Employment Are Told," October 15, 1943.

114. "The Nigerian Boy of Today," *West African Pilot*, August 30, 1942.

115. NAI, COMCOL 1, 2471, "Juvenile Delinquency in Lagos by Donald Faulkner," 1941.

116. "Hooliganism and Worse," *Nigerian Daily Times*, November 6, 1940.

117. Olatunji Otusanya, "Guides for Visiting Sailors," letter to the editor, *Daily Service*, November 25, 1940.

118. "Clean-Up Lagos," *Nigerian Daily Times*, July 29, 1943; Awolowo, *Awo*, 82.

119. "The Jaguda Boys," *West African Pilot*, April 21, 1938.

120. NAI, CSO/37457, "Boma Boys Acting as Touts to Seamen and Passenger: Activities of, 1935–1943."

121. "Two Men Exchanged Cuffs over Young Girl at Taiwo Street," *West African Pilot*, August 4, 1938.

122. Father, "Sailors and 'Boma Boys,'" *West African Pilot*, August 21, 1940; "'Boma Boy' Who Robbed Seaman Receives 9 Months and 12 Months' Police Supervision," *West African Pilot*, October 28, 1940.

123. "The 'Boma Boy' Problem," *African Mirror*, August 14, 1940.

124. "The Underworld of Lagos," *Nigerian Daily Times*, September 9, 1940; D. D. Ola, "Guides for Visiting Sailors," letter to the editor, *Nigerian Daily Times*, November 20, 1940; "Boma Boy Sells Vulture to a Seaman Who Wanted Fowl," *West African Pilot*, June 3, 1943.

125. NAI, COMCOL 1, 2471, "History Sheet for Victor," March 7, 1941.

126. "Boma Boy Robs Seaman of Ten Shillings Note," *West African* Pilot, February 21, 1938.

127. NAI, COMCOL 1, 2471, "History Sheet for Felix Bolaji" and "History Sheet for Jack Morris," March 7, 1941.

CHAPTER 3. CHILDHOOD INNOCENCE,
ADULT CRIMINALITY

1. NAI, COMCOL 1, 2844, "Child Welfare: Prostitution and Child Marriage," May 1943.

2. NAI, COMCOL 1, 2844, "Informant to the Colony Welfare Officer," July 10, 1943.

3. See the following editorials in the *Lagos Daily News*: "Nigerian Women and Social Work," April 7, 1932; "Educated Women and Native Industry," April 14, 1932; "The Education of Nigerian Women," May 12, 1932; "The Education of Muslim Girls," May 14, 1932; "Education of Children," May 12, 1932; "Training in Domestic Work," May 14, 1932; "Nigerian Women and Social Work: The Girl Aina," April 8, 1932; "Vocation for Women," October 10, 1932; "What Women Can Do," September 21, 1931. See also from the *Nigerian Daily Times*: "Children Are Treasures," July 27, 1932; "Children of the Dark Continent," May 4, 1931; "What Could Be Done with the Boys?" May 25, 1933.

4. For more on the ideas of childhood, modernity, and colonial progress, see Aderinto, "Researching Colonial Childhoods."

5. Fadipe, *The Sociology of the Yoruba*, 100–105; Talbot, *The Peoples of Southern Nigeria*, 2:388–415; Talbot, *The Peoples of Southern Nigeria*, 3:538–61; Talbot, *Life in Southern Nigeria*, 26–29, 38–39, 126–27; Aries, *Centuries of Childhood*; Cunningham, *Children and Childhood in Western Society since 1500*; Colin, *A History of Childhood*; Mintz, *Huck's Raft*; Fass, ed., *The Routledge History of Childhood in the Western World*.

6. Byfield, "Pawns and Politics," 199.

7. NAI, Kwale Dist. 1, "Acting Colony Welfare Officer Bankole Wright to the District Officer, Kwale: Juvenile Prostitution in Lagos H. H. 169 & 170," February 28, 1944.

8. NAI, COMCOL 1, 2786, "'Madam Folly's Case," July 22, 1944.

9. NAI, COMCOL 1, 2844, "The Commissioner of the Colony to the Honourable, the Chief Secretary to the Government: Child Prostitution," May 21, 1946.

10. House-Midamba and Ekechi, eds., *African Market Women and Economic Power*.

11. Leith-Ross, *Stepping-Stones*, 83; Leith-Ross, *African Women*.

12. T. Ayinla Dis., "The Hawkers and the Buyers," *Nigerian Daily Times*, April 25, 1932; from the *West African Pilot*: "7 Female Hawkers Are Fined 10s. Each," June 28, 1939; "Unemployed Cyclist Injured Girl Hawkers," July 12, 1941; "Food Hawking in Lagos," April 1, 1942; "Our Girl Hawkers," September 18, 1942; "Our Girl Hawkers," September 26, 1942; "Magistrate Warns All Parents of Hawkers," March 27, 1945.

13. NAI, COMCOL 1, 498, "Mrs. Obasa to the Resident of Lagos," August 6, 1926.

14. "Problem of the Girl Hawkers," *Nigerian Daily Times*, May 20, 1930.

15. The criminality of girls was treated as a particularly worrisome development that had to be attended to. See the following stories from the *Nigerian Daily Times*: "Girl Criminals: Veteran Doctor Suggests a Solution," August 20, 1932; "The Girl Criminal," August 22, 1932; "Girl Housebreaker Sentenced: Twelve Months Eighth Conviction," August 18, 1932; "Ex-Convent Girl in Court," August 18, 1932; "Another Girl Criminal: Young Husband's Plea to Magistrate," August 24, 1932; "Welfare of Women and Girls," September 10, 1932; "Another Girl Kidnapped," September 14, 1932. See also from the *West African Pilot*: "Young Girls Bound Over for Stealing Tin Corned Beef," August 18, 1938, and "13 Year Old Girl Is Arraigned for Stealing the Sum of 15/- [15 shillings]," December 16, 1938.

16. See from the *Comet*: Sogidi, "Save the Future Mothers," September 21, 1935; [a Muslim], "Save the Future Mothers," October 5, 1935; Kabiboy, "Girl Hawkers' Morals," October 19, 1935; C.O.O., "Girl Hawkers' Morals," October 26, 1935.

17. Sogidi, "Save the Future Mothers," *Comet*, September 21, 1935; Kabiboy, "Girl Hawkers' Morals," *Comet*, October 19, 1935.

18. Kabiboy, "Girl Hawkers' Morals," *Comet*, October 19, 1935.

19. C.O.O., "Girl Hawkers' Morals," *Comet*, October 26, 1935.

20. Ibid.

21. Kabiboy, "Girl Hawkers' Morals," *Comet*, October 19, 1935; [a Muslim], "Save the Future Mothers," *Comet*, October 5, 1935.

22. "Three Girls for £9: Lashes for Enticing a Child," *Nigerian Daily Times*, June 10, 1932.

23. From the *West African Pilot*: "Hungry Jaguda Boys Rob Girl Hawker of Her Fish," September 12, 1938; "Fisherman Who Arrested Girl Hawker Is Held and Imprisoned," July 1, 1943.

24. NAI, COMCOL 1, "Hawking by Children in Lagos: Faulkner to the President of the Lagos Town Council," September 1942.

25. NAI, COMCOL 1, 2844, "Child Prostitution in Lagos by Alison Izzett, Lady Welfare Officer," May 15, 1946.

26. From the *West African Pilot*: "Young Girl Found Dead on Race Course: Foul Play Suspected; Information Requested by Police," March 15, 1945. Other stories about sexual assaults of girl hawkers include "Street Hawking by Young Girls," *West African Pilot*, June 20, 1946; "Eleven Year Old Girl Hawker Found Dead in Public Garden," *West African Pilot*, June 20, 1946.

27. "Young Girl Found Dead on Race Course: Foul Play Suspected; Information Requested by Police," *West African Pilot*, March 15, 1945.

28. "Eleven Year Old Girl Hawker Found Dead in Public Garden," *West African Pilot*, June 20, 1946.

29. For a discussion of slavery and trafficking in other parts of Africa, see Lawrance and Roberts, eds., *Trafficking in Slavery's Wake*.

30. Mabogunje, *Urbanization in Nigeria*, 239.

31. "Street Indecencies," *Lagos Daily News*, May 27, 1932.

32. "Women's Welfare League's Protest against Moral Danger Proves a Big Success: Government Will Be Asked to Forbid Hawking by Girls of Tender Age," *Daily Service*, August 10, 1944.

33. Ibid.

34. Ibid.; "Mrs Abayomi Attributes Prostitution to Laziness, Undue Gaiety, and Unemployment," *West African Pilot*, August 10, 1944.

35. "Female Hawkers," *West African Pilot*, June 28, 1939.

36. NAI, COMCOL 1, 2844, "Child Marriage," February 1943.

37. Fadipe, *The Sociology of the Yoruba*, 65–86; Johnson, *The History of the Yorubas*, 113–17.

38. The commercialization of African marriage was not unique to Nigeria. See Parkin and Nyamwaya, eds., *Transformations of African Marriage*.

39. This estimate was derived from newspaper stories and reports on bride-price published during the 1930s and 1940s. According to Ojo, the "scarcity of women" in the Ekiti region due to warfare and slavery pushed marriage payment up in the early years of the twentieth century. See Ojo, "Slavery, Marriage, and Gender Relations in Eastern Yorubaland," 151.

40. Debate over marriage payment received adequate publicity in the *Eastern Nigerian Guardian*, *West African Pilot*, and *Southern Nigeria Defender* during the 1930s and 1940s. See from the *West African Pilot*: "This Dowry Problem," July 29, 1938; "The Dowry System," February 21, 1939; "Bride-Price at Awka," August 24, 1946. See also "Youth of Awo-Omama Will Boycott Their Girls, Want Bride Price Be Reduced," *Nigerian Spokesman*, January 8, 1948; "Bride Price in Iboland," *Daily Comet*, July 7, 1949.

41. Oral interview, Mrs. Johnson, Lagos, June 19, 2008.

42. NAI, COMCOL 1, 2844, "The District Officer of Kukuruku Division to the Welfare Officer," October 13, 1943.

43. NAI, COMCOL 1, 2844, "Colony Welfare Officer to the District Officer of Kukuruku Division," October 23, 1943.

44. NAI, COMCOL 1, 2844, "Ogbo Abuyola to the Colonial Welfare Office," July 12, 1946.

45. Ibid.

46. NAI, COMCOL 1, 2844, "District Officer of Kukuruku Division to the Colony Welfare Officer," October 6, 1943.

47. See from the *West African Pilot*: "Seducer of 15 Yrs. Old Girl Charged," September 15, 1938; "Man Found Guilty of Abduction Is Bound Over for Twelve Months," November 29, 1938; "Man Charged with Stealing 10-Year-Old Child Is Committed to Assizes for Trial," November 5, 1941; "Man Abducts Young Damsel and Runs into Vichy Territory," October 15, 1941; "Offences of Child Stealing," January 2, 1942; "Man Imprisoned for Stealing a Young Girl Loses Appeal," February 3, 1942; "New Law Will Check Child Stealing in the Protectorate," August 20, 1942; "13-Year-Old

Hawker Plants Self in Man's Home as His Wife," May 3, 1943; "Native Doctor Uses 'Tanda' to Court Girl: He Pays £25 Fine," September 24, 1943.

48. "Seducer of 15 Yrs. Old Girl Charged," *West African Pilot*, September 15, 1938.

49. "Man Found Guilty of Abduction Is Bound Over for Twelve Months," *West African Pilot*, November 29, 1938.

50. "Native Doctor Uses 'Tanda' to Court Girl: He Pays £25 Fine," *West African Pilot*, September 24, 1943.

51. "Man Abducts Young Damsel and Runs into Vichy Territory," *West African Pilot*, October 15, 1941.

52. "13-Year-Old Hawker Plants Self in Man's Home as His Wife," *West African Pilot*, May 3, 1943.

53. NAI, COMCOL 1, 2844, "Lance Corporal E. Ogbe's Report," November 11, 1946.

54. NAI, COMCOL 1, 2844, "Child Prostitution in Lagos by Alison Izzett, Lady Welfare Officer."

55. Ibid.

56. Ibid.

57. NAI, COMCOL 1, "Rose Ojenughe to Welfare Officer," November 21, 1946.

58. Ibid.

59. NAI, COMCOL 1, 2844, "District Officer of Okitipupa Division to the Colony Welfare Officer," November 20, 1946.

60. NAI, COMCOL 1, 2844, "Bernard to the Colony Welfare Officer," June 24, 1944.

61. NAI, COMCOL 1, 2844, Donald Faulkner, "Child Prostitution in Lagos," July 1943.

62. This unscientific myth transcends Africa—even in Britain during the late nineteenth and early twentieth centuries, some men believed that sexual intercourse with virgins could cure VD. And in the era of HIV/AIDS, widespread stories of underage prostitution and rape of virgins centered on this myth.

63. "Mrs Abayomi Attributes Prostitution to Laziness, Undue Gaiety, and Unemployment," *West African Pilot*, August 10, 1944.

64. NAI, COMCOL 1, 2844, "Child Prostitution in Lagos, by Alison Izzett."

65. NAI, MH (Fed) 1/1, 5021 (Confidential), "West African Governors' Conference," March 1942.

66. "Leg. Co. Adjourns Sin Die: Bill against 'Boma Boys' Passed: Dr. Carr Advocates Adjustment of Educational Policy," *Nigerian Daily Times*, January 16, 1941.

67. NAI, COMCOL 1, 2844, "Child Prostitution in Lagos by Donald Faulkner."

68. Ibid.

69. NAI, COMCOL 1, 2844, "Child Welfare-Prostitution and Child Marriage," May 1943.

70. NAI, COMCOL 1, 2786 vol. 2, "Report upon Methods of Training Young Offenders in Nigeria, 1951 by W. W. Llewellin," April 1951.

71. NAI, COMCOL 1, 2844, "Donald Faulkner to the President of Lagos Town Council," September 1942.

72. NAI, COMCOL 1, 2844, Donald Faulkner, "Social Welfare and Juvenile Delinquency in Lagos," n.d.

73. See, among others, Bailey, *Delinquency and Citizenship*; Rose, *Governing the Soul*.

CHAPTER 4. THE SEXUAL SCOURGE
OF IMPERIAL ORDER

1. NAI, N 1088, "Senior Sanitary Officer to the General Staff Officer, WAFF," April 1918.

2. See, among others, Skelley, *The Victorian Army at Home*; Trustram, *Women of the Regiment*.

3. Judith Walkowitz's book *Prostitution and Victorian Society* remains a classic on the subject. See also Bartley, *Prostitution*. For the application of the CDAs to some British colonies in Asia, see Levine, *Prostitution, Race, and Politics*.

4. Jochelson, *The Colour of Disease*; Jeater, *Marriage, Perversion, and Power*.

5. Gilman, *Difference and Pathology*, 76–127.

6. Baronov, *The African Transformation of Western Medicine*, 77–123.

7. See, among others, Ukpabi, *The Origin of the Nigerian Army*; Ubah, *Colonial Army and Society in Northern Nigeria*.

8. NAI, COMCOL 1, N 1088/1918, "Venereal Disease in the Nigerian Regiment—the Commandant to the Director of Medical and Sanitary Service, 1918."

9. Ibid.

10. NAI, COMCOL 1, N 1088/1918, "Venereal Disease in the Military, 1918."

11. Ibid.

12. NAI, COMCOL 1, N 1088/1918, "Senior Sanitary Officer to the General Staff Officer," April 20, 1918.

13. "Africans and Commissions in the Army," *Daily Service*, June 19, 1943; "Discrimination in the Army," *Daily Service*, January 13, 1945.

14. Olusanya, "The Role of Ex-Servicemen in Nigerian Politics," 225.

15. Ibid.

16. NAI, CSO/N 628/1919, "Infliction of Corporal Punishment on Native Soldiers: Stoppage of, 1920"; NAI, MH 54/S.1/vol. 3, "British Federation against Venereal Disease, Report," 1930–31.

17. The following four were commissioned the following year: Lieutenant J. T. Aguiyi-Ironsi, who would later become Nigeria's first military head of state and one of the victims of the July 1966 coup, and Lieutenants Bassey, Sey, and Ademulegun. The number increased to twelve by 1954. See Ubah, *Colonial Army and Society in Northern Nigeria*, 234–35.

18. NAI, COMCOL 1, N 1088/1918, "Venereal Disease: Minutes of Meeting on," February 17, 1919.

19. Ibid.

20. Ibid.

21. Ibid.

22. Ibid.

23. NAI, CSO 17/12845, "Discipline and Order in the Force, 1921/1922 Report."

24. NAI, CSO N 1088/1918, "Flint to the CSG," February 21, 1919.

25. Ibid.

26. NAI, CSO N 1088/1918, "CSG to the DMSS," February 26, 1919.

27. Ibid.

28. NAI, CSO N 1088/1918, "Flint to the CSG," April 22, 1918.

29. NAI, MH (Fed) 54/S.1, "VD in the Troops," 1919.

30. NAI, MH (Fed) 54/S.1, "Flogging of Troops," June 1920.

31. NAI, CSO N 1088, "Venereal Disease," 1923.

32. Ibid.

33. NAI, MH (Fed) N 1098, "Irrigation and Early Treatment Center: Establishment of," June 1925.

34. NAI, MH 54 vol. 1, "Troops' Diseases and Welfare: Control of," January 25, 1939.

35. Ibid.

36. Ibid.

37. Crowder, *West Africa under Colonial Rule*, 490.

38. NAI, COMCOL 1, 2383 vol. 4, "Military Accommodation in Lagos," 1940–46.

39. NAI, MH 544, "Venereal Disease among African Troops—West African Governors' Conference to the Honourable Chief Secretary, Lagos," March 18, 1942.

40. Ibid.

41. NAI, MH 54 vol. 2, "Venereal Diseases," July 13, 1941.

42. Ibid.

43. NAI, MH (Fed) 1/1, 6304A, "Venereal Diseases: Control of," 1941.

44. NAI, MH 54 vol. 2, "Venereal Diseases," July 13, 1941.

45. Ibid.; emphasis added.

46. NAI, MH 54/Si/vol. 1, "Solicitor General to the Acting Governor," September 1941.

47. NAI, CSO 26, 03338 vol. 2, "Secretary of State for the Colonies to the Government Administering Nigeria," October 28, 1921.

48. NAI, COMCOL 1, 3/21, "Alleged Military Irregularities," March 25, 1940; NAI, CSO 26/41837, "Disturbances by Soldiers." See the following news and editorials from the *West African Pilot*: "Young Soldier Is Sentenced to Two Months for Assault," April 1, 1941; "Soldier Charged with Manslaughter Is Released on Bail," June 3, 1943.

49. NAI, CSO 18/1920, "Colonial Office to Sir Hugh Clifford," November 18, 1919.

50. Ibid.

51. For more on politics between African and European doctors, see Patton, *Physicians, Colonial Racism, and Diaspora in West Africa*.

52. NAI, CSO 18/1920, "Memo by the CS," January 28, 1920.

53. Schram, *A History of the Nigerian Health Services*.

54. NAI, CSO 18/1920, "Memorandum by E. E. Maples," December 10, 1919.

55. "Mrs Abayomi Attributes Prostitution to Laziness, Undue Gaiety, and Unemployment," *West African Pilot*, August 10, 1944; NAI, COMCOL 1, 2844, "Child Prostitution in Lagos by Alison Izzett, the Lady Welfare Officer."

56. See also Laoye, "The Concept of Magun among the Yoruba." Public opinion is still very much divided on the power of *magun* in contemporary Nigeria. This debate is the main theme of a popular Yoruba movie titled *Magun* (Thunderbolt).

57. NAI, CSO 18/1920, "W. Best to the S.S.P.," January 14, 1920.

58. NAI, CSO 18/1920, "Memorandum by E. E. Maples."

59. NAI, CSO 18/1920, "W. Best to the S.S.P.," January 14, 1920.

60. NAI, CSO 18/1920, "Memorandum by E. E. Maples."

61. Ibid.

62. NAI, CSO 18/1920, "W. Best to the S.S.P.," January 14, 1920.

63. Levine, *Prostitution, Race, and Politics*, 63–64.

64. NAI, COMCOL 1, 894 vol. 1, "Unemployment in Lagos, 1921–1931."

65. NAI, COMCOL 1, 237 vol. 3, "Plague in Lagos," 1932–35. For public health problems and infrastructural development in Lagos, see the following, among others, Bigon, *A History of Urban Planning*, 131–85; Mabogunje, *Urbanization in Nigeria*, 257–64; Schram, *A History of the Nigerian Health Services*, 193–215.

66. NAI, COMCOL 1, 1348, "Outbreak of Epidemics in the Colony," 1932–47; Bigon, *History of Urban Planning*, 131.

67. NAI, COMCOL 1, 981 vol. 1, "Anti-Mosquito Campaign Lagos," 1930–51.

68. The *Lagos Weekly Record* took sanitary problems and mortality in Lagos as a core component of its anticolonial sentiments. Information on mortality rate and public health problems can be found in the following editorials and news items: "Cholera Epidemic," October 1, 1892; "The Mortality of the Town," August 11, 1894.

69. McCulloch, "The Management of Venereal Disease in a Settler Society."

70. Musisi, "The Politics of Perception or Perception of Politics?" 95–115; Tuck, "Venereal Disease, Sexuality and Society in Uganda," 191–204; McCurdy, "Urban Threats," 212–33; Jackson, "'When in the White Man's Town,'" 191–213.

71. NAI, COMCOL 1, 994, "Lord Passfield to Governor of Nigeria," March 8, 1930.

72. NAI, COMCOL 1, 994, "A. Burns to Lord Passfield," July 31, 1930.

73. Ibid.

74. Ibid.

75. "Advert," *Lagos Daily News*, March 3, 1932. This advertisement appeared on nearly a daily basis in early 1932.

76. NAI, COMCOL 1, 994, "Memorandum on VD."

77. Patton, *Physicians, Colonial Racism, and Diaspora in West Africa*, 14–23.

78. Ibid. For a history of medicine in Nigeria, see, among others, Schram, *A History of the Nigerian Health Services*.

79. Vaughan, *Curing Their Ills*, 129–54.

Chapter 5. Sexualized Laws, Criminalized Bodies

1. The colonialists' position included the following laws: Unlicensed Guide (Prohibition) Ordinance, in *Annual Volume of the Laws of Nigeria Containing All Legislation Enacted during the Year 1941* (Lagos: Government Printer, 1942), A143–A150; Venereal Diseases Ordinance, 1943, in *Annual Volume of the Laws of Nigeria Containing All Legislation Enacted during the Year 1943* (Lagos: Government Printer, 1944), A110–A116; Children and Young Persons Ordinance, in *Annual Volume of the Laws of Nigeria, Legislation Enacted during 1943* (Lagos: Government Printer, 1944), A424–A444; Criminal Code (Amendment) Ordinance, 1944, in *Annual Volume of Laws of Nigeria, Legislation Enacted during the Year 1944* (Lagos: Government Printer, 1945), A52–A57.

2. Mann and Roberts, eds., *Law in Colonial Africa*, 3.

3. I arrive at this conclusion through critical examination of the content and legalistic provisions in the full compilation of *Annual Volumes of the Laws of Nigeria.*

4. Wheare, *The Nigerian Legislative Council.*

5. *The Undesirable Advertisement Ordinance: Legislative Council Debates—Tenth Session, June 1932* (Lagos: Government Printer, 1932), 33–34; *Unlicensed Guides (Prohibition) Ordinance: Legislative Council Debates—Eighteenth Session, January 1941* (Lagos: Government Printer, 1943), 138; *Reading of an Ordinance to Amend the Unlicensed Guide Ordinance: Legislative Council Debates—Nineteenth Session, September 1941* (Lagos: Government Printer, 1943), 44–45; *The Venereal Diseases Ordinance, 1943: Legislative Council Debates—Twenty-first Session, March 1943* (Lagos: Government Printer, 1943), 65–66; *The Children and Young Persons Ordinance, 1943: Legislative Council Debates—Twenty-first Session, August 1943* (Lagos: Government Printer, 1943), 38–40; *The Criminal Code (Amendment) Ordinance, 1944: Legislative Council Debates—Twenty-second Session, March 1944* (Lagos: Government Printer, 1945), 52–53.

6. The strength of the Legislative Council of Nigeria varied from year to year but never exceeded 50 (28–29 British official members and 20–21 African unofficial members). See Wheare, *The Nigerian Legislative Council*, 42–87.

7. Margery Perham, "Editor's Introduction," in ibid., vii.

8. See the following news items and editorials from the *West African Pilot*: "Hotel Girls Suffering from V.D. Will Be Affected by New Bill," March 9, 1943; "A Check on Venereal Disease," March 9, 1943; "The Young Persons Ordinance," July 21, 1943; "Juvenile Courts Will Be Set Up to Try Young Delinquents," July 21, 1943; "The V.D. Ordinance, 1943," November 5, 1943; "Venereal Disease," March 21, 1945; "Free Clinic for Venereal Disease," March 22, 1945; "Venereal Disease," April 30, 1945; "Pity the Idle Loiterers," May 16, 1941; "Unlicensed Guides Bill," September 22, 1941; "Unlicensed Guides," January 30, 1942; "Unlicensed Guides," September 29, 1942; "Prostitution Given Legal Definition," March 8, 1944; "Women Will Not Be Guilty of Offence for Addressing 3 Men within 1 Hour," March 24, 1944; "Writer Welcomes Recent Law on Prostitution," March 10, 1944; "Prostitution Given a Legal Definition," March 8, 1944; "New Girls' Hostel Is Opened at Yaba Estate," February 3, 1945; "Welfare Department and Juvenile Delinquency," January 26, 1946; "Juvenile Court and Remand Home," February 11, 1946; "Help to Combat Juvenile Delinquency," April 30, 1946; "Children and Young People's Ordinance," July 6, 1946; "Women's Party Wants Public Informed before Operation of New Juvenile Law," July 15, 1946.

9. Coker, *Landmarks of the Nigerian Press*, 20.

10. Morris, "How Nigeria Got Its Criminal Code."

11. "Leg. Co. Adjourns Sin Die: Bill against 'Boma Boys' Passed: Dr. Carr Advocates Adjustment of Educational Policy," *Nigerian Daily Times,* January 16, 1941; Unlicensed Guide (Prohibition) Ordinance (1941), A148–A149; NAI, COMCOL 1, "Loitering," 1944–45.

12. "Leg. Co. Adjourns Sin Die: Bill against 'Boma Boys' Passed: Dr. Carr Advocates Adjustment of Educational Policy," *Nigerian Daily Times*, January 16, 1941.

13. "Short Shrift for 'Boma Boys,'" *Nigerian Daily Times*, January 16, 1941.

14. Unlicensed Guide (Prohibition) Ordinance (1941), A148–A149.

15. "Reading of an Ordinance to Amend the Unlicensed Guide Ordinance."

16. See from the *West African Pilot*: "European Officer Is Fined 5 Pounds for Traffic Offence," January 9, 1939; "European Is Fined 10 Pounds for Obstructing a Police Officer," May 3, 1939, 1, 8; "2 European Soldiers Are Fined for Assaulting Civilians and P.C. [police constable]," March 5, 1943; see from the *Daily Service*: "European Seaman Pleads Guilty to Possessing 3 Bottles of Illicit Gin," November 11, 1941; "European Sailor Gets £4 Fine for Assaulting Police Constable," November 27, 1941; "Seaman Is Fined £50 for Receiving 20 Shillings under False Pretenses," June 3, 1941; "European Army Man Gets Four Months for Willful Damage and Stoning Africans," February 14, 1947; "European Sailor Is Fined £10 for Theft," October 18, 1946; "European Is Charged over Sleeper Theft," September 7, 1946.

17. "Four Seamen Who Refused to Defend Themselves Are Fined," *West African Pilot*, November 24, 1941.

18. "European Sailor Assaults Police Constable and Pays £17.10s Fine," *West African Pilot*, February 27, 1943.

19. "RAF European Assaults Police Constable: He Pays £25 Fine," *West African Pilot*, February 9, 1943.

20. "European Is Fined £12 for Assaulting African Co-Worker," *West African Pilot*, July 25, 1938.

21. "Sailor Who Preferred Women to His Health Is Imprisoned," *West African Pilot*, August 30, 1944.

22. "Criminal Code (Amendment) Ordinance, 1944," A53.

23. Ibid., A54–A55.

24. Ibid.

25. "Women Will Not Be Guilty of Offence for Addressing 3 Men within 1 Hour," *West African Pilot*, March 24, 1944.

26. Ibid.

27. Ibid.

28. "40 Hotel Girls Convicted," *West African Pilot*, January 1, 1955.

29. "Man and Woman Gaoled for Prostitution," *Daily Service*, August 17, 1944.

30. "Man Is Arraigned in Court for Living on Prostitutes' Earnings: Women Are Involved," *West African Pilot*, September 3, 1943.

31. NAI, COMCOL 1, 2471, "Director of Prison to the Honourable Chief Secretary to the Government: Juvenile Delinquency in Lagos," July 21, 1941; NAI, COMCOL 1, 2471, "Juvenile Delinquency in Lagos," 1941.

32. NAI, Oyo Prof., 4113, "A Report to His Excellency the Governor of Nigeria: Crime and Its Treatment in the Colony and Protectorate, 1944."

33. Ibid.

34. "Children and Young Persons Ordinance," *West African Pilot*, July 6, 1946. For more on Britain's Children and Young Persons Act of 1933, see Arthur, *Young Offenders and the Law*, chapter 2.

35. NAI, Oshogbo Prof., "Treatment of Juvenile Offenders," April 17, 1931.

36. Criminal Code (Amendment) Ordinance, 1944, A53.

37. NAI, COMCOL 1, 2844, "Regulation to Prevent Children Trading in the Streets."

38. Ibid.

39. Children and Young Persons Ordinance, A425.

40. Ibid.

41. Ibid., A437.

42. "Young Girl of Ten Represents 'Mother' to 3 Little Kiddies," *West African Pilot*, June 22, 1943.

43. Children and Young Persons Ordinance, A436–A440.

44. Criminal Code (Amendment) Ordinance, 1944, A53.

45. The Criminal Code Act of Nigeria (Section 218) 1960 Amendment, 3209.

46. NAI, Oyo Prof., 4113, "A Report to His Excellency the Governor of Nigeria."

47. Criminal Code (Amendment) Ordinance, 1944, A56.

48. Children and Young Persons Ordinance, A432–A438.

49. NAI, COMCOL 1, 2786, "Probation Officer to the Manager of Elder Dempster Lines," August 2, 1946.

50. NAI, COMCOL 1, 2844, "Report Under Section 76 (B) of Criminal Procedure (Amendment) Ordinance No.11 of 1937," May 10, 1946.

51. Children and Young Persons Ordinance, A425.

52. NAI, COMCOL 1, 2844, "Colony Welfare Officer to the Public Relations Officer," June 25, 1946.

53. Ibid.

54. NAI, COMCOL 1, 2786 vol. 1, "District Officer of Urhobo Division to the Commissioner of the Colony," August 13, 1946; NAI, COMCOL 1, 2786 vol. 1, "Colony Welfare Officer to the District Officer of Urhobo Division," August 20, 1946.

55. NAI, Ijebu Prof., C.103, "Child Prostitution," 1944; NAI, Owo Div., 703, "Child Prostitution," 1943–46; NAI, Ondo Div., 686, "Child Prostitution," 1943–46; NAI, Oyo Prof., 3562, "Measures against Prostitution"; NAI, Kwale Dist., I 49, "(1) Social Welfare (2) Traffic in Women and Children and Obscene Publications (3) Child Betrothals." See also "Ijebu Igbo Town Council Discusses Child Prostitution," *Nigerian Daily Times*, September 16, 1943.

56. The only information that tended to be available about provincial girls included the names of their parents and family compound, along with dates of births, school information, and other important life dates.

57. NAI, Kwale Dist., I 49, "Moral Welfare Work with the Women and Girls of the Warri Province," n.d.

58. NAI, COMCOL 1, 2844, "District Officer of Kukuruku Division to the Colony Welfare Officer," October 6, 1943.

59. Ibid.

60. NAI, COMCOL 1, 2844, "Child Welfare: Prostitution and Child Marriage," 1943.

61. NAI, Kwale Dist., I, "Child Prostitution."

62. Byfield, "Women, Marriage, Divorce and the Emerging Colonial State in Abeokuta (Nigeria)."

63. NAI, COMCOL 1, 2471, "Juvenile Delinquency: Commissioner of the Colony to the Chief Secretary to the Government," July 23, 1941.

64. The 134 prisons included both government and native authority prisons. NAI, Oyo Prof., 4113, "A Report to His Excellency the Governor of Nigeria."

65. NAI, MH 54 vol. 1, "Undesirable Advertisement Ordinance, 1932."

66. Ibid.

67. Ibid.

68. See advertisements for drugs in a bilingual newspaper, *Akede Eko*, in the early 1930s.

69. NAI, MH 54 vol. 1, "Officer Administering the Government of Nigeria to the Secretary of State for the Colonies," November 14, 1932.

70. NAI, MH 54 vol. 1, "Extract from the Proceedings of the Medical Conference Held at Accra—December 1925."

71. NAI, MH 54 vol. 1, "Director of Medical and Sanitary Service to the Third Medical Conference—Agendum No. 10 Anti-Venereal Work," March 10, 1926.

72. Venereal Diseases Ordinance, 1943, A112.

73. Ibid., A113–A116.

74. From the *West African Pilot*: "Venereal Disease," March 21, 1945; "Venereal Disease," April 30, 1945.

75. NAI, COMCOL 1, 2608/S.5, "Port Welfare Committee—VD among Seamen," 1923.

76. NAI, COMCOL 1, 248, "Constitution of Owerri Union, Lagos Branch, 1940," 21.

77. Ibid.

78. NAI, COMCOL 1, 248/58, "Constitution of Efik Ladies Union, 1940."

79. NAI, COMCOL 1, 248/58, "Calabar Ladies Union, 1943."

80. NAI, COMCOL 1, 248/ S. 130, "Colony Welfare Officer to the Secretary of Calabar Improvement League," January 21, 1944.

81. NAI, COMCOL 1, 2796, "Colony Welfare Officer to the District Officer, Calabar," August 5, 1943.

82. NAI, COMCOL 1, 248/76, "Secretary of Urhobo Progress Union to the Welfare Officer," August 7, 1943.

83. NAI, COMCOL 1, 248/76, "Notice."

84. NAI, COMCOL 1, 248/76, "Colony Welfare Officer to the Honourable Secretary, Urhobo Progress Union," October 2, 1943.

85. NAI, COMCOL 1, 248/76, "Urhobo Progress Union to the Colony Welfare Officer," October 11, 1943.

86. NAI, COMCOL 1, 248/77, "Obubra Improvement Union—Minutes of Meeting," May 15, 1943.

87. NAI, COMCOL 1, 2844, "The Okpe Union to the Colony Welfare Officer," December 3, 1943.

88. Ibid.

89. NAI, COMCOL 1, 248/58, "Efik Ladies Union to the Commissioner of the Colony," May 10, 1940.

90. NAI, COMCOL 1, 248/S 130, "Colony Welfare Officer to the Secretary of Calabar Improvement League," January 27, 1944.

91. NAI, MH 54, "Handwriting Memo among Colonial Officers, 2 November 1932."

CHAPTER 6. MEN, MASCULINITIES, AND THE POLITICS OF SEXUAL CONTROL

1. "Moral Degeneracy in Lagos," *Lagos Daily News*, May 10, 1929; from the *Comet*: Sogidi, "Save the Future Mothers," September 21, 1935; [a Muslim], "Save the Future

Mothers," October 5, 1935; Kabiboy, "Girl Hawkers' Morals," October 19, 1935; C.O.O., "Girl Hawkers' Morals," October 26, 1935; from the *West African Pilot*: "Red Light District," December 17, 1937; "Woman Sentenced to Prison: She Runs Akunakuna House," December 24, 1937.

2. "Pity the Idle Loiterers," *West African Pilot*, May 16, 1941.

3. "Unlicensed Guides," *West African Pilot*, September 29, 1942.

4. "Unlicensed Guides Bill," *West African Pilot*, September 22, 1941.

5. NAI, COMCOL 1, 2786, "Wait and Get Immediate Picture Takers to the Commissioner of the Colony," July 19, 1946.

6. Ibid.

7. Ibid.

8. "The 'Boma Boy' Menace," *Nigerian Daily Times*, August 12, 1943.

9. See the following stories from the *Daily Service*: Civis! "The Law of Loitering," December 27, 1944; Ade Tee, "The Police as Prosecutors," February 4, 1943; "Loitering," November 13, 1944; F.R.A. Williams, "Is Everybody Equal before the Law?" November 14, 1944; "Police Criticised on Loitering," November 15, 1944; "Women's Party Meets Police Officer," December 18, 1944; "Oppression or Protection?" November 14, 1944; "The Police Has Got It," April 8, 1947; "C[ommissioner] of Police Asks Rudeness of Police to Be Reported," March 24, 1943; "Are All Idlers and Loiterers?" August 5, 1944; "Cases of Loitering at the Police Court," November 16, 1944; from the *West African Pilot*: "Loiterers and the Local Police," November 29, 1944; "The Essence of the Law," July 28, 1943. See also the following stories from the *Comet*: "Smoke Out the Prostitutes," June 24, 1944; "Re: Irresponsible Women," July 31, 1944.

10. "The Law of Loitering," *Daily Service*, December 27, 1947.

11. "Are All Idlers and Loiterers?" *Daily Service*, August 5, 1944.

12. NAI, COMCOL 1, 2043, "Extract of the Minutes of the Meeting of the Oba and Chiefs with the COC at Iga Idunganran on Monday, November 6, 1945."

13. F.R.A. Williams, "Is Everybody Equal before the Law?" *Daily Service*, November 14, 1944.

14. Ibid.; "The Essence of the Law," *West African Pilot*, July 28, 1943.

15. "Police Criticised on Loitering," *Daily Service*, November 15, 1944.

16. Ibid.; NAI, COMCOL 1, 2043, "Meeting of the Oba and Chiefs with the COC."

17. "The Essence of the Law," *West African Pilot*, July 28, 1943.

18. See from the *West African Pilot*: "False Informants," September 8, 1943; "Manufactured Prostitutes," September 17, 1943.

19. "'Loitering' Police Impersonator Gaoled," *Daily Service,* November 21, 1944.

20. NAI, COMCOL 1, 2498, "Office of the Assistant Superintendent Colony 'A' Division to the Superintendent the Nigeria Police," August 1, 1941. Various parts of Nigeria established vigilante groups and "irregular" police forces in response to escalating crime. See Tamuno, *The Police in Modern Nigeria*, 108.

21. "Ashogbon's Police Force," *Daily Service*, August 6, 1946.

22. NAI, COMCOL 1, 2498, "J. G. C. Allen to Superintendent of Police," August 7, 1946.

23. "Ashogbon Police: Statement of Commissioner of the Colony," *Nigerian Daily Times*, August 19, 1946; "End of Case against 'Ashogbon Police': First and Third Accused Found Guilty and Sentenced," *Nigerian Daily Times*, September 24, 1946; "Allen

Says Only Nigeria Police Is Genuine," *Daily Comet*, August 19, 1946; "Ashogbon Police Force Is Virtually Disbanded: Colony Commissioner Says They Have No Authority to Arrest," *Daily Service*, August 19, 1946; "Public Now Warned about Mock 'Police,'" *West African Pilot*, August 19, 1946.

24. NAI, COMCOL 1, 2498, "Notes on the Ashogbon," August 7, 1946.

25. See from the *Daily Service*: "Three Women Who Profiteered Are Fined 10/, 20/, and 30/ Respectively," December 21, 1942; "Woman Who Profiteered in Gari Is Sentenced to 2 Months," November 21, 1942.

26. "Our Bribery Series: An Aftermath," *West African Pilot*, February 28, 1944.

27. See from the *Daily Service*: "Police Constable Is Found Guilty of Stealing," February 18, 1941; "Constable with 14 Years of Clean Record Is Fined £10 or 1 Month," March 28, 1941; "Special Constable Egbe Who Received 2/- [2 s.] Bribe Is Sentenced to 3 Months," April 2, 1943; "2 Police Constables Face Charge of Official Corruption," June 2, 1943; "Police Constable Who Smuggled Case of Cigarettes Is Sentenced 4 months," March 1, 1943; "C. [Commissioner] of Police Asked Rudeness of Police to Be Reported," March 24, 1943; "Police Constable's Appeal Is Dismissed," October 13, 1944; "P.C. [Police Constable] Who Swallows £5 Notes Is Gaoled," October 14, 1944; "2 Policemen Face Trial for Bribery," November 22, 1944.

28. "P.C. Who Swallows £5 Notes Is Gaoled," *Daily Service*, October 14, 1944.

29. See from the *West African Pilot*: "Policing the Police," June 28, 1943; "Two Police Constables Face Terms for Corruption," June 28, 1943; "Sergeant Uzor Is Discharged on Alleged Bribery Charge," April 6, 1943; see also from the *Nigerian Daily Times*: "Police Constable Charged with Recurring Bribe," February 13, 1941; "Sergeant and Police on Corruption Charge," March 4, 1943; "Regular and Special Constable on Corruption Charge," January 15, 1943; from the *Daily Service*: "2 Police Constables Face Charge of Official Corruption," June 2, 1943; "Bail Is Now Granted C.I.D. Cpl. and 6 Others Involved in Fraud Case," March 19, 1943; "Special Constable Egbe Who Received 2/- [2 s.] Bribe Is Sentenced to 3 Months," April 2, 1943.

30. "Policing the Police," *West African Pilot,* June 28, 1943.

31. "Leg. Co. Adjourns Sin Die: Bill against 'Boma Boys' Passed: Dr. Carr Advocates Adjustment of Educational Policy," *Nigerian Daily Times*, January 16, 1941.

32. "Bribery, Prostitution and Theft in Nigeria," *West African Pilot*, June 28, 1944.

33. Ekwensi, *People of the City*, 40; "Social Morality," *Daily Service*, May 1, 1945.

34. T. Babs F. Opayemi, "Social Evil and the 'Big Guns,'" *Daily Service*, September 29, 1944; "Hotel Girls Complain They Are Being Pestered by Some Big Gun Patrons," *Eastern Nigerian Guardian*, June 9, 1944; "Those Demoralising Night Clubs," *West African Pilot*, January 28, 1948.

35. "Law and Prostitution," *Daily Service*, March 14, 1945.

36. "The Law of Loitering," *Daily Service*, December 27, 1947.

37. "Police Raids for Night Clubs," *West African Pilot*, April 3, 1948.

38. "Those Demoralising Night Clubs," *West African Pilot*, January 28, 1948.

39. See from the *West African Pilot*: "Northern Nigerian Chiefs Will Tax Prostitutes," June 7, 1942; "Taxation of Prostitutes," June 22, 1942; "These Common Prostitutes," June 30, 1943; "Fighting the Social Scourge," August 11, 1943; "Government Asked to Reform Rather Than Repatriate Common Prostitutes," November 4, 1943; "The Logic of Repatriating Prostitutes," March 30, 1944; "The Repatriation Craze," May 1, 1944; "An

Approach to Prostitution," July 4, 1944; "Prostitution: A Curable Problem," August 4, 1944; "Mrs Abayomi Attributes Prostitution to Laziness, Undue Gaiety, and Unemployment," August 10, 1944; "The Problem of Prostitution," August 11, 1944.

40. "Oged Macaulay Suggests Licensing of Prostitution," *Daily Comet*, November 30, 1944.

41. See from the *West African Pilot*: "Logic of Repatriating Prostitutes," March 30, 1944; "Repatriation Craze," May 1, 1944; "Government Asked to Reform Rather Than Repatriate Common Prostitutes," November 4, 1943. See also "Re: Irresponsible Women," *Comet*, May 31, 1944; "Re: Irresponsible Women," *Comet*, August 23, 1944; "Repatriation of Prostitutes," *Southern Nigeria Defender*, May 22, 1944; "J. E. Osoroh Feels That Repatriating Prostitutes Is Not the Right Thing," *Southern Nigeria Defender*, May 4, 1944.

42. "Repatriation of Prostitutes," *Nigerian Spokesman*, June 21, 1943.

43. Mr. I.O.W. Oriaku, "Evil Practices Create 'Surplus Women,'" *West African Pilot*, September 20, 1945; "Cause of Surplus Women," *West African Pilot*, February 7, 1946.

44. Dennis C. Osadebay, "The Problem of the 'Surplus Woman,'" *West African Pilot*, September 15, 1945.

45. Ibid.

46. Ibid.

47. "The 'Surplus' Woman," *West African Pilot*, October 20, 1945.

48. Mbonu Ojike, review of *Surplus Women*, *West African Pilot*, September 11, 1948.

49. "Prostitution Must Be Tackled from Its Roots," *Southern Nigeria Defender*, March 7, 1944.

50. "Mr. S. L. Akintola Lectures Large Audience on Men, Women, and Divorce: He Says Relations between Man and Woman Determines National Solidarity of a Country," *Daily Service*, November 11, 1944. Akintola was the managing editor of the *Daily Service* between 1943 and 1946. See his biography: Osuntokun, *Chief S. Ladoke Akintola*, 13.

51. "Mr. S. L. Akintola Lectures Large Audience on Men, Women, and Divorce: He Says Relations between Man and Woman Determines National Solidarity of a Country," *Daily Service*, November 11, 1944.

52. Olu Adeyemi, "Prostitution in Nigeria," *Daily Service*, July 10, 1944.

53. "Prostitution," *Daily Service*, December 1, 1944.

54. For more on transnational prostitution, see Aderinto, "Journey to Work." See also NAI, CSO, 36005 vol. 1, "Prince Eikineh, President of Nigerian Youth Movement, Gold Coast Branch to the President Nigerian Youth Movement, Lagos," June 28, 1939.

55. See from the *Nigerian Spokesman*: "This Question of Prostitution," May 31, 1944; "Considering Prostitution," June 15, 1944; "About the Prostitutes," June 17, 1944; "Encouraging Prostitution (1)," June 20, 1944; "Encouraging Prostitution (2)," June 21, 1944; "Child Marriage Problem," September 21, 1944; "Child Marriage," June 29, 1945; "Child Marriage," June 30, 1945; "2 Undesirables Fail to Quit Township Jailed," May 22, 1952; "Prostitutes and the Nation," January 28, 1953; "Problems of Prostitution," January 30, 1953; "Prostitution and Our Nation," January 31, 1953; "Prostitution and Our Nation," February 13, 1953; "Clearing Prostitutes from the Township," June 10, 1953; "Problems of Prostitution," June 13, 1953; "Hotels or Brothels," November 6, 1953.

56. Coker, *Landmarks of the Nigerian Press*, 20.

57. See from the *West African Pilot*: "Sexual Hygiene," April 19, 1941; "Sexual Laxity," May 17, 1943; "Writer Pleads for a Proper Handling of Subject of Sex," May 22, 1943; "Rape," October 11, 1944; "'Brains' to Discuss Sex Education: Elites Will Feature," July 11, 1946.

58. "Sexology," *Eastern Nigeria Guardian*, March 12, 1940.

59. "Girl Hawker," *Nigerian Daily Times*, December 29, 1947.

60. NAI, COMCOL 1, 2844 vol. 2, "Handwriting Memo by the Commissioner of the Colony," n.d.

61. See from the *West African Pilot*: "Food Hawking in Lagos," April 1, 1942; "Our Girl Hawkers," September 18, 1942; "Our Girl Hawkers," September 26, 1942; "Street Trading," August 21, 1943; "Magistrate Warns All Parents of Hawkers," March 27, 1945; "Hawkers and Public Health," April 5, 1949; "Moral Dangers in the Community," *Nigerian Daily Times*, November 24, 1944; "Street Hawking by Young Girls," *Daily Service*, June 20, 1946.

62. NAI, Oyo Prof. 1, 3562, "Extract from the Minutes of Ibadan Native Authority Inner Council Meeting," March 20, 1944.

63. Ibid.

64. NAI, Oyo Prof. 1, "District Officer to the Senior Resident Oyo Province," March 29, 1944.

65. NAI, Ijebu Prof., J.P.C. 103, "Child Prostitution," March 1944.

66. NAK, Kano Prof. 1, 186/MSWCA, "Child Prostitution and Child Marriage: Secretary Northern Province to Resident Kano Province," June 22, 1946.

67. NAK, Kano Prof. 1, 186/MSWCA, "The Criminal Code (Amendment) Bill: Secretary of Northern Province to the Resident of Kano Province," July 10, 1946.

68. I searched through Ajisafe's premier book, which documents the laws and customs of the Yoruba, but did not see a phrase like "child marriage"; see Ajisafe, *The Laws and Customs of the Yoruba People*.

69. "The Colony Welfare Office to the District Officer, Owerri," February 26, 1944.

70. Jean-Baptiste, "'These Laws Should Be Made by Us'"; Allman, "Rounding up Spinsters"; and Simelane, "The State, Chiefs and the Control of Female Migration in Colonial Swaziland," among others, examine the colonial state and the campaign by African male elders to regulate women's reproduction, social status, wealth, and sexuality through English and customary laws.

71. NAE, AIDIST 2.1.373, "Egbisim Improvement Union to the District Officer, Obubra Division," April 3, 1948.

72. See the entries on prostitution in the Simple List of documents of Calabar, Ogoja, and Owerri Provinces deposited in the National Archives, Enugu.

73. NAI, MH 54 vol. 1, "The Nigerian Apothecary Society to the Director of Medical and Sanitary Service," May 30, 1932.

74. Ibid.

75. Ibid.

76. Ibid.

77. Ibid.

78. Arifalo and Ogen, "C. C. Adeniyi-Jones"; Sklar, *Nigerian Political Parties*, 43–48.

79. NAI, MH 54 vol. 1, May 22, 1934.

80. NAI, MH 54 vol. 1, October 11, 1934.

81. Ibid.

82. NAI, MH 54 vol. 1, October 10, 1934.

83. NAI, MH 54 vol. 1, October 11, 1934.

84. NAI, COMCOL 1, 857 vol. 1, "Local Native Doctors."

85. Adeloye, *African Pioneers of Modern Medicine*, 131–58.

86. Ibid., 288–90.

87. For more on Yoruba healers associations in colonial southwestern Nigeria, see Washington-Weik, "The Resiliency of Yoruba Traditional Healing."

88. NAI, 857 vol. 1, "Petition to the DMSS," May 17, 1933.

89. Patton, *Physicians, Colonial Racism, and Diaspora*, 89.

90. NAI, "UAO Petition," August 15, 1934.

91. Ibid.

92. "Venereal Disease as a Social Problem," *Daily Service*, March 27, 1945.

93. Ibid.

94. Ibid.

95. Lagos newspapers covered this story. See the following news stories, editorials, and reports from the *Daily Service* in April 1945: "Reader Says, 'Magun is Poison,'" April 3; "Is 'Magun' Mere Superstition?" April 3; "Dr. Abayomi Offers 50 Pounds to One Who Can Successfully Demonstrate 'Magun,'" April 4.

96. NAI, MH (Fed) 1/1, 6304, "Lieutenant R. W. Theakstone to the DMSS," June 30, 1945.

97. "The V.D. Ordinance, 1943," *West African Pilot*, November 5, 1943.

98. "The VD Menace," *Daily Service*, May 19, 1945.

99. "Clean-Up Lagos," *Nigerian Daily Times*, July 29, 1943.

100. Dr. K. Abayomi, "Venereal Disease as a Social Problem," *Daily Service*, March 27, 1945.

101. *Daily Service*, August 10, 1944.

102. Lasekan, *Nigeria in Cartoons*, 35–36.

103. "Hotel Girls Suffering from VD Will Be Affected by New Bill," *West African Pilot*, March 9, 1943.

104. Oral interview, Madam Tawa Abasi, June 11, 2008.

105. NAI, MH (Fed) 1/1, "Annual Report of the DMSS," 1943–44.

106. Ibid.

107. Oral interview, Mr. Timothy Adisa, June 12, 2008.

108. NAI, MH (Fed) 1/1, 6304, "Monthly Report by Dr. Taylor," June 1946.

109. NAI, MH (Fed) 1/1, 6304, "Dr. Taylor to the DMSS," June 2, 1946.

110. NAI, MH (Fed) 1/1, 6304, "Taylor to the DMSS," July 1946.

CHAPTER 7. LAGOS ELITE WOMEN AND THE STRUGGLE FOR LEGITIMACY

1. NAI, COMCOL 1, 2786, "Obasa to the Chief Secretary to the Government," October 13, 1941.

2. See from the *Daily Service*: "Imprisonment of Women for Profiteering," November 6, 1942; "Penalties Inflicted for Profiteering," December 1, 1942; "Woman Who Profiteered

NOTES TO CHAPTER 7

in Pirate Cigarettes is Fined £5.10," December 29, 1942; "Three Women Who Profiteered Are Fined 10/, 20/, and 30/ Respectively," December 21, 1942; "Woman Who Profiteered in Gari Is Sentenced to 2 Months," November 21, 1942; "Lady Caught at Pullen Rice Stall," January 22, 1944.

3. For more on this, see, Aderinto, "Isaac Fadoyebo at The Battle of Nyron."

4. Johnson, "Female Leadership during the Colonial Period"; Johnson, "Grassroots Organizing"; NAI, COMCOL 1, 4030, "Prosecution for Profiteering Offenses," 1941–44.

5. Mba, *Nigerian Women Mobilized*, 225–33.

6. See NAI, COMCOL 1, 248/121, "Proceedings of a Meeting of Women Held in the Schoolroom of St. Paul's Church Breadfruit Street on Monday September 13, 1943."

7. For various opinions, see, among others, Olu Adeyemi, "Prostitution in Nigeria," *Daily Service*, July 10, 1944; "Re: Irresponsible Women," *Comet*, May 31, 1944; "Re: Irresponsible Women," *Comet*, August 23, 1944; "Nigeria Wants Night Club Reforms," *West African Pilot*, February 4, 1948; "Prostitution: The Editorial," *Daily Service*, December 1, 1944.

8. Oyinkan Abayomi, "Modern Womanhood," *Daily Service*, December 10, 1935.

9. "Miss Kofo Moore Defends Her Sex," *West African Pilot*, November 24, 25, 26, 29, 30, and December 1, 1937.

10. See the manifestos of the Nigerian Women's Party: "Women's Party Hold Grand Meeting," *Daily Service*, August 24, 1944.

11. "The Women's Welfare Council Club," *Daily Service*, October 27, 1944.

12. Levine, *Prostitution, Race, and Politics*; Walkowitz, *Prostitution and Victorian Society*.

13. T. Babs F. Opayemi, "Social Evil and the Big Guns," *Daily Service*, September 29, 1944.

14. "Mrs Abayomi Attributes Prostitution to Laziness, Undue Gaiety, and Unemployment," *West African Pilot*, August 10, 1944; "Women's Welfare League's Protest Meeting against Moral Danger Proves a Big Success," *Daily Service*, August 10, 1944.

15. See from the *Daily Service*: "The Lagos Women's Party Demands Equal Pay for Men and Women," November 15, 1944; "Representatives of Women's Party Interview LTC Secretary," December 18, 1944; "Women's Party Meets Police Officer," December 18, 1944.

16. See from the *West African Pilot*: "Women's Party Will Have Provincial Offices," December 18, 1944; "Women's Party and the Provinces," December 19, 1944; "Nigerian Women's Party Meets Oshogbo Women in Town Hall," March 30, 1946; "Making the Women's Party Truly Nigerian," June 4, 1946.

17. "The Lagos Women's Party Demands Equal Pay for Men and Women," *Daily Service*, November 15, 1944.

18. Ibid.; "Representatives of Women's Party Interview LTC Secretary," *Daily Service*, December 18, 1944; "Women's Party Meets Police Officer," *Daily Service*, December 18, 1944.

19. "Representatives of Women's Party Interview LTC Secretary," *Daily Service*, December 18, 1944.

20. Ibid.

21. "Women's Party Meets Police Officer," *Daily Service*, December 18, 1944.

22. Ibid.

23. "Policewomen for Nigeria," *Daily Service*, August 10, 1944; "Moral Danger in the Community," *Nigerian Daily Times*, November 24, 1944; Mr. P. I. Omo Ananigie, "Wanted: Women Police Constables," *West African Pilot*, January 23, 1948; Mr. N. O. Olaniyan, "Women Police Constables: Not Wanted," *West African Pilot*, January 30, 1946.

24. NAI, COMCOL 1, 43399, "Commissioner of Police to the Chief Secretary to the Government," December 1, 1944.

25. Ibid.

26. Ibid.

27. NAI, COMCOL 1, 43399, "Nigerian Women's Party to the Governor of Nigeria," January 5, 1945.

28. "Leg. Co. Adjourns Sin Die: Bill against 'Boma Boys' Passed: Dr. Carr Advocates Adjustment of Educational Policy," *Nigerian Daily Times*, January 16, 1941.

29. "Magistrate Warns Policewoman," *West African Pilot*, September 22, 1956.

30. See NAI, CSO 26/03338 vols. 1 and 2, "International Convention for the Suppression of White Slave Traffic"; NAI, CSO 26/27837, "Annual Report on Traffic in Women and Children and Obscene Language/Publication."

31. For more on Nigeria and the UN conventions on trafficking in women and children, see Aderinto, "'The Problem of Nigeria Is Slavery.'"

32. NAI, COMCOL 1, 248/107, "H. Millicent Douglas, Honorary Secretary of the Women's Welfare Council to the Governor of Nigeria," October 11, 1942.

33. Ibid.

34. Ibid.

35. NAI, COMCOL 1, 248/107, "H. Millicent Douglas, Secretary of the WWC to the Commissioner of the Colony," January 19, 1943.

36. NAI, COMCOL 1, 248/107, "Bankole-Wright to the Comcol," January 13, 1943.

37. Ibid.

38. NAI, COMCOL 1, 248/107, "The Women's Welfare Council to the Commissioner of the Colony," January 19, 1943; NAI, COMCOL 1, 2705, "European Ladies: Employment of," 1942–46; NAI, COMCOL 1, 3007, "Employment of African Ladies," 1942–46.

39. NAI, COMCOL 1, 248/107, "The Women's Welfare Council to the Commissioner," 1942.

40. Ibid.

41. Ibid.

42. NAI, COMCOL 1, 248/107, "Commissioner of the Colony to the Honorable Secretary Women's Welfare Council," February 2, 1943.

43. Ibid.

44. NAI, COMCOL 1, 248/107, "Women's Welfare Council to the Commissioner of the Colony," October 10, 1944; NAI, COMCOL 1, 284/107, "Faulkner to Commissioner of the Colony," October 14, 1944.

45. NAI, COMCOL 1, 284/107, "Faulkner to Commissioner of the Colony," October 14, 1944.

46. NAI, COMCOL 1, 248/107, "Social Welfare Officer to the Women's Welfare Council," October 17, 1944.

47. NAI, COMCOL 1, 3080, "Commissioner of the Colony to Mrs. O. M. Abayomi," February 1945.

48. NAI, COMCOL 1, 3080, "Commissioner of the Colony to Mrs. T. A. Manuwa," July 28, 1945.

49. The only concession the women won was the appointment of Dorcas Doherty as the matron of the Girls' Hostel in 1943; however, she was fired after serving less than two years in this position. In her sack letter following Faulkner's ten-point query, the commissioner of the colony accused her of being "too old," "inactive," "not observant enough," and unable to adjust to modern methods of girls' rehabilitation. NAI, COM-COL 1, 2782, "Commissioner of the Colony to Mrs. Dorcas," November 8, 1944.

50. NAI, COMCOL 1, 2786, "Petition to the Government Re: Nos. 4 and 21 on pages 730 and 739 of Gazette Nos. 36 vol. 33 of June 27, 1946," October 3, 1946.

51. Ibid.

52. Ibid.

53. Ibid.

54. NAI, COMCOL 1, 2786, "Memo Addressed to the CWO," October 15, 1946.

55. Ibid.

56. NAI, COMCOL 1, 2786, "Re-Petition," October 28, 1946.

57. NAI, COMCOL 1, 248/107, "H. Millicent Douglas to the Governor of Nigeria."

58. NAI, COMCOL 1, 2471, "Director of Prisons to the Honourable Chief Secretary to the Government: Juvenile Delinquency in Lagos," July 21, 1941.

59. Ibid.

60. Ibid.

61. Ibid.

62. Ibid.

63. "A Female Member of the LTC," *West African Pilot*, June 26, 1944; "Women's Party Honours President," *Daily Service*, July 2, 1944.

EPILOGUE: PROSTITUTION AND TRAFFICKING IN THE AGE OF HIV/AIDS

1. "National Agency for Prohibition of Traffic in Persons and Other Related Matters," *Federal Government of Nigeria Official Gazette* 90, no. 89 (2003): 57–73. See also "National Agency for the Prohibition of Traffic in Persons and Other Related Matters," http://www.naptip.gov.ng/legal.html.

2. "32 Prostitutes Sentenced to Jail in Lagos," August 9, 2012, http://www.informationg .com/2012/08/32workers-sentenced-to-jail-in-lagos.html.

3. "Abused! Kids as Sex Objects," *Nigerian Tribune*, September 16, 1994; Debo Abdulai and Biodun Oyeleye, "Where Teenagers Hawk Sex," *Nigerian Tribune*, July 21, 1997; Emeka Madunagu, "Child Trafficking: Nigeria, Others to Get $94m US Aid," *Punch*, July 17, 2001; Austeen Osumah, "SWAAN Decries High Teenage Prostitution," *Post Express*, December 15, 2001; Tunde Thompson, "Tales of Child-Trafficking," *Guardian*, July 28, 2002; "The Children Also Become Sex Slaves," *Nigerian Tribune*, April 4, 2009.

4. National Population Commission, Nigeria, http://www.population.gov.ng/.

5. Tessy Eneji and Emman Chukwu-Anukwu, "Student Prostitution Booms," *Nigerian Tribune*, April 24, 1993; "The Campus Connection," *Vintage Tribune*, March 23, 1995; Kenneth Okpomo, "Student Prostitutes," *Post Express*, October 1, 1997; Sam Nwaoko, "The Emerging Face of Prostitution in Universities," *Nigerian Tribune*, July 2, 2000; "Educated Prostitutes," *Nigerian Tribune*, January 21, 2001; Tolu Rowaiye, "The Big Babes of UNILAG: A Peep into Their Weird Lifestyle," *Punch*, June 2, 2001.

6. Emmanuel Chidiogo, "Ten Undergraduates on Trial for Prostitution," *Daily Times*, September 20, 2011, http://dailytimes.com.ng/article/ten-undergraduates-trial-prostitution.

7. Prof. Elizabeth Balogun, "80% of Prostitutes in Ogun State Are Undergraduates," Ladun Liadi's Blog, November 8, 2012, http://ladunliadi.blogspot.com/2012/11/80-of-prostitutes-in-ogun-state-are.html.

8. Kunli Falayi, "Immigration Investigates Chinese Sex Workers," *Punch*, August 27, 2012, http://www.punchng.com/metro/immigration-investigates-chinese-sex-workers/.

9. Agbola, *The Architecture of Fear*.

10. Soyinka, *The Beatification of Area Boy*.

11. Ekpenyong, "Social Inequalities, Collusion, and Armed Robbery in Nigerian Cities."

12. "100,000 Police Officers Carry Handbags for Wives of Moneybags and Politicians," *Nigeria Police Watch*, October 19, 2011, http://www.nigeriapolicewatch.com/2011/10/100000-police-officers-carry-handbags-for-wives-of-moneybags-and-politicians/.

13. *Nwa Baby (Ashawo Remix)*.

14. *The Prostitutes*.

15. Ibid.

16. Aderinto, "'The Problem of Nigeria Is Slavery.'"

17. "60 Nigerian Prostitutes, Others Detained," *Nigerian Tribune*, October 19, 1994; Chika Nwoko, "Alleged Prostitution: 13 Nigerian Ladies Deported from Spain," *Third Eye*, August 25, 1996.

18. Chris Anana, "10,000 Nigerians Prostitute in Italy, Says Envoy," *Post Express*, July 6, 2000.

19. Dijk, "'Voodoo' on the Doorstep"; Achebe, "The Road to Italy"; Olaniyi, "No Way Out"; Cole, "Reducing the Damage."

20. WOTCLEF, "About Us," http://wotclef.org.ng/index.php?option=com_content&view=article&id=79&Itemid=27.

21. "National Agency for the Prohibition of Traffic in Persons and Other Related Matters," 65.

22. http://www.naptip.gov.ng/legal.html.

23. "Criminal Code Act of Nigeria," 3209.

24. "National Agency for Prohibition of Traffic in Persons and Other Related Matters," 64.

25. "Nigerian Girls in the Street of Athens," http://www.youtube.com/watch?v=GCMhrhB0VMQ.

26. Emeka Madunagu, "Child Trafficking: Nigeria, Others to Get $94m US Aid," *Punch*, July 17, 2001.

27. U.S. Department of State, "Trafficking in Persons Report," http://www.state.gov/j/tip/rls/tiprpt/.

28. Ray Okosun, "Italy Donates $2.5m to Nigeria," *Post Express*, January 30, 2000.

29. Akanbi and Jekayinfa, "From Sincerity to Deception."

30. "Idia Renaissance," http://www.idia-renaissance.org/projects.html.

31. "Role of First Ladies in Nigeria"; "First Lady: Between Legality and Thirst for Power"; "Nigerian First Ladies and the Love of Money," *Nigeria Politico*, http://nigeriapolitico.com/greedyamazons.html.

32. Nasidi and Harry, "The Epidemiology of HIV/AIDS in Nigeria," 18.

33. Akinwale, "From Denial to Acceptance."

34. Ibid., 392–96.

35. Quoted in Geshekter, "A Critical Reappraisal of African AIDS Research and Western Sexual Stereotypes."

36. Caldwell, Caldwell, and Quiggin, "The Social Context of AIDS in Sub-Saharan Africa."

37. Onwuliri and Jolayemi, "Reaching Vulnerable and High-Risk Groups in Nigeria," 314.

38. Folarin and Oyefara, "Investigation of the Variables Influencing the Use of Condoms"; Orubuloye, "Sexual Networking, Use of Condoms and Perception of STDs and HIV/AIDS Transmission."

39. Orubuloye, "Sexual Networking, Use of Condoms and Perception of STDs and HIV/AIDS Transmission," 217.

40. Onwuliri and Jolayemi, "Reaching Vulnerable and High-Risk Groups in Nigeria," 314.

41. Adebajo et al., *Knowledge, Attitudes, and Sexual Behaviour among the Nigerian Military*, 1.

42. Ekong, "HIV/AIDS and the Military," 560.

43. Ibid., 1.

44. Okeke, Onwasigwe, and Ibegbu, "The Effect of Age on Knowledge of HIV/AIDS"; Hussain and Akande, "Sexual Behaviour and Condom Use among Nigerian Soldiers in Ilorin, Kwara State, Nigeria"; Nwokoji and Ajuwon, "Knowledge of AIDS and HIV-Related Sexual Behavior among Nigerian Naval Personnel."

45. "Microbes and Morals—an Unlikely Love Affair," by Professor Bakare, see Akinwale Aboluwade, "Don Advocates Registration of Sex Workers," *Punch*, April 8, 2012.

BIBLIOGRAPHY

Archives

National Archives, Ibadan

ABEPROF 1–9 Abeokuta Provincial Office, Second Accession
Chief Secretary's Office Records
COMCOL 1–15 Commissioner of the Colony Office, Lagos
COMCOL 1 Commissioner of the Colony Office, Lagos, Criminal Record Books, 1910–55
IBADAN PROF 1–4 Ibadan Provincial Office
IJE PROF 1–10 Ijebu Provincial Office
ONDO DIV 1–5 Ondo Divisional Office
OYO PROF 1 Oyo Provincial Office
Simple List of Ministry of Justice Paper
Simple List of Papers from the Federal Ministry of Health, Lagos, REF M. FED
Simple List of Papers from Federal Ministry of Health, Red No MHFED 1/1 1/21 2nd Accession
Simple List of the West African Frontier Force
Special List of Records on the Origins and Development of the Nigerian Medical and Sanitary Services, 1861–1960

National Archives, Enugu

ABADIST 1–22 Aba District Office
CALPROF 1–54 Calabar Provincial Office
OBUBDIST 1–15 Obubra District Office
OGONDIST 1–3 Ogoni District Office
MINJUST 1–30 Ministry of Justice

National Archives, Kaduna

List of Papers Removed from Kano Native Authority
List of Papers Removed from the Provincial Office, Kano Prof. Second Collection

Premiers' Office, Kaduna, 2nd Collection
Simple List of Documents Removed from Ministry of Social Welfare and Community
    Development, Kaduna
SNP 6 Secretariat, Northern Provinces. Confidential Annual Numerical Minute Papers
SNP 12 Civil Secretary's Office
SNP 19 Confidential Annual Subject Files

Newspapers

Comet, 1935–44
Daily Service, 1939–50
Daily Trust, 1990–2013
Eastern Nigeria Guardian, 1941–55
Lagos Daily News, 1925–32
Lagos Standard, 1890–1910
Lagos Weekly Records, 1890–1910
Nigerian Spokesman, 1945–55
Nigerian Tribune, 1990–2013
Post Express, 1990–2010
Punch, 1990–2013
Southern Nigeria Defender, 1943–50
West African Pilot, 1937–60

Published Primary Documents

*Annual Report of the Department of Social Welfare, Western Region for the Year
    1957–1958*. Lagos: Government Printer, 1959.
*The Children and Young Persons Ordinance: Annual Volume of the Laws of Nigeria,
    Legislation Enacted during 1943*. Lagos: Government Printer, 1944.
*The Children and Young Persons Ordinance, 1943: Legislative Council Debates—
    Twenty-First Session, August 1943*. Lagos: Government Printer, 1943.
*The Criminal Code (Amendment) Ordinance 1944: Annual Volume of Laws of Ni-
    geria, Legislation Enacted during the Year 1944*. Lagos: Government Printer, 1945.
*The Criminal Code (Amendment) Ordinance, 1944: Legislative Council Debates—
    Twenty-Second Session, March 1944*. Lagos: Government Printer, 1945.
*The National Agency for Prohibition of Traffic in Persons and Other Related Matters.
    Federal Government of Nigeria Official Gazette* 90, no. 89 (2003): 57–73.
*Reading of an Ordinance to Amend the Unlicensed Guide Ordinance: Legislative Coun-
    cil Debates—Nineteenth Session, September 1941*. Lagos: Government Printer, 1943.
Report of the Cost of Living Committee, Lagos, Nigeria 1942. London: Crown Agents
    for the Colonies on Behalf of the Government of Nigeria, 1942.
Selected Judgments of the West African Court of Appeal, 1946/1949. Lagos: Crown
    Agent, 1956.
*The Undesirable Advertisement Ordinance: Legislative Council Debates—Tenth Ses-
    sion, June 1932*. Lagos: Government Printer, 1932.

The Unlicensed Guide (Prohibition) Ordinance: Annual Volume of the Laws of Nigeria Containing All Legislation Enacted during the Year 1941. Lagos: Government Printer, 1942.

Unlicensed Guides (Prohibition) Ordinance: Legislative Council Debates—Eighteenth Session, January 1941. Lagos: Government Printer, 1943.

The Venereal Diseases Ordinance, 1943: Annual Volume of the Laws of Nigeria Containing All Legislation Enacted during the Year 1943. Lagos: Government Printer, 1944.

The Venereal Diseases Ordinance, 1943: Legislative Council Debates—Twenty-first Session, March 1943. Lagos: Government Printer, 1943.

Videos

Magun (Thunderbolt). 2000. Nigeria: Opomulero Mainframe Productions, VCD.

Nwa Baby (Ashawo Remix). Music by Flavor Obaino. 2010. Nigeria: Music and 2nite Entertainment, DVD.

The Prostitutes. Directed by Fred Amata. 2001. Nigeria: Kingsley Ogoro Productions, VCD.

Books, Articles, and Dissertations

Achebe, Nwando. "'And She Became a Man': King Ahebi Ugbabe in the History of Enugu-Ezike, Northern Igboland, 1880–1948." In *Men and Masculinities in Modern African History,* edited by Stephan F. Miescher and Lisa A. Lindsay, 52–68. Portsmouth, N.H.: Heinemann, 2003.

———. "The Road to Italy: Nigerian Sex Workers at Home and Abroad." *Journal of Women's History* 15, no. 4 (2004): 178–85.

———. "The Day I 'Met' Ahebi Ugbabe, Female King of Enugu-Ezike, Nigeria." *Journal of Women's History* 21, no. 4 (2009): 134–37.

———. "When Deities Marry: Indigenous 'Slave' Systems Expanding and Metamorphosing in the Igbo Hinterland." In *African Systems of Slavery,* edited by Stephanie Beswick and Jay Spaulding, 105–33. Trenton, N.J.: Africa World Press, 2010.

———. *The Female King of Colonial Nigeria: Ahebi Ugbabe.* Bloomington: Indiana University Press, 2011.

Adebajo, Sylvia B., et al. *Knowledge, Attitudes, and Sexual Behaviour among the Nigerian Military Concerning HIV/AIDS and STDs.* Nigeria: Policy Project, 2002.

Adefuye, Ade, Babatunde Agiri, and Jide Osuntokun, eds. *History of the Peoples of Lagos State.* Lagos: Lantern Books, 1987.

Adeloye, Adelola. *African Pioneers of Modern Medicine: Nigerian Doctors of the Nineteenth Century.* Ibadan: University Press, 1985.

Aderibigbe, A. B., ed. *Lagos: The Development of an African City.* Lagos: Longman, 1975.

Aderinto, Saheed. "Dangerous Aphrodisiac, Restless Sexuality: Venereal Disease, Biomedicine, and Protectionism in Colonial Lagos, Nigeria." *Journal of Colonialism and Colonial History* 13, no. 3 (2012). *Project MUSE,* March 11, 2013, http://o-muse.jhu.edu.wncln.wncln.org/.

———. "Of Gender, Race, and Class: The Politics of Prostitution in Lagos, Nigeria, 1923–1958." *Frontiers: A Journal of Women's Studies* 33, no. 3 (2012): 71–92.

———. "Of Historical Visibility and Epistemology: History and Historians of Nigerian Women." In *The Third Wave of Historical Scholarship on Nigeria: Essays in Honor of Ayodeji Olukoju,* edited by Saheed Aderinto and Paul Osifodunrin, 128–51. Newcastle upon Tyne: Cambridge Scholars Publishing, 2012.

———. "'The Problem of Nigeria is Slavery, Not White Slave Traffic': Globalization and the Politicization of Prostitution in Southern Nigeria, 1921–1955." *Canadian Journal of African Studies* 46, no. 2 (2012): 1–22.

———. "Representing 'Tradition,' Confusing 'Modernity': Love and Mental Illness in Yoruba (Nigerian) Video Films." In *Mental Illness in Popular Media: Essays on the Representation of Disorders,* edited by Lawrence Rubin, 256–69. Jefferson, N.C.: MacFarland, 2012.

———. "Researching Colonial Childhoods: Images and Representations of Children in the Nigerian Newspaper Press, 1925–1950." *History in Africa: A Journal of Method* 39 (2012): 241–66.

———. "Isaac Fadoyebo at The Battle of Nyron: African Voices from the First and Second World Wars, c. 1914–1945." In *African Voices of the Global Past: 1500 to the Present,* edited by Trevor Getz, 107–38. Boulder, Colo.: Westview Press, 2014.

———. "Journey to Work: Transnational Prostitution in Colonial British West Africa." *Journal of the History of Sexuality* 24, no.1 (forthcoming 2015).

———. "'O! Sir I Do Not Know Either to Kill Myself or to Stay': Childhood Emotion, Poverty, and Literary Culture in Nigeria, 1900–1960." *Journal of the History of Childhood and Youth* 8 (forthcoming 2015).

Adesina, Segun. "The Development of Western Education." In *Lagos: The Development of an African City,* edited by A. B. Aderibigbe, 125–40. Lagos: Longman, 1975.

Adewoye, Omoniyi. *The Legal Profession in Nigeria, 1865–1962.* Lagos: Longman, 1977.

Adeyi, Olusoji, Phyllis J. Kanki, Oluwole Odutola, and John A. Idoko, eds. *AIDS in Nigeria: A Nation on the Threshold.* Cambridge, Mass.: Harvard Center for Population and Development Studies, 2006.

Agbola, Tunde. *The Architecture of Fear: Urban Design and Construction Response to Urban Violence in Lagos, Nigeria.* Ibadan: IFRA, 1997.

Aghatise, E. "Trafficking for Prostitution in Italy: Possible Effects of Government Proposals for Legalization of Brothels." *Violence against Women* 10, no. 10 (2005): 1126–55.

Agiri, Babatunde. "Kola in Western Nigeria, 1850–1950: A History of the Cultivation of Cola Nitida in Egba-Owode, Ijẹbu-Rẹmọ, Iwo and Ọta Areas." Ph.D. diss., University of Wisconsin, 1972.

Ahire, Philip Terdoo. *Imperial Policing: The Emergence and Role of the Police in Colonial Nigeria, 1860–1960.* Milton Keynes: Open University Press, 1991.

Ajayi, J. F. Ade. *Christian Missions in Nigeria, 1841–1891: The Making of a New Elite.* Evanston, Ill.: Northwestern University Press, 1965.

Ajisafe, A. K. *The Laws and Customs of the Yoruba People.* London: Trubner and Company, 2003 [1927].

Akanbi, Grace, and Alice Jekayinfa. "From Sincerity to Deception: First Ladies 'Pet Project' of Empowering Rural Women and Children through Education in Nigeria." *European Journal of Humanities and Social Sciences* 5, no. 1 (2011): 180–93.

Akintoye, S. A. *Revolution and Power Politics in Yorubaland, 1840–1893: Ibadan Expansion and the Rise of Ekitiparapo*. London: Longman, 1971.

Akinwale, Akeem Ayofe. "From Denial to Acceptance: HIV/AIDS in Nigeria since the 1980s." In *The Third Wave of Historical Scholarship on Nigeria: Essays in Honor of Ayodeji Olukoju*, edited by Saheed Aderinto and Paul Osifodunrin, 392–405. Newcastle upon Tyne: Cambridge Scholars Publishing, 2012.

Akyeampong, Emmanuel. "Sexuality and Prostitution among the Akan of the Gold Coast c. 1650–1950." *Past & Present*, no. 156 (1997): 144–73.

Alaja-Browne, Afolabi. "The Origin and Development of Juju Music." *The Black Perspective in Music* 17, nos. 1–2 (1989): 55–72.

Alao, Akin. *Statesmanship on the Bench: The Judicial Career of Sir Adetokunbo Ademola (CJN), 1939–1972*. Trenton, N.J.: Africa World Press, 2007.

Albert, Isaac Olawale. "The Emics and Etics: Insider/Outsider Binary in Nigeria's Migration History." In *The Third Wave of Historical Scholarship on Nigeria: Essays in Honor of Ayodeji Olukoju*, edited by Saheed Aderinto and Paul Osifodunrin, 118–27. Newcastle upon Tyne, UK: Cambridge Scholars Publishing, 2012.

Allman, Jean. "Of 'Sprinters,' 'Concubines' and 'Wicked Women': Reflections on Gender and Social Change in Colonial Asante." *Gender and History* 3, no. 2 (1991): 176–89.

———. "Adultery and the State in Asante: Reflections on Gender, Class, and Power from 1800 to 1950." In *The Cloth of Many Colored Silks: Papers on History and Society, Ghanaian and Islamic, in Honor of Ivor Wilks*, edited by John Hunwick and Nancy Lawler, 27–65. Evanston, Ill.: Northwestern University Press, 1996.

———. "Rounding up Spinsters: Gender Chaos and Unmarried Women in Colonial Asante." *Journal of African History* 37, no. 2 (1996): 195–214.

Amadiume, Ifi. *Male Daughters, Female Husbands: Gender and Sex in an African Society*. London: Zed Books, 1987.

Amoko, Apollo. "The 'Missionary Position' and the Postcolonial Polity, or, Sexual Difference in the Field of Kenyan Colonial Knowledge." *Callalo* 24, no. 1 (2001): 310–24.

Anderson, David M. *Bodies and Souls: Female Circumcision and Christian Missions in Colonial Kenya, 1900–1939*. Cape Town: University of Cape Town, Centre for African Studies, 1994.

Aries, Philippe. *Centuries of Childhood: A Social History of Family Life*. Translated from the French by Robert Baldick. New York: Vintage Books, 1962.

Arifalo, S. O., and Olukoya Ogen. "C. C. Adeniyi-Jones, 1876–1957: A Forgotten National Hero." *AMU: Akungba Journal of the Humanities* 1 (2006): 1–19.

Arnfred, Signe, ed. *Re-Thinking Sexualities in Africa*. Uppsala: Nordiska Afrikainstitutet, 2004.

Arthur, Raymond. *Young Offenders and the Law: How the Law Responds to Youth Offending*. London: Routledge, 2010.

Awe, Bolanle. "The Iyalode in the Traditional Yoruba Political System." In *Sexual Stratification: A Cross Cultural View*, edited by Alice Schlegel, 144–60. New York: Columbia University Press, 1977.

———. "Writing Women into History: The Nigerian Experience." In *Writing Women's History: International Perspectives*, edited by Karen Offen, Ruth Roach Pierson, and Jane Rendall, 211–20. Bloomington: Indiana University Press, 1991.

———, ed. *Nigerian Women in Historical Perspective*. Lagos: Sankore Publishers Bookcraft, 1992.

Awolowo, Obafemi. *Awo: The Autobiography of Chief Obafemi Awolowo*. Cambridge: Cambridge University Press, 1960.

Ayandele, E. A. *The Missionary Impact on Modern Nigeria, 1842–1914: A Political and Social Analysis*. London: Longman, 1966.

Bailey, Victor. *Delinquency and Citizenship: Reclaiming the Young Offender, 1914–1948*. Oxford: Clarendon, 1987.

Baker, Pauline H. *Urbanization and Political Change: The Politics of Lagos, 1917–1967*. Berkeley: University of California Press, 1974.

Ballhatchet, Kenneth. *Race, Sex, and Class under the Raj: Imperial Attitudes and Policies and Their Critics, 1793–1905*. London: Weidenfeld and Nicolson, 1980.

Barber, Karin, ed., trans., and with an introduction. *Print Culture and the First Yoruba Novel: I. B. Thomas's 'Life Story of Me, Segilola' and Other Texts*. Leiden: Brill, 2012.

Barkan, Joel D., Michael L. McNulty, and M.A.O. Ayeni. "Hometown' Voluntary Associations, Local Development, and the Emergence of Civil Society in Western Nigeria." *Journal of Modern African Studies* 29, no. 3 (1991): 457–80.

Barkow, Jerome H. "The Institution of Courtesanship in the Northern States of Nigeria." *Geneva Afrique* 10, no. 1 (1971): 59–73.

Barnes, Sandra T. *Patrons and Power: Creating a Political Community in Metropolitan Lagos*. Manchester: Manchester University Press, 1986.

Barnes, Teresa A. "The Fight for Control of Women's Mobility in Colonial Zimbabwe, 1900–1939." *Signs* 17, no. 3 (1992): 586–608.

———. *"We Women Worked So Hard": Gender, Urbanization, and Social Reproduction in Colonial Harare, Zimbabwe, 1930–1956*. Portsmouth, N.H.: Heinemann, 1999.

Baronov, David. *The African Transformation of Western Medicine and the Dynamics of Global Cultural Exchange*. Philadelphia: Temple University Press, 2008.

Barrera, Giulia. "Colonial Affairs: Italian Men, Eritrean Women, and the Construction of Racial Hierarchies in Colonial Eritrea (1885–1941)." Ph.D. diss., Northwestern University, 2002.

Barret-Ducrocq, Francoise. *Love in the Time of Victoria: Sexuality and Desire among Working-Class Men and Women in Nineteenth-Century London*. New York: Penguin Books, 1989.

Barrett, John. "The Rank and File of the Colonial Army in Nigeria, 1914–1918." *Journal of Modern African Studies* 15, no. 1 (1977): 105–15.

Barrymore, Francis. "The Contagious Diseases Acts Reconsidered." *Social History of Medicine* 3 (1990): 197–215.

Bartley, Paula. *Prostitution: Prevention and Reform in England, 1860–1914*. London: Routledge, 2000.

Bell, Shannon. *Reading, Writing, and Rewriting the Prostitute Body*. Bloomington: Indiana University Press, 1994.

Berger, Mark T. "Imperialism and Sexual Exploitation: A Response to Ronald Hyam's 'Empire and Sexual Opportunity.'" *Journal of Imperial and Commonwealth History* 17, no. 1 (1988): 83–89.

Bigon, Liora. *A History of Urban Planning in Two West African Colonial Capitals: Residential Segregation in British Lagos and French Dakar (1850–1930)*. Lewiston, N.Y.: Edwin Mellen Press, 2009.

Bonner, P. L. *Desirable or Undesirable Sotho Women? Liquor, Prostitution and the Migration of Sotho Women to the Rand, 1920–1945*. Johannesburg: University of Witwatersrand, African Studies Institute, 1988.

Bryder, Linda. "Sex, Race and Colonialism: An Historiographical Review." *The International History Review* 20, no. 4 (1998): 806–22.

Buckley, Roger Norman. *Slaves in Red Coats: The British West India Regiments, 1795–1815*. New Haven, Conn.: Yale University Press, 1979.

Bujra, Janet M. "Sexual Politics in Atu." *Cahiers d'études africaines* 65 (1977): 13–39.

Burke, Timothy. *Lifebuoy Men, Lux Women: Commodification, Consumption, and Cleanliness in Modern Zimbabwe*. Durham, N.C.: Duke University Press, 1996.

Byfield, Judith. "Pawns and Politics: The Pawnship Debate in Western Nigeria." In *Pawnship in Africa: Debt Bondage in Historical Perspective*, edited by Toyin Falola and Paul E. Lovejoy, 187–216. Boulder, Colo.: Westview Press, 1994.

———. "Women, Marriage, Divorce and the Emerging Colonial State in Abeokuta (Nigeria), 1892–1904." *Canadian Journal of African Studies* 30, no. 1 (1996): 32–51.

———. *The Bluest Hands: A Social and Economic History of Women Dyers in Abeokuta (Nigeria), 1890–1940*. Portsmouth, N.H.: Heinemann, 2002.

———. "Taxation, Women, and the Colonial State: Egba Women's Protest in Abeokuta (Nigeria), 1918–1948." *Meridians: A Journal on Feminism, Race, and Transnationalism* 3, no. 1 (2003): 250–77.

———. "Feeding the Troops: Abeokuta (Nigeria) and World War II." *African Economic History* 35 (2007): 77–87.

Byfield, Judith A., LaRay Denzer, and Anthea Morrison, eds. *Gendering the African Diaspora: Women, Culture, and Historical Change in the Caribbean and Nigerian Hinterland*. Bloomington: Indiana University Press, 2010.

Caldwell, John C., Pat Caldwell, and Pat Quiggin. "The Social Context of AIDS in Sub-Saharan Africa." *Population and Development Review* 15, no. 2 (1989): 185–234.

Callaway, Barbara. *Muslim Hausa Women in Nigeria: Tradition and Change*. Syracuse, N.Y.: Syracuse University Press, 1987.

Callaway, Helen. *Gender, Culture, and Empire: European Women in Colonial Nigeria*. Urbana: University of Illinois Press, 1987.

Caplan, Patricia. *The Cultural Construction of Sexuality*. London: Tavistock, 1987.

Chuku, Gloria. "From Petty Traders to International Merchants: A Historical Account of the Role of Three Igbo Women of Nigeria in Trade and Commerce, 1886 to 1970." *African Economic History* 27 (1999): 1–22.

———. *Igbo Women and Economic Transformation in Southeastern Nigeria, 1900–1960*. New York: Routledge, 2005.

———. "Igbo Women and Political Participation in Nigeria, 1800s-2005." *International Journal of African Historical Studies* 42, no. 1 (2009): 81–103.

———. "Igbo Women and the Production of Historical Knowledge: An Examination of Unwritten and Written Sources." In *Emergent Themes and Methods in African*

Studies: Essays in Honor of Adiele E. Afigbo, edited by Toyin Falola and Adam Paddock, 255–78. Trenton, N.J.: Africa World Press, 2009.

———. "'Crack Kernels, Crack Hitler': Export Production Drive and Igbo Women during the Second World War." In *Gendering the African Diaspora: Women, Culture, and Historical Change in the Caribbean and Nigerian Hinterland,* edited by Judith Byfield, LaRay Denzer, and Anthea Morrison, 219–44. Bloomington: Indiana University Press, 2010.

Clarke, Peter B. *West Africans at War, 1914–1918–1938–1945: Colonial Propaganda and Its Cultural Aftermath.* London: Ethnographica, 1986.

Clayton, Anthony, and David Killingray. *Khaki and Blue: Military and Police in British Colonial Africa.* Athens: Ohio University Center for International Studies, 1989.

Cohen, Abner. *Custom and Politics in Urban Africa: A Study of Hausa Migrants in Yoruba Towns.* London: Routledge and Kegan Paul, 1969.

Coker, Folarin. *A Lady: A Biography of Lady Oyinkan Abayomi.* Ibadan: Evans Brothers Nigeria Publishers Limited, 1987.

Coker, Increase H. E. *Landmarks of the Nigerian Press: An Outline of the Origins and Development of the Newspaper Press in Nigeria, 1859 to 1965.* Lagos: Daily Times Press, 1968.

Cole, Catherine M., Takyiwaa Manuh, and Stephan Miescher, eds. *Africa after Gender?* Bloomington: Indiana University Press, 2007.

Cole, Jeffrey. "Reducing the Damage: Dilemma of Anti-Trafficking Efforts among Nigerian Prostitutes in Palermo." *Anthropologica* 48, no. 2 (2006): 217–28.

Cole, Jennifer, and Lynn M. Thomas, eds. *Love in Africa.* Chicago: University of Chicago Press, 2009.

Cole, Patrick. *Modern and Traditional Elites in the Politics of Lagos.* Cambridge: Cambridge University Press, 1975.

Coleman, J. S. *Nigeria: Background to Nationalism.* Berkeley: University of California Press, 1958.

Cooper, Frederick. "Conflict and Connection: Rethinking Colonial African History." *American Historical Review* 99, no. 5 (1994): 1516–45.

Cooter, Roger, ed. *In the Name of the Child: Health and Welfare, 1800–1940.* London: Routledge, 1992.

Cornwell, Gareth. "George Webb Hardy's the *Black Peril* and the Social Meaning of 'Black Peril' in Early Twentieth-Century South Africa." *Journal of Southern African Studies* 22, no. 3 (1996): 441–53.

Crowder, Michael. *West Africa under Colonial Rule.* London: Hutchinson, 1968.

Cunningham, Hugh. *Children and Childhood in Western Society since 1500.* London: Longman, 1995.

Dalla, Rochelle L., et al., eds., *Global Perspectives on Prostitution and Sex Trafficking: Africa, Asia, Middle East, and Oceania.* Lanham, Md.: Lexington Books, 2011.

Denzer, LaRay. "Women in Government Service in Colonial Nigeria, 1863–1945." *Working Papers in African Studies, 136,* African Studies Center, Boston University, 1989.

———. "Domestic Science Training in Yorubaland, Nigeria." *In African Encounters with Domesticity,* edited by Karen Tranberg Hansen, 116–39. New Brunswick, N.J.: Rutgers University Press, 1992.

———. "Yoruba Women: A Historiographical Study." *International Journal of African Historical Studies* 27, no. 1 (1994): 1–39.

———. *The Iyalode in Ibadan Politics and Society, c. 1850–1997*. Ibadan: HRC, 1998.

———. *Folayegbe M. Akintunde-Ighodalo: A Public Life*. Ibadan: Sam Bookman Publishers, 2002.

———. "Fela, Women, Wives." In *Fela: From West Africa to West Broadway*, edited by Trevor Schoonmaker, 111–43. New York: Palgrave Macmillan, 2003.

———. "Intersections: Nigerian Episodes in the Careers of Three West Indian Women." In *Gendering the African Diaspora: Women, Culture, and Historical Change in the Caribbean and Nigerian Hinterland*, edited by Judith Byfield, LaRay Denzer, and Anthea Morrison, 245–84. Bloomington: Indiana University Press, 2010.

Dirasse, Laketch. *The Commoditization of the Female Sexuality: Prostitution and Socio-Economic Relations in Addis Ababa, Ethiopia*. New York: AMS Press, 1991.

Donaldson, Laura E. *Decolonizing Feminisms: Race, Gender & Empire Building*. Chapel Hill: University of North Carolina Press, 1992.

Eales, Kathy. *Rehabilitating the Body Politic: Black Women, Sexuality, and the Social Order in Johannesburg*. Johannesburg: University of Witwatersrand, African Studies Institute, 1990.

Echeruo, Michael J. C. *Victorian Lagos: Aspects of Nineteenth Century Lagos Life*. London: Macmillan, 1977.

Ejikeme, Anene. "Catholic Women in Colonial Nigeria." In *The Human Tradition in Modern Britain*, edited by Caroline Litzenberger and Eileen Groth Lyon, 221–34. Wilmington, Del.: Scholarly Resources Books, 2006.

Ekong, Ernest. "HIV/AIDS and the Military." In *AIDS in Nigeria: A Nation on the Threshold*, edited by Olusoji Adeyi, Phyllis J. Kanki, Oluwole Odutola, and John A. Idoko, 559–65. Cambridge, Mass.: Harvard Center for Population and Development Studies, 2006.

Ekpenyong, Stephen. "Social Inequalities, Collusion, and Armed Robbery in Nigerian Cities." *British Journal of Criminology* 29, no. 1 (1989): 21–34.

Ekpootu, Mfon Umoren. "Contestation of Identity: Colonial Policing of Female Sexuality in the Cross River Region of Southern Nigeria." *Inkanyiso: Journal of Humanities and Social Sciences* 5, no. 1 (2013): 72–80.

Ekwensi, Cyprian. *People of the City*. London: Andre Dakers Limited, 1954.

Enemo, Eleazor Obiakonwa. "The Social Problems of Nigeria." *Africa: Journal of International African Institute* 18, no. 3 (1948): 190–98.

Epprecht, Marc. *"This Matter of Women Is Getting Bad": Gender, Development and Politics in Colonial Lesotho*. Pietermaritzburg: University of Natal Press, 2000.

———. *Hungochani: The History of a Dissident Sexuality in Southern Africa*. Montreal: McGill-Queen's University Press, 2004.

———. *Heterosexual Africa? The History of an Idea from the Age of Exploration to the Age of AIDS*. Athens: Ohio University Press, 2008.

Etherington, Norman. "Natal's Black Rape Scare of the 1870s." *Journal of Southern African Studies* 15, no. 1 (1988): 36–53.

Fadipe, N. A. *The Sociology of the Yoruba*. Edited with an introduction by F. O. Okediji and O. O. Okediji. Ibadan: University of Ibadan Press, 1970.

Fafunwa, A. Babatunde. *History of Education in Nigeria.* Ibadan: NPS Educational, 1974.

Fajana, Adewunmi. *Education in Nigeria, 1842–1939: An Historical Analysis.* London: Longman, 1978.

Fakoyede, Taiwo, ed. *F.R.A. Williams through the Cases.* Lagos: Longman, 2000.

Falola, Toyin, "Lebanese Traders in Southwestern Nigeria, 1900–1960." *African Affairs* 89, no. 357 (1990): 523–53.

Falola, Toyin, and Saheed Aderinto. *Nigeria, Nationalism, and Writing History.* Rochester, N.Y.: University of Rochester Press, 2010.

Fass, Paula S., ed. *The Routledge History of Childhood in the Western World.* New York: Routledge, 2013.

Fatayi-Williams, Atanda. *Faces, Cases and Places: Memoirs by Fatayi Williams Nigerian Jurist.* London: Butterworths, 1983.

Flint, J. E. *Sir George Goldie and the Making of Nigeria.* London: George & Allen, 1960.

Folarin, Bamidele, and John Lekan Oyefara. "Investigation of the Variables Influencing the Use of Condoms among Prostitutes in Lagos." *Nigerian Journal of Business and Social Sciences* 1 (2007): 44–55.

Foucault, Michel. *The History of Sexuality,* vol. I. Translated by Robert Hurley. New York: Vintage Books, 1978.

Fourchard, Laurent. "Urban Poverty, Urban Crime, and Crime Control: The Lagos and Ibadan Cases, 1929–1945." In *African Urban Spaces in Historical Perspective,* edited by Steven J. Salm and Toyin Falola, 287–316. Rochester, N.Y.: University of Rochester Press, 2005.

———. "Lagos and the Invention of Juvenile Delinquency in Nigeria, 1920–1960." *Journal of African History* 47, no. 1 (2006): 115–37.

———. "A New Name for an Old Practice: Vigilante in South Western Nigeria." *Africa: Journal of the International African Institute* 78, no. 1 (2008): 6–40.

Frederiksen, Bodil Folke. "Jomo Kenyatta, Marie Bonaparte, and Bronislaw Malinowski on Clitoridectomy and Female Sexuality." *History Workshop Journal* 65 (2008): 3–48.

Gaitskell, Deborah L. "Race, Gender and Imperialism: A Century of Black Girls' Education in South Africa." Johannesburg: University of Witwatersrand, African Studies Institute, 1988.

Gann, L. H., and P. Duignan, eds. *African Proconsuls, European Governors in Africa.* New York: Free Press, 1978.

George, Abosede. "Feminist Activism and Class Politics: The Example of the Lagos Girl Hawker Project." *Women's Studies Quarterly* 35, no. 3 & 4 (2007): 128–43.

———. "Within Salvation: Girl Hawkers and the Colonial State in Development Era Lagos." *Journal of Social History* 44, no. 3 (2011): 837–59.

Geshekter, Charles L. "A Critical Reappraisal of African AIDS Research and Western Sexual Stereotypes." Paper presented at the General Assembly Meeting Council for the Development of Social Science Research in Africa [CODESRIA], Dakar, December 14–18, 1998 [revised May 5, 1999].

Ghosh, Durba. *Sex and the Family in Colonial India: The Making of Empire.* Cambridge: Cambridge University Press, 2006.

Gilman, Sander. *Difference and Pathology: Stereotypes of Sexuality, Race, and Madness.* Ithaca, N.Y.: Cornell University Press, 1985.

Glaser, Clive. *Bo-Tsotsi: The Youth Gangs of Soweto, 1935–1976*. Portsmouth, N.H.: Heinemann, 2000.

———. "Managing the Sexuality of Urban Youth: Johannesburg, 1920s–1960s." *International Journal of African Historical Studies* 38, no. 2 (2005): 301–27.

Greiger, Susan. "Women and African Nationalism." *Journal of Women's History* 2, no. 1 (1990): 227–44.

Griffiths, Claire. *Colonial Subjects: Race and Gender in French West Africa*. Bradford: Emerald Group Publishing, 2006.

Haggis, Jane. "Gendering Colonialism or Colonising Gender? Recent Women's Studies Approaches to White Women and the History of British Colonialism." *Women's Studies International Forum* 13, nos. 1–2 (1990): 105–15.

Hansen, Karen Tranberg, ed. *African Encounters with Domesticity*. New Brunswick, N.J.: Rutgers University Press, 1992.

Harrison, Fraser. *The Dark Angel: Aspects of Victorian Sexuality*. London: Sheldon Press, 1977.

Harrison, Mark. *Public Health in British India: Anglo-Indian Preventive Medicine, 1859–1914*. Cambridge: Cambridge University Press, 1994.

Hasting, A.C.G. *Nigerian Days*. London: John Lane, 1925.

Hay, Margaret Jean. "Queens, Prostitutes, and Peasants: Historical Perspectives on African Women, 1971–1986." *Canadian Journal of African Studies* 22, no. 3 (1988): 431–47.

Heap, Simon. "Jaguda Boys: Pickpocketing in Ibadan, 1930–1960." *Urban History* 24 (1997): 324–43.

———. "'Their Days Are Spent in Gambling and Loafing, Pimping for Prostitutes, and Picking Pockets': Male Juvenile Delinquents in Lagos Island, 1920s–1960s." In *The Third Wave of Historical Scholarship on Nigeria: Essays in Honor of Ayodeji Olukoju*, edited by Saheed Aderinto and Paul Osifodunrin, 274–305. Newcastle upon Tyne: Cambridge Scholars Publishing, 2012.

Heaton, Matthew. *Black Skin, White Coats: Nigerian Psychiatrists, Decolonization, and the Globalization of Psychiatry*. Athens: Ohio University Press, 2013.

Hendrick, Harry. *Child Welfare: England, 1872–1969*. London: Routledge, 1994.

Heyningen, Elizabeth. "The Social Evil in the Cape Colony, 1868–1902: Prostitution and the Contagious Diseases Acts." *Journal of Southern African Studies* 10, no. 2 (1984): 170–91.

Heywood, Colin. *A History of Childhood: Children and Childhood in the West from Medieval to Modern Times*. Cambridge: Polity Press, 2001.

Hobsbawm, E. J. *Nations and Nationalism since 1780: Programme, Myth, Reality*. Cambridge: Cambridge University Press, 1990.

Hodgson, Dorothy L., and Sheryl A. McCurdy, eds. *"Wicked" Women and the Reconfiguration of Gender in Africa*. Portsmouth, N.H.: Heinemann, 2001.

House-Midamba, Bessie, and Felix K. Ekechi, eds. *African Market Women and Economic Power: The Role of Women in African Economic Development*. Westport, Conn.: Greenwood Press, 2005.

Hussain, N.A.A., and T. M. Akande. "Sexual Behaviour and Condom Use among Nigerian Soldiers in Ilorin, Kwara State, Nigeria." *African Journal of Clinical and Experimental Microbiology* 10, no. 2 (2009): 128–35.

Hutchinson, John, and Anthony D. Smith, eds. *Nationalism*. Oxford: Oxford University Press, 1994.

Hyam, Ronald. "Concubinage and Colonial Service: The Crewe Circular (1909)." *Journal of Imperial and Commonwealth History* 14, no. 3 (1986): 170–86.

———. *Empire and Sexuality: The British Experience*. Manchester: Manchester University Press, 1990.

Iliffe, John. *The African Poor: A History*. Cambridge: Cambridge University Press, 1987.

Jackson, Lynette A. "'When in the White Man's Town': Zimbabwean Women Remember *Chibeura*." In *Women in African Colonial Histories*, edited by Jean Allman, Susan Geiger, and Nakanyinke Musisi, 191–215. Bloomington: Indiana University Press, 2002.

Jean-Baptiste, Rachael. "'These Laws Should Be Made by Us': Customary Marriage Law, Codification, and Political Authority in Twentieth-Century Colonial Gabon." *Journal of African History* 49, no. 2 (2008): 217–40.

Jeater, Diana. *Marriage, Perversion and Power: The Construction of Moral Discourse in Southern Rhodesia, 1894–1920*. Oxford: Clarendon, 1993.

Jochelson, Karen. *The Colour of Disease: Syphilis and Racism in South Africa, 1880–1950*. New York: Palgrave, 2001.

Johnson, Cheryl. "Female Leadership during the Colonial Period: Madam Alimotu Pelewura and the Lagos Market Women." *Tarikh* 7, no. 1 (1980): 1–10.

———. "Grassroots Organizing: Women in Anti-colonial Activity in Southwestern Nigeria." *African Studies Review* 25 (June–September 1982): 137–57.

Johnson, Cheryl, and Nina Emma Mba. *For Women and the Nation: Funmilayo Ransome-Kuti of Nigeria*. Urbana: University of Illinois Press, 1997.

Johnson, Samuel. *The History of the Yorubas: From the Earliest Times to the Beginning of the British Protectorate* [1921]. London: Routledge, 1966.

Kaler, Amy. *Running After Pills: Politics, Gender, and Contraception in Colonial Zimbabwe*. Portsmouth, N.H.: Heinemann, 2003.

Kanogo, Tabitha. *African Womanhood in Colonial Kenya, 1900–1950*. Athens: Ohio University Press, 2005.

Killingray, David. "The Idea of a British Imperial African Army." *Journal of African History* 20, no. 3 (1979): 421–36.

———. "The Maintenance of Law and Order in British Colonial Africa." *African Affairs* 85, no. 340 (July 1986): 112–42.

Klausen, Susanne Maria. *Race, Maternity, and the Politics of Birth Control in South Africa, 1910–1939*. Basingstoke: Palgrave Macmillan, 2004.

Kopytoff, Jean H. *A Preface to Modern Nigeria: The "Sierra Leonians" in Yoruba, 1830–1890*. Madison: University of Wisconsin Press, 1965.

Korieh, Chima J. "The Invisible Farmer? Women, Gender, and Colonial Agricultural Policy in the Igbo Region of Nigeria, c. 1913–1954." *African Economic History* 29 (2001): 117–62.

———. *The Land Has Changed: History, Society, and Gender in Colonial Eastern Nigeria*. Calgary: University of Calgary Press, 2010.

Laoye, J. A. "The Concept of Magun among the Yoruba." *Acta Ethnographica Academia Scientiarum Hungaricae* 23 (1974): 352–55.

Lasekan, Akinola. *Nigeria in Cartoons*. Lagos: Ijaiye Press, 1944.

Law, Robin. *The Oyo Empire, c. 1600–1836: A West African Imperialism in the Era of the Atlantic Slave Trade.* Oxford: Clarendon, 1977.

Lawrance, Benjamin N., and Richard L. Roberts, eds. *Trafficking in Slavery's Wake: Law and the Experience of Women and Children.* Athens: Ohio University Press, 2012.

Leith-Ross, Sylvia. *African Women: A Study of Ibo of Nigeria.* London: Faber and Faber, 1939.

———. *Stepping-Stones: Memoirs of Colonial Nigeria, 1907–1960.* London: Peter Owen, 1983.

Levine, Philippa. *Prostitution, Race and Politics: Policing Venereal Disease in the British Empire.* London: Routledge, 2003.

Lindsay, Lisa A. "'To Return to the Bosom of Their Fatherland': Brazilian Immigrants in Nineteenth Century Lagos." *Slavery and Abolition* 15 (1994): 22–50.

———. *Working with Gender: Wage Labor and Social Change in Southwestern Nigeria.* Portsmouth, N.H.: Heinemann, 2003.

———. "A Tragic Romance, A Nationalist Symbol: The Case of the Murdered White Lover in Colonial Nigeria." *Journal of Women's History* 17, no. 2 (2005): 118–41.

Little, Kenneth. *West African Urbanization: A Study of Voluntary Associations in Social Change.* Cambridge: Cambridge University Press, 1965.

———. *African Women in Towns: An Aspect of Africa's Social Revolution.* Cambridge: Cambridge University Press, 1973.

Lloyd, Peter C. *Africa in Social Change: West African Societies in Transition.* New York: Praeger, 1968.

Loatan, A. B. "Brazilian Influence on Lagos." *Nigeria Magazine* 69 (1961): 157–65.

Losi, John B. *History of Lagos.* Lagos: Tika Tore Press, 1914.

Lovejoy, Paul. "Concubinage and the Status of Women Slaves in Early Colonial Northern Nigeria." *Journal of African History* 29, no. 2 (1988): 245–66.

Mabogunje, Akin L. *Urbanization in Nigeria.* New York: Africana Publishing Corporation, 1968.

MacKenzie, Megan H. *Female Soldiers in Sierra Leone: Sex, Security, and Post-Conflict Development.* New York: New York University Press, 2012.

Magubane, Zine. *Bringing the Empire Home: Race, Class, and Gender in Britain and Colonial South Africa.* Chicago: University of Chicago Press, 2004.

McClintock, Anne. *Imperial Leather: Race, Gender, and Sexuality in the Colonial Contest.* New York: Routledge, 1995.

McCulloch, Jock. "The Management of Venereal Disease in a Settler Society: Colonial Zimbabwe, 1900–30." In *Histories of Sexually Transmitted Diseases and HIV/AIDS in Sub-Saharan Africa,* edited by Philip W. Setel, Milton Lewis, and Maryinez Lyons, 195–201. Westport, Conn.: Greenwood Press, 1999.

———. *Black Peril, White Virtue: Sexual Crime in Southern Rhodesia, 1902–1935.* Bloomington: Indiana University Press, 2000.

McCurdy, Sheryl A. "Urban Threats: Manyema Women, Low Fertility, and Venereal Diseases in Tanganyika, 1926–1936." In *"Wicked" Women and the Reconfiguration of Gender in Africa,* edited by Dorothy L. Hodgson and Sheryl A. McCurdy, 212–33. Portsmouth, N.H.: Heinemann, 2001.

Mann, Kristin. *Marrying Well: Marriage, Status and Social Change among the Educated Elite in Colonial Lagos.* Cambridge: Cambridge University Press, 1985.

————. *Slavery and the Birth of an African City: Lagos, 1760–1900*. Bloomington: Indiana University Press, 2007.

Mann, Kristin, and Richard L. Roberts, eds. *Law in Colonial Africa*. Portsmouth, N.H.: Heinemann, 1991.

Marris, Peter. *Family and Social Change in an African City: A Study of Rehousing in Lagos*. Evanston, Ill.: Northwestern University Press, 1962.

Mason, Michael. *The Making of Victorian Sexuality*. Oxford: Oxford University Press, 1994.

Mba, Nina Emma. *Nigerian Women Mobilized: Women's Political Activity in Southern Nigeria, 1900–1965*. Berkeley: University of California Press, 1982.

McHugh, Paul. *Prostitution and Victorian Social Reform*. London: Croom Helm, 1980.

McIntosh, Marjorie Keniston. *Yoruba Women, Work, and Social Change*. Bloomington: Indiana University Press, 2009.

McIntyre, W. D. "Commander Glover and the Colony of Lagos, 1861–1873." *Journal of African History* 4, no. 1 (1953): 57–79.

Miller, Nevil. "Glover Hall, Old and New." *The Nigerian Field* 31 (1966): 75–80.

Mintz, Steven. *Huck's Raft: A History of American Childhood*. Cambridge, Mass.: Belknap Press, 2004.

Moore, Kofoworola Aina. "The Story of Kofoworola Aina Moore of the Yoruba Tribe, Nigeria." In *Ten Africans*, edited by Margery Perham, 323–43. London: Faber and Faber, 1936.

Morgan, Ruth, and Saskia Wieringa, eds. *Tommy Boys, Lesbian Men and Ancestral Wives: Female Same-Sex Practices in Africa*. Johannesburg: Jacana, 2005.

Morris, H. F. "How Nigeria Got Its Criminal Code." *Journal of African Law* 14, no. 3 (1970): 137–54.

Mosse, George L. *Nationalism and Sexuality: Middle-Class Morality and Sexual Norms in Modern Europe*. Madison: University of Wisconsin Press, 1985.

Muffett, D. J. M. *Empire Builder Extraordinary Sir George Goldie: His Philosophy of Government and Empire*. Douglas: Shearwater Press, 1978.

Murray, Stephen O., and Will Roscoe, eds. *Boy-Wives and Female Husbands: Studies in African Homosexualities*. New York: St. Martin's Press, 1998.

Musisi, Nakanyinke. "The Politics of Perception or Perception of Politics? Colonial and Missionary Representation of Baganda Women, 1900–1945." In *Women in African Colonial Histories*, edited by Jean Allman, Susan Geiger, and Nakanyinke Musisi. Bloomington: Indiana University Press, 2002.

Naanen, Benedict B. "The Itinerant Gold Mines: Prostitution in the Cross River Basin of Nigeria, 1930–1950." *African Studies Review* 34, no. 2 (1991): 57–79.

Nasidi, Abdulsalami, and Tekena O. Harry. "The Epidemiology of HIV/AIDS in Nigeria." In *AIDS in Nigeria: A Nation on the Threshold*, edited by Olusoji Adeyi, Phyllis J. Kanki, Oluwole Odutola, and John A. Idoko, 17–36. Cambridge, Mass.: Harvard Center for Population and Development Studies, 2006.

Nast, Heidi J. *Concubines and Power: Five Hundred Years in a Northern Nigerian Palace*. Minneapolis: University of Minnesota Press, 2005.

Niven, Rex. *Nigerian Kaleidoscope: Memoirs of a Colonial Servant*. London: C. Hurst, 1982.

Njoku, Raphael Chijioke. *African Cultural Values: Igbo Political Leadership in Colonial Nigeria, 1900–1966*. New York: Routledge, 2006.

Nnaemeka, Obioma, ed. *Sisterhood, Feminisms, and Power: From Africa to the Diaspora*. Trenton, N.J.: Africa World Press, 1998.

———, ed. *Female Circumcision and the Politics of Knowledge: African Women in Imperialist Discourses*. Westport, Conn.: Praeger, 2005.

Notkola, Veijo, and Harri Siiskonen. *Fertility, Mortality and Migration in Sub-Saharan Africa: The Case of Ovamboland in North Namibia, 1925–1990*. New York: St. Martin's Press, 2000.

Nwokoji, Ugboga Adaji, and Ademola J. Ajuwon. "Knowledge of AIDS and HIV-Related Sexual Behavior among Nigerian Naval Personnel." *BMC Public Health* 4 (24): 1–9.

Ochonu, Moses E. "'Native Habits Are Difficult to Change': British Medics and the Dilemmas of Biomedical Discourses and Practice in Early Colonial Northern Nigeria." *Journal of Colonialism and Colonial History* 5, no. 1 (2004). *Project MUSE*, March 11, 2013, http://o-muse.jhu.edu.wncln.wncln.org/.

———. *Colonial Meltdown: Northern Nigeria in the Great Depression*. Athens: Ohio University Press, 2009.

Ogbomo, Onaiwu. *When Men and Women Mattered: A History of Gender Relations among the Owan of Nigeria*. Rochester, N.Y.: University of Rochester Press, 1997.

Ojo, Olatunji. "More than Farmers' Wives: Yoruba Women and Cash Crop Production, c. 1920–1957." In *The Transformation of Nigeria: Essays in Honor of Toyin Falola*, edited by Adebayo Oyebade, 383–404. Trenton, N.J.: Africa World Press, 2002.

———. "Beyond Diversity: Women, Scarification, and Yoruba Identity." *History in Africa: A Journal of Method* 35 (2008): 347–74.

———. "Slavery, Marriage, and Gender Relations in Eastern Yorubaland, 1875–1920." In *Gendering the African Diaspora: Women, Culture, and Historical Change in the Caribbean and Nigerian Hinterland*, edited by Judith A. Byfield, LaRay Denzer, and Anthea Morrison, 144–76. Bloomington: Indiana University Press, 2010.

Okeke, C. E., C. N. Onwasigwe, and M. D. Ibegbu. "The Effect of Age on Knowledge of HIV/AIDS and Risk Related Behaviours among Army Personnel." *African Health Sciences* 12, no. 3 (2012): 291–96.

Okonkwo, Rina. *Protest Movements in Lagos, 1908–1930*. Lewiston, N.Y.: Edwin Mellen Press, 1995.

Olaniyi, Rasheed. "No Way Out: The Trafficking of Women in Nigeria." *Agenda*, no. 55 (2003): 45–52.

Olukoju, Ayodeji. "Elder Dempster and the Shipping Trade of Nigeria during the First World War." *Journal of African History* 33, no. 2 (1992): 255–71.

———. "The Cost of Living in Lagos, 1914–45." In *Africa's Urban Past*, edited by Richard Rathbone and David Anderson, 126–43. Oxford: James Currey, 2000.

———. *Infrastructure Development and Urban Facilities in Lagos, 1861–2000*. Ibadan: IFRA, 2003.

———. "The Segregation of Europeans and Africans in Colonial Nigeria." In *Security, Crime, and Segregation in West African Cities*, edited by Laurent Fourchard and Isaac Olawale Albert, 263–86. Paris: IFRA, 2003.

Olusanya, G. O. "The Sabon-Gari System in the Northern State of Nigeria." *Nigeria Magazine Literary Supplement*, no. 94 (1967): 18–24.

———. "The Role of Ex-Servicemen in Nigerian Politics." *Journal of Modern African Studies* 6, no. 2 (1968): 221–32.

Omorodion, Francisca Isi. "Vulnerability of Nigerian Secondary School to Human Sex Trafficking in Nigeria." *African Journal of Reproductive Health* 13, no. 2 (2009): 33–48.

Omu, Fred I. A. *Press and Politics in Nigeria, 1880–1937*. Atlantic Highlands, N.J.: Humanities Press, 1978.

Onwuliri, Viola Adaku, and Oluwatoyin M. Jolayemi, "Reaching Vulnerable and High-Risk Groups in Nigeria." In *AIDS in Nigeria: A Nation on the Threshold*, edited by Olusoji Adeyi, Phyllis J. Kanki, Oluwole Odutola, and John A. Idoko, 309–22. Cambridge, Mass.: Harvard Center for Population and Development Studies, 2006.

Orubuloye, I. O. "Sexual Networking, Use of Condoms and Perception of STDs and HIV/AIDS Transmission among Migrant Sex Workers in Lagos, Nigeria." In *Sexual Cultures and Migration in the Era of AIDS: Anthropological and Demographic Perspectives*, edited by Gilbert Herdt, 216–24. Oxford: Oxford University Press, 1997.

Osuntokun, Akinjide. *Chief S. Ladoke Akintola: His Life and Times*. London: Frank Cass, 1984.

Oyewumi, Oyeronke. *The Invention of Women: Making an African Sense of Western Gender Discourses*. Minneapolis: University of Minnesota Press, 1997.

Pape, John. "Black and White: The 'Perils of Sex' in Colonial Zimbabwe." *Journal of Southern African Studies* 16, no. 4 (1990): 699–720.

Parker, Andrew, Mary Russo, Doris Sommer, and Patricia Yaeger, eds. *Nationalisms and Sexualities*. New York: Routledge, 1992.

Parkin, David, and David Nyamwaya, eds. *Transformations of African Marriage*. Manchester: Manchester University Press, 1989.

Parpart, Jane L. "Sexuality and Power on the Zambian Copperbelt, 1926–1964." *Working Papers in African Studies, 10*, African Studies Center. Boston University, 1986.

———. "'Where Is Your Mother?': Gender, Urban Marriage, and Colonial Discourse on the Zambian Copperbelt, 1924–1945." *International Journal of African Historical Studies* 27, no. 2 (1994): 241–71.

Parsons, Timothy. "All Askaris Are Family Men: Sex, Domesticity and Discipline in the King's African Rifles, 1902–1964." In *Guardians of Empire*, edited by David Killingray and David Omissi, 157–78. Manchester: Manchester University Press, 1999.

———. *The African Rank-and-File: Social Implications of Colonial Military Service in the King's African Rifles, 1902–1964*. Portsmouth, N.H.: Heinemann, 1999.

Patton, Adell. *Physicians, Colonial Racism, and Diaspora in West Africa*. Gainesville: University Press of Florida, 1996.

Paxton, Nancy L. *Writing under the Raj: Gender, Race, and Rape in the British Colonial Imagination, 1830–1947*. New Brunswick, N.J.: Rutgers University Press, 1999.

Pedersen, Susan. "National Bodies, Unspeakable Acts: The Sexual Politics of Colonial Policy-Making." *Journal of Modern History* 63, no. 4 (1991): 646–80.

Peil, Margaret. *Lagos: The City Is the People*. Boston: G. K. Hall & Co., 1991.

Phillips, Richard. "Heterogeneous Imperialism and the Regulation of Sexuality in British West Africa." *Journal of the History of Sexuality* 14, no. 3 (2005): 291–315.

———. "Histories of Sexuality and Imperialism: What's the Use?" *History Workshop Journal* 63, no. 1 (2007): 136–53.

Pierce, Steven. "Farmers and 'Prostitutes': Twentieth-Century Problems of Female Inheritance in Kano Emirate, Nigeria." *Journal of African History* 44, no. 3 (2005): 463–86.

Pittin, Renee I. *Women and Work in Northern Nigeria: Transcending Boundaries*. New York: Palgrave Macmillan, 2002.

Ray, Carina. "The 'White Wife Problem': Sex, Race, and the Contested Politics of Repatriation to Interwar British West Africa." *Gender and History* 21, no. 3 (2009): 628–46.

———. "Sex Trafficking, Prostitution, and the Law in Colonial British West Africa, 1911–1943." In *Trafficking in Slavery's Wake: Law and the Experience of Women and Children in Africa*, edited by Benjamin N. Lawrance and Richard L. Roberts, 101–20. Athens: Ohio University Press, 2012.

Robertson, Stephen. *Crimes against Children: Sexual Violence and Legal Culture in New York City, 1880–1960*. Chapel Hill: University of North Carolina Press, 2005.

Rose, Nikolas S. *Governing the Soul: The Shaping of the Private Self*. London: Routledge, 1990.

Rosiji, Gbemi. *Lady Ademola: A Portrait of a Pioneer*. Lagos: EnClair Publishers Limited, 1996.

Ross, Robert. "Oppression, Sexuality and Slavery at the Cape of Good Hope." *Historical Reflections* 6, no. 2 (1979): 421–33.

Rotimi, Kemi. *The Police in a Federal State: The Nigerian Experience*. Lagos: College Press, 2001.

Scully, Pamela. "Rape, Race, and Colonial Culture: The Sexual Politics of Identity in the Nineteenth-Century Cape Colony, South Africa." *American Historical Review* 100, no. 2 (1995): 335–59.

Schmidt, Elizabeth. *Peasants, Traders, and Wives: Shona Women in the History of Zimbabwe, 1870–1939*. Portsmouth, N.H.: Heinemann, 1992.

———. "Race, Sex, and Domestic Labor: The Question of African Female Servants in Southern Rhodesia, 1900–1939." In *African Encounters with Domesticity*, edited by Karen Tranberg Hansen, 221–41. New Brunswick, N.J.: Rutgers University Press, 1992.

Schram, Ralph. *A History of the Nigerian Medical Services*. Ibadan: Ibadan University Press, 1971.

Setel, Phillip W., Milton Lewis, and Maryinez Lyons, eds. *History of Sexually Transmitted Diseases and HIV/AIDS in Sub-Saharan Africa*. Westport, Conn.: Greenwood Press, 1999.

Shadle, Brett L. *"Girl Cases": Marriage and Colonialism in Gusiiland, Kenya, 1890–1970*. Portsmouth, N.H.: Heinemann, 2006.

Shaw, Carolyn M. *Colonial Inscriptions: Race, Sex, and Class in Kenya*. Minneapolis: University of Minnesota Press, 1995.

Simelane, Hamilton Sipho. "The State, Chiefs and the Control of Female Migration in Colonial Swaziland, c.1930s-1950s." *Journal of African History* 45, no. 1 (2004): 103–24.

Skelley, Ramsay. *The Victorian Army at Home.* London: Croom Helm, 1977.

Sklar, Richard L. *Nigerian Political Parties: Power in an Emergent African Nation.* Princeton, N.J.: Princeton University Press, 1963.

Smith, Mary F. *Baba of Karo: A Woman of the Muslim Hausa.* New Haven, Conn.: Yale University Press, 1981.

Smith, M. G. "The Hausa System of Social Status." *Africa* 29 (1959): 239–53.

Smith, Robert S. *The Lagos Consulate, 1851–1861.* London: Macmillan, 1978.

Soyinka, Wole. *The Beatification of Area Boy: A Lagosian Kaleidoscope.* London: Methuen, 1995.

Stoler, Ann Laura. *Race and the Education of Desire: Foucault's History of Sexuality and the Colonial Order of Things.* Durham, N.C.: Duke University Press, 1995.

———. *Carnal Knowledge and Imperial Power: Race and the Intimate in Colonial Rule.* Berkeley: University of California Press, 2002.

Summers, Carol. "Intimate Colonialism: The Imperial Production of Reproduction in Uganda, 1907–1925." *Signs* 16, no. 4 (1991): 787–807.

Talbot, Percy Amaury. *Life in Southern Nigeria: The Magic, Belief, and Customs of the Ibibio Tribe.* New York: Barnes and Noble, 1967 [1923].

———. *The Peoples of Southern Nigeria*, vol. 2. London: Frank Cass, 1969 [1923].

———. *The Peoples of Southern Nigeria*, vol. 3. London: Frank Cass, 1969 [1923].

Taliani, Simona. "Coercion, Fetishes and Suffering in the Daily Lives of Young Nigerian Women in Italy." *Africa* 82, no. 4 (2012): 579–608.

Tamuno, Tekena. "The Role of the Legislative Council in the Administration of Lagos, 1886–1913." *Journal of the Historical Society of Nigeria* 4, no. 4 (1969): 555–70.

———. *The Police in Modern Nigeria, 1861–1965: Origins, Development, and Role.* Ibadan: Ibadan University Press, 1970.

———. *Herbert Macaulay, Nigerian Patriot.* London: Heinemann Educational Publishers, 1976.

Thomas, Greg. *The Sexual Demon of Colonial Power.* Bloomington: Indiana University Press, 2007.

Thomas, Lynn M. *The Politics of the Womb: Women, Reproduction, and the State in Kenya.* Berkeley: University of California Press, 2003.

Thompson, J. Malcolm. "Colonial Policy and the Family Life of Black Troops in French West Africa, 1817–1904." *International Journal of African Historical Studies* 23, no. 3 (1990): 423–53.

Tijani, Hakeem Ibikunle. *Union Education in Nigeria: Labor, Empire, and Decolonization since 1945.* New York: Palgrave Macmillan, 2012.

Trotter, Henry. *Sugar Girls and Seamen: A Journey into the World of Dockside Prostitution in South Africa.* Athens: Ohio University Press, 2011.

Trustram, Myna. *Women of the Regiment: Marriage and the Victorian Army.* Cambridge: Cambridge University Press, 1984.

Tuck, Michael W. "Venereal Disease, Sexuality and Society in Uganda." In *Sex, Sin, and Suffering: Venereal Disease and European Society since 1870*, edited by Roger Davidson and Lesley A. Hall, 191–204. London: Routledge, 2001.

Ubah, C. N. *Colonial Army and Society in Northern Nigeria*. Kaduna: Baraka Press, 1998.

Uchendu, Victor C. "Concubinage among Ngwa Igbo of Southern Nigeria." *Africa* 35, no. 2 (1965): 187–97.

Ukpabi, Sam C. *The Origin of the Nigerian Army: A History of the West African Frontier Force, 1897–1914*. Zaria: Gaskiya Corp., 1987.

Van Allen, Judith. "'Sitting on a Man': Colonialism and the Lost Political Institutions of Igbo Women." *Canadian Journal of African Studies* 6, no. 2 (1972): 165–81.

Van Den Bersselaar, Dmitri. "Imagining Home: Migration and the Igbo Village in Colonial Nigeria." *Journal of African History* 46, no. 1 (2005): 51–73.

Van Dijk, Rijk. "'Voodoo' on the Doorstep: Young Nigerian Prostitutes and Magic Policing in the Netherlands." *Africa* 71, no. 4 (2001): 558–86.

van Onselen, Charles. *Studies in the Social and Economic History of the Witwatersrand, 1886–1914*, vol. 1: *New Babylon*. London: Longman, 1982.

Vaughan, Megan. *Curing Their Ills: Colonial Power and African Illness*. Cambridge: Polity Press, 1991.

Walkowitz, Judith R. *Prostitution and Victorian Society: Women, Class and the State*. Cambridge: Cambridge University Press, 1980.

———. *City of Dreadful Delight: Narratives of Sexual Danger in Late-Victorian London*. Chicago: University of Chicago Press, 1992.

Washington-Weik, Natalie A. "The Resiliency of Yoruba Traditional Healing, 1922–1955." Ph.D. diss., University of Texas, 2009.

Waterman, Christopher Alan. *Juju: A Social History and Ethnography of an African Popular Music*. Chicago: University of Chicago Press, 1990.

Watts, Sheldon J. *Epidemics and History: Disease, Power and Imperialism*. New Haven, Conn.: Yale University Press, 1997.

Webster, J. B. *The African Churches among the Yoruba, 1888–1922*. Oxford: Clarendon, 1964.

Wheare, Joan. *The Nigerian Legislative Council*. London: Faber & Faber, 1949.

White, E. Frances. *Sierra Leone's Settler Women Traders: Women on the Afro-European Frontier*. Ann Arbor: University of Michigan Press, 1987.

White, Luise. *The Comforts of Home: Prostitution in Colonial Nairobi*. Chicago: University of Chicago Press, 1990.

White, O. "Miscegenation and Colonial Society in French West Africa, c. 1900–1960." Ph.D. diss., Oxford University, 1996.

Williams, Atanda Fatayi. *Faces, Cases and Places: Memoirs by Fatayi Williams, Nigerian Jurist*. London: Butterworths, 1983.

Wilson-Haffenden, J. R. "'Espousal Fee': An Alternative Term for 'Bride-Price.'" *Man* 31, no. 166 (1931): 163–64.

Woollacott, Angela. *Gender and Empire*. New York: Palgrave Press, 2006.

Zedomi, Patience Anne. "Women in the Lagos Newspaper Press, 1930–1966." B.A. long essay, University of Ibadan, 1987.

INDEX

SAHEED ADERINTO is an assistant professor of history at Western Carolina University and coauthor of *Nigeria, Nationalism, and Writing History*.

The University of Illinois Press
is a founding member of the
Association of American University Presses.

Composed in 10/13 Sabon
by Lisa Connery
at the University of Illinois Press
Designed by Dennis Roberts
Manufactured by Sheridan Books, Inc.

University of Illinois Press
1325 South Oak Street
Champaign, IL 61820-6903
www.press.uillinois.edu